GREAT
CRICKET
MATCHES

1772-1800

Edited by John Bryant

First published in Great Britain by
Association of Cricket Statisticians and Historians
Cardiff CF11 9XR
© ACS, 2010

John Bryant has asserted his right under the Copyright, Designs and Patents Act 1988 to be identified as the author of this work.

All Rights Reserved. No part of this publication may be reproduced, stored in a retrieval system, or transmitted in any form, or by any means, electronic, mechanical, photocopying, recording or otherwise without the prior permission in writing of the Copyright holders, nor be otherwise circulated in any form, or binding or cover other than in which it is published and without a similar condition including this condition being imposed on the subsequent publisher.

British Library Cataloguing-in-Publication Data.
A catalogue record for this book is available from the British Library.

ISBN: 978 1 905138 99 9
Typeset by Limlow Books

Contents

	Page
Acknowledgements	4
List of Illustrations	5
Matches in 1744	9
Preface	12
The Matches 1772-1800	33
The 'Lost' Great Matches	271
Supplementary Notes	274
Register of Matches	279
Register of Grounds	281
1802 Match	282
Index of Scorecards	284
Index of Players	286
Abbreviations and Sources	295

Acknowledgements

Nothing I can write here as editor can begin to do justice to the immense contribution made by others to this publication.

The original categorisation of matches was the work of an ACS working party of eleven members, one of whom, sadly, will never see the results in book form. On 11 July 2010 Don Ambrose passed away at the age of 78. Don contributed a wealth of biographical information to support the intricate process of player identification, but his shrewd advice was of even greater value. Indeed, it may fairly be said that each member of the working party made a distinctive and valuable contribution. This may have been in the form of knowledge or advice, or access to relevant material; some members constructively challenged a general view, or offered a markedly different approach, ensuring that prevailing views were not accepted without fresh scrutiny. For me to mention indivuals is invidious but unavoidable.

The role of Keith Warsop has been absolutely fundamental. He and I jointly wrote the article in the Cricket Statistician that began the formal process in March 2009, but that article was itself the fruit of what was already a lengthy collaboration. And Keith has remained at the centre of the process, endlessly commenting, reviewing, researching and checking. Without him this publication would not have been possible.

Without Martin Wilson, on the other hand, the publication would probably still have been possible but it would have been infinitely less valuable. For it was Martin, more than anyone, that undertook the sheer hard work of checking newspapers and other contemporary sources. In the process he turned up innumerable well-attested variations to previously accepted scores, all of them meticulously sourced. And it is entirely thanks to Martin that this book is able to include the full score of an additional 'great' match, which had remained lost since its original newspaper publication in 1778.

I was delighted when the eminent writer and historian David Frith agreed to join the working party. I knew he would provide valuable insights and knowledge from a lifetime or researching and writing about the game, but what I had not expected was his generous offer to assist with illustrative material from his own collection. In this connexion I must also thank MCC for freely giving permission for the use of images from its vast collection, including the wonderfully evocative sketches of famous cricketers of the 1790s by George Shepheard.

Pete Griffiths and Philip Bailey have also been supportive throughout, not only in their contributions to the original working party but also during the process of getting the matches into a fit state to print.

And after all that, what is left for me to claim as editor? Only this: that responsibility for any and all errors is unequivocally mine.

List of Illustrations

1) Cricket at Moulsey Hurst: A match in progress, circa 1790. Unknown artist: attributed to circle of Paul Sandby. With thanks to MCC Photo Library.

2) Thomas Lord batting. Drawing by George Shepheard. With thanks to MCC Photo Library.

3) John Frederick Sackville, 3rd Duke of Dorset. David Frith Collection.

4) Match at the White Conduit, Islington, circa 1787, by an unknown artist.

5) Tom Walker, 'Old Everlasting'. Drawing by George Shepheard. With thanks to MCC Photo Library.

6) William Beldham, 'Silver Billy'. Drawing by George Shepheard. With thanks to MCC Photo Library.

7) David Harris. Drawing by George Shepheard. With thanks to MCC Photo Library.

8) The Bat and Ball Inn. David Frith Collection.

9) Edward Stevens, 'Lumpy'. Knole House Estate.

10) Lord Frederick Beauclerk. Drawing by George Shepheard. With thanks to MCC Photo Library.

11) Col Charles Lennox and Capt Edward Bligh. Drawing by George Shepheard. With thanks to MCC Photo Library.

12) The evolution of the bat. David Frith Collection.

13) Articles of the Game of Cricket. David Frith Collection.

14) The grave of Edward 'Lumpy' Stevens. Photograph by David Frith.

Cricket at Moulsey Hurst
A match in progress, circa 1790.
Unknown artist: attributed to circle of Paul Sandby.
With thanks to MCC Photo Library.

Matches in 1744

The scores on the following two pages date from 1744 and are the earliest known examples of full scores. They are included because of their obvious importance and interest, but it should be stressed that, as explained in the Preface, they are not formally classified as 'great' matches by the Association of Cricket Statisticians and Historians.

One day only is given for each match and this is thought likely to be correct. It was still common at the time for a two-innings-a-side game to be completed in a single day if the weather was good.

The first match is between London and Slindon. The latter is a small Sussex village located not far from Goodwood House, country seat of the preeminent cricket patron the 2nd Duke of Richmond. The village was home to many leading cricketers and has some claim to be the Hambledon of its day.

Indeed, the Hambledon comparison is not an idle one. Hambledon itself lies less than twenty miles to the west on the other side of the Hampshire border. And Richard Nyren, the Hambledon Club's 'head and right arm' as he was later described, was baptised at Slindon's next-door village of Eartham in 1734, the nephew of the celebrated Slindon cricketer Richard Newland. Another Slindon cricketer, Edward Aburrow, was the father of the Hambledon player of the same name.

Both Richard Newland and Edward Aburrow appear for Slindon in the 1744 match against London, but on this occasion the village team is reinforced by a number of men from father afield such as John and Joseph Harris and John Bryant. It has been pointed out that in the famous match between England and Kent on 18 June, all but one of the England side had appeared for either London or Slindon on 2 June. The earlier match may therefore have been in the nature of a trial to help select the England team to play Kent.

In the event, Kent beat England by one wicket after Thomas Waymark dropped the catch that would have given England victory: 'The erring Ball, amazing to be told! Slip'd thro' his out-stretch'd Hand, and mock'd his Hold.' The quote is from *Cricket: an Heroic Poem* by James Love, which celebrated this famous game and which went through three editions, the last as late as 1770. The poem, which gives many additional details about the players and the match, is now most readily found in Volume I of Ian Maun's *From Commons to Lord's: A Chronology of Cricket 1700-1799*.

LONDON v SLINDON

Played at Honourable Artillery Company Ground, Finsbury, June 2, 1744.

Slindon won by 55 runs.

SLINDON

1	E.Aburrow	5		0
2	J.Bryant	5		10
3	R.Newland	0		0
4	A.Newland	0		22
5	Ridgway	6		
6	Joseph Harris	13		14
7	G.Jackson	19		1
8	John Harris	18		47
9	Norris	13		
10	Andrews	7		4
11	G.Smith	8		
	Byes	8		4
		102	(6 wickets, declared)	102

FoW (1): 1- , 2- , 3- , 4- , 5- , 6- , 7- , 8- , 9- , 10-102
FoW (2): 1- , 2- , 3- , 4- , 5- , 6-

LONDON

1	Howlett	1	5
2	S.Dingate	0	19
3	W.Sawyer	4	4
4	Maynard	8	6
5	Bennett	11	7
6	T.Faulkner	1	0
7	T.Waymark	13	16
8	Butler	18	0
9	Green	11	12
10	Hoder	6	0
11	Collins	2	1
	Byes	4	
		79	70

FoW (1): 1- , 2- , 3- , 4- , 5- , 6- , 7- , 8- , 9- , 10-79
FoW (2): 1- , 2- , 3- , 4- , 5- , 6- , 7- , 8- , 9- , 10-70

Umpires:

It would appear that Slindon must have declared, even though no such thing was known, or else they batted after winning. The report says '55 notches beat by and three men to go in'

ENGLAND v KENT

Played at Honourable Artillery Company Ground, Finsbury, June 18, 1744.

Kent won by one wicket.

ENGLAND

1	John Harris	b Hodsoll	0	b	4
2	S.Dingate	b Hodsoll	3	b Hodsoll	11
3	A.Newland	b	0	b Hodsoll	3
4	E.Aburrow	b Hodsoll	0	c Danes	2
5	Green	b	0	b	5
6	T.Waymark	b	7	b Hodsoll	9
7	J.Bryant	st Kips	12	c Kips	7
8	R.Newland	not out	18	c Sackville	15
9	Joseph Harris	b Hodsoll	0	b Hodsoll	1
10	G.Smith	c Bartram	0	b	8
11	J.Newland	b	0	not out	5
	Byes				
			40		70

FoW (1): 1- , 2- , 3- , 4- , 5- , 6- , 7- , 8- , 9- , 10-40
FoW (2): 1- , 2- , 3- , 4- , 5- , 6- , 7- , 8- , 9- , 10-70

KENT

1	Lord J.P.Sackville	c Waymark	5	b	3
2	R.Colchin	b	7	b	9
3	Mills	b	0	c and b	6
4	W.Hodsoll	b	0	not out	5
5	J.Cutbush	c Green	3	not out	7
6	Bartram	b	2	b	0
7	Danes	b	6	c Smith	0
8	W.Sawyer	c Waymark	0	b	5
9	Kips	b	12	b	10
10	J.Mills	not out	7	b	2
11	*V.Romney	b	11	b	8
	Byes				3
			53	(9 wickets)	58

FoW (1): 1- , 2- , 3- , 4- , 5- , 6- , 7- , 8- , 9- , 10-53
FoW (2): 1- , 2- , 3- , 4- , 5- , 6- , 7- , 8- , 9-

Kent Bowling

	O	M	R	W	O	M	R	W
Hodsoll				4				4

Umpires:

SB incorrectly has the year for this match as 1746.

Four batsmen in the England first innings (Green, Waymark, A.Newland, J.Newland) and three batsmen in the England second innings (John Harris, Green and Smith) were bowled by Mills - but which Mills is unknown. Four batsmen in the Kent first innings (the first Mills, Hodswell, Kips and Romney) and three batsmen in the Kent second innings (Sackville, Kips and Romney) were bowled by Harris - but which Harris is unknown. Three batsmen in the Kent first innings (Colchin, Bartram and Danes) and four batsmen in the Kent second innings (Colchin, Bartram, Sawyer, the second Mills) were bowled by Newland - but which Newland is unknown.

Preface

The game of cricket has attracted the attention of many eminent social and sporting historians. Their published works contain many differences of opinion and emphasis about the origins and evolution of the game, but all agree that something recognisable as cricket first emerged no later than the mid sixteenth century somewhere in the counties of Kent, Surrey and Sussex in the south-eastern corner of England. Only later did it spread to the rest of England, ultimately going on to become the global game we see today.

The period covered by this book, broadly the last three decades of the eighteenth century, was crucial to this development. By 1770, cricket had already moved a long way from its lowly origins. It had for many decades attracted the interest and patronage of the nobility and gentry, and it had become popular in London and other places beyond its traditional heartland. Nevertheless, in the 1770s the game's rural origins were still dominant and the greatest force on the cricket field was the celebrated club based at Hambledon in the Hampshire Downs. By 1800, however, the focus of the game had shifted emphatically to London, and in particular to the Marylebone Cricket Club and its new ground developed and managed by a professional cricketer, Thomas Lord.

Thomas Lord batting.
Drawing by George Shepheard.
With thanks to MCC Photo Library.

Many histories of the game have addressed these pivotal decades, and this book does not aspire to jostle such crowded territory. Instead of narrative history, it aims to contribute essential documentary background: the full scores of the most important matches of the period, so far as they can be assembled after a lapse of more than two centuries.

Others have, of course, been here before. As long ago as 1799, William Epps of Rochester published *A Collection of All the Grand Matches of Cricket played in England within Twenty Years, viz. 1771 to 1791*. From 1790 to 1803 Samuel Britcher produced an annual containing the scores of major matches, and in 1823 Henry Bentley published a book of matches played between 1786 and 1822. Finally, in 1862 Arthur Haygarth began to issue his monumental *Scores and Biographies*, the first volume of which (referred to in these notes simply as 'SB') covered matches from 1744 to 1826.

Ever since, for statisticians and historians in search of scores from the period, *Scores and Biographies* has been the first port of call. But nearly a century and a half after Haygarth, it is time to revisit the subject. Scholarship of the period has advanced markedly since his day. Researchers such as F.S. Ashley-Cooper, G.B. Buckley and H.T. Waghorn uncovered much important new material, and the process has continued up to the present time, with their modern successors much assisted by the availability of newspapers and other records on the internet.

The time has come to seek to draw all this work together and put it into print. The result is a collection of 237 'great' matches. The great majority of these featured in *Scores and Biographies*, but every one has been checked and reviewed and in some cases, very significant alterations have been made that may well disconcert more conservative readers. Nevertheless, every change is traced back to sources as close as possible to the time and place of the match in question, and where sources differ (as they almost always do, if only in detail), reasons are given for preferring one to another.

No one is more aware than the compilers of this book of the immense amount of work that historians and statisticians have put in to recording and researching this fascinating period of the game's evolution. This is a process that is still going on, and to which readers are encouraged to contribute. We hope that agreeing a list of 'great' matches will help to promote interest in and understanding of the period, besides bringing to fruition a project of match classification that inspired the Association of Cricket Statisticians and Historians (ACS) from its foundation.

Classification of the matches

The following sections set out the reasoning behind the classification of the 237 'great' matches presented in this book. They refer to, and draw substantially from, an article that appeared in the ACS's journal, the *Cricket Statistician*, in March 2009.

The classification of eighteenth-century matches must be seen in the context of the classification of major cricket more generally. This is an issue that has concerned statisticians ever since the emergence of the concept of 'first-class cricket' as a distinct and definable body of matches.

The term 'first-class cricket' had acquired this specialised meaning long before it was officially defined by the Imperial Cricket Conference (as it then was) in 1947, but the ICC specifically stated that its definition was not to apply retrospectively. For matches before 1947, accordingly, statisticians had to arrive at their own definition. This was not so daunting a prospect as it might appear, because the overwhelming majority of possible matches were part of recognised first-class tournaments, or were ruled on by national boards or MCC, or were the subject of general agreement among statisticians about their inclusion or exclusion. For a stubborn minority of marginal games, however, no such consensus emerged and practice varied between statisticians.

One of the founding aims of the ACS was to agree a list of first-class matches so that statisticians should have a common basis for their work. This exercise was first carried back to 1864 and then extended to 1801, although for the earlier period the matches were described as 'important' because the term 'first-class' was not in use at that time. The ACS published guides setting out the details of its approach to match classification in all the cricketing countries. For the British Isles, there were two guides, one covering matches since 1864 and the other, all earlier games.

A Guide to Important Cricket Matches Played in the British Isles 1707-1863, published in 1981, included a list of 'important' matches played between 1801 and 1863, with extensive notes on the issues involved and the various teams. It did not, however, attempt to classify 18th-century cricket in the same way, explaining that it was separated from later cricket by a 'very definite diminution of matches during the first twenty years of the 19th century' and adding that because so many 18th-century scores are missing, 'it is much more difficult to gauge the standard of the players'. Accordingly, the Guide included a list of 18th-century matches but did not classify them.

Nearly thirty years later, the ACS returned to this issue and concluded that there are legitimate reasons for carrying match classification back beyond 1801. In the first place, the lull to which the Guide refers was centred not on 1800 but somewhat later, on the period 1811-13 when the war with France was at its height. Matches in the first decade of the 19th century are best seen as the tail-end of the vibrant cricket scene of the late 18th century, and in this context the year 1800 represents no sort of logical dividing-point. Moreover, knowledge of the 18th-century game has advanced significantly since the Guide was published in 1981 so that it is now possible to arrive at a more informed assessment of the quality of players.

Accordingly, in March 2009 the *Cricket Statistician* carried a long article by John Bryant and Keith Warsop, setting out a classification of matches in the 18th century based on the principle that the general approach applied to matches from 1801 should be maintained for the earlier period, so far as possible in 18th-century conditions.

At the Association's Annual General Meeting at Cardiff in March 2009, the matter was discussed and it was agreed to invite statisticians with an interest in this subject to form a small group to consider and, if thought fit, amend the list of 228 definite, and 8 possible, matches proposed in the article.

This group consisted, fittingly perhaps given the subject matter, of eleven members:

> Don Ambrose   Dennis Lambert
> Philip Bailey   David Main
> John Bryant   Keith Warsop
> David Frith   Martin Wilson
> Peter Griffiths   Peter Wynne-Thomas
> Bob Harragan

The group agreed to take the list of 236 matches as its starting point. Group members were invited to propose matches, or categories of match, for addition or deletion. Several suggestions were made and lively discussions ensued.

It became clear that the opinions of members of the group were informed by different approaches to the topic that varied quite widely from one member to the next. As discussion progressed, however, it also became clear that these different approaches tended to lead members to very similar conclusions about the specific matches to be included on the proposed list.

The eventual conclusion was that the 8 matches originally identified as doubtful should all be included. These matches aside, no consensus emerged for any of the additions or deletions suggested by various members of the group. Consequently it was agreed that the list of 236 matches, as set out in the *Cricket Statistician* in March 2009, should stand as the recommendation of the group. Further research has since uncovered an additional match in 1778 that clearly qualifies for inclusion, raising the total to 237; this match is the subject of an article by its discoverer, Martin Wilson, in the March 2010 edition of the *Cricket Statistician*.

There was some discussion among the group about the treatment of 'odds' matches, which were a common feature of the period. This has always been a controversial issue among statisticians, and in the end the group was guided by the ACS's established approach for similar matches in the 19th century, which is to include only the most outstanding instances. The final list includes only eight matches involving odds, all of them between an England team and either Hampshire (one match) or Surrey (seven matches). In no case do the odds exceed XIV against XI, and it is an interesting comment on the balance of 18th-century cricketing power than in each case it is England, rather than the county, that receives the odds.

The list includes only matches for which a scorecard is available, although it should be noted that there are reports of at least 11 additional matches that would appear to be strong candidates for inclusion if a full score came to light. Additional research into the period is going on all the time, and the ACS will review the list in the light of any new information.

It is stressed that although the list of matches was agreed by the group, this should not be taken to imply that every member agreed with all decisions regarding match classification. It was agreed, however, that the proposed list represented a consensus view of the group as a whole.

Regarding terminology, it was agreed that to reflect contemporary usage these games should be described as 'great' matches.

The start date: Why 1772?

It may well be asked: why begin in 1772?

If the question is specific – why 1772 rather than 1771 or 1773? – the answer is one of simple practicality. 1772 is the year when a continuous record of scores begins. After this date, full scores of matches are available, sometimes in quite large numbers, for each season; but before it, they scarcely exist. The handful of scores that chance to have survived from before 1772 are of matches that have no claim to 'great' status, with two exceptions. These two matches, which both date from June 1744, are printed on pages 10 and 11. They undoubtedly merit an 'honourable mention' but they are so far separated in time from later scores that to include them in the list would be pointless.

If the question is more general – why begin around this time? – there is good evidence that the game was undergoing transformational change in the years around 1770. The practice of bowling the ball through the air, instead of rolling it along the ground as formerly, precipitated a rush of further changes: the bat completed its evolution to its modern upright form, the laws restricted its width for the first time, the third stump was introduced, and the first lbw law appeared. All these developments, coming in such short order, must have revolutionised the game. In other words, the date of 1772, although imposed by the lack of earlier scores, is defensible in terms of cricket history.

Pattern of matches during the period

The matches we are interested in fall in the years 1772-1800, but this period is divided into two distinct phases separated by a marked lull, with only one 'great' match in 1784 and none at all in 1785.

Phase 1 starts in 1772 and peters out in 1784. In this period, games by the three major county teams of Hampshire, Kent and Surrey against each other and against England set what might be considered a 'gold standard' for great matches at the time. Games involving these three counties are so sharply differentiated from more run-of-the-mill matches that there is very little difficulty in distinguishing them. Only a handful of doubtful matches date from this period.

John Frederick Sackville, 3rd Duke of Dorset and patron of Kent cricket.
David Frith Collection.

Phase 2 runs from 1785 to 1800 (and beyond, but that is outside the scope of the present exercise). In this phase, the focus of activity shifts more and more to London and particularly to Lord's; far more teams and players are involved in potential 'great' matches and classification becomes altogether more complicated. By far the majority of dubious matches fall in this phase.

After 1785, the principal new teams are the Marylebone Cricket Club (MCC) and its forerunner the White Conduit Club (WCC); Middlesex; Essex/Hornchurch; Berkshire/Oldfield; and Sussex/Brighton. The fact that these teams play chiefly against each other, and that matches against the established teams of Hampshire, Kent and Surrey are relatively rare, can obscure the fact that the quality of the new teams is a long way below that of the established ones. However, occasional matches make the disparity clear: when WCC plays Kent in 1786 it is reinforced by no fewer than six top professionals and for several years thereafter MCC enjoys the assistance of between three and five top professionals in all its matches against any of the older counties. Only towards the end of our period does the gap seem to close. Middlesex played Kent in 1796 with only one given man and the next year MCC played Hampshire with no given men at all, but Hampshire and Kent were clearly in decline by this time.

This is not the only evidence. In 1791 Middlesex received odds of XXII against XI in playing Hampshire; in 1793 it enjoyed the same odds against England (i.e., a Hambledon side), as did Essex/Hornchurch; and in 1794 Middlesex had odds of XXII against XII in playing England. All these matches are excluded from the list because the odds are so long. Note too that in all these games the XXIIs contain enough familiar names to suggest they are fairly representative (these matches are in SB pp113, 153, 156, 160, 162, 167). There is nothing like this when the established counties play England or each other; in fact, it is the England side, not the county, that often receives odds. All the evidence underlines the point that, at least until the mid-1790s, there is a large gap in quality between the established teams and the new ones.

This is not to say that the new teams cannot be included. But it does suggest that they are toward the lower end of the standard for 'great' matches and this must be borne in mind when assessing their performances against each other. On this basis the new teams may be summarised as follows.

New teams emerging 1785-1800

This section summarises the principal new teams that emerged in the latter part of the period. It should be noted that apparent club sides such as Hornchurch seem also to have organised county games with no discernible change in personnel, in a similar way to Nottingham and Nottinghamshire in the nineteenth century. The side is referred to as Essex/Hornchurch, and similar comments apply to Sussex/Brighton and Berkshire/Oldfield.

- **White Conduit Club and Marylebone Cricket Club** – The key point here is that WCC/MCC is not a fixed quantity because the team was frequently reinforced with professionals, the number and quality of whom is in fact a very useful guide to contemporary opinion of how strong the opposition was expected to be. Provided account is taken of which professionals, if any, were engaged, performance against WCC/MCC is critical evidence in assessing the possible status of other teams. In its very early games against strong opposition, WCC was very heavily reinforced: in both matches against Kent in 1786 by six of the leading professionals in England; and in its matches against Essex/Hornchurch in 1787 by the Moulsey Hurst club (SB refers to the team in the Hornchurch games simply as Moulsey Hurst but contemporary evidence proves it was a joint team of WCC and Moulsey).

A match at the White Conduit, Islington, circa 1787, by an unknown artist.
Frontispiece to Cricket Scores, Notes &c from 1730-1773 by *H.T.Waghorn.*

- **Middlesex** – This was clearly the strongest of the new counties, with far more matches over a longer period than the others. MCC almost always engaged very strong professionals when playing Middlesex. The odds employed against Hampshire and England remind us not to exaggerate the strength of Middlesex, and the early games in 1787 and 1789 appear to be weaker than the rest, but from a perspective of the period as a whole Middlesex matches clearly merit inclusion. For the distinction between Middlesex and the Thursday Club, see notes on the latter below.

- **Berkshire/Oldfield** – For the four seasons 1792-95 this team, on the whole, held its own against respectable MCC teams and it achieved a remarkable triumph by beating a good Kent side in 1794. During this period it was at least the equal of Middlesex and is included. However, earlier 'Berkshire' matches in 1783 and 1785 are more difficult to classify. In the 1785 game against Hornchurch, the side is full of good players, so much so that it scarcely looks like a Berkshire team at all. But it must be questionable whether Hornchurch, which is marginal even in later years as outlined below, can be considered 'great' in 1785. Certainly it was badly beaten in this game, which is on balance, and not without reservations, excluded from the list. The 1783 game can likewise be excluded because of the opposition, in this case Chertsey.

- **Sussex/Brighton** – This team enjoyed a fleeting presence in 'great' matches – one game in 1791 and five in 1792 – but the results are good and the matches are included despite the large number of lesser-known players in the Sussex/Brighton team.

- **Essex/Hornchurch** – This team was overwhelmed by 'Berkshire' in 1785 and also lost in 1787 to Middlesex, itself very marginal at this date. Also in 1787, it played and lost against a combined side of WCC and Moulsey Hurst in three matches (the score of one of which has not survived). From 1789 it played regularly with reasonable results against MCC teams that tended to be weaker than those selected against other opposition on the fringe of 'great' status – compare for instance MCC teams v Hornchurch on 13 June 1791 and v Gentlemen of Kent on 2 June 1791. On the credit side, it played home and away against Kent in 1792 (but Kent won comfortably) and its results in 1793, and the standard of MCC opposition, were probably better than at any previous time; but ironically this was its final year (and yet it still (with Hertfordshire) played XXII v Hambledon/England). Essex/Hornchurch is the most marginal of the new teams but on balance, and with some misgivings, its matches against MCC, Middlesex and Kent are included. Note the exclusion of the two matches against a combined MCC/Hertfordshire team in 1791: the Hertfordshire element in the combined team is significant, especially in the Hornchurch match (where Britcher calls it simply 'Herts').

Other marginal teams

We now turn to teams of more marginal status. The starting point here, as elsewhere, is the approach taken in the ACS Guide.

- **Chertsey, Moulsey Hurst, Hambledon Town** – The Guide accepts that in exceptional circumstances matches by club sides may be included. The most instructive precedents (because the closest in time) are Epsom and Godalming. Epsom in 1814-19 was playing county sides (treating Brighton as equivalent to Sussex) and the Guide remarks that at least some of the games were regarded as 'the great matches of their year'. The Guide could have added that although Surrey did play one match in 1815 and another in 1817, it was not very active and indeed the game generally seems to have been at a low ebb, so there was something of a vacuum for a club like Epsom to fill. In the case of Godalming in 1821-25, the Guide refers to the team as 'perhaps not quite representative of Surrey as a whole' but points out that it was 'reinforced by some non-Godalming men' and argues that its inclusion is justified by results. Again, it could have added that there were no Surrey matches at all during Godalming's period as an 'important' side. The Guide's approach to Epsom and Godalming can be applied to 18th-century games. The 1773 Hambledon Town match against Surrey is very clearly on a different footing to Hampshire matches of the period; a number of Hampshire men are missing from the Hambledon side, while Surrey at this period would have included given men against a full Hampshire team. Similarly, Chertsey in 1775 against 'London', although full of good players and clearly the leading club in Surrey, is significantly different from the county side. Chertsey's 1778 match against England, however, is a special case: Chertsey fields virtually a Surrey team (T.White (of Reigate) is the only major absentee) and although entitling the opposition as 'England' is highly optimistic (even allowing for 'barring Hants'), it certainly includes some outstanding players along with some lesser lights.

Accordingly, this match is included. There might be some argument for including a match by Chertsey against Berkshire in 1783 in view of the lack of Surrey games at this time, but this match is a far cry from the later successes of Epsom and Godalming against recognised county sides. The danger of including this sort of match is well illustrated by the Moulsey Hurst game against Uxbridge on 8 June 1789; a glance at the Surrey team in the game against Kent starting two days later shows the gulf between even a strong club like Moulsey and a genuine Surrey side. However, in 1787 a joint team of Moulsey Hurst and WCC played and beat Essex/Hornchurch in three matches. The score of one of these is unfortunately lost but the other two are included: note that SB calls the team in these two games simply 'Moulsey Hurst' but it has been established it was a joint team of WCC and Moulsey and this raises the standard sufficiently to merit inclusion.

- **London** – A handful of possible games involve a team named 'London'. There does not appear to be any organising body or any continuity between them so it is assumed that 'London' was merely a convenient label for what are effectively select sides. The match in 1775 against Chertsey includes some good players on both sides but the standard is lowered by the large number of lesser-known names; whilst in the 1789 game v Middlesex, both sides are effectively from the same county (the London team is mostly if not wholly from Middlesex and the Middlesex team looks suspiciously like Uxbridge). Apart from these, there are four games v MCC, in 1794 (2), 1797 and 1798. The MCC sides, on the whole, are not strong and the London teams are variable in composition (for instance only two of the 1797 team reappear in 1798). Looking at the teams in detail, the 1797 match is significantly stronger than the others. The London team consists of recognised Middlesex players reinforced by two good professionals, and it is the only one to be included.

- **Thursday** – The Thursday Club played at Lord's, included many Middlesex players, and is sometimes referred to as 'the Middlesex Club'. It is hardly surprising, then, that Thursday sides are so often confused with those representing the county of Middlesex. However, it is possible to distinguish them. Apart from the team composition, it is relevant to look at the opposition; a match against another county is likely to have been Middlesex rather than Thursday. For matches against MCC, it is helpful to see whether the latter required 'cracks' as given men and, if so, who they were. Against Thursday, MCC would make do with professionals such as Lord and Fennex but against Middlesex big guns such as Beldham and T.Walker are brought in. This is valuable evidence of how strongly contemporaries rated the opposition and it shows that Middlesex was regarded as a different (and tougher) proposition than Thursday. The one exception is in June 1798 when MCC boldly put out a side with no professionals at all against a team that, looking at its

Tom Walker, 'Old Everlasting'
the leading batsman in England for many years
from about 1786.
Drawing by George Shepheard.
With thanks to MCC Photo Library.

personnel, is clearly Middlesex rather than Thursday. Middlesex won by ten wickets.

- **Other metropolitan clubs** – This refers to four matches, all in 1796, between combinations of various metropolitan clubs (see SB pp 201, 204, 206, 210). The Guide specifically refers (p12) to 'good quality metropolitan club matches' as a category of game that should not be included. These matches appear to come into this category, although it should be pointed out that the two between MCC and a combined Montpelier/Thursday side (24 June and 13 July) are of a relatively high standard and include some professionals. It is possible that these games were arranged in place of the usual MCC v Middlesex fixtures, which did not come off in 1796. However, they are not included because they are not on quite the same footing as the only two London club matches included after 1801, MCC v Homerton in 1808 and MCC v St John's Wood in 1814, which incorporated respectively seven and ten of the leading professionals of the day. Note for instance that the Guide excludes the 1810 game between MCC and Homerton even though the latter includes three strong professionals.

- **Old Etonians** – Three games are included, two in 1791 (v Gentlemen of England and v MCC) and one in 1793 (v Old Westminsters). The games against MCC and Old Westminsters include respectively eight and twelve professionals as given men; while the game against Gentlemen of England includes most of the leading amateurs of the day, plus two professionals. The Guide similarly includes Old Etonian games in 1816 and 1817.

- **Select teams** – Matches between select sides are common in the period from 1787 and have been included or excluded based on the strength of the teams. The 1798 Beauclerk v Whitehead match has reasonably good teams but is omitted because it was a single innings affair in which play stopped as soon as a result was achieved.

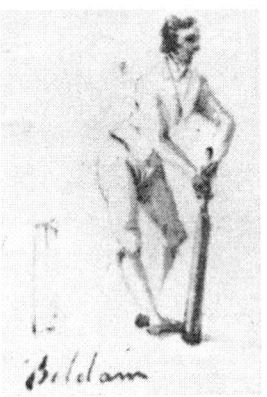

William Beldham, 'Silver Billy',
the greatest all-rounder of his day.
Drawing by George Shepheard.
With thanks to MCC Photo Library.

David Harris,
the celebrated fast bowler.
Drawing by George Shepheard.
With thanks to MCC Photo Library.

Kent teams

Kent teams present special problems and require a separate discussion. The issue is not with the county side itself, which is of course 'great' throughout the period, but with teams that appear, at least on the face of it, to represent less than the full county.

- **Gentlemen of Kent** – The Guide on p8 sets out an approach based on the involvement of Gentlemen of Kent in the Canterbury Festival, which began in 1842, long after our period. The Guide also includes a handful of earlier matches going back to 1827. In that match the Gentlemen had professional reinforcement, which makes it a close parallel to the 1791 game v MCC, which is included. The Gentlemen of Kent also played home and away v WCC in 1785 but both teams were very weak, with no professionals at all on either side ('T.Taylor Esq', playing for Gentlemen of Kent, has sometimes been identified with Thomas Taylor, the Hampshire professional, but this is incorrect). The first 'important' match in which Gentlemen of Kent play without a professional is not until 1833, nearly half a century later. Indeed, even as an amateur side, the Gentlemen of 1785 are weak: only one member of the side (Hosmer) had been even a fringe member of the full Kent team. The 1785 games are excluded.

- **East Kent v West Kent** – There are eight matches in this category, some of which are also billed as matches between the various sponsors, the Duke of Dorset, Sir Horace Mann and Stephen Amherst. The games fall in 1780 (2), 1781 (2), 1783, 1789 (2), 1790. On the face of it, these matches have the character of internal Kent games of the type that the Guide states (p10) should not be included. Indeed, East Kent v West Kent is specifically mentioned. However, although the majority of players involved are from Kent, the teams are generally reinforced by a number of leading cricketers from outside the county. Even the lesser players are usually recognised Kent cricketers on the fringe of the county side. They were evidently serious contests, one lasting five days and two others four days, and the Coxheath game in 1789 was important enough for the game England XIII v Hampshire to be suspended to allow players to take part. The inclusion of significant numbers of leading non-Kent men differentiates these games from the 19th-century East v West Kent games. It should be noted too that the Guide includes two matches Gents of Notts v Players of Notts in 1842 and 1844 on the basis that the Gents are strengthened by players from outside the county. On balance, therefore, these games are included.

Other excluded matches

For completeness' sake, it should be added that there are a few games that have occasionally been mentioned as candidates but that appear to fall well below any reasonable standard for inclusion.

These include a so-called MCC v WCC match in 1788. On the face of it, this is MCC's first recorded match and one of pivotal importance, symbolising its taking over the reins from WCC. Closer scrutiny suggests otherwise: the MCC side is a strong all-amateur team but WCC is full of unknowns. Moreover, other evidence suggests that so far from one club taking over from the other, MCC and WCC are effectively one and the same, and certainly WCC was playing home matches at Lord's the previous season.

Matches involving northern and midland teams have also occasionally been put forward. It is true that Leicester and Nottingham played XI-a-side against MCC in 1791. However, these MCC sides were nothing like so good as the teams MCC would field against major southern counties, and it is significant that Leicester and Nottingham were both badly beaten. Indeed, the next year Nottingham played XXII against an equally moderate MCC team, and still lost. Slightly after our period, in 1803, Hampshire, by then a shadow of its former self, was able to beat by an innings a combined team of Nottingham and Leicester reinforced by Beauclerk (who top-scored in both innings and took two of the four Hampshire wickets for which the bowler is recorded). The evidence is clear that midland and northern sides were of much lower standard than the main southern teams so they are excluded, although the historical importance of their matches is acknowledged.

Presentation of scores

In order to be consistent with each other and with other ACS publications, the scores are presented in the normal ACS style. Although this means that scores are presented with many gaps, for instance in the bowling analyses and in the fall of wickets, it has the merit of making it immediately clear, in relation to any particular score, not only what is known but also, equally importantly, what is not known.

Team nomenclature

The nomenclature of teams is a recurring problem and one that sometimes attracts controversy. Original sources are often highly inconsistent, not only using different titles for very similar matches but also, often, using different titles for the same match. Moreover, the original team titles, in keeping with 18th-century style in other matters such as book titles, are often very descriptive and wordy by modern standards. So the fact that a team may be described in this book simply as, say, 'Surrey', does not exclude the possibility that its original title may have been far longer.

A further complicating factor is that teams are often named after their patron or sponsor, even if the team itself is plainly intended to represent a county or other recognised cricketing entity.

The use of 'given men' as a way of balancing the teams (or, sometimes, as a way of strengthening both teams) was common practice well into the 19th century. It adds to the potential for confusion, particularly in the early part of our period, when only a few counties were involved at top level. A team playing against Hampshire might be described in one source as 'England', in another as 'Kent with three given men', and in yet another as 'Kent and Surrey combined'. Since any given men in the Kent team would in all likelihood come from Surrey, and since an England team opposed to Hampshire would consist mainly of Kent and Surrey players in any case, the difference between the various titles is likely to be marginal.

Finally, where a single club is dominant within a county, there may be no clear distinction between the two. For instance, during our period the Hornchurch club was preeminent in Essex and the team organised by the club can be variously described under either title without any discernible difference in personnel. In the next century a similar situation arose with Nottingham and Nottinghamshire and in other cases, and this book follows the established ACS practice of classifying the match according to the strength of the side, whilst reflecting the contemporary title.

In attempting to make sense of this, and title teams and matches in a clear and consistent way, a degree of streamlining and rationalisation is inevitable. Apart from any other factors, insistence on the use of full titles would render it impossible to index matches and players' appearances in any coherent way. In all the circumstances, the best advice is to focus on the composition and strength of teams and not give undue attention to the matter of titles.

Hambledon and Hampshire

This brings us to the fascinating question of the relationship between the famous Hambledon Club and the county of Hampshire.

Many persons on first becoming interested in the history of cricket must be excited by stories of how the tiny village of Hambledon vied against and overcame the might of All England. It is a fine story, appealing to the romantic in all of us. And like many of the best legends, it is all the more potent for containing much more than a grain of truth. The Hambledon Club did indeed organise a team that played England and often won; and it is also true that Hambledon men formed the kernel of the side. Admittedly some of its best players came from places farther afield, and Hambledon itself probably qualified by the standards of the day to be called a small town rather than a village, but it was certainly not a celebrated or eminent place except for cricket, and even when greater knowledge has deprived the story of a little of its romance the achievements of the Hambledon Club remain remarkable.

Regarding the teams it organised, however, there is clear and substantial contemporary evidence that these were intended as Hampshire rather than Hambledon. It is true that the team is titled 'Hambledon' in some sources, but this is for the same reason that Kent and Surrey teams are often labelled 'Dorset' or 'Tankerville': they are called after their sponsor. The only difference is that the sponsor is a club rather than a nobleman. When, exceptionally, the team is intended to represent Hambledon Town, the sources are very clear in drawing the distinction and it is duly reflected in the composition of the side.

The Bat and Ball Inn, next to Broad Halfpenny Down.
Richard Nyren was landlord during a crucial phase in the development of Hambeldon cricket.
David Frith Collection.

Accordingly, in this book teams organised by the Hambledon Club are usually titled Hampshire. This remains the case even when, after about 1783, a number of very talented players emerged from the western end of Surrey and were drawn to the Hambledon Club (itself evidence that the club's reach extended far beyond its eponymous home). While the evidence is not clear-cut, the club minutes seem to imply that these players, despite coming from just over the county boundary, should be regarded as eligible to play in county matches in which the club was engaged. In this connexion it may be significant that the Surrey side, which might have been expected to claim these players, had been in abeyance since 1779 and did not resume until 1788.

Sobriquets, aliases, and other issues of player identification

Edward Stevens, 'Lumpy',
firmly established as the leading bowler in England
when scores begin to be regularly preserved in
1772.
Knole House Estate.

It was common for leading players of this period to acquire familiar sobriquets or nicknames by which they were widely known: 'Buck' (Peter Stewart), 'Silver Billy' (William Beldham) and so on. Sometimes these appear in place of the player's real name even in formal scores, and in the case of 'Lumpy', the leading bowler in England when our scores begin in 1772, this practice is universal. However, all players are shown in this book under their real names, even though this means that Lumpy features more prosaically as Edward Stevens.

A similar issue arises with amateurs, especially during the later part of our period, who often appear under aliases. Probably they did not want it to be evident in the newspapers that they were playing cricket when they doubtless should have been otherwise engaged. These aliases can present a significant problem with identifying the participants in matches, but it is believed that most of them have been pinned down. And from a safe distance of over two centuries, one can say with confidence that taking an active part in the development of important cricket was almost certainly a more rewarding and worthwhile activity than whatever else they were supposed to be doing.

A large number of lesser players (and one or two more significant ones) are known only by their surname, without even an identifying initial. In some of these cases, however, the player's place of origin, or home club, is known and this is indicated in a footnote against his first appearance.

While we believe that most players have been identified, there remain some particularly knotty problems: in particular, the two players named John Wood, one from Pirbright (Surrey) and the other from Seal (Kent), who both played in the 1770s. We have, at least provisionally, assigned each appearance to a specified player, giving our reasons in the footnotes.

Notes on the accuracy of scores

We have striven throughout to give the fullest and most accurate version of the score that we can. This has frequently required us to choose between different versions in the sources. To approach this task in as consistent a way as possible, we have evolved certain guidelines.

These are set out below. It is stressed that they are not in order of priority. Where they come into conflict, the choice is a matter of judgment. It is not possible to say that any one factor will automatically take priority over another.

- For any given match, a single source should be the 'lead'. This does not prevent the 'lead' source from being supplemented by relevant additional information from other credible sources, provided they are consistent with the 'lead' version. It does mean, however, that sources should not normally be mixed and matched by taking, say, the first innings from one source and the second innings from another. On the very rare occasions that we have combined parts of two versions, a note explains the circumstances.

- Preference should be given to the fullest version of the score.

- Preference should be given to primary sources over secondary sources.

- Preference should be given to the most proximate version of the score. A newspaper that was local to the match venue is likely to have had access to reliable information; whereas a newspaper in a distant town will probably have got its information from intermediate sources.

- Preference should be given to contemporary versions of the score, which will often be found in newspapers. For scores from 1790 on, Britcher offers a near-contemporary source that should normally be given priority over later sources such as SB.

- Occasionally, a score contains a serious internal contradiction. Such a score is to be treated with great caution.

- Where there is a conflict between these guidelines, a decision will have to be made about which version is likely to represent the fullest and most accurate record of the match. This is a matter of judgment; it is unlikely that we shall be able to say that any particular factor, e.g. the fulness of the score, should always take priority over any other, e.g. the proximity of the source.

For each match there is a footnote outlining issues relating to the version of the score that is presented, and referring to any other versions available.

The scores in the current volume differ in very many particulars from previously accepted versions, especially those found in volume 1 of *Scores and Biographies*. Many of these changes are minor, perhaps relating only to the batting order (and see the separate note below for the issues involved in batting orders). We have also been able to give better dates for many matches, showing that virtually all of those for which a single day is given in SB in fact continued for two or more days. In addition, we have resolved all the cases where SB suggests, most implausibly, that play took place on a Sunday.

*Lord Frederick Beauclerk,
a formidable character both on and off the field of
play.
Drawing by George Shepheard.
With thanks to MCC Photo Library.*

*Col Charles Lennox (later 4th Duke of Richmond)
and Capt Edward Bligh,
two leading gentleman cricketers.
Drawing by George Shepheard.
With thanks to MCC Photo Library.*

In a number of cases, however, we have made significant alterations to well-known scores. Although we recognise that some of these changes may be controversial, they are justified by an objective application of the guidelines we have outlined, and we believe that the scores presented here, taken as a whole, constitute the fullest, most accurate and most reliable record that has ever been assembled of major cricket during this crucial phase in the development of the game.

However, we acknowledge that a book such as this can never represent the last word on its subject. Errors will always creep in despite all efforts to exclude them. More fundamentally, research is continuing and will undoubtedly uncover new information that questions, or contradicts, the version of events that is presented here.

Batting orders

The issue of batting orders requires a separate note.

The settled convention in presenting cricket scores is to list teams in first-innings batting order. Although this convention also existed in the 18th century, it had not become fully established and several sources use other approaches.

Some, for instance, list the team in order of social rank, with the dukes and earls at the top, followed by the 'Honourables', then the ordinary 'Esquires', with the lowly professionals bringing up the rear. Although it is obviously most unlikely that the team batted in this way, the order cannot be described as 'wrong'; it is probably quite correct, by its own lights, and while it is not a batting order, it reflects the values of its day.

Sometimes 'given men' are listed at the end, even though they are often leading batsmen who will have actually have gone in near the top of the order. In some cases, the side appears to be listed in the order of getting out (as opposed to the order of going in), which can have the paradoxical effect that the top scorer, if he batted through most of the innings, is listed at or near the bottom rather than near the top as we should expect. At least one card lists the teams in order of score, from highest to lowest. And there is some evidence that Epps took advantage of the great consistency of team selection in the 1770s to carry the same list of names forward from match to match without altering the order. This would have meant that only the score and method of dismissal had to be altered for each match, rather than the whole assembled block of type. It must have saved a lot of time, but unfortunately it means that Epps contains many batting orders that make little sense in the context of the match. The same problem affects other publications (notably *Scores and Biographies*) that have relied on Epps as a source.

Reference to contemporary sources, especially newspapers, has often revealed batting orders that appear to be preferable to those in SB. In assessing this we have had regard to factors such as, for instance, where the not-out batsman is listed and his score. Thus, we know that if the man listed third scored 0 not out in a total of 150, it is most unlikely that the team is given in batting order. Lists with noblemen at the top are similarly suspect, although this should not be carried too far: the scores show that the Duke of Dorset, for instance, although hardly up to professional standard, was far from incompetent as a batsman and he may indeed have opened the innings on occasion. So in the end, where sources give different batting orders it has to be a matter of judgment which to prefer.

Subject to all these caveats, we have attempted to list teams in the order that seems most plausible overall, and we have been able to improve the order in a very large number of matches, especially compared with the versions in *Scores and Biographies*. However, we have made no attempt to 'force' a plausible order when no source provides one. Users of this book are therefore advised to treat batting orders with a degree of caution. Given the inconsistent approach of contemporary sources, it should be accepted that many will remain incorrect, or at least unproven, and the batting order cannot be regarded as such a fundamental part of the score as, for instance, batsmen's totals and modes of dismissal.

Second-innings batting order is even more uncertain. A glance at many scores is sufficient to show that it was very common for teams to vary their order at the second attempt, but in only a handful of cases have we been able to find satisfactory evidence allowing us to show a definite second-innings order.

Continuity and change: cricket then and now

Any reader accustomed to modern cricket scorecards, but coming to the 18th-century game for the first time, is likely to be struck not by how different everything is but by how familiar it seems.

At first glance, the scorecards do indeed look very similar to what a modern cricket follower would expect: there are two teams consisting of (usually) eleven players, to each of whom is ascribed an individual score and means of dismissal in each of two innings. The individual totals are added and a result is given by so many runs or wickets.

A second glance might reveal some differences. Bowlers receive credit only when a batsman is bowled, almost never for other types of dismissal such as catches and lbw. And the bowling figures themselves are nugatory; in fact, they contain nothing but what can be derived from the batting details (which is very little).

But what of the game itself? If it were possible for a modern cricket follower to attend an eighteenth-century 'great' match, would it be the change or the continuity that was more striking?

To take this question first at the most basic level, the elements of continuity are profound. Take a look at paintings from the period. There are two sets of stumps, each defended by a player equipped with a wooden bat against adversaries scattered around the field of play, one of whom projects a small, hard ball from near one set of stumps towards the other, while two umpires oversee the game. Against these similarities, the differences pale almost into insignificance: this is cricket.

The surroundings were generally much more open than today, with no demarcated boundary to the field of play and, even at the biggest matches, very little organised accommodation for large numbers of spectators. A sound hit might send the ball a long distance, forcing the fielders to scramble to recover it from some nearby bushes or among the crowd. The modern concept of a boundary did not exist, although it was foreshadowed both in the allowance of six runs if the fielding side called 'lost ball', and in local rules, varying from ground to ground, that might make a certain allowance of runs, usually three, if the ball struck some defined obstacle such as a refreshment tent (a 'booth ball'). But in general, the word 'run' should be understood in its most literal sense of a dash between the wickets, so that a large innings was a feat of physical stamina as well as sustained skill and concentration: 18th-century batsmen would have considered it a great luxury to be able to stand at the crease watching a well-struck ball whistle to the boundary for four.

Some other proceedings would be strange to a modern cricketer. After 1774, the visiting team would normally have choice of innings, the toss being used only on rare occasions such as when teams met at a neutral venue. (This was a change from the laws of 1744, which stipulated that 'the party that wins the toss up may order which side shall go in first at his Option'. It was not until the early 19th century that the toss was restored as the standard method of deciding choice of innings.)

Teams arriving to play a match would not find themselves presented with the close-mown, lovingly-prepared batting strip that we expect today. Instead, the visiting captain would choose to have stumps pitched anywhere within 30 yards of a point stipulated by the home team, so the pitch would be no different from any other part of the playing area. Choosing a suitable pitch must have been a great art: an unwise selection would condemn the team to a torrid experience with the bat and in all likelihood a very low score.

Although a poem of 1773 refers to cricketers' 'milk-white vestments', the tradition of cricket 'whites' was not yet fully established. Players seem generally to have worn comfortable, relatively loose-fitting clothes, tending to be light rather than dark in shade. A typical outfit would be a tunic and knee breeches, the latter being, according to Haygarth's comment on a match of 1786, 'of course in use now by everyone'.

As for protective equipment, it can be readily summarised. There was none. Batsmen and wicket-keepers had no gloves, pads, or other physical protection. Robert Robinson, clearly a man far in advance of his time, apparently tried to bat wearing a primitive type of pads but he 'was laughed out of his invention.' (Pycroft, *The Cricket Field*, p145).

At this period (and for many years later), the over consisted of four balls. Bowling would, of course, have been 'underhand'. This meant in essence that the hand must be kept below the shoulder, although not with any particular expectation that the arm must be straight. By the time our period begins in 1772, bowlers had already made the transition from 'bowling' in its original sense – that is, rolling the ball along the ground in the manner familiar from skittles and bowls, although perhaps at greater speed than is usual in those sports – in favour of the more modern practice of projecting the ball through the air, and pitching it near the batsman.

The emergence of pitched bowling is a crucial development in the evolution of the game, arguably even more so than the later shift first to roundarm bowling, then to overarm. It is deeply frustrating that evidence is so sparse of exactly when and how this transition took place. A poetic account of a school match in 1756 shows that both types of bowling were in use at that time, although the danger need hardly be stressed of placing too much reliance on a single account of a game between schoolboys. At any rate, pitched bowling seems to have become general by the 1760s, probably as bowlers such as the celebrated 'Lumpy' Stevens learned to exploit the novel factors of 'length' and 'break' that the new technique opened up.

The bat, which in the 1720s had still been shaped like a hockey stick in order to meet a ball approaching (perhaps rapidly) at or near ground level, evolved through the middle part of the century to its familiar upright shape. A bat dated to 1774, preserved at Lord's, is strikingly modern in its overall appearance.

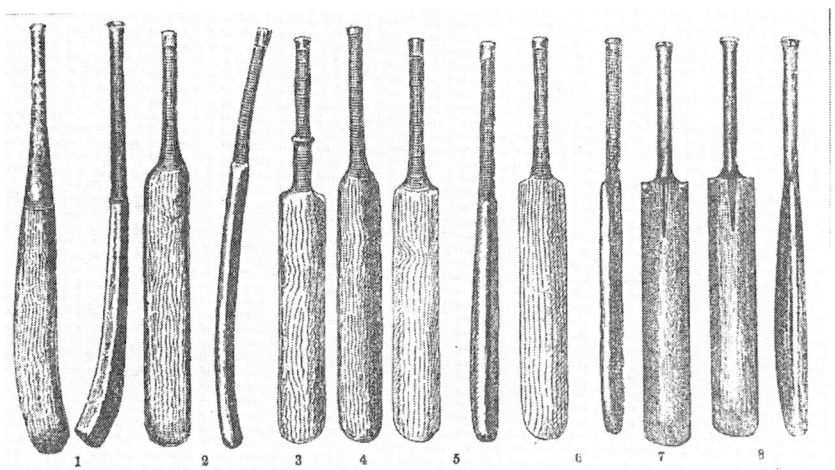

The evolution of the bat.
(1) 1743: The bat has begun to develop from the old 'hockey stick' shape, but still exhibits a marked curvature. (2) 1771: The bat approaches its modern shape, but it was still a single piece of wood, weighing (in this case) a hefty 5 lbs. (3) 1790: A bat with a modified handle to meet the requirements of its owner, who had a crippled hand. (4) 1792: John Ring's bat. (5) 1800: Weight about 2 lbs, 12 oz. (6) 1827. (7) and (8) are later bats displaying a spliced handle.
David Frith Collection.

The new code of laws adopted in 1774 was the first to restrict the width of the bat. Modern research has failed to confirm the story that this followed an incident in which Thomas White came to play with a bat as wide as the wicket, and the document dated 1771, in which the width restriction was allegedly ordained by the Hambledon Club, is definitely a forgery.

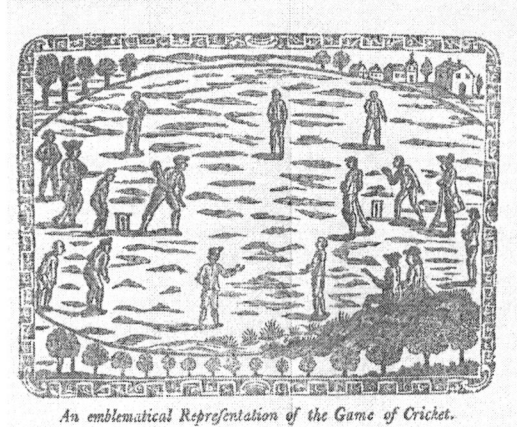
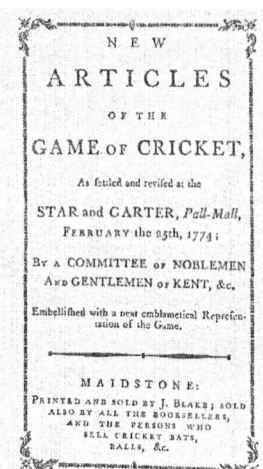

An emblematical Reprefentation of the Game of Cricket.

The title page for the 1774 code of laws, together with an 'emblematical representation' of the game. David Frith Collection.

Another innovation in the laws of 1774 is the provision for a batsman to be out leg-before-wicket, but it remained a very rare form of dismissal for many years. It is possible that early instances were recorded simply as bowled.

In 1772 there were still only two stumps with a single bail, and it was possible for the ball to pass cleanly through the gap (which was not out). It is uncertain exactly when the third stump was added: Haygarth gives the date as 1775 based on an account by John Nyren. There are references to three stumps at the end of the 1776 season, while the announcement of a match in 1777 states that three stumps will be used 'to shorten the game'. In the same year the diarist and cricket enthusiast John Baker reports as a 'new thing' three stumps in a single wicket game. The change may have come in gradually, players using whichever style of stumps and bails was available, over a few years between about 1775 and 1780 (maybe later in lesser matches).

It may be of interest to compare a few of the principal 'weights and measures' in the laws of 1774 with the code of 2000, which prevails today.

	Laws of 1774	Laws of 2000
Weight of ball	5½ to 5¾ ounces	5½ to 5¾ ounces
Maximun width of bat	4¼ inches	4¼ inches
Height of stumps	22 inches	28 inches
Width of wicket*	6 inches	9 inches
Distance between bowling and popping creases	46 inches	48 inches
Distance between wickets	22 yards	22 yards

* These measures are not strictly comparable. The 2000 code defines the overall width of the wicket directly; the code of 1774 did it indirectly, by defining the length of the single bail.

It will be seen that the wicket has grown both taller and wider, but overall the degree of continuity is remarkable. It would, of course, be mischievous, and entirely unfair to the game's modern legislators, to add that the 1774 code consisted of 843 words, while the 2000 code required a modest increase to 27,557 (not including the diagrams).[1]

Scoring was modest: an 18th-century score should be at least doubled to arrive at a modern equivalent. An individual score of fifty was not uncommon, but a century was a rare feat: the 'conversion rate', as a modern batting coach might term it, was extremely low. When in 1777 James Aylward scored 167, ironically in the very match that was advertised as being played with a third stump 'to shorten the game', the feat was looked upon as almost miraculous, and the record that it set remained unsurpassed, at least in top cricket, for over forty years.

Because scoring was slower and matches generally shorter, fewer bowlers were needed. It seems it was not uncommon for a team to use the same two bowlers throughout an innings, or indeed the whole match. A bowler might change ends, but only once in any innings (although there was nothing to stop him, in changing ends, from bowling two overs in succession).

Wicket-keeping was a distinct role, recognised as such in the laws, and by the 1770s, if not before, some players were beginning to specialise in it. However, it remained common throughout the period for players to bowl and keep wicket in the same innings. Long stop – that is, near the boundary behind the wicket-keeper – was very much a recognised position, in which players might specialise. Its prevalence may be taken as evidence more of the bumpiness of pitches rather than the inadequacy of wicket-keepers or the inaccuracy of bowlers.

The teams would take their innings in strict alternation: there was no follow-on. There were also no declarations: or, rather, the laws made no provision for them. There are, however, a few occasions where an ascendant team appears to have given up its innings in order to have a go at bowling the other side out.

Matches were almost always played out. Given the relatively modest scoring, this seldom took more than two or three days in good conditions; but weather interference, or unusually heavy scoring, could extend a match to five or six days or even longer. Eighteenth-century cricketers showed commendable persistence in giving a match as much time as it needed to come to a definite conclusion, returning day after day after weather interruptions or an intervening Sunday even when the result was a foregone conclusion. This may be on account of the wagers laid not only on the result of the match but also on one player's score against another's; but whatever the reason, an unfinished game was a rarity.

---

1 The word count for 1774 includes the laws for the settlement of bets. The count for 2000 includes updates to 2008 and comprises the preamble, the numbered laws, and the appendices. It does not include regulations by the ICC, ECB, and other governing bodies; nor does it include the Duckworth-Lewis provisions. The ACS is grateful to MCC for supplying the modern laws in a format that allowed an electronic word count. (The laws of 1774 were counted manually.)

*The grave of Edward 'Lumpy' Stevens at Walton-on-Thames.
The inscription, now barely legible, gives his date of death as
7 September 1819 and his age as 84.
Photograph taken by David Frith in 1967.*

The Matches
1772-1800

HAMPSHIRE v ENGLAND

Played at Broad Halfpenny Down, Hambledon, June 24, 25, 1772.

Hampshire won by 53 runs.

HAMPSHIRE

1	T.Brett	11			2
2	W.Yalden	5			9
3	J.Small, sen	78	(4)		34
4	T.Sueter	2	(3)		9
5	R.Nyren	9			4
6	G.Leer	1			0
7	J.Edmeads	0			6
8	P.Stewart	12	(9)		11
9	E.Aburrow	27	(8)		0
10	W.Hogsflesh	0			4
11	W.Barber	1			
	Byes				
		146			79

FoW (1): 1- , 2- , 3- , 4- , 5- , 6- , 7- , 8- , 9- , 10-146
FoW (2): 1- , 2- , 3- , 4- , 5- , 6- , 7- , 8- , 9- , 10-79

ENGLAND

1	T.White	35			6
2	J.Fuggles	5	(5)		12
3	J.Minchin	16			1
4	R.Miller	11			0
5	Gill	5	(11)		2
6	W.Palmer	13			8
7	T.May	15			18
8	Childs	2	(2)		0
9	J.Frame	2	(10)		4
10	E.Stevens	5	(8)		7
11	R.May	0	(9)		5
	Byes				
		109			63

FoW (1): 1- , 2- , 3- , 4- , 5- , 6- , 7- , 8- , 9- , 10-109
FoW (2): 1- , 2- , 3- , 4- , 5- , 6- , 7- , 8- , 9- , 10-63

Umpires: Toss:

Close of Play: 1st day: .

The dismissal details are not available. Hampshire had Edmeads and Yalden as given men. It is notable that there are no byes in the match. This is unlikely to be correct: some reports give the margin as 47 runs (but without any further details) and it is possible the discrepancy results from byes omitted from the score.

(Variant) DC shows this as a three-day game commencing 23 June, with no play on the first day, but no contemporary source could be found to corroborate this. SB incorrectly gives Miller as Joseph in this and other matches.

ENGLAND v HAMPSHIRE

Played at Merrow Down, Guildford, July 23, 24, 1772.

Hampshire won by 62 runs.

HAMPSHIRE

1	T.Brett	3	2
2	W.Yalden	68	49
3	J.Small, sen	1	30
4	T.Sueter	21	5
5	R.Nyren	16	0
6	G.Leer	2	0
7	J.Edmeads	5	17
8	P.Stewart	11	7
9	E.Aburrow	10	0
10	W.Barber	5	0
11	W.Hogsflesh	2	8
	Byes	8	4
		152	122

FoW (1): 1- , 2- , 3- , 4- , 5- , 6- , 7- , 8- , 9- , 10-152
FoW (2): 1- , 2- , 3- , 4- , 5- , 6- , 7- , 8- , 9- , 10-122

ENGLAND

1	E.Stevens		0	1
2	J.Fuggles		21	3
3	R.Simmons		27	3
4	J.Minchin		0	13
5	R.Miller		30	26
6	J.Boorman		18	0
7	T.Pattenden		15	4
8	T.May		5	3
9	J.Frame	c	1	10
10	Page	b	0	3
11	R.May	not out	0	7
	Byes		9	13
			126	86

FoW (1): 1- , 2- , 3- , 4- , 5- , 6- , 7- , 8- , 9-126, 10-126
FoW (2): 1- , 2- , 3- , 4- , 5- , 6- , 7- , 8- , 9- , 10-86

Umpires: Toss:

Close of Play: 1st day: England (1) 126-8 (Frame 1*, Page 0*).

John Baker's diary says Frame c, Page b, and confirms that both were out without addition at beginning of day 2. The batting order appears to be correct, so this means R.May was not out. Other dismissal details are not available. Hampshire had Edmeads and Yalden as given men. Page is one of two brothers from Guildford, John or William. The ground is sometimes called Guildford Bason ('bason' is an 18th-century variant spelling of 'basin').

ENGLAND v HAMPSHIRE

Played at Bourne Paddock, Bishopsbourne, August 19, 20, 1772.

England won by two wickets.

HAMPSHIRE

1	T.Brett	11	0
2	T.Sueter	26	11
3	G.Leer	29	7
4	J.Small, sen	22	48
5	P.Stewart	13	12
6	T.Ridge	4	8
7	W.Barber	0	2
8	W.Hogsflesh	0	1
9	W.Yalden	4	1
10	J.Edmeads	7	4
11	E.Aburrow	0	6
	Byes	7	13
		123	113

FoW (1): 1- , 2- , 3- , 4- , 5- , 6- , 7- , 8- , 9- , 10-123
FoW (2): 1- , 2- , 3- , 4- , 5- , 6- , 7- , 8- , 9- , 10-113

ENGLAND

1	E.Stevens	14		12
2	R.May	3		
3	J.Wood (Pirbright)	0		20
4	T.Pattenden	20		4
5	J.Minchin	24		9
6	R.Simmons	3		1
7	J.Fuggles	0		1
8	R.Miller	14	not out	17
9	T.White	8		5
10	W.Palmer	29		14
11	J.Boorman	0	not out	2
	Byes	21		16
		136	(8 wickets)	101

FoW (1): 1- , 2- , 3- , 4- , 5- , 6- , 7- , 8- , 9- , 10-136
FoW (2): 1- , 2- , 3- , 4- , 5- , 6- , 7- , 8-

England Bowling

	O	M	R	W		O	M	R	W
Stevens									
May									

Hampshire Bowling

	O	M	R	W		O	M	R	W
Brett									
Stewart									
Barber									
Hogsflesh									
Aburrow									

Umpires: Toss:

Close of Play: 1st day: England (1) 136-8.

The title has been accepted as England v Hampshire. Although the match announcement says Kent, as does the poem reproduced in SB, match reports are clear for England rather than Kent. This is supported by the composition of the team, which includes Minchin, Palmer, Stevens and White. Therefore Wood is probably John Wood of Surrey. Hampshire had Edmeads and Yalden as given men. Dismissal details are not available. The bowlers were: Hampshire - Brett from one end unchanged, Stewart, Barber, Hogsflesh and Aburrow from the other (it will be noted that Nyren is not playing); England - Stevens and May unchanged. A report notes, 'Lumpy [Stevens] had the honour of bowling out Small, which had not been done for some years,' but does not say in which innings.

(Variant) In this and other matches, SB incorrectly gives John Wood of Surrey as Thomas.

SURREY v KENT

Played at Laleham Burway Cricket Ground, June 21, 22, 1773.

Surrey won by 34 runs.

SURREY
1	Earl of Tankerville	b	15	b		2
2	R.Stone	b	35	b		2
3	M.Lewis	b	2	b		9
4	J.T.de Burgh	b	0	b		0
5	J.Edmeads	c	11	b		0
6	W.Yalden	b	9	b		0
7	E.Stevens	run out	10	b		11
8	J.Wood (Pirbright)	b	3	c		6
9	T.White	not out	44	not out		22
10	W.Palmer	b	8	c		3
11	R.Francis	b	30	b		9
	Byes		8			5
			175			69

FoW (1): 1- , 2- , 3- , 4- , 5- , 6- , 7- , 8- , 9- , 10-175
FoW (2): 1- , 2- , 3- , 4- , 5- , 6- , 7- , 8- , 9- , 10-69

KENT
1	Duke of Dorset	b	14	b		6
2	Sir H.Mann	b	1	b		8
3	Sir J.B.Davis	b	23	not out		4
4	E.Hussey	b	7	b		9
5	R.Miller	b	4	b		18
6	T.Pattenden	run out	25	b		4
7	F.Booker	b	2	b		4
8	R.N.Newman	not out	28	b		0
9	J.Fuggles	c	3	b		6
10	T.May	b	20	run out		10
11	J.Wheeler	b	1	b		0
	Byes		5			8
			133			77

FoW (1): 1- , 2- , 3- , 4- , 5- , 6- , 7- , 8- , 9- , 10-133
FoW (2): 1- , 2- , 3- , 4- , 5- , 6- , 7- , 8- , 9- , 10-77

Kent Bowling
	O	M	R	W	O	M	R	W
Dorset								
Wheeler								

Surrey Bowling
	O	M	R	W	O	M	R	W
Stevens								
Wood								

Umpires: Toss:

Close of Play: 1st day: .

Bowlers for England: Dorset and Wheeler; for Surrey: Stevens and Wood. The sources give details of how players were dismissed, but not by whom. Teams are listed by social status: nobility, gentry, then 'other ranks'. Lewis in the Surrey side is assumed to be M.Lewis, whom a report in the *Hampshire Chronicle* includes in the Surrey team for a match against Hambledon Town in August, with 'Lewis, Esq' down to play for Hambledon (thus contradicting SB, which gives the Lewises the other way round).

(Variant) RM also gives each player's means of dismissal (bowled, caught, run out) for this match, but not by whom the dismissal was effected. It differs in some details from the LlEP version above and is given for all 11 in each innings, i.e. no not outs, so the RM score is less reliable and LlEP's identification of Pattenden as Thomas rather than William is also preferred.

ENGLAND v HAMPSHIRE

Played at Sevenoaks Vine Cricket Club Ground, June 28, 29, 1773.

England won by an innings and 51 runs.

HAMPSHIRE

1	T.Brett	b Stevens	26	c Minchin	1
2	G.Leer	run out (Stevens)	14	not out	15
3	T.Sueter	b Stevens	11	c Stevens	9
4	P.Stewart	run out (Minchin)	5	b J.Wood (Pirbright)	0
5	W.Yalden	b J.Wood (Pirbright)	5	b Stevens	0
6	J.Aylward	c Minchin	4	b Stevens	13
7	W.Hogsflesh	c Simmons	4	c J.Wood (Pirbright)	0
8	J.Small, sen	c Stevens	3	run out (Simmons)	4
9	R.Nyren	c White	2	c Minchin	5
10	E.Aburrow	not out	2	b Stevens	2
11	W.Barber	b R.May	1	b J.Wood (Pirbright)	0
	Byes				
			77		49

FoW (1): 1- , 2- , 3- , 4- , 5- , 6- , 7- , 8- , 9- , 10-77
FoW (2): 1- , 2- , 3- , 4- , 5- , 6- , 7- , 8- , 9- , 10-49

ENGLAND

1	R.Miller	c Barber	73
2	R.Simmons	b Brett	20
3	T.May	b Barber	16
4	J.Minchin	hit wkt	15
5	J.Wood (Seal)	b Hogsflesh	14
6	J.Wood (Pirbright)	b Hogsflesh	12
7	R.May	not out	10
8	T.White	b Nyren	7
9	T.Pattenden	c Hogsflesh	1
10	E.Stevens	b Brett	6
11	Childs	b Hogsflesh	1
	Byes		2
			177

FoW (1): 1- , 2- , 3- , 4- , 5- , 6- , 7- , 8- , 9- , 10-177

England Bowling

	O	M	R	W		O	M	R	W
Stevens				2					3
J.Wood (Pirbright)				1					2
R.May				1					

Hampshire Bowling

	O	M	R	W
Brett				2
Nyren				1
Hogsflesh				3
Barber				1

Umpires: Toss:

Close of Play: 1st day: England (1) ?-? (Miller not out, Simmons not out).

Both Woods played for England. They are separately identified in the batting but no source identifies which was involved in the dismissals. They are attributed to Wood of Surrey, who generally bowled with much more success than Wood of Kent, and was the better-known player. Hampshire had Yalden as a given man. The teams are listed in descending order of scores.

ENGLAND v HAMPSHIRE

Played at Honourable Artillery Company Ground, Finsbury, July 2, 3, 1773.

England won by six wickets.

HAMPSHIRE
1	T.Brett	1		14
2	R.Nyren	0		14
3	†T.Sueter	29		32
4	J.Small, sen	58		25
5	J.Aylward	8		1
6	W.Hogsflesh	2		14
7	P.Stewart	10		5
8	W.Yalden	4		2
9	E.Aburrow	0		3
10	W.Barber	15		25
11	G.Leer	0		3
	Byes	5		16
		132		154

FoW (1): 1- , 2- , 3- , 4- , 5- , 6- , 7- , 8- , 9- , 10-132
FoW (2): 1- , 2- , 3- , 4- , 5- , 6- , 7- , 8- , 9- , 10-154

ENGLAND
1	E.Stevens		5		
2	J.Frame		11		
3	†J.Wood (Pirbright)		15		
4	Childs		38		
5	T.White		24		1
6	S.Colchin		1		9
7	J.Boorman		5		55
8	J.Wood (Seal)		5	not out	0
9	W.Bullen		1		1
10	Read		13		
11	W.Palmer	not out	52	not out	30
	Byes		17		4
			187	(4 wickets)	100

FoW (1): 1- , 2- , 3- , 4- , 5- , 6- , 7- , 8- , 9- , 10-187
FoW (2): 1- , 2- , 3- , 4-

England Bowling
	O	M	R	W	O	M	R	W
Stevens								
Frame								

Hampshire Bowling
	O	M	R	W	O	M	R	W
Brett								
Nyren								

Umpires: Toss:

Close of Play: 1st day: .

Wicket-keepers were Sueter and Wood (Pirbright); longstops Leer and Palmer; England bowlers Stevens and Frame; Hampshire bowlers Brett and Nyren. The dismissal details are not available. The teams are listed with bowlers first, followed by wicket-keepers; the order in which they batted is not known, although clearly Palmer, listed at 11 for England, came in much higher.

KENT v SURREY

Played at Bourne Paddock, Bishopsbourne, July 19, 20, 21, 1773.

Surrey won by 153 runs.

SURREY

1	Earl of Tankerville	b T.May	0	c Davis		3
2	W.Bartholomew	c Simmons	3	b Miller		10
3	M.Lewis	b Dorset	0	not out		21
4	R.Stone	b Dorset	12	b Miller		24
5	E.Stevens	b Miller	6	b Miller		8
6	J.Wood (Pirbright)	c Mann	6	c R.May		6
7	W.Palmer	c Davis	22	c Dorset		38
8	T.White	b Dorset	5	c Hussey		60
9	W.Yalden	not out	17	b Dorset		1
10	Childs	b T.May	0	b Dorset		3
11	R.Francis	b Dorset	5	c Wood		36
	Byes		1			7
			77			217

FoW (1): 1- , 2- , 3- , 4- , 5- , 6- , 7- , 8- , 9- , 10-77
FoW (2): 1- , 2- , 3- , 4- , 5- , 6- , 7- , 8- , 9- , 10-217

KENT

1	Duke of Dorset	b Wood	25	b Wood		1
2	Sir H.Mann	b Wood	3	c Tankerville		22
3	Sir J.B.Davis	b Wood	4	c Lewis		0
4	E.Hussey	not out	0	b Wood		0
5	R.Miller	c Yalden	13	run out		10
6	R.Simmons	b Stevens	5	c Yalden		4
7	R.May	b Wood	0	not out		3
8	T.May	b Stevens	4	c Childs		5
9	G.Louch	c Stone	5	b Stevens		26
10	T.Pattenden	c Lewis	0	b Stevens		1
11	J.Wood (Seal)	c Wood	1	c Bartholomew		9
	Byes		3			
			63			78

FoW (1): 1- , 2- , 3- , 4- , 5- , 6- , 7- , 8- , 9- , 10-63
FoW (2): 1- , 2- , 3- , 4- , 5- , 6- , 7- , 8- , 9- , 10-78

Kent Bowling

	O	M	R	W		O	M	R	W
Dorset				4					2
T.May				2					
Miller				1					3

Surrey Bowling

	O	M	R	W		O	M	R	W
Stevens				2					2
Wood				4					2

Umpires: Toss: Surrey

Close of Play: 1st day: Kent (1) 55-5; 2nd day: Surrey (2) 65-2 (Palmer 36*, White 2*).

At the close of day 2, Stone and Yalden were the men out. The teams are listed by social status. See the Supplementary Note on page 274 for more details about this match.

HAMPSHIRE v ENGLAND

Played at Broad Halfpenny Down, Hambledon, August 4, 5, 1773.

England won by nine wickets.

HAMPSHIRE

1	T.Ridge	b Dorset	0	c Yalden		24
2	T.Davis	run out	30	b Stevens		7
3	J.Small, sen	b Stevens	16	run out		22
4	J.Aylward	b Stevens	18	b Stevens		4
5	W.Hogsflesh	b Stevens	6	b Dorset		0
6	R.Nyren	b Dorset	5	not out		6
7	T.Sueter	b Dorset	2	b Dorset		39
8	G.Leer	b Dorset	2	c Simmons		13
9	W.Barber	not out	2	b Stevens		1
10	R.Francis	b Wood	2	c Palmer		6
11	R.Purchase	b Stevens	1	c Miller		17
	Byes		5			1
			89			140

FoW (1): 1- , 2- , 3- , 4- , 5- , 6- , 7- , 8- , 9- , 10-89
FoW (2): 1- , 2- , 3- , 4- , 5- , 6- , 7- , 8- , 9- , 10-140

ENGLAND

1	R.Stone	b Hogsflesh	0			
2	W.Palmer	c Ridge	68			
3	J.Minchin	c Ridge	11			
4	T.White	b Purchase	69			
5	R.Miller	b Hogsflesh	18			
6	Duke of Dorset	c Barber	3			
7	W.Yalden	b Purchase	0	not out		10
8	R.Simmons	c Nyren	3	c Hogsflesh		13
9	T.Pattenden	b Purchase	1	not out		4
10	E.Stevens	b Purchase	1			
11	J.Wood (Pirbright)	not out	17			
	Byes		11			1
			202	(1 wicket)		28

FoW (1): 1- , 2- , 3- , 4- , 5- , 6- , 7- , 8- , 9- , 10-202
FoW (2): 1- (2)

England Bowling

	O	M	R	W	O	M	R	W
Stevens				4				3
Dorset				4				2
Wood				1				

Hampshire Bowling

	O	M	R	W	O	M	R	W
Hogsflesh				2				
Purchase				4				

Umpires: Toss:

Close of Play: 1st day: .

Hampshire had Francis as a given man. Simmons scored 7 with one hit.

KENT v SURREY

Played at Sevenoaks Vine Cricket Club Ground, August 16, 17, 18, 1773.

Kent won by six wickets.

SURREY

#	Batsman	Dismissal	Runs	Dismissal (2)	Runs
1	J.Wood (Pirbright)	c Simmons	16	b Frame	5
2	W.Palmer	run out	20	c Simmons	20
3	T.White	c Wood	59	c Minchin	0
4	R.Francis	b Fish	14	b Frame	9
5	Earl of Tankerville	b Dorset	13	c Frame	18
6	W.Yalden	b Booker	8	b Dorset	3
7	C.Phillips	c Miller	14	c Simmons	3
8	Childs	run out	0	b Dorset	8
9	Page	b Booker	2	c Minchin	1
10	E.Stevens	not out	8	b Frame	0
11	Blake	b Booker	8	not out	0
	Byes		9		3
			171		70

FoW (1): 1- , 2- , 3- , 4- , 5- , 6- , 7- , 8- , 9- , 10-171
FoW (2): 1- , 2- , 3- , 4- , 5- , 6- , 7- , 8- , 9- , 10-70

KENT

#	Batsman	Dismissal	Runs	Dismissal (2)	Runs
1	G.Louch	c Phillips	0	c Francis	0
2	J.Wood (Seal)	b Stevens	37	not out	5
3	J.Minchin	c Yalden	21	c Page	32
4	R.Miller	b White	42	not out	32
5	Duke of Dorset	c Yalden	14	b White	23
6	R.Simmons	b Wood	0		
7	F.Booker	c Wood	0		
8	R.N.Newman	b Wood	1		
9	J.Frame	c White	6		
10	J.Fish	c Francis	14		
11	T.Pattenden	not out	1	c Stevens	6
	Byes		6		2
			142	(4 wickets)	100

FoW (1): 1- , 2- , 3- , 4- , 5- , 6- , 7- , 8- , 9- , 10-142
FoW (2): 1- , 2- , 3- , 4-

Kent Bowling

	O	M	R	W	O	M	R	W
Dorset				1				2
Booker				3				
Fish				1				
Frame								3

Surrey Bowling

	O	M	R	W	O	M	R	W
Stevens				1				
Wood				2				
White				1				1

Umpires: Toss: Kent

Close of Play: 1st day: ; 2nd day: .

Kent had Minchin as a given man. See the Supplementary Note on page 274 for more details about this match.

SURREY v HAMPSHIRE

Played at Laleham Burway Cricket Ground, September 16, 17, 18, 1773.

Surrey won by eight wickets.

HAMPSHIRE

1	J.Aylward	b Francis	11	c Attfield	36
2	T.Brett	b Wood	0	b Wood	8
3	J.Small, sen	b Wood	0	c Yalden	3
4	T.Sueter	b Francis	13	b White	19
5	G.Leer	c Tankerville	0	c Minchin	17
6	J.Bayley	c Stevens	4	b White	19
7	P.Stewart	c Francis	8	run out	10
8	T.Davis	c Tankerville	0	c Tankerville	4
9	R.Purchase	b Wood	1	b Stevens	8
10	W.Hogsflesh	not out	0	not out	6
11	J.Frame	b Francis	0	c White	12
	Byes		1		3
			38		145

FoW (1): 1- , 2- , 3- , 4- , 5- , 6- , 7- , 8- , 9- , 10-38
FoW (2): 1- , 2- , 3- , 4- , 5- , 6- , 7- , 8- , 9- , 10-145

SURREY

1	W.Palmer	b Brett	6		
2	J.Wood (Pirbright)	c Stewart	7		
3	R.Miller	b Frame	37	not out	30
4	T.White	c Small	17	not out	10
5	J.Minchin	c Purchase	29		
6	Earl of Tankerville	b Hogsflesh	0	b Brett	3
7	R.Francis	b Frame	4		
8	W.Yalden	c Sueter	0		
9	E.Stevens	c Stewart	11		
10	H.Attfield	not out	4		
11	Childs	c Bayley	0	c Brett	18
	Byes		5		3
			120	(2 wickets)	64

FoW (1): 1- , 2- , 3- , 4- , 5- , 6- , 7- , 8- , 9- , 10-120
FoW (2): 1- , 2-

Surrey Bowling

	O	M	R	W	O	M	R	W
Francis				3				
Wood				3				1
White								2
Stevens								1

Hampshire Bowling

	O	M	R	W	O	M	R	W
Brett				1				1
Frame				2				
Hogsflesh				1				

Umpires: Toss:

Close of Play: 1st day: ; 2nd day: .

Hampshire had Frame and Bayley (sometimes spelt 'Bailey') as given men; Surrey had Miller and Minchin. Rain prevented much play on day 2.

(Variant) HCC says the match went into a 5th day but HC appears to disprove this.

HAMPSHIRE v SURREY

Played at Broad Halfpenny Down, Hambledon, September 27, 28, 1773.

Surrey won by an innings and 60 runs.

HAMPSHIRE

1	T.Brett	10	10
2	J.Frame	9	3
3	J.Aylward	3	33
4	J.Small, sen	1	1
5	R.Nyren	0	0
6	T.Sueter	22	4
7	P.Stewart	2	6
8	T.Davis	6	3
9	R.Purchase	0	6
10	J.Bayley	24	1
11	G.Leer	5	12
	Byes	1	3
		83	82

FoW (1): 1- , 2- , 3- , 4- , 5- , 6- , 7- , 8- , 9- , 10-83
FoW (2): 1- , 2- , 3- , 4- , 5- , 6- , 7- , 8- , 9- , 10-82

SURREY

1	E.Stevens	14
2	J.Wood (Pirbright)	18
3	T.White	2
4	W.Palmer	14
5	W.Yalden	88
6	Childs	5
7	R.Miller	39
8	J.Minchin	10
9	R.Francis	14
10	H.Attfield	8
11	W.Bartholomew	6
	Byes	7
		225

FoW (1): 1- , 2- , 3- , 4- , 5- , 6- , 7- , 8- , 9- , 10-225

Surrey Bowling

	O	M	R	W	O	M	R	W
Stevens								
Wood								

Hampshire Bowling

	O	M	R	W
Brett				
Nyren				

Umpires: Toss:

Close of Play: 1st day: .

Hampshire had Bayley and Frame as given men; Surrey had Miller and Minchin. The dismissal details are not available. Bowlers were: Surrey - Stevens and Wood; Hants - Brett and Nyren.

HAMPSHIRE v ENGLAND

Played at Broad Halfpenny Down, Hambledon, June 22, 23, 24, 1774.

Hampshire won by an innings and 52 runs.

ENGLAND
1	Duke of Dorset	19	6
2	Earl of Tankerville	18	35
3	R.Stone	14	4
4	J.Minchin	37	38
5	R.May	7	6
6	R.Miller	3	26
7	J.Wood (Pirbright)	10	0
8	T.White	5	0
9	W.Palmer	0	6
10	Childs	2	6
11	W.Yalden	1	0
	Byes	6	6
		122	133

FoW (1): 1- , 2- , 3- , 4- , 5- , 6- , 7- , 8- , 9- , 10-122
FoW (2): 1- , 2- , 3- , 4- , 5- , 6- , 7- , 8- , 9- , 10-133

HAMPSHIRE
1	E.Aburrow	9
2	J.Small, sen	47
3	E.Stevens	22
4	G.Leer	12
5	T.Sueter	67
6	R.Nyren	21
7	J.Aylward	37
8	R.Francis	29
9	P.Stewart	11
10	R.Purchase	37
11	T.Brett	9
	Byes	6
		307

FoW (1): 1- , 2- , 3- , 4- , 5- , 6- , 7- , 8- , 9- , 10-307

Umpires:

Close of Play: 1st day: ; 2nd day: .

It is assumed that R.May and Wood of Pirbright played for England, rather than T.May and Wood of Seal. Hampshire had Stevens as a given man. Dismissal details are not available. This was the first 'great' match played after the adoption of a new code of laws in February 1774. In contrast to the earlier code of 1744, which had provided for choice of innings to be decided by a toss, the 1774 code gave the choice to the visiting team, although a toss might still be used in rare cases such as a match at a neutral venue. Given the difficulty of identifying the cases where a toss may still have taken place, the reference to a toss has been omitted from all scores from this point. The toss was restored early in the 19th century: probably around 1810, although the exact date is uncertain.

(Variant) RM gives dates as 22, 23 June only: also England (1) byes 0, total 116; Hants (1) Francis 49, total 327; margin innings & 78. These are numerically large departures from the Epps version as given above, which is confirmed by several newspapers. SB incorrectly gives the venue as Laleham Burway.

ENGLAND v HAMPSHIRE

Played at Sevenoaks Vine Cricket Club Ground, July 7, 8, 1774.

Hampshire won by 169 runs.

HAMPSHIRE

1	J.Aylward	run out	29	c Minchin	61
2	R.Francis	b Bullen	4	b J.Wood (Pirbright)	1
3	J.Small, sen	b Bullen	10	run out	20
4	T.Sueter	c Bullen	12	b Bullen	30
5	G.Leer	b Frame	28	b J.Wood (Pirbright)	14
6	R.Nyren	b Bullen	10	c Minchin	18
7	P.Stewart	not out	14	b Colchin	7
8	E.Stevens	c J.Wood (Pirbright)	21	b Colchin	11
9	E.Aburrow	b Bullen	8	b J.Wood (Pirbright)	7
10	T.Brett	b Bullen	2	not out	4
11	R.Purchase	c White	0	b Colchin	0
	Byes		1		9
			139		182

FoW (1): 1- , 2- , 3- , 4- , 5- , 6- , 7- , 8- , 9- , 10-139
FoW (2): 1- , 2- , 3- , 4- , 5- , 6- , 7- , 8- , 9- , 10-182

ENGLAND

1	Earl of Tankerville	c Small	1	b Stevens	5
2	R.Stone	c Small	0	b Brett	3
3	W.Bullen	b Stevens	7	b Stevens	1
4	J.Minchin	b Purchase	6	b Stevens	8
5	R.Miller	b Nyren	16	c Sueter	12
6	S.Colchin	not out	10	c Leer	19
7	T.White	b Brett	17	c Nyren	4
8	W.Palmer	c Small	3	b Stevens	5
9	J.Wood (Seal)	b Nyren	27	c Brett	3
10	J.Frame	b Brett	1	b Purchase	3
11	J.Wood (Pirbright)	b Stevens	0	not out	0
	Byes				1
			88		64

FoW (1): 1- , 2- , 3- , 4- , 5- , 6- , 7- , 8- , 9- , 10-88
FoW (2): 1- , 2- , 3- , 4- , 5- , 6- , 7- , 8- , 9- , 10-64

England Bowling

	O	M	R	W	O	M	R	W
Frame				1				
Bullen				5				1
Wood								3
Colchin								3

Hampshire Bowling

	O	M	R	W	O	M	R	W
Stevens				2				4
Brett				2				1
Nyren				2				
Purchase				1				1

Umpires:

Close of Play: 1st day: .

Hampshire had Stevens as a given man. SB reasonably suggests that Wood of Pirbright took the wickets.

47

SURREY v HAMPSHIRE

Played at Merrow Down, Guildford, July 20, 21, 1774.

Hampshire won by seven wickets.

SURREY

1	Muggeridge	b Nyren	0	b Nyren		0
2	T.White	c Nyren	13	b Brett		1
3	H.Attfield	b Brett	2	b Brett		16
4	J.Miller	b Brett	3	b Nyren		1
5	R.Miller	c Aburrow	3	c Nyren		2
6	J.Edmeads	b Brett	5	b Brett		10
7	W.Palmer	not out	26	b Francis		2
8	W.Yalden	b Brett	0	b Francis		8
9	E.Stevens	b Hogsflesh	3	not out		13
10	J.Wood (Pirbright)	b Brett	0	b Brett		12
11	T.Quiddington	b Hogsflesh	3	b Francis		5
	Byes		3			6
			61			76

FoW (1): 1- , 2- , 3- , 4- , 5- , 6- , 7- , 8- , 9- , 10-61
FoW (2): 1- , 2- , 3- , 4- , 5- , 6- , 7- , 8- , 9- , 10-76

HAMPSHIRE

1	J.Small, sen	c Muggeridge	28	b Stevens		8
2	J.Aylward	b Wood	15	c Stevens		5
3	R.Francis	c Attfield	8	b Wood		14
4	T.Sueter	run out	11	not out		10
5	G.Leer	b Wood	0	not out		9
6	P.Stewart	b White	0			
7	E.Aburrow	not out	6			
8	T.Brett	b White	4			
9	W.Hogsflesh	c Yalden	0			
10	R.Nyren	b Stevens	11			
11	R.Purchase	b White	7			
	Byes		2			
			92	(3 wickets)		46

FoW (1): 1- , 2- , 3- , 4- , 5- , 6- , 7- , 8- , 9- , 10-92
FoW (2): 1- , 2- , 3-

Hampshire Bowling

	O	M	R	W	O	M	R	W
Brett				5				4
Nyren				1				2
Hogsflesh				2				
Francis								3

Surrey Bowling

	O	M	R	W	O	M	R	W
Stevens				1				1
Wood				2				1
White				3				

Umpires:

Close of Play: 1st day: .

Surrey had Miller as a given man, almost certain to be Richard Miller. The other is assumed to be his brother Joseph - although R.Miller is associated chiefly with Kent, the brothers originally came from Caterham and J.Miller may still have been living there. Muggeridge of Epsom.

KENT v HAMPSHIRE

Played at Sevenoaks Vine Cricket Club Ground, August 8, 9, 10, 1774.

Kent won by an innings and 25 runs.

HAMPSHIRE

1	T.Ridge	b Stevens	2	c Simmons		1
2	R.Francis	b Stevens	3	b Bullen		9
3	J.Small, sen	b Stevens	18	not out		55
4	T.Sueter	c Waller	0	c Waller		12
5	R.Nyren	c Simmons	3	b Booker		3
6	G.Leer	c White	4	b Booker		17
7	J.Aylward	b Dorset	1	run out		16
8	W.Hogsflesh	not out	3	b White		3
9	E.Aburrow	b Stevens	9	b Stevens		25
10	T.Brett	c Bullen	1	c Stevens		11
11	R.Purchase	c Booker	1	c Colchin		11
	Byes		1			6
			46			169

FoW (1): 1- , 2- , 3- , 4- , 5- , 6- , 7- , 8- , 9- , 10-46
FoW (2): 1- , 2- , 3- , 4- , 5- , 6- , 7- , 8- , 9- , 10-169

KENT

1	Duke of Dorset	c Small	77
2	Waller	b Nyren	2
3	R.Simmons	b Brett	1
4	E.Stevens	c Aylward	7
5	R.Miller	c Purchase	95
6	S.Colchin	b Brett	0
7	T.White	b Hogsflesh	0
8	T.Pattenden	b Francis	24
9	W.Brazier	run out	0
10	F.Booker	c Brett	22
11	W.Bullen	not out	8
	Byes		4
			240

FoW (1): 1- , 2- , 3- , 4- , 5- , 6- , 7- , 8- , 9- , 10-240

Kent Bowling

	O	M	R	W		O	M	R	W
Stevens				4					1
Dorset				1					
Booker									2
Bullen									1
White									1

Hampshire Bowling

	O	M	R	W
Brett				2
Nyren				1
Hogsflesh				1
Francis				1

Umpires:

Close of Play: 1st day: ; 2nd day: .

Kent had Colchin, Stevens and White as given men. Waller of Maidstone.

49

HAMPSHIRE v KENT

Played at Broad Halfpenny Down, Hambledon, August 15, 16, 17, 18, 1774.

Kent won by four wickets.

HAMPSHIRE

1	T.Ridge	c Brazier	1	b White		8
2	J.Small, sen	c Brazier	45	c Waller		8
3	T.Sueter	b Stevens	3	c Bullen		9
4	G.Leer	b Stevens	14	b White		0
5	R.Nyren	b Colchin	35	b Colchin		20
6	J.Aylward	b Stevens	30	c Colchin		4
7	P.Stewart	b Booker	7	b Stevens		5
8	E.Aburrow	c Colchin	20	c Dorset		33
9	T.Brett	c Colchin	0	b Colchin		8
10	R.Francis	not out	14	run out		22
11	W.Barber	c Simmons	0	not out		5
	W.Hogsflesh					
	Byes		5			7
			174			129

FoW (1): 1- , 2- , 3- , 4- , 5- , 6- , 7- , 8- , 9- , 10-174
FoW (2): 1- , 2- , 3- , 4- , 5- , 6- , 7- , 8- , 9- , 10-129

KENT

1	Duke of Dorset	b Brett	5			
2	Waller	b Brett	6			
3	R.Simmons	not out	6	b Hogsflesh		4
4	E.Stevens	b Barber	3			
5	R.Miller	c Brett	40	c Hogsflesh		45
6	S.Colchin	b Barber	25	not out		1
7	T.White	b Aburrow	1	b Brett		50
8	T.Pattenden	c Small	35	b Nyren		14
9	W.Brazier	b Nyren	4	not out		5
10	F.Booker	c Nyren	7	run out		3
11	W.Bullen	b Brett	27	b Nyren		2
	Byes		9			12
			168	(6 wickets)		136

FoW (1): 1- , 2- , 3- , 4- , 5- , 6- , 7- , 8- , 9- , 10-168
FoW (2): 1- , 2- , 3- , 4- , 5- , 6-

Kent Bowling

	O	M	R	W	O	M	R	W
Stevens				3				1
Colchin				1				2
Booker				1				
White								2

Hampshire Bowling

	O	M	R	W	O	M	R	W
Brett				3				1
Nyren				1				2
Barber				2				
Aburrow				1				
Hogsflesh								1

Umpires:

Close of Play: 1st day: ; 2nd day: ; 3rd day: .

W.Hogsflesh was a full substitute for Hampshire, replacing W.Barber who had sprained his leg. Kent had Colchin, Stevens and White as given men.

KENT v HAMPSHIRE

Played at Sevenoaks Vine Cricket Club Ground, June 14, 15, 1775.

Kent won by 110 runs.

KENT

1	Duke of Dorset	b Brett	20	c Francis		10
2	W.Bullen	c Francis	1	c Sueter		4
3	T.Pattenden	c Aylward	7	b Brett		72
4	J.Wood (Seal)	b Hogsflesh	3	not out		7
5	R.Miller	b Nyren	8	c Aylward		7
6	W.Brazier	b Brett	1	b Brett		31
7	F.Booker	c Taylor	23	c Sueter		14
8	T.White	b Hogsflesh	25	c Sueter		26
9	E.Stevens	b Brett	0	c Aburrow		6
10	R.Simmons	c Francis	11	b Small		1
11	R.May	not out	3	b Nyren		3
	Byes		2			13
			104			194

FoW (1): 1- , 2- , 3- , 4- , 5- , 6- , 7- , 8- , 9- , 10-104
FoW (2): 1- , 2- , 3- , 4- , 5- , 6- , 7- , 8- , 9- , 10-194

HAMPSHIRE

1	T.Ridge	b Booker	4	b Stevens		0
2	R.Francis	c Simmons	1	b May		1
3	J.Small, sen	b Stevens	3	c Simmons		14
4	T.Sueter	c Bullen	15	b Stevens		5
5	G.Leer	c Miller	27	c Bullen		?
6	R.Nyren	b White	11	b Stevens		3
7	J.Aylward	b Stevens	38	b Stevens		0
8	W.Hogsflesh	run out	7	not out		3
9	E.Aburrow	b Stevens	36	b Stevens		1
10	T.Brett	not out	6	b May		1
11	T.Taylor	run out	3	b May		0
	Byes		6			1
			157			31

FoW (1): 1- , 2- , 3- , 4- , 5- , 6- , 7- , 8- , 9- , 10-157
FoW (2): 1- , 2- , 3- , 4- , 5- , 6- , 7- , 8- , 9- , 10-31

Hampshire Bowling

	O	M	R	W	O	M	R	W
Brett				3				2
Nyren				1				1
Hogsflesh				2				
Small								1

Kent Bowling

	O	M	R	W	O	M	R	W
Stevens				3				5
Booker				1				
White				1				
May								3

Umpires:

Close of Play: 1st day: .

Kent had Stevens and White as given men.

HAMPSHIRE v KENT

Played at Broad Halfpenny Down, Hambledon, June 29, 30, 1775.

Hampshire won by nine wickets.

KENT
1	Duke of Dorset	14		0
2	W.Bullen	7		6
3	T.Pattenden	14		4
4	W.Bowra	14		10
5	R.Miller	5		71
6	W.Brazier	0		2
7	F.Booker	3		4
8	S.Colchin	1		13
9	E.Stevens	5		7
10	R.Simmons	0		18
11	R.May	14		0
	Byes	7		12
		84		147

FoW (1): 1- , 2- , 3- , 4- , 5- , 6- , 7- , 8- , 9- , 10-84
FoW (2): 1- , 2- , 3- , 4- , 5- , 6- , 7- , 8- , 9- , 10-147

HAMPSHIRE
1	R.Francis	7	not out	10
2	J.Small, sen	14		
3	Francis	2		3
4	T.Sueter	37		
5	G.Leer	79		
6	R.Nyren	14		
7	J.Aylward	14		
8	W.Barber	8		
9	E.Aburrow	5		2
10	T.Brett	2		
11	T.Taylor	28		
	Byes	9		3
		219	(1 wicket)	18

FoW (1): 1- , 2- , 3- , 4- , 5- , 6- , 7- , 8- , 9- , 10-219
FoW (2): 1-

Umpires:

Close of Play: 1st day: .

Francis, playing for Hampshire, is assumed to be a brother of R.Francis, but no details are known. The dismissal details are not known. Kent had Colchin and Stevens as given men.

SURREY v HAMPSHIRE

Played at Laleham Burway Cricket Ground, July 6, 7, 8, 1775.

Surrey won by 69 runs.

SURREY

1	H.Attfield	b Brett	5	run out		15
2	R.Miller	b Brett	0	c Dorset		42
3	T.White	c Small	0	b Brett		0
4	J.Minchin	c Small	8	b Barber		45
5	W.Palmer	c Taylor	15	c Taylor		1
6	Earl of Tankerville	b Barber	0	b Brett		26
7	W.Yalden	b Brett	2	b Brett		6
8	W.Edmeads	b Brett	13	c Brett		2
9	E.Stevens	b Brett	9	b Brett		3
10	T.Quiddington	not out	11	b Barber		20
11	J.Wood (Pirbright)	b Brett	12	not out		2
	Byes		1			1
			76			163

FoW (1): 1- , 2- , 3- , 4- , 5- , 6- , 7- , 8- , 9- , 10-76
FoW (2): 1- , 2- , 3- , 4- , 5- , 6- , 7- , 8- , 9- , 10-163

HAMPSHIRE

1	J.Aylward	c Edmeads	1	c Yalden		38
2	E.Aburrow	c Wood	4	c Tankerville		0
3	J.Small, sen	c White	4	c Yalden		2
4	G.Leer	c Yalden	4	c Edmeads		26
5	Duke of Dorset	b Wood	0	b Wood		18
6	T.Sueter	c Yalden	11	c Yalden		11
7	R.Francis	b Wood	3	c Attfield		16
8	T.Taylor	b Stevens	8	b Stevens		5
9	T.Brett	c Yalden	3	b Wood		0
10	R.Nyren	c Stevens	12	c White		0
11	W.Barber	not out	0	not out		3
	Byes		1			
			51			119

FoW (1): 1- , 2- , 3- , 4- , 5- , 6- , 7- , 8- , 9- , 10-51
FoW (2): 1- , 2- , 3- , 4- , 5- , 6- , 7- , 8- , 9- , 10-119

Hampshire Bowling

	O	M	R	W	O	M	R	W
Brett				6				4
Barber				1				2

Surrey Bowling

	O	M	R	W	O	M	R	W
Stevens				1				1
Wood				2				2

Umpires:

Close of Play: 1st day: ; 2nd day: .

A contemporary handwritten score in Chertsey Museum (local to Laleham Burway) gives a much better order for Hampshire, and correctly cites the name of the match promoter, Mr Porter (SB says 'Barber'). Edmeads is given as 'Edmeads, jun' in SB, i.e. presumably William rather than the usual man, John. Surrey had Miller and Minchin as given men. Dorset made a hit for 5.

HAMPSHIRE v SURREY

Played at Broad Halfpenny Down, Hambledon, July 13, 14, 15, 17, 1775.

Hampshire won by 273 runs.

HAMPSHIRE
1	Duke of Dorset	8	6
2	J.Small, sen	38	138
3	R.Francis	45	0
4	T.Sueter	6	0
5	G.Leer	21	2
6	R.Nyren	12	97
7	J.Aylward	1	2
8	W.Barber	9	26
9	E.Aburrow	0	7
10	T.Brett	19	69
11	T.Taylor	8	1
	Byes	1	7
		168	355

FoW (1): 1- , 2- , 3- , 4- , 5- , 6- , 7- , 8- , 9- , 10-168
FoW (2): 1- , 2- , 3- , 4- , 5- , 6- , 7- , 8- , 9- , 10-355

SURREY
1	Earl of Tankerville		2	12
2	R.Miller		15	1
3	T.White		7	8
4	J.Minchin		7	2
5	W.Yalden		26	25
6	J.Wood (Pirbright)		22	0
7	H.Attfield		39	15
8	E.Stevens		4	4
9	J.Edmeads		6	0
10	T.Quiddington		2	0
11	W.Palmer	not out	0	40
	Byes		5	8
			135	115

FoW (1): 1- , 2- , 3- , 4- , 5- , 6- , 7- , 8- , 9- , 10-135
FoW (2): 1- , 2- , 3-78, 4- , 5- , 6- , 7- , 8- , 9- , 10-115

Umpires:

Close of Play: 1st day: ; 2nd day: ; 3rd day: Surrey (2) 78-3 (Palmer 22*).

Hampshire had Dorset as a given man. Surrey had Miller and Minchin as given men. The score in the *Reading Mercury* is preferred because it gives much the fullest available version of this famous match in which Small made the first recorded century in top cricket. Although, like other versions, it unfortunately contains no details of dismissals, it gives a complete final innings; it also increases Small's score from 136 to 138 among many other changes, all of which, in view of the relative fullness of the score, are accepted for consistency. Other versions of the score give three days only with the Surrey (2) total as 78-3, suggesting that Surrey conceded. The RM score shows that the game continued on a fourth day, which has been assumed to be 17 July (16 July was a Sunday): it was certainly during that week because the RM score appeared on 24 July. Nothing in RM contradicts the statement in the *General Evening Post* that play on day 3 continued until 8pm, when it must have got too dark to continue, and 78-3 has been accepted as the score at that point, with Palmer 22* and Tankerville, Yalden and Attfield the men out.

(Variant) SB says it is 'believed Small carried his bat' but this is unconfirmed.

HAMPSHIRE v KENT

Played at Molesey Hurst, June 5, 6, 7, 1776.

Hampshire won by 152 runs.

HAMPSHIRE

1	R.A.Veck	c Bowra	6	c May	12
2	J.Aylward	b Dorset	13	c Miller	30
3	T.Sueter	b May	36	b May	4
4	J.Small, sen	c Bowra	38	c Bullen	44
5	T.Taylor	run out	0	b White	41
6	R.Nyren	c May	18	c Bullen	13
7	R.Francis	b May	10	b Dorset	16
8	T.Brett	c Colchin	43	c White	0
9	T.Davis	c Bullen	40	b Dorset	13
10	P.Stewart	not out	15	not out	7
11	W.Barber	b May	0	b May	3
	Byes		6		3
			225		186

FoW (1): 1- , 2- , 3- , 4- , 5- , 6- , 7- , 8- , 9- , 10-225
FoW (2): 1- , 2- , 3- , 4- , 5- , 6- , 7- , 8- , 9- , 10-186

KENT

1	W.Palmer	b Barber	2	b Barber	0
2	T.Pattenden	b Barber	0	b Brett	38
3	R.Miller	c Sueter	15	b Brett	39
4	W.Bowra	c Veck	2	b Nyren	19
5	T.White	b Barber	3	b Brett	0
6	Duke of Dorset	run out	3	c Sueter	3
7	W.Brazier	b Nyren	3	b Brett	49
8	S.Colchin	c Barber	0	b Taylor	14
9	F.Booker	c Stewart	4	run out	15
10	R.May	run out	12	not out	16
11	W.Bullen	not out	10	c Small	3
	Byes		1		8
			55		204

FoW (1): 1- , 2- , 3- , 4- , 5- , 6- , 7- , 8- , 9- , 10-55
FoW (2): 1- , 2- , 3- , 4- , 5- , 6- , 7- , 8- , 9- , 10-204

Kent Bowling

	O	M	R	W	O	M	R	W
May				3				2
Dorset				1				2
White								1

Hampshire Bowling

	O	M	R	W	O	M	R	W
Nyren				1				1
Barber				3				1
Brett								4
Taylor								1

Umpires:

Close of Play: 1st day: ; 2nd day: .

Kent had Colchin, Palmer and White as given men. The 18th-century spelling of Moulsey has been modernised as Molesey.

(Variant) HCC calls Dorset's team 'England' but contemporary sources prove it was Kent with three given men.

KENT v HAMPSHIRE

Played at Sevenoaks Vine Cricket Club Ground, June 25, 26, 1776.

Hampshire won by 75 runs.

HAMPSHIRE

1	J.Aylward	b Dorset	6	b White		3
2	J.Small, sen	b Dorset	45	c Bullen		7
3	G.Leer	b Stevens	0	c Bowra		1
4	T.Sueter	c Booker	5	run out		13
5	T.Brett	c Bullen	3	not out		1
6	E.Aburrow	c Bowra	8	c Brazier		5
7	R.Francis	c Booker	47	b White		9
8	T.Taylor	c Booker	42	c Booker		14
9	W.Barber	not out	4	c Boorman		0
10	R.Nyren	c Dorset	70	c Bullen		19
11	R.A.Veck	c Bullen	0	b Stevens		10
	Byes		11			2
			241			84

FoW (1): 1- , 2- , 3- , 4- , 5- , 6- , 7- , 8- , 9- , 10-241
FoW (2): 1- , 2- , 3- , 4- , 5- , 6- , 7- , 8- , 9- , 10-84

KENT

1	Duke of Dorset	b Brett	6	c Nyren		2
2	E.Stevens	b Nyren	6	b Barber		2
3	R.Miller	c Small	4	c Sueter		6
4	W.Bowra	b Brett	1	c Small		20
5	W.Bullen	c Francis	29	b Brett		0
6	W.Brazier	c Veck	34	not out		19
7	T.Pattenden	c Small	0	c Aburrow		6
8	J.Boorman	not out	13	c Francis		9
9	F.Booker	run out	41	c Taylor		6
10	T.White	hit wkt	23	c Sueter		0
11	J.Wood (Seal)	b Nyren	9	b Nyren		2
	Byes		7			5
			173			77

FoW (1): 1- , 2- , 3- , 4- , 5- , 6- , 7- , 8- , 9- , 10-173
FoW (2): 1- , 2- , 3- , 4- , 5- , 6- , 7- , 8- , 9- , 10-77

Kent Bowling

	O	M	R	W	O	M	R	W
Stevens				1				1
Dorset				2				
White								2

Hampshire Bowling

	O	M	R	W	O	M	R	W
Brett				2				1
Nyren				2				1
Barber								1

Umpires:

Close of Play: 1st day: .

Kent had Stevens and White as given men.

RM has many differences including one huge one (Hants (1) Nyren 7 not 70, total 177 not 241) but other newspapers confirm the score as given.

(Variant) The diarist Richard Hayes reports that Dorset opened the bowling with a maiden 'but soon hitting began' and goes on to say that Dorset took two good catches. LEP reports that Dorset took three catches, but surviving versions of the score show only one. It is possible that Aylward and Small ought to be 'c Dorset' rather than 'b Dorset', but in view of the uncertainty the score has been left unaltered.

HAMPSHIRE v KENT

Played at Broad Halfpenny Down, Hambledon, July 2, 3, 4, 1776.

Kent won by four wickets.

HAMPSHIRE

1	J.Aylward	c Wood	5	b Stevens	19
2	J.Small, sen	c Bowra	12	b White	57
3	G.Leer	b Stevens	21	b White	23
4	T.Sueter	c Wood	6	c White	16
5	T.Brett	not out	0		
	T.Davis			not out	0
6	E.Aburrow	b Stevens	0	b Wood	7
7	R.Francis	b Stevens	3	b Wood	13
8	T.Taylor	c Bullen	20	b White	22
9	R.Nyren	b Stevens	6	b Stevens	36
10	R.A.Veck	c Brazier	14	b Stevens	14
11	W.Barber	c Bullen	0	b White	8
	Byes				6
			87		221

FoW (1): 1- , 2- , 3- , 4- , 5- , 6- , 7- , 8- , 9- , 10-87
FoW (2): 1- , 2- , 3- , 4- , 5- , 6- , 7- , 8- , 9- , 10-221

KENT

1	Duke of Dorset	c Barber	34	b Francis	1
2	E.Stevens	not out	0		
3	R.Miller	c Leer	16	c Sueter	12
4	W.Bowra	b Francis	31	b Francis	0
5	W.Bullen	b Brett	3		
6	W.Brazier	b Brett	36	b Francis	17
7	T.Pattenden	b Brett	20	b Francis	14
8	J.Boorman	c Sueter	0	not out	38
9	F.Booker	b Taylor	6	not out	17
10	T.White	b Taylor	4	b Brett	38
11	J.Wood (Seal)	b Barber	4		
	Byes		9		10
			163	(6 wickets)	147

FoW (1): 1- , 2- , 3- , 4- , 5- , 6- , 7- , 8- , 9- , 10-163
FoW (2): 1- , 2- , 3- , 4- , 5- , 6-

Kent Bowling

	O	M	R	W	O	M	R	W
Stevens				4				3
White								4
Wood								2

Hampshire Bowling

	O	M	R	W	O	M	R	W
Brett				3				1
Barber				1				
Francis				1				4
Taylor				2				

Umpires:

Close of Play: 1st day: ; 2nd day: .

T.Davis was a full substitute for Hampshire, replacing T.Brett. Kent had Stevens and White as given men.

KENT v HAMPSHIRE

Played at Sevenoaks Vine Cricket Club Ground, July 15, 16, 17, 1776.

Hampshire won by six wickets.

KENT

#	Batsman	Dismissal	Score	2nd innings	Score
1	Duke of Dorset	c Aylward	9	b Francis	0
2	E.Stevens	b Nyren	8	(11) not out	0
3	R.Miller	c Nyren	27	(4) c Veck	21
4	W.Bowra	c Veck	37	(6) b Francis	8
5	W.Bullen	b Brett	4	(7) run out	0
6	W.Brazier	c Taylor	33	(5) c Francis	17
7	T.Pattenden	c Small	8	(2) b Brett	3
8	J.Boorman	not out	5	(3) b Brett	6
9	F.Booker	c Small	1	c Taylor	2
10	T.White	c Leer	9	(8) run out	11
11	J.Wood (Seal)	b Nyren	7	(10) c Leer	0
	Byes		6		1
			154		69

FoW (1): 1- , 2- , 3- , 4- , 5- , 6- , 7- , 8- , 9- , 10-154
FoW (2): 1- , 2- , 3- , 4- , 5- , 6- , 7- , 8- , 9- , 10-69

HAMPSHIRE

#	Batsman	Dismissal	Score	2nd innings	Score
1	E.Aburrow	b Stevens	5		
2	R.A.Veck	c Stevens	10		
3	J.Small, sen	not out	59	c Wood	2
4	T.Sueter	c Stevens	8	c Wood	13
5	J.Aylward	c Bullen	13	c Boorman	0
6	R.Nyren	b Stevens	5	not out	22
7	T.Taylor	b Wood	8		
8	G.Leer	c Stevens	5	not out	47
9	R.Francis	c Boorman	9	c Bowra	5
10	T.Brett	b Wood	5		
11	T.Davis	b Wood	1		
	Byes		2		5
			130	(4 wickets)	94

FoW (1): 1- , 2- , 3- , 4- , 5- , 6- , 7- , 8- , 9- , 10-130
FoW (2): 1- , 2- , 3- , 4-

Hampshire Bowling

	O	M	R	W	O	M	R	W
Brett				1				2
Nyren				2				
Francis								2

Kent Bowling

	O	M	R	W	O	M	R	W
Stevens				2				
Wood				3				

Umpires:

Close of Play: 1st day: ; 2nd day: .

Kent had Stevens and White as given men.

HAMPSHIRE v KENT

Played at Chidden Holt, Hambledon, July 22, 23, 24, 1776.

Kent won by five wickets.

HAMPSHIRE

1	T.Brett	c Booker	0	c Booker		0
2	J.Small, sen	b Wood	20	b Stevens		10
3	J.Aylward	b Stevens	14	c Boorman		9
4	T.Sueter	run out	2	c White		11
5	G.Leer	c Wood	0	b Stevens		18
6	R.Francis	b Stevens	12	c Booker		9
7	R.Nyren	b White	15	b White		12
8	T.Taylor	b Stevens	0	c Booker		5
9	R.A.Veck	not out	14	c Yalden		8
10	E.Aburrow	c Wood	6	not out		25
11	W.Barber	c Pattenden	4	c Yalden		3
	Byes		2			3
			89			113

FoW (1): 1- , 2- , 3- , 4- , 5- , 6- , 7- , 8- , 9- , 10-89
FoW (2): 1- , 2- , 3- , 4- , 5- , 6- , 7- , 8- , 9- , 10-113

KENT

1	J.Boorman	b Brett	0	c Brett		12
2	W.Yalden	b Brett	31	b Brett		15
3	Duke of Dorset	b Brett	5	not out		13
4	J.Bayton	b Brett	5			
5	W.Brazier	b Francis	6	not out		19
6	T.White	c Nyren	14	c Francis		3
7	T.Pattenden	c Sueter	1	c Small		4
8	W.Bowra	c Francis	36			
9	F.Booker	c Taylor	2	c Barber		0
10	J.Wood (Seal)	c Small	3			
11	E.Stevens	not out	16			
	Byes		17			1
			136	(5 wickets)		67

FoW (1): 1- , 2- , 3- , 4- , 5- , 6- , 7- , 8- , 9- , 10-136
FoW (2): 1- , 2- , 3- , 4- , 5-

Kent Bowling

	O	M	R	W	O	M	R	W
Stevens				3				2
White				1				1
Wood				1				

Hampshire Bowling

	O	M	R	W	O	M	R	W
Brett				4				1
Francis				1				

Umpires:

Close of Play: 1st day: ; 2nd day: .

Kent had Stevens, White and Yalden as given men. The team also included Bayton (also Boyton or Boynton), assumed to be John although George is possible. He was not a Kent man but is known to have been associated with the Hambledon Club; Buckly notes press reports that Pattenden and Bayton replaced R.Miller and J.Minchin in the Kent team. The ground name has been modernised: in the 18th century it was 'Cheden'.

(Variant) SB has the visitors as England but several newspapers confirm that it was Kent with three of Surrey.

SURREY v HAMPSHIRE

Played at Laleham Burway Cricket Ground, August 6, 7, 8, 1776.

Surrey won by one wicket.

HAMPSHIRE

1	T.Brett	b Stevens	0	run out	0
2	R.May	b Wood	6	b White	11
3	R.Nyren	b Stevens	7	c Tankerville	4
4	J.Small, sen	b Wood	7	b Stevens	2
5	T.Sueter	c Yalden	1	b Wood	1
6	G.Leer	c Tankerville	8	c Edmeads	6
7	R.Francis	b Stevens	10	b Wood	10
8	R.A.Veck	c Yalden	6	c Yalden	16
9	E.Aburrow	not out	4	c White	20
10	T.Taylor	b Stevens	9	run out	19
11	J.Aylward	c Muggeridge	29	not out	82
	Byes		7		5
			94		176

FoW (1): 1- , 2- , 3- , 4- , 5- , 6- , 7- , 8- , 9- , 10-94
FoW (2): 1- , 2- , 3- , 4- , 5- , 6- , 7- , 8- , 9- , 10-176

SURREY

1	Earl of Tankerville	b Brett	15	b Brett	4
2	H.Attfield	c Francis	0	b Brett	5
3	T.White	run out	58	c Small	20
4	W.Yalden	b Brett	0	c May	20
5	Muggeridge	c Small	4	c May	7
6	W.Palmer	b Brett	2	b Francis	5
7	W.Brazier	c Taylor	14	c Taylor	3
8	J.Edmeads	not out	13	b Taylor	14
9	W.Bowra	run out	19	b Francis	2
10	J.Wood (Pirbright)	c Veck	0	not out	19
11	E.Stevens	b Nyren	11	not out	19
	Byes		5		12
			141	(9 wickets)	130

FoW (1): 1- , 2- , 3- , 4- , 5- , 6- , 7- , 8- , 9- , 10-141
FoW (2): 1- , 2-19, 3- , 4- , 5- , 6- , 7- , 8- , 9-87

Surrey Bowling

	O	M	R	W	O	M	R	W
Stevens				4				1
Wood				2				2
White								1

Hampshire Bowling

	O	M	R	W	O	M	R	W
Brett				3				2
Nyren				1				
Francis								2
Taylor								1

Umpires:

Close of Play: 1st day: Surrey (1) 141 all out; 2nd day: Surrey (2) 19-2 (Attfield 4*).

Hampshire had May as a given man, Surrey had Bowra and Brazier. Surrey's last pair, Stevens and Wood, added 43 runs to win the match. The Hampshire team is not in batting order. In Hampshire (2), the newspapers give the order as Small, Sueter, Francis, Leer, Nyren, Taylor, Veck, Aburrow, Brett, May, Aylward, which is probably the order of dismissal. The newspapers' order for Surrey seems more plausible and has been accepted (although Tankerville may be listed first as patron); changes in Surrey (2) are not known, although Muggeridge and Palmer were the men out at the end of day 2.

HAMPSHIRE v SURREY

Played at Broad Halfpenny Down, Hambledon, August 26, 27, 28, 1776.

Hampshire won by 197 runs.

HAMPSHIRE

1	J.Small, sen	b Wood	85	run out	35
2	J.Aylward	c Tankerville	45	c White	59
3	G.Leer	b Stevens	1	c Yalden	4
4	T.Sueter	c sub (T.Quiddington)	1	b Stevens	5
5	T.Brett	not out	1	not out	15
6	E.Aburrow	b Stevens	49	b Wood	2
7	R.Francis	c Yalden	5	c Wood	0
8	T.Taylor	c Yalden	10	b Wood	2
9	S.Colchin	run out	6	b Stevens	7
10	R.Nyren	c Edmeads	21	c Stevens	1
11	R.A.Veck	b Stevens	46	b Stevens	22
	Byes		3		3
			273		155

FoW (1): 1- , 2- , 3- , 4- , 5- , 6- , 7- , 8- , 9- , 10-273
FoW (2): 1- , 2- , 3- , 4- , 5- , 6- , 7- , 8- , 9- , 10-155

SURREY

1	E.Stevens	b Nyren	2	run out	3
2	Earl of Tankerville	run out	8	c Nyren	15
3	W.Yalden	b Nyren	10	b Nyren	23
4	W.Bowra	b Colchin	34		
	T.Quiddington			not out	14
5	J.Edmeads	b Francis	5	b Francis	47
6	J.Minchin	b Nyren	0		
	W.Yalden			c Francis	14
7	W.Palmer	b Nyren	0	c Sueter	0
8	Muggeridge	b Francis	0	run out	1
9	H.Attfield	b Nyren	8	b Francis	28
10	T.White	b Colchin	1	c Colchin	1
11	J.Wood (Pirbright)	not out	11	b Brett	1
	Byes		4		1
			83		148

FoW (1): 1- , 2- , 3- , 4- , 5- , 6- , 7- , 8- , 9- , 10-83
FoW (2): 1- , 2- , 3- , 4- , 5- , 6- , 7- , 8- , 9- , 10-148

Surrey Bowling

	O	M	R	W	O	M	R	W
Stevens				3				3
Wood				1				2

Hampshire Bowling

	O	M	R	W	O	M	R	W
Nyren				5				1
Francis				2				2
Colchin				2				
Brett								1

Umpires:

Close of Play: 1st day: ; 2nd day: .

T.Quiddington was a full substitute for Surrey, replacing W.Bowra who was ill. Quiddington must have caught Sueter in Surrey (1) as a substitute fielder since he had not replaced Bowra at this stage. Hampshire had Colchin as a given man; Surrey had Bowra as a given man. W.Yalden was allowed to bat twice in Surrey (2), replacing J.Minchin who was ill. Minchin is sometimes cited as a given man for Surrey but Buckley has established that he was residing at Chertsey by 1776 and was regarded as a Surrey man.

ENGLAND v HAMPSHIRE

Played at Sevenoaks Vine Cricket Club Ground, June 18, 19, 20, 1777.

Hampshire won by an innings and 168 runs.

ENGLAND
1	W.Bullen	c Tankerville	13	b Nyren		2
2	T.Pattenden	b Brett	38	c Sueter		0
3	R.Miller	c Small	27	b Brett		23
4	J.Minchin	not out	60	b Taylor		12
5	T.White	c Veck	8	run out		10
6	Duke of Dorset	b Brett	0	c Tankerville		5
7	W.Yalden	c Small	6	c Nyren		8
8	W.Bowra	b Brett	2	b Taylor		4
9	F.Booker	c Brett	8	b Brett		2
10	E.Stevens	b Brett	1	not out		2
11	J.Wood (Pirbright)	b Brett	1	b Nyren		1
	Byes		2			
			166			69

FoW (1): 1- , 2- , 3- , 4- , 5- , 6- , 7- , 8- , 9- , 10-166
FoW (2): 1- , 2- , 3- , 4- , 5- , 6- , 7- , 8- , 9- , 10-69

HAMPSHIRE
1	R.A.Veck	b Stevens	16
2	J.Aylward	b Bullen	167
3	J.Small, sen	c White b Stevens	33
4	Earl of Tankerville	b Wood	3
5	T.Sueter	b Wood	46
6	G.Leer	b Wood	7
7	T.Taylor	c Bullen b Wood	32
8	R.Nyren	b Stevens	37
9	R.Francis	c and b Wood	26
10	E.Aburrow	c Minchin b Bullen	22
11	T.Brett	not out	9
	Byes		5
			403

FoW (1): 1- , 2- , 3- , 4- , 5- , 6- , 7- , 8- , 9- , 10-403

Hampshire Bowling
	O	M	R	W	O	M	R	W
Brett				5				2
Nyren								2
Taylor								2

England Bowling
	O	M	R	W
Stevens				3
Wood				5
Bullen				2

Umpires:

Close of Play: 1st day: Hampshire (1) ?-? (Aylward not out); 2nd day: Hampshire (1) ?-? (Aylward not out).

This is a famous match. Aylward's score of 167 set a record that remained unbeaten, at least in top cricket, until 1820. Haygarth quotes from a printed bill of the match that 'Aylward went in at 5 o'clock on Wednesday, and was not out till after 3 on Friday.' Ironically, the announcement of this match in the *Kentish Gazette* stated that 'to shorten the game' three stumps would be used. Another strikingly modern feature, unique for this period, is that in the Hampshire innings the name of the bowler is added when a batsman is caught.

HAMPSHIRE v ENGLAND

Played at Broad Halfpenny Down, Hambledon, July 7, 8, 9, 10, 1777.

England won by 28 runs.

ENGLAND

1	W.Yalden	b Brett	1	c Taylor	44
2	J.Wood (Pirbright)	b Francis	9	b Small	0
3	R.Miller	b Francis	4	b Brett	65
4	J.Minchin	b Brett	21	b Brett	16
5	W.Bowra	run out	2	b Francis	6
6	W.Bullen	b Brett	1	c Sueter	27
7	Duke of Dorset	c Tankerville	2	b Small	0
8	R.Clifford	b Brett	7	run out	4
9	T.White	b Nyren	3	b Small	3
10	F.Booker	b Nyren	5	c Nyren	29
11	E.Stevens	not out	1	not out	5
	Byes		4		8
			60		207

FoW (1): 1- , 2- , 3- , 4- , 5- , 6- , 7- , 8- , 9- , 10-60
FoW (2): 1- , 2- , 3- , 4- , 5- , 6- , 7- , 8- , 9- , 10-207

HAMPSHIRE

1	J.Aylward	c Miller	16	b Wood	0
2	R.A.Veck	b White	54	not out	0
3	J.Small, sen	b Wood	3	run out	8
4	T.Sueter	c Wood	21	c Yalden	1
5	G.Leer	c Yalden	15	c Wood	0
6	Earl of Tankerville	run out	0	c Miller	7
7	T.Taylor	b Stevens	0	b Stevens	2
8	R.Nyren	b White	18	c Yalden	17
9	E.Aburrow	b Stevens	25	run out	2
10	R.Francis	b Dorset	35	b Stevens	6
11	T.Brett	not out	6	c Bullen	1
	Byes		1		1
			194		45

FoW (1): 1- , 2- , 3- , 4- , 5- , 6- , 7- , 8- , 9- , 10-194
FoW (2): 1- , 2- , 3- , 4- , 5- , 6- , 7- , 8- , 9- , 10-45

Hampshire Bowling

	O	M	R	W	O	M	R	W
Brett				4				2
Nyren				2				
Francis				2				1
Small								3

England Bowling

	O	M	R	W	O	M	R	W
Stevens				2				2
Dorset				1				
Wood				1				1
White				2				

Umpires:

Close of Play: 1st day: ; 2nd day: ; 3rd day: .

Owing to injury, Veck went in late in Hampshire (2). England won after being 134 behind on first innings.

ENGLAND v HAMPSHIRE

Played at Laleham Burway Cricket Ground, July 22, 23, 24, 25, 26, 1777.

Hampshire won by 39 runs.

HAMPSHIRE

#	Batsman	Dismissal	Score	Dismissal (2)	Score (2)
1	R.A.Veck	b Lamborn	2	c Edmeads	9
2	E.Aburrow	c White	0	b Stevens	22
3	J.Small, sen	c Edmeads	28	b Stevens	14
4	J.Aylward	c Edmeads	17	c Tankerville	0
5	T.Sueter	c Yalden	7	b Wood	20
6	G.Leer	b Wood	0	b Wood	69
7	Duke of Dorset	b Lamborn	37	c Tankerville	16
8	R.Francis	c Wood	0	run out	4
9	R.Nyren	b Lamborn	10	c Bullen	9
10	T.Taylor	not out	0	c Yalden	20
11	T.Brett	b Stevens	6	not out	0
	Byes		8		4
			115		187

FoW (1): 1- , 2- , 3- , 4- , 5- , 6- , 7- , 8- , 9- , 10-115
FoW (2): 1- , 2- , 3- , 4- , 5- , 6- , 7- , 8- , 9- , 10-187

ENGLAND

#	Batsman	Dismissal	Score	Dismissal (2)	Score (2)
1	W.Bullen	b Brett	3	c Aburrow	38
2	J.Minchin	retired hurt	7		
	H.Attfield	run out	16	b Brett	0
3	R.Miller	c Francis	0	c Francis	2
4	Earl of Tankerville	b Dorset	34	b Nyren	21
5	W.Yalden	c Veck	1	not out	29
6	W.Bowra	b Brett	28	b Nyren	8
7	T.White	b Dorset	24	c Small	6
8	J.Edmeads	c Sueter	14	b Brett	5
9	E.Stevens	not out	7	b Brett	3
10	J.Wood (Pirbright)	b Brett	5	run out	4
11	Lamborn	b Brett	0	b Brett	3
	Byes		4		1
			143		120

FoW (1): 1- , 2- , 3- , 4- , 5- , 6- , 7- , 8- , 9- , 10-143
FoW (2): 1- , 2- , 3- , 4- , 5- , 6- , 7- , 8- , 9- , 10-120

England Bowling

	O	M	R	W	O	M	R	W
Stevens				1				2
Wood				1				2
Lamborn				3				

Hampshire Bowling

	O	M	R	W	O	M	R	W
Brett				4				4
Dorset				2				
Nyren								2

Umpires:

Close of Play: 1st day: ; 2nd day: ; 3rd day: ; 4th day: .

H.Attfield was a full substitute for England, replacing J.Minchin who injured his knee. Hampshire had the Duke of Dorset as a given man.

A return was planned for 4 August at Kilmiston Down (near Alresford) but Tankerville chose to pay forfeit and the game did not take place.

ENGLAND v HAMPSHIRE

Played at Merrow Down, Guildford, August 18, 19, 20, 1777.

Hampshire won by one wicket.

ENGLAND

1	J.Minchin	not out	33	b Mann	0
2	W.Bullen	b Nyren	0	b Mann	20
3	Earl of Tankerville	b Brett	1	b Nyren	46
4	R.Miller	run out	2	b Mann	65
5	W.Yalden	c Taylor	6	b Brett	42
6	W.Bowra	b Nyren	5	run out	12
7	J.Edmeads	b Brett	1	c Francis	6
8	C.Phillips	b Nyren	0	c Veck	20
9	E.Stevens	run out	1	not out	6
10	J.Wood (Pirbright)	b Brett	0	run out (Brett)	17
11	Lamborn	b Nyren	1	c Aylward	10
	Byes				7
			50		251

FoW (1): 1- , 2- , 3- , 4- , 5- , 6- , 7- , 8- , 9- , 10-50
FoW (2): 1- , 2- , 3- , 4- , 5- , 6- , 7- , 8- , 9- , 10-251

HAMPSHIRE

1	R.A.Veck	c Yalden	1	c Bullen	17
2	R.Francis	c Tankerville	15	b Stevens	9
3	J.Aylward	c Bowra	30	b Stevens	0
4	J.Small, sen	c Minchin	14	c Wood	33
5	T.Sueter	b Wood	14	not out	11
6	N.Mann	c Bullen	27	c Edmeads	15
7	T.Taylor	c Edmeads	19	c Wood	58
8	R.Nyren	b Stevens	4	not out	8
9	E.Aburrow	b Stevens	3	b Stevens	9
10	T.Brett	not out	3	b Bullen	3
11	W.Barber	b Stevens	0	b Stevens	0
	Byes		2		8
			132	(9 wickets)	171

FoW (1): 1- , 2- , 3- , 4- , 5- , 6- , 7- , 8- , 9- , 10-132
FoW (2): 1- , 2- , 3- , 4- , 5- , 6- , 7- , 8- , 9-

Hampshire Bowling

	O	M	R	W	O	M	R	W
Brett				3				1
Nyren				4				1
Mann								3

England Bowling

	O	M	R	W	O	M	R	W
Stevens				3				4
Wood				1				
Bullen								1

Umpires:

Close of Play: 1st day: ; 2nd day: .

The Dorset papers at the Kent Archive Office, Maidstone, give a full score with additional information, attributing blame for run-outs (Miller (1) - Minchin's fault; Bowra (2) - Tankerville's fault) which, apart from being interesting in itself, gives valuable information about who was batting in partnership. The Dorset papers also tell us that Wood (2) was 'thrown out by Brett', which is assumed to mean run out, and that Aylward (2) and Barber (2) were out first ball. These details tend to increase confidence in the general reliability of the score, besides adding colour and interest. One can almost sense the delight of England's backers when Stevens removed the dangerous Aylward first ball.

HAMPSHIRE v ENGLAND

Played at Broad Halfpenny Down, Hambledon, September 8, 9, 10, 1777.

England won by 56 runs.

ENGLAND
1	W.Bullen	c Leer	45	b Brett		34
2	W.Bowra	b Nyren	4	b Nyren		19
3	Earl of Tankerville	b Brett	13	b Mann		21
4	R.Miller	b Mann	52	b Veck		39
5	W.Yalden	b Mann	7	c Brett		10
6	J.Bayton	b Brett	1	c Francis		13
7	J.Edmeads	b Brett	10	not out		34
8	S.Colchin	c Francis	2	c Mann		4
9	W.Bedster	not out	6	run out		0
10	E.Stevens	b Brett	2	c Francis		5
11	Lamborn	b Brett	2	c Francis		2
	Byes		3			7
			147			188

FoW (1): 1- , 2- , 3- , 4- , 5- , 6- , 7- , 8- , 9- , 10-147
FoW (2): 1- , 2- , 3- , 4- , 5- , 6- , 7- , 8- , 9- , 10-188

HAMPSHIRE
1	R.A.Veck	c Edmeads	15	b Colchin		16
2	T.Taylor	c Bayton	1	b Lamborn		13
3	J.Aylward	b Stevens	29	c sub (Goodwin)		47
4	J.Small, sen	b Lamborn	16	b Stevens		30
5	T.Sueter	c Bullen	5	b Colchin		0
6	G.Leer	b Lamborn	9	c Tankerville		3
7	R.Francis	c Bullen	24	b Lamborn		1
8	R.Nyren	b Lamborn	6	not out		15
9	N.Mann	b Stevens	5	b Stevens		9
10	E.Aburrow	b Lamborn	0	b Colchin		5
11	T.Brett	not out	1	c Bullen		1
	Byes		6			22
			117			162

FoW (1): 1- , 2- , 3- , 4- , 5- , 6- , 7- , 8- , 9- , 10-117
FoW (2): 1- , 2- , 3- , 4- , 5- , 6- , 7- , 8- , 9- , 10-162

Hampshire Bowling
	O	M	R	W	O	M	R	W
Brett				5				1
Nyren				1				1
Mann				2				1
Veck								1

England Bowling
	O	M	R	W	O	M	R	W
Stevens				2				2
Lamborn				4				2
Colchin								3

Umpires:

Close of Play: 1st day: ; 2nd day: .

The Dorset papers are again the source. Unfortunately they do not give a full score for Hampshire (2), although they note that Colchin took 3 in 5 balls and Aylward and Veck 'got near 80'; since their scores add to 63, this implies that a large proportion of the 22 byes occurred during their partnership. These details are consistent with the score for Hampshire (2) in the *Hampshire Chronicle*, which is therefore accepted despite the normal reluctance to mix sources.

ENGLAND v HAMPSHIRE

Played at Honourable Artillery Company Ground, Finsbury, September 15, 16, 17, 1777.

Hampshire won by 130 runs.

HAMPSHIRE

1	R.A.Veck	c Bullen	18	c Stevens	78
2	E.Aburrow	b Stevens	5	not out	1
3	J.Aylward	c Yalden	58	c Edmeads	28
4	J.Small, sen	c Yalden	4	c Yalden	1
5	T.Sueter	b Stevens	19	b Colchin	11
6	R.Nyren	b Stevens	15	b Colchin	9
7	T.Taylor	b Stevens	26	b Bullen	8
8	G.Leer	b Stevens	15	b Stevens	33
9	R.Francis	run out	11	c Pemmell	4
10	N.Mann	b Stevens	2	c Edmeads	9
11	Baker	not out	0	c Edmeads	1
	Byes		13		28
			186		211

FoW (1): 1- , 2- , 3- , 4- , 5- , 6- , 7- , 8- , 9- , 10-186
FoW (2): 1- , 2- , 3- , 4- , 5- , 6- , 7- , 8- , 9- , 10-211

ENGLAND

1	W.Bullen	c Aburrow	5	c Aburrow	2
2	W.Bowra	b Mann	8	b Nyren	9
3	Earl of Tankerville	c Francis	14	c Small	22
4	R.Miller	c Taylor	21	c Aylward	11
5	W.Yalden	b Nyren	0	b Taylor	10
6	J.Edmeads	b Taylor	21	b Francis	14
7	W.Bedster	b Taylor	19	c Aylward	28
8	Pemmell	not out	18	b Mann	4
9	S.Colchin	run out	26	b Nyren	8
10	E.Stevens	run out	3	c Nyren	6
11	Lamborn	c Aburrow	7	not out	3
	Byes		8		
			150		117

FoW (1): 1- , 2- , 3- , 4- , 5- , 6- , 7- , 8- , 9- , 10-150
FoW (2): 1- , 2- , 3- , 4- , 5- , 6- , 7- , 8- , 9- , 10-117

England Bowling

	O	M	R	W	O	M	R	W
Stevens				6				1
Bullen								1
Colchin								2

Hampshire Bowling

	O	M	R	W	O	M	R	W
Nyren				1				2
Mann				1				1
Taylor				2				1
Francis								1

Umpires:

Close of Play: 1st day: England (1) 32-2 (Tankerville 5*, Miller 14*); 2nd day: Hampshire (2) 121-4.

Again, the Dorset papers supply additional information, assigning blame for two run-outs (Colchin (1), his fault; Stevens (1), Pemmell's fault) and telling us that Baker (1) did not face a ball, and Yalden (1) was out first ball. Second-innings orders are not known, but Veck and Aylward shared a 3rd-wicket partnership of 57 in Hampshire (2), and Tankerville and Miller opened in England (2). The England no 8 is also spelt Pemel and Pennell but Pemmell seems to be the most frequent version. This is the final 'great' match played at this historic ground, although it remains in existence and is still used for cricket.

ENGLAND v HAMPSHIRE

Played at Sevenoaks Vine Cricket Club Ground, June 29, 30, 1778.

Hampshire won by three wickets.

ENGLAND

1	R.Clifford	b Francis	10	b Nyren		15
2	E.Stevens	b Mann	11	b Brett		4
3	R.Miller	run out	0	b Brett		32
4	J.Minchin	c Taylor	0	c Sueter		12
5	W.Bowra	run out	14	b Nyren		2
6	T.White	b Brett	13	b Mann		11
7	J.Wood (Pirbright)	b Francis	7	not out		7
8	W.Yalden	c Taylor	19	run out		22
9	Lamborn	not out	2	c Veck		4
10	W.Bullen	b Brett	5	c Aburrow		6
11	F.Booker	b Mann	0	b Mann		4
	Byes		7			3
			88			122

FoW (1): 1- , 2- , 3- , 4- , 5- , 6- , 7- , 8- , 9- , 10-88
FoW (2): 1- , 2- , 3- , 4- , 5- , 6- , 7- , 8- , 9- , 10-122

HAMPSHIRE

1	J.Small, sen	c Yalden	1	b Lamborn		6
2	T.Sueter	b Stevens	3	not out		2
3	G.Leer	c Yalden	4			
4	R.Nyren	b Stevens	3	c Yalden		38
5	R.Francis	b Lamborn	24	c Stevens		0
6	R.A.Veck	c Wood	2	not out		53
7	T.Taylor	c Minchin	0	c Wood		5
8	E.Aburrow	not out	1	b Lamborn		0
9	T.Brett	c Wood	0			
10	W.Bedster	c Minchin	12	c Yalden		7
11	N.Mann	b Stevens	16	c Yalden		19
	Byes		5			10
			71	(7 wickets)		140

FoW (1): 1- , 2- , 3- , 4- , 5- , 6- , 7- , 8- , 9- , 10-71
FoW (2): 1- , 2- , 3- , 4- , 5- , 6- , 7-

Hampshire Bowling

	O	M	R	W	O	M	R	W
Brett				2				2
Francis				2				
Mann				2				2
Nyren								2

England Bowling

	O	M	R	W	O	M	R	W
Stevens				3				
Lamborn				1				2

Umpires:

Close of Play: 1st day: .

Hampshire had Bedster as a given man.

HAMPSHIRE v ENGLAND

Played at Stoke Down, Alresford, July 6, 7, 1778.

England won by 45 runs.

ENGLAND

1	W.Bullen	b Nyren	0	not out	12
2	W.Bedster	b Francis	3	b Brett	34
3	R.Miller	c Sueter	1	b Nyren	9
4	J.Minchin	b Taylor	31	run out	0
5	T.White	b Taylor	33	b Nyren	16
6	W.Bowra	run out	2	run out	29
7	W.Yalden	not out	24	c Taylor	10
8	F.Booker	b Taylor	2	c Francis	3
9	E.Stevens	c Taylor	19	b Nyren	11
10	J.Wood (Pirbright)	b Mann	26	c Aburrow	0
11	Lamborn	b Mann	0	b Nyren	1
	Byes		2		5
			143		130

FoW (1): 1- , 2- , 3- , 4- , 5- , 6- , 7- , 8- , 9- , 10-143
FoW (2): 1- , 2- , 3- , 4- , 5- , 6- , 7- , 8- , 9- , 10-130

HAMPSHIRE

1	E.Aburrow	b Lamborn	14	b Lamborn	0
2	R.Francis	b Lamborn	0	b Stevens	23
3	T.Sueter	b Lamborn	22	not out	17
4	R.A.Veck	c Wood	7	c Stevens	7
5	J.Small, sen	not out	49	b Stevens	4
6	T.Taylor	b Lamborn	1	b Lamborn	5
7	N.Mann	c Yalden	7	b Lamborn	0
8	G.Leer	b Stevens	17	c Yalden	2
9	R.Nyren	c Miller	5	b Stevens	3
10	R.Stone	run out	0	run out	0
11	T.Brett	c Bullen	19	b Wood	12
	Byes		11		3
			152		76

FoW (1): 1- , 2- , 3- , 4- , 5- , 6- , 7- , 8- , 9- , 10-152
FoW (2): 1- , 2- , 3- , 4- , 5- , 6- , 7- , 8- , 9- , 10-76

Hampshire Bowling

	O	M	R	W	O	M	R	W
Nyren				1				4
Francis				1				
Taylor				3				
Mann				2				
Brett								1

England Bowling

	O	M	R	W	O	M	R	W
Stevens				1				3
Lamborn				4				3
Wood								1

Umpires:

Close of Play: 1st day: .

CHERTSEY v ENGLAND

Played at Laleham Burway Cricket Ground, September 10, 11, 1778.

Chertsey won by an innings and 25 runs.

ENGLAND
1	Boltwood	c Bedster	27	b Stevens		7
2	S.Colchin	b Lamborn	0	b Stevens		4
3	R.Miller	b Stevens	5	c Minchin		29
4	J.Aylward	run out	1	b Lamborn		5
5	J.Boorman	c Bedster	0	b Lamborn		7
6	Mansfield	c Minchin	2	not out		15
7	C.Phillips	c Mills	6	b Lamborn		2
8	W.Bullen	b Stevens	2	c Attfield		2
9	Pemmell	c Bedster	2	b Lamborn		2
10	Polden	not out	2	b Lamborn		8
11	Irons	b Lamborn	4	b Lamborn		0
	Byes		14			7
			65			88

FoW (1): 1- , 2- , 3- , 4- , 5- , 6- , 7- , 8- , 9- , 10-65
FoW (2): 1- , 2- , 3- , 4- , 5- , 6- , 7- , 8- , 9- , 10-88

CHERTSEY
1	J.Edmeads	b Bullen	20
2	T.Swayne	b Polden	5
3	W.Yalden	b Polden	49
4	E.Stevens	not out	24
5	H.Attfield	b Polden	24
6	J.Minchin	c Pemmell	12
7	W.Bartholomew	b Mansfield	9
8	W.Bedster	c Aylward	9
9	R.Simmons	b Boorman	6
10	Lamborn	b Bullen	6
11	Mills	b Polden	2
	Byes		12
			178

FoW (1): 1- , 2- , 3- , 4- , 5- , 6- , 7- , 8- , 9- , 10-178

Chertsey Bowling
	O	M	R	W	O	M	R	W
Stevens				2				2
Lamborn				2				6

England Bowling
	O	M	R	W
Bullen				2
Boorman				1
Mansfield				1
Polden				4

Umpires:

Close of Play: 1st day: .

Although Chertsey matches have generally not been included, an exception is made in this case because of the strength of the Chertsey team: almost a full Surrey side except for T.White. The England team excluded Hampshire, but it includes some strong players alongside a few lesser lights. It is possible that Irons is to be identified with John I'ons, who scored 197 in a match in 1783, according to the *Sporting Magazine* in 1795. A return match was advertised for the Artillery Ground on 15 September but no details have been found and it may not have taken place.

HAMPSHIRE v SURREY

Played at Broad Halfpenny Down, Hambledon, September 24, 25, 1778.

Hampshire won by four wickets.

SURREY

1	H.Attfield	b Mann	1	b Nyren	7
2	W.Bedster	not out	63	b Nyren	10
3	R.Miller	c Taylor	3	not out	59
4	T.White	b Nyren	28	c Taylor	3
5	J.Minchin	c Sueter	3	run out	6
6	W.Yalden	b Nyren	0	c Veck	20
7	R.Simmons	b Francis	0	b Nyren	2
8	Mills	b Francis	1	b Mann	20
9	J.Edmeads	run out	8	b Nyren	6
10	E.Stevens	run out	3	b Mann	21
11	Lamborn	b Taylor	1	b Brett	2
	Byes		4		10
			115		166

FoW (1): 1- , 2- , 3- , 4- , 5- , 6- , 7- , 8- , 9- , 10-115
FoW (2): 1- , 2- , 3- , 4- , 5- , 6- , 7- , 8- , 9- , 10-166

HAMPSHIRE

1	P.Stewart	b Lamborn	3		
2	J.Small, sen	b Stevens	10	c Yalden	15
3	R.A.Veck	c Attfield	6	b Stevens	46
4	T.Taylor	c Attfield	8	b Lamborn	7
5	N.Mann	b Stevens	31	not out	3
6	T.Sueter	c Stevens	9	b Stevens	49
7	R.Francis	b Stevens	19	not out	4
8	G.Leer	c Stevens	8	c Stevens	9
9	R.Nyren	c Attfield	8		
10	E.Aburrow	not out	10		
11	T.Brett	b Stevens	15	b Stevens	6
	Byes		8		8
			135	(6 wickets)	147

FoW (1): 1- , 2- , 3- , 4- , 5- , 6- , 7- , 8- , 9- , 10-135
FoW (2): 1- , 2- , 3- , 4- , 5- , 6-

Hampshire Bowling

	O	M	R	W	O	M	R	W
Mann				1				2
Nyren				2				4
Francis				2				
Taylor				1				
Brett								1

Surrey Bowling

	O	M	R	W	O	M	R	W
Lamborn				1				1
Stevens				4				3

Umpires:

Close of Play: 1st day: .

The full score of this match, which escaped Epps, Haygarth, Ashley-Cooper and Waghorn, was discovered by Martin Wilson. It was reproduced in the ACS journal in March 2010, which is believed to have been its first appearance in print since its initial publication in the *General Advertiser* for 1 October 1778. Surrey had Miller as a given man. If the batting order is correct (and it looks very plausible), Bedster carried his bat in Surrey (1).

SURREY v HAMPSHIRE

Played at Laleham Burway Cricket Ground, October 6, 7, 8, 1778.

Surrey won by 147 runs.

SURREY

1	J.Edmeads	run out	1	c Francis		12
2	W.Yalden	c Small	24	b Brett		14
3	J.Minchin	b Brett	75	b Mann		17
4	E.Stevens	b Brett	0	not out		4
5	Lamborn	b Brett	0	c Leer		0
6	H.Attfield	b Mann	18	b Brett		0
7	W.Bedster	b Taylor	48	b Nyren		19
8	Muggeridge	c Taylor	4	b Mann		3
9	T.White	not out	23	c Stewart		1
10	Mills	run out	1	b Mann		10
11	R.Miller	b Taylor	42	c Nyren		20
	Byes		2			5
			238			105

FoW (1): 1- , 2- , 3- , 4- , 5- , 6- , 7- , 8- , 9- , 10-238
FoW (2): 1- , 2- , 3- , 4- , 5- , 6- , 7- , 8- , 9- , 10-105

HAMPSHIRE

1	H.Bonham	b Stevens	4	st Yalden		9
2	J.Small, sen	b Stevens	6	run out		3
3	R.Nyren	b Lamborn	0	c White		0
4	N.Mann	b Lamborn	2	b Stevens		4
5	T.Brett	c Muggeridge	6	c Minchin		0
6	E.Aburrow	c Yalden	0	b Stevens		10
7	P.Stewart	b Lamborn	3	not out		0
8	T.Taylor	not out	18	b Lamborn		5
9	R.Francis	b Lamborn	15	b Stevens		11
10	G.Leer	b Lamborn	31	c Edmeads		17
11	T.Sueter	b Lamborn	17	b Stevens		20
	Byes		5			10
			107			89

FoW (1): 1- , 2- , 3- , 4- , 5- , 6- , 7- , 8- , 9- , 10-107
FoW (2): 1- , 2- , 3- , 4- , 5- , 6- , 7- , 8- , 9- , 10-89

Hampshire Bowling

	O	M	R	W	O	M	R	W
Brett				3				2
Taylor				2				
Mann				1				3
Nyren								1

Surrey Bowling

	O	M	R	W	O	M	R	W
Stevens				2				4
Lamborn				6				1

Umpires:

Close of Play: 1st day: Surrey (1) 120-3; 2nd day: .

Surrey had Miller as a given man.

The version above is supported by two newspapers and substantially by Epps (except that he has Nyren (1) with 9, probably a copying error), but Chertsey Museum holds a manuscript and printed scorecard giving very different details, viz: Surrey (2) Minchin 19, byes 2, total 104; Hampshire (2) Aburrow b Lamborn 0, Leer 18, Sueter 11, byes 7, total 68; margin 167 runs. Some sources give the losing team as England but the above is as in Epps and SB.

HAMPSHIRE v ENGLAND

Played at Stoke Down, Alresford, June 14, 15, 1779.

Hampshire won by six wickets.

ENGLAND

1	W.Bullen	run out	5	c Sueter	4
2	W.Bedster	c Small	23	b Mann	26
3	R.Miller	b Nyren	23	c Sueter	25
4	J.Minchin	c Small	7	c Small	17
5	B.Rimmington	b Nyren	2	b Nyren	18
6	W.Bowra	c Aylward	9	c Tankerville	9
7	Mills	b Nyren	5	b Nyren	34
8	R.Clifford	b Nyren	3	c Tankerville	34
9	F.Booker	not out	1	c Aburrow	7
10	E.Stevens	run out	0	not out	4
11	Lamborn	b Francis	0	c Nyren	0
	Byes		2		1
			80		179

FoW (1): 1- , 2- , 3- , 4- , 5- , 6- , 7- , 8- , 9- , 10-80
FoW (2): 1- , 2- , 3- , 4- , 5- , 6- , 7- , 8- , 9- , 10-179

HAMPSHIRE

1	Earl of Tankerville	c Booker	6	b Lamborn	12
2	J.Small, sen	b Stevens	16	b Stevens	11
3	J.Aylward	b Lamborn	12	b Stevens	27
4	R.A.Veck	b Stevens	30	not out	39
5	T.Sueter	b Stevens	44		
6	T.Taylor	b Stevens	10		
7	G.Leer	c Bedster	2		
8	E.Aburrow	b Lamborn	11	not out	25
9	R.Francis	c Bowra	0		
10	N.Mann	b Lamborn	4		
11	R.Nyren	not out	0	b Bullen	6
	Byes		2		5
			137	(4 wickets)	125

FoW (1): 1- , 2- , 3- , 4- , 5- , 6- , 7- , 8- , 9- , 10-137
FoW (2): 1- , 2- , 3- , 4-

Hampshire Bowling

	O	M	R	W	O	M	R	W
Nyren				4				2
Francis				1				
Mann								1

England Bowling

	O	M	R	W	O	M	R	W
Stevens				4				2
Lamborn				3				1
Bullen								1

Umpires:

Close of Play: 1st day: .

ENGLAND v HAMPSHIRE

Played at Sevenoaks Vine Cricket Club Ground, June 23, 24, 25, 26, 1779.

Hampshire won by an innings and 89 runs.

ENGLAND
1	W.Bedster	c Small	22	b Francis		37
2	Mills	b Mann	3	c Sueter		7
3	R.Miller	hit wkt	0	b Mann		0
4	W.Bullen	b Mann	1	not out		5
5	J.Minchin	b Nyren	3	run out		4
6	W.Bowra	b Nyren	0	c Mann		11
7	W.Yalden	b Nyren	0	c Mann		2
8	R.Clifford	b Mann	2	c Veck		12
9	T.White	c Taylor	3	b Nyren		6
10	Lamborn	c Mann	1	b Mann		0
11	E.Stevens	not out	21	b Mann		3
	Byes					
			56			87

FoW (1): 1- , 2- , 3- , 4- , 5- , 6- , 7- , 8- , 9- , 10-56
FoW (2): 1- , 2- , 3- , 4- , 5- , 6- , 7- , 8- , 9- , 10-87

HAMPSHIRE
1	E.Aburrow	b Bullen	16
2	J.Aylward	b Bullen	13
3	J.Small, sen	b Lamborn	3
4	Earl of Tankerville	b Stevens	6
5	R.A.Veck	b Lamborn	79
6	N.Mann	b Lamborn	56
7	R.Francis	b Lamborn	1
8	T.Taylor	b Lamborn	13
9	T.Sueter	c Bowra	11
10	G.Leer	c Yalden	9
11	R.Nyren	not out	14
	Byes		11
			232

FoW (1): 1- , 2- , 3- , 4- , 5- , 6- , 7- , 8- , 9- , 10-232

Hampshire Bowling
	O	M	R	W	O	M	R	W
Nyren				3				1
Mann				3				3
Francis								1

England Bowling
	O	M	R	W
Stevens				1
Lamborn				5
Bullen				2

Umpires:

Close of Play: 1st day: ; 2nd day: ; 3rd day: .

SURREY v KENT

Played at Laleham Burway Cricket Ground, August 9, 10, 11, 1779.

Kent won by five wickets.

SURREY

1	Earl of Tankerville	c Bowra	11	c Bowra	16
2	W.Bedster	b Bullen	0	c Boorman	20
3	Lamborn	b Boorman	0	b Bullen	3
4	J.Minchin	run out	40	c Miller	11
5	R.Simmons	b May	2	b Bullen	3
6	J.Edmeads	c Booker	20	c Pattenden	3
7	W.Yalden	c Rimmington	27	b Bullen	3
8	Berwick	b Boorman	1	not out	9
9	Mills	c Bowra	11	c Aylward	9
10	H.Attfield	b Boorman	7	c Bullen	25
11	E.Stevens	not out	4	b May	3
	Byes				3
			123		108

FoW (1): 1- , 2- , 3- , 4- , 5- , 6- , 7- , 8- , 9- , 10-123
FoW (2): 1- , 2- , 3- , 4- , 5- , 6- , 7- , 8- , 9- , 10-108

KENT

1	J.Boorman	b Lamborn	0		
2	R.A.Veck	c Yalden	55	b Stevens	9
3	J.Aylward	c Yalden	4	c Yalden	11
4	W.Bullen	b Lamborn	17	not out	19
5	F.Booker	b Stevens	1		
6	W.Bowra	c Lamborn	15	not out	11
7	R.Clifford	b Stevens	1		
8	R.Miller	b Stevens	25	b Lamborn	25
9	B.Rimmington	b Lamborn	15	c Yalden	6
10	T.Pattenden	c Bedster	4	b Lamborn	7
11	R.May	not out	2		
	Byes		2		3
			141	(5 wickets)	91

FoW (1): 1- , 2- , 3- , 4- , 5- , 6- , 7- , 8- , 9- , 10-141
FoW (2): 1- , 2- , 3- , 4- , 5-

Kent Bowling

	O	M	R	W		O	M	R	W
Boorman				3					
Bullen				1					3
May				1					1

Surrey Bowling

	O	M	R	W		O	M	R	W
Stevens				3					1
Lamborn				3					2

Umpires:

Close of Play: 1st day: ; 2nd day: .

Kent had Aylward and Veck as given men.

(Variant) SB notes that in two other accounts the score varies in twenty places, but gives no details. Epps actually gives two versions of this match: one dated 9 August as above, the other dated 30 August with many minor variants.

HAMPSHIRE v ENGLAND

Played at Broad Halfpenny Down, Hambledon, August 23, 1779.

Hampshire won by 149 runs.

HAMPSHIRE

1	E.Aburrow	2	b Lamborn		9
2	N.Mann	45	b Lamborn		23
3	J.Small, sen	66	b Stevens		6
4	R.A.Veck	8	b Bullen		14
5	T.Sueter	10	c Bullen		24
6	G.Leer	2	c Yalden		58
7	T.Taylor	6	b Lamborn		2
8	Berwick	0	not out		10
9	P.Stewart	4	b Stevens		2
10	R.Nyren	1	c Aylward		14
11	W.Bowra	16	b Lamborn		12
	Byes	7			8
		167			182

FoW (1): 1- , 2- , 3- , 4- , 5- , 6- , 7- , 8- , 9- , 10-167
FoW (2): 1- , 2- , 3- , 4- , 5- , 6- , 7- , 8- , 9- , 10-182

ENGLAND

1	W.Bedster	8	b Nyren		2
2	Earl of Tankerville	0	c Nyren		12
3	W.Yalden	10	b Berwick		0
4	H.Attfield	17	c Veck		16
5	R.Miller	0	b Mann		37
6	J.Minchin	0	b Nyren		4
7	Lamborn	0	b Mann		0
8	W.Bullen	3	b Mann		6
9	E.Stevens	4	not out		1
10	R.Clifford	17	c Aburrow		3
11	J.Aylward	51	b Nyren		3
	Byes	2			4
		112			88

FoW (1): 1- , 2- , 3- , 4- , 5- , 6- , 7- , 8- , 9- , 10-112
FoW (2): 1- , 2- , 3- , 4- , 5- , 6- , 7- , 8- , 9- , 10-88

Bowling

	O	M	R	W		O	M	R	W
Lamborn									4
Stevens									2
Bullen									1

Bowling

	O	M	R	W		O	M	R	W
Nyren									3
Berwick									1
Mann									3

Umpires:

The first innings dismissal details are not available. Hampshire had Berwick and Bowra as given men. The scoring suggests that the match must have continued into at least a second day. Clearly Aylward did not bat last for England, but no better order is available.

(Variant) SB notes that another account says the match was played at Chertsey.

ENGLAND v HAMPSHIRE

Played at Molesey Hurst, September 13, 14, 15, 16, 1779.

Hampshire won by two wickets.

ENGLAND

1	H.Attfield	b Nyren	9		46
2	W.Bedster	b Nyren	1		7
3	J.Aylward	c Bowra	4		6
4	R.Miller	b Mann	7		34
5	J.Minchin	b Berwick	0		34
6	W.Yalden	c Berwick	0		25
7	W.Bullen	c Taylor	35		12
8	J.Edmeads	c Veck	0		0
9	E.Stevens	b Nyren	2		52
10	R.Clifford	c Taylor	33		21
11	Lamborn	not out	0	not out	3
	Byes				2
			91		242

FoW (1): 1- , 2- , 3- , 4- , 5- , 6- , 7- , 8- , 9- , 10-91
FoW (2): 1- , 2- , 3- , 4- , 5- , 6- , 7- , 8- , 9- , 10-242

HAMPSHIRE

1	G.Leer	c Bullen	21		10
2	T.Taylor	c Bedster	81		3
3	J.Small, sen	c Yalden	5		9
4	R.A.Veck	c Bedster	3		43
5	N.Mann	b Bedster	37		1
6	T.Sueter	b Bullen	5	not out	11
7	W.Bowra	b Stevens	5		6
8	E.Aburrow	run out	0		35
9	R.Nyren	b Stevens	2	not out	23
10	Berwick	b Stevens	1		19
11	P.Stewart	not out	6		
	Byes		6		2
			172	(8 wickets)	162

FoW (1): 1- , 2- , 3- , 4- , 5- , 6- , 7- , 8- , 9- , 10-172
FoW (2): 1- , 2- , 3- , 4- , 5- , 6- , 7- , 8-

Hampshire Bowling

	O	M	R	W	O	M	R	W
Nyren				3				
Mann				1				
Berwick				1				

England Bowling

	O	M	R	W	O	M	R	W
Stevens				3				
Bedster				1				
Bullen				1				

Umpires:

Close of Play: 1st day: ; 2nd day: ; 3rd day: .

Hampshire had Berwick and Bowra as given men. The second innings dismissal details are not available.

DUKE OF DORSET'S XI v SIR H.MANN'S XI

Played at Sevenoaks Vine Cricket Club Ground, June 27, 28, 1780.

Sir H.Mann's XI won by seven wickets.

DUKE OF DORSET'S XI
1	Duke of Dorset	0	b Berwick		6
2	Earl of Tankerville	4	c Yalden		1
3	J.Minchin	13	b Berwick		5
4	W.Bedster	8	c Aylward		11
5	F.Booker	0	c Aylward		7
6	W.Bowra	33	b Gibson		4
7	W.Bullen	8	b Berwick		34
8	H.Attfield	1	not out		13
9	T.Pattenden	9	c Aylward		0
10	J.Boorman	13	c Stone		6
11	E.Stevens	2	c Berwick		0
	Byes	2			5
		93			92

FoW (1): 1- , 2- , 3- , 4- , 5- , 6- , 7- , 8- , 9- , 10-93
FoW (2): 1- , 2- , 3- , 4- , 5- , 6- , 7- , 8- , 9- , 10-92

SIR H.MANN'S XI
1	R.Stone	9			
2	W.Yalden	0	c Bedster		15
3	Berwick	1	b Bullen		10
4	R.Miller	13	not out		24
5	J.Aylward	47	not out		12
6	R.May	4			
7	R.Clifford	8	b Stevens		20
8	Mills	4			
9	R.Hosmer	6			
10	B.Rimmington	11			
11	Gibson	0			
	Byes	2			
		105	(3 wickets)		81

FoW (1): 1- , 2- , 3- , 4- , 5- , 6- , 7- , 8- , 9- , 10-105
FoW (2): 1- , 2- , 3-

Sir H.Mann's X Bowling

	O	M	R	W	O	M	R	W
Berwick								3
Gibson								1

Duke of Dorset's XI Bowling

	O	M	R	W	O	M	R	W
Bullen								1
Stevens								1

Umpires:

Close of Play: 1st day: .

The first innings dismissal details are not available. In the absence of distinguishing initials or any other evidence the appearances by May and Rimmington have been attributed to the best-known players of those names. This is the first of 8 matches between teams representing (broadly) East and West Kent, although also involving many leading players from outside the county. See the introduction for notes regarding the treatment of these games. Match titles vary from one source to another: sometimes the sides are named as East and West Kent, sometimes after the patrons involved. The titles used here have been taken from SB.

(Variant) KG has significant differences, viz: Dorset (2) Bedster 12, Attfield 12; Mann (2) Stone 11, Berwick 2, Miller not out 34, Hosmer 9, Rimmington 20, byes 5, total 81-3. However, it does not say who was not out in Mann (2) apart from Miller and it has no dismissal details in either innings, so Epps is preferred as representing a more complete score, although KG is a more proximate source.

SIR H.MANN'S XI v DUKE OF DORSET'S XI
Played at Bourne Paddock, Bishopsbourne, August 21, 22, 23, 1780.

Duke of Dorset's XI won by 9 runs.

DUKE OF DORSET'S XI

1	R.Stanford	b Gibson	9	c Miller		10
2	W.Bullen	b Clifford	0	c Clifford		30
3	W.Bedster	b Clifford	23	b Gibson		24
4	Earl of Tankerville	c Yalden	30	c Hosmer		9
5	F.Booker	b Clifford	2	not out		20
6	W.Bowra	b Gibson	0	c Yalden		1
7	W.Pattenden	b Gibson	15	b Clifford		29
8	T.Pattenden	b Clifford	0	c Aylward		7
9	J.Boorman	b Gibson	6	b Gibson		4
10	E.Stevens	not out	10	b Gibson		25
11	R.N.Newman	b Gibson	2	b Clifford		0
	Byes					
			97			159

FoW (1): 1- , 2- , 3- , 4- , 5- , 6- , 7- , 8- , 9- , 10-97
FoW (2): 1- , 2- , 3- , 4- , 5- , 6- , 7- , 8- , 9- , 10-159

SIR H.MANN'S XI

1	R.Stone	b Stevens	4	b Bullen		8
2	T.Rimmington	b Boorman	17	b Stevens		9
3	B.Rimmington	b Stevens	62	b Bedster		16
4	J.Aylward	run out	0	c Bedster		16
5	R.Miller	c Bullen	3	b Bedster		10
6	R.Hosmer	c Booker	36	b Stevens		3
7	R.Clifford	c Bullen	1	c Bowra		2
8	Mills	run out	8	b Bedster		5
9	W.Yalden	not out	9	not out		22
10	Gibson	c Newman	1	c Stevens		8
11	R.May	run out	0	c Bedster		0
	Byes		4			3
			145			102

FoW (1): 1- , 2- , 3- , 4- , 5- , 6- , 7- , 8- , 9- , 10-145
FoW (2): 1- , 2- , 3- , 4- , 5- , 6- , 7- , 8- , 9- , 10-102

Sir H.Mann's XI Bowling

	O	M	R	W	O	M	R	W
Clifford				4				2
Gibson				5				3

Duke of Dorset's XI Bowling

	O	M	R	W	O	M	R	W
Stevens				2				2
Boorman				1				
Bedster								3
Bullen								1

Umpires:

Close of Play: 1st day: ; 2nd day: .

ENGLAND v HAMPSHIRE

Played at Bourne Paddock, Bishopsbourne, August 30, 31, September 1, 1780.

England won by 166 runs.

ENGLAND

1	T.Rimmington	b Nyren	25	run out		7
2	W.Bedster	b Mann	12	b Lamborn		8
3	W.Bullen	c Tankerville	7	c Small		12
4	J.Aylward	b Nyren	9	b Nyren		24
5	B.Rimmington	b Lamborn	4	c Small		4
6	R.Miller	c Small	7	b Aburrow		37
7	W.Bowra	b Veck	31	c Mann		1
8	W.Yalden	c Freemantle	52	b Lamborn		34
9	R.Clifford	b Nyren	25	c Taylor		7
10	E.Stevens	c Sueter	6	not out		4
11	Berwick	not out	6	b Freemantle		5
	Byes		13			1
			197			144

FoW (1): 1- , 2- , 3- , 4- , 5- , 6- , 7- , 8- , 9- , 10-197
FoW (2): 1- , 2- , 3- , 4- , 5- , 6- , 7- , 8- , 9- , 10-144

HAMPSHIRE

1	E.Aburrow	c Bullen	0	b Stevens		36
2	H.Attfield	b Clifford	13	run out		1
3	N.Mann	b Stevens	6	b Clifford		32
4	T.Taylor	b Clifford	2	c T.Rimmington		0
5	J.Small, sen	c Stevens	22	b Stevens		19
6	Earl of Tankerville	b Clifford	4	c Aylward		2
7	R.A.Veck	c Aylward	7	b Clifford		2
8	T.Sueter	c Berwick	14	b Clifford		0
9	R.Nyren	c Bullen	4	c Bowra		0
10	J.Freemantle	not out	1	c Aylward		0
11	Lamborn	b Clifford	2	not out		3
	Byes		5			
			80			95

FoW (1): 1- , 2- , 3- , 4- , 5- , 6- , 7- , 8- , 9- , 10-80
FoW (2): 1- , 2- , 3- , 4- , 5- , 6- , 7- , 8- , 9- , 10-95

Hampshire Bowling

	O	M	R	W	O	M	R	W
Nyren				3				1
Mann				1				
Lamborn				1				2
Veck				1				
Freemantle								1
Aburrow								1

England Bowling

	O	M	R	W	O	M	R	W
Stevens				1				2
Clifford				4				3

Umpires:

Close of Play: 1st day: ; 2nd day: .

Hampshire had Attfield and Lamborn as given men.

HAMPSHIRE v ENGLAND

Played at Stoke Down, Alresford, September 20, 21, 22, 1780.

England won by 51 runs.

ENGLAND

1	B.Rimmington	b Lamborn	7	b Nyren	38
2	W.Bullen	b Lamborn	0	b Freemantle	15
3	R.Miller	c Mann	50	c Small	3
4	J.Aylward	c Nyren	26	b Nyren	3
5	T.Rimmington	c Mann	0	b Lamborn	3
6	W.Bedster	c Mann	24	c Nyren	10
7	W.Bowra	c Freemantle	3	run out (Taylor)	1
8	W.Yalden	b Lamborn	0	c Nyren	4
9	Berwick	c Wood	2	not out	4
10	E.Stevens	b Lamborn	31	b Nyren	4
11	R.Clifford	not out	33	b Nyren	12
	Byes		3		4
			179		101

FoW (1): 1- , 2- , 3- , 4- , 5- , 6- , 7- , 8- , 9- , 10-179
FoW (2): 1- , 2- , 3- , 4- , 5- , 6- , 7- , 8- , 9- , 10-101

HAMPSHIRE

1	J.Small, sen	c Yalden	0	b Stevens	6
2	Earl of Tankerville	b Clifford	3	c Aylward	2
3	R.A.Veck	b Stevens	16	c Bullen	23
4	N.Mann	c Clifford	30	b Stevens	10
5	E.Aburrow	run out	42	run out	1
6	T.Sueter	b Stevens	36	b Clifford	6
7	R.Nyren	b Stevens	11	not out	4
8	T.Taylor	c Stevens	17	b Stevens	2
9	J.Freemantle	b Clifford	4	b Stevens	0
10	J.Wood (Pirbright)	b Stevens	5	b Stevens	1
11	Lamborn	not out	0	b Stevens	4
	Byes		5		1
			169		60

FoW (1): 1- , 2- , 3- , 4- , 5- , 6- , 7- , 8- , 9- , 10-169
FoW (2): 1- , 2- , 3- , 4- , 5- , 6- , 7- , 8- , 9- , 10-60

Hampshire Bowling

	O	M	R	W	O	M	R	W
Lamborn				4				1
Nyren								4
Freemantle								1

England Bowling

	O	M	R	W	O	M	R	W
Stevens				4				6
Clifford				2				1

Umpires:

Close of Play: 1st day: ; 2nd day: .

Hampshire had Lamborn and Wood as given men. The *Morning Post* batting orders marginally improve on those in SB: Clifford at 11 with a score of 33* would normally be suspect but Stevens at 10 made 31 so there was probably a large last-wicket stand.

HAMPSHIRE v KENT

Played at Stoke Down, Alresford, June 6, 7, 8, 9, 1781.

Hampshire won by eight wickets.

KENT

1	R.Miller	b Mann	16	c Taylor		14
2	T.Rimmington	b Lamborn	0	b Mann		4
3	J.Aylward	b Lamborn	25	c Bedster		73
4	M.Rimmington	b Lamborn	2	not out		16
5	W.Bullen	b Mann	16	b Mann		1
6	R.Clifford	b Lamborn	22	b Lamborn		48
7	B.Rimmington	b Lamborn	1	b Nyren		31
8	W.Bowra	not out	13	b Mann		8
9	W.Yalden	b Mann	0	b Nyren		7
10	J.Boorman	b Lamborn	1	b Freemantle		17
11	E.Stevens	b Lamborn	1	b Mann		12
	Byes		4			1
			101			232

FoW (1): 1- , 2- , 3- , 4- , 5- , 6- , 7- , 8- , 9- , 10-101
FoW (2): 1- , 2- , 3- , 4- , 5- , 6- , 7- , 8- , 9- , 10-232

HAMPSHIRE

1	W.Bedster	c Yalden	5	b Bowra		49
2	E.Aburrow	c Clifford	11			
3	J.Small, sen	b Stevens	47			
4	R.A.Veck	c B.Rimmington	12			
5	N.Mann	b Clifford	10	b Stevens		73
6	T.Sueter	c M.Rimmington	66			
7	G.Leer	c Bullen	15			
8	T.Taylor	c Yalden	12	not out		1
9	R.Nyren	b Stevens	8			
10	J.Freemantle	not out	19	not out		5
11	Lamborn	c Clifford	0			
	Byes		1			
			206	(2 wickets)		128

FoW (1): 1- , 2- , 3- , 4- , 5- , 6- , 7- , 8- , 9- , 10-206
FoW (2): 1- , 2-

Hampshire Bowling

	O	M	R	W	O	M	R	W
Lamborn				7				1
Mann				3				4
Nyren								2
Freemantle								1

Kent Bowling

	O	M	R	W	O	M	R	W
Stevens				2				1
Clifford				1				
Bowra								1

Umpires:

Close of Play: 1st day: ; 2nd day: ; 3rd day: .

Hampshire had Bedster and Lamborn as given men. Kent had Stevens and Yalden as given men.

WEST KENT v EAST KENT

Played at Sevenoaks Vine Cricket Club Ground, June 20, 21, 1781.

West Kent won by ten wickets.

EAST KENT

1	R.Miller	c Sueter	29	b Stevens	0
2	R.Clifford	b Stevens	32	b Bullen	5
3	J.Small, sen	c Sueter	5	c Sueter	3
4	R.Hosmer	b Stevens	9	not out	37
5	R.A.Veck	c Sueter	5	c Wood	5
6	B.Rimmington	c Sueter	23	c Bowra	1
7	Pemmell	c Stevens	0	b Bedster	7
8	W.Pattenden	b Bedster	12	c Sueter	6
9	M.Rimmington	c Stevens	11	c Stevens	9
10	Holness	b Bedster	9	c Bullen	0
11	Lamborn	not out	1	c Mann	6
	Byes				5
			136		84

FoW (1): 1- , 2- , 3- , 4- , 5- , 6- , 7- , 8- , 9- , 10-136
FoW (2): 1- , 2- , 3- , 4- , 5- , 6- , 7- , 8- , 9- , 10-84

WEST KENT

1	W.Bedster	c Veck	1		
2	N.Mann	b Clifford	21	not out	37
3	T.Sueter	b Lamborn	34		
4	J.Wood (Seal)	b Clifford	2		
5	W.Bullen	b Lamborn	7	not out	26
6	W.Bowra	c Pemmell	18		
7	T.Pattenden	not out	50		
8	R.Stanford	b Clifford	6		
9	Webb	c Hosmer	17		
10	Mills	b Clifford	0		
11	E.Stevens	b Lamborn	0		
	Byes		2		
			158	(no wicket)	63

FoW (1): 1- , 2- , 3- , 4- , 5- , 6- , 7- , 8- , 9- , 10-158

West Kent Bowling

	O	M	R	W	O	M	R	W
Stevens				2				1
Bedster				2				1
Bullen								1

East Kent Bowling

	O	M	R	W	O	M	R	W
Clifford				4				
Lamborn				3				

Umpires:

Close of Play: 1st day: .

East Kent had Lamborn, Small and Veck as given men; West Kent had Mann, Mills, Stevens and Sueter. Webb was from the Isle of Thanet. Holness (or Houness) may have been from Maidstone.

(Variant) SB has T.Rimmington, but KG gives M. and, as a local newspaper, is assumed to be in a better position to know its Rimmingtons.

KENT v HAMPSHIRE

Played at Bourne Paddock, Bishopsbourne, July 18, 19, 20, 1781.

Kent won by 150 runs.

KENT

#	Batsman	Dismissal	Runs	Dismissal 2	Runs 2
1	W.Bullen	c Sueter	4	b Nyren	13
2	R.Clifford	b Nyren	26	b Freemantle	57
3	J.Aylward	c Veck	29	c Sueter	25
4	Webb	b Lamborn	8	c Taylor	2
5	B.Rimmington	b Lamborn	11	c Sueter	20
6	W.Bowra	b Lamborn	15	b Freemantle	10
7	R.Miller	c Nyren	29	run out	14
8	T.Pattenden	c Taylor	15	c Taylor	16
9	Hogben	b Nyren	13	c Aburrow	15
10	W.Yalden	not out	18	b Mann	0
11	E.Stevens	b Freemantle	7	not out	10
	Byes		6		4
			181		186

FoW (1): 1- , 2- , 3- , 4- , 5- , 6- , 7- , 8- , 9- , 10-181
FoW (2): 1- , 2- , 3- , 4- , 5- , 6- , 7- , 8- , 9- , 10-186

HAMPSHIRE

#	Batsman	Dismissal	Runs	Dismissal 2	Runs 2
1	W.Bedster	b Stevens	0	c Clifford	3
2	E.Aburrow	b Stevens	5	c Yalden	5
3	T.Taylor	b Clifford	6	b Stevens	3
4	J.Small, sen	c Clifford	7	c Yalden	17
5	R.A.Veck	c Yalden	2	c Stevens	26
6	T.Sueter	c Clifford	3	run out	14
7	N.Mann	c Bullen	2	c Yalden	7
8	G.Leer	not out	14	b Stevens	53
9	R.Nyren	b Clifford	5	b Stevens	22
10	J.Freemantle	c Clifford	1	b Stevens	6
11	Lamborn	c Clifford	8	not out	0
	Byes		6		2
			59		158

FoW (1): 1- , 2- , 3- , 4- , 5- , 6- , 7- , 8- , 9- , 10-59
FoW (2): 1- , 2- , 3- , 4- , 5- , 6- , 7- , 8- , 9- , 10-158

Hampshire Bowling

	O	M	R	W	O	M	R	W
Nyren				2				1
Lamborn				3				
Freemantle				1				2
Mann								1

Kent Bowling

	O	M	R	W	O	M	R	W
Stevens				2				4
Clifford				2				

Umpires:

Close of Play: 1st day: ; 2nd day: .

Kent had Stevens and Yalden as given men; Hampshire had Bedster and Lamborn as given men. Hogben of Rochester.

HAMPSHIRE v KENT

Played at Broad Halfpenny Down, Hambledon, July 30, 31, August 1, 1781.

Kent won by 34 runs.

KENT

1	W.Bullen	b Purchase	5	run out		54
2	R.Clifford	b Nyren	66	c Sueter		13
3	J.Aylward	b Purchase	6	b Veck		28
4	W.Bedster	run out	7	c Sueter		1
5	W.Bowra	b Purchase	29	not out		42
6	R.Miller	b Nyren	45	run out		10
7	B.Rimmington	b Nyren	21	c Nyren		15
8	T.Pattenden	b Nyren	0	c Veck		2
9	Hogben	b Lamborn	12	run out		3
10	J.Boorman	not out	5	c Veck		17
11	Webb	b Lamborn	2	b Nyren		0
	Byes		17			3
			215			188

FoW (1): 1- , 2- , 3- , 4- , 5- , 6- , 7- , 8- , 9- , 10-215
FoW (2): 1- , 2- , 3- , 4- , 5- , 6- , 7- , 8- , 9- , 10-188

HAMPSHIRE

1	G.Leer	c Webb	14	c Clifford		10
2	N.Mann	b Bullen	51	not out		38
3	J.Small, sen	b Bullen	0	c Bowra		33
4	R.Nyren	b Bullen	5	c Bowra		3
5	T.Sueter	run out	22	b Bullen		0
6	T.Taylor	b Bullen	35	c Aylward		28
7	E.Aburrow	b Bullen	3	c Clifford		10
8	R.A.Veck	c Bowra	26	b Clifford		44
9	J.Freemantle	b Bullen	11	b Clifford		5
10	R.Purchase	not out	5	c Bowra		2
11	Lamborn	c Bullen	4	c Aylward		0
	Byes		10			10
			186			183

FoW (1): 1- , 2- , 3- , 4- , 5- , 6- , 7- , 8- , 9- , 10-186
FoW (2): 1- , 2- , 3- , 4- , 5- , 6- , 7- , 8- , 9- , 10-183

Hampshire Bowling

	O	M	R	W	O	M	R	W
Nyren				4				1
Lamborn				2				
Purchase				3				
Veck								1

Kent Bowling

	O	M	R	W	O	M	R	W
Bullen				6				1
Clifford								2

Umpires:

Close of Play: 1st day: ; 2nd day: .

Hampshire had Lamborn as a given man; Kent had Bedster as a given man.

SIR H.MANN'S XI v DUKE OF DORSET'S XI

Played at Bourne Paddock, Bishopsbourne, August 8, 9, 10, 11, 1781.

Duke of Dorset's XI won by 107 runs.

DUKE OF DORSET'S XI

#	Batsman	Dismissal	Runs	Dismissal (2)	Runs
1	T.Sueter	c Hogben	58	b Lamborn	56
2	W.Bedster	c Aylward	19	c Small	20
3	Earl of Tankerville	c Hogben	11	b Clifford	9
4	W.Bowra	b Clifford	5	b Clifford	3
5	W.Bullen	c Martin	10	run out	36
6	T.Pattenden	not out	29	b Clifford	6
7	W.Yalden	c Pattenden	17	b Lamborn	5
8	R.Stanford	b Lamborn	4	not out	11
9	J.Boorman	b Clifford	0	b Lamborn	3
10	N.Mann	b Clifford	4	c Pattenden	21
11	E.Stevens	b Lamborn	12	c Hogben	13
	Byes		2		1
			171		184

FoW (1): 1- , 2- , 3- , 4- , 5- , 6- , 7- , 8- , 9- , 10-171
FoW (2): 1- , 2- , 3- , 4- , 5- , 6- , 7- , 8- , 9- , 10-184

SIR H.MANN'S XI

#	Batsman	Dismissal	Runs	Dismissal (2)	Runs
1	J.Small, sen	b Stevens	21	c Yalden	28
2	J.Aylward	b Boorman	36	b Stevens	44
3	R.Clifford	b Stevens	24	c Bullen	3
4	R.Miller	c Stanford	31	b Bullen	3
5	Hodges	b Bullen	7	run out	1
6	B.Rimmington	c Bullen	3	c Bedster	3
7	W.Pattenden	b Stevens	13	b Stevens	3
8	Hogben	b Stevens	1	b Stevens	15
9	T.Martin	c Stevens	2	not out	0
10	Lamborn	not out	2	b Stevens	0
11	Webb	c Stevens	3	run out	0
	Byes		4		1
			147		101

FoW (1): 1- , 2- , 3- , 4-63, 5- , 6- , 7- , 8- , 9- , 10-147
FoW (2): 1- , 2- , 3- , 4- , 5- , 6- , 7- , 8- , 9- , 10-101

Sir H.Mann's XI Bowling

	O	M	R	W	O	M	R	W
Lamborn				2				3
Clifford				3				3

Duke of Dorset's XI Bowling

	O	M	R	W	O	M	R	W
Stevens				4				4
Bullen				1				1
Boorman				1				

Umpires:

Close of Play: 1st day: ; 2nd day: ; 3rd day: Sir H.Mann's XI (2) 63-4 (Aylward 28*).

Sueter was the first to score two separate fifties in a 'great' match. In Mann (2), Small, Clifford, Miller and Hodges were the men out at the end of day 3. Batting orders are from Epps.

(Variant) KG gives different orders, viz: Dorset - Tankerville, Stevens, Bullen, Bowra, Bedster, Yalden, Sueter, Pattenden, Boorman, Stanford, Mann; Mann - Aylward, Miller, Clifford, Hodges, Small, Lamborn, Rimmington, Webb, Hogben, Pattenden, Martin. These are less satisfactory as regards the first innings; they may be second-innings orders but this is unclear so they have not been incorporated into the score.

KENT v HAMPSHIRE

Played at Bourne Paddock, Bishopsbourne, August 27, 28, 1781.

Hampshire won by 8 runs.

HAMPSHIRE

1	N.Mann	c Bullen	16	b Bowra		17
2	G.Leer	c Hogben	2	run out		11
3	T.Sueter	c Boorman	16	c sub (R.Simmons)		13
4	R.A.Veck	b Bullen	2	c Aylward		14
5	J.Small, sen	run out	5	c Clifford		14
6	R.Purchase	b Clifford	0	b Bullen		24
7	E.Aburrow	c Bullen	4	b Bowra		3
8	J.Freemantle	c Aylward	3	b Clifford		8
9	R.Nyren	b Clifford	7	not out		1
10	Lamborn	b Clifford	2	c Aylward		0
11	T.Skinner	not out	3	b Clifford		0
	Byes					1
			60			106

FoW (1): 1- , 2- , 3- , 4- , 5- , 6- , 7- , 8- , 9- , 10-60
FoW (2): 1- , 2- , 3- , 4- , 5- , 6- , 7- , 8- , 9- , 10-106

KENT

1	Webb	b Lamborn	0	run out		4
2	R.Clifford	b Lamborn	5	b Lamborn		4
3	B.Rimmington	run out	7	b Purchase		0
4	W.Bullen	b Lamborn	0	c Mann		21
5	W.Bedster	c Purchase	3	not out		8
6	R.Miller	c Leer	3	b Nyren		1
7	W.Bowra	b Nyren	17	b Nyren		2
8	J.Aylward	c Leer	32	c Leer		21
9	Hogben	b Lamborn	13	b Lamborn		5
10	T.Pattenden	b Nyren	5	b Nyren		4
11	J.Boorman	not out	0	c Veck		0
	Byes		3			
			88			70

FoW (1): 1- , 2- , 3- , 4- , 5- , 6- , 7- , 8- , 9- , 10-88
FoW (2): 1- , 2- , 3- , 4- , 5- , 6- , 7- , 8- , 9- , 10-70

Kent Bowling

	O	M	R	W	O	M	R	W
Clifford				3				2
Bullen				1				1
Bowra								2

Hampshire Bowling

	O	M	R	W	O	M	R	W
Nyren				2				3
Lamborn				4				2
Purchase								1

Umpires:

Close of Play: 1st day: .

Hampshire had Lamborn as a given man.

KENT v HAMPSHIRE

Played at Sevenoaks Vine Cricket Club Ground, July 3, 4, 5, 1782.

Kent won by four wickets.

HAMPSHIRE

1	J.Small, sen	c Booker	2	c Bowra	15
2	R.A.Veck	c Bullen	7	c Aylward	0
3	N.Mann	b Stevens	6	c Bullen	13
4	E.Aburrow	c Clifford	8	b Clifford	6
5	H.Attfield	not out	16	b Clifford	6
6	G.Leer	c Bowra	1	c Hosmer	25
7	T.Taylor	c Booker	0	c Booker	6
8	W.Hall	b Clifford	4	not out	2
9	R.Francis	b Stevens	10	b Stevens	15
10	D.Harris	c Aylward	27	c Bullen	1
11	T.Sueter	c Bullen	5	b Clifford	48
	Byes		1		3
			87		140

FoW (1): 1- , 2- , 3- , 4- , 5- , 6- , 7- , 8- , 9- , 10-87
FoW (2): 1- , 2- , 3- , 4- , 5- , 6- , 7- , 8- , 9- , 10-140

KENT

1	W.Brazier	b Harris	1	c Attfield	0
2	E.Stevens	b Aburrow	17		
3	W.Bowra	b Harris	4	c Leer	48
4	W.Bedster	c Harris	25	c Aburrow	12
5	F.Booker	not out	29		
6	R.Clifford	c Taylor	0	b Mann	15
7	J.Aylward	c Francis	3	run out	17
8	W.Bullen	c Francis	5	not out	11
9	J.Ring	c Small	3	b Mann	3
10	R.Hosmer	c Hall	6	not out	20
11	T.Pattenden	b Mann	7		
	Byes		2		
			102	(6 wickets)	126

FoW (1): 1- , 2- , 3- , 4- , 5- , 6- , 7- , 8- , 9- , 10-102
FoW (2): 1- , 2- , 3- , 4- , 5- , 6-

Kent Bowling

	O	M	R	W	O	M	R	W
Stevens				2				1
Clifford				1				3

Hampshire Bowling

	O	M	R	W	O	M	R	W
Harris				2				
Mann				1				2
Aburrow				1				

Umpires:

Close of Play: 1st day: ; 2nd day: Kent (2) 109-6 (Bullen 5*, Hosmer 9*).

Kent had Bedster and Stevens as given men. A contemporary scorecard gives an unfinished version of this match that supports the version in the *Kentish Gazette* as above except that it has Ring's score in Kent (2) as 2 rather than 3. The scorecard gives the dates as 3, 4 July only, so it has been accepted as representing the position at the close of play on the second day. No total is given for the innings in progress (Kent (2)), but Bullen and Hosmer are shown as 5*and 9* respectively, which implies a score of 190-6 at that point.

HAMPSHIRE v KENT

Played at Stoke Down, Alresford, July 11, 12, 13, 15, 1782.

Kent won by 145 runs.

KENT
1	W.Bullen	b Harris	5	b Harris		4
2	R.Clifford	c Freemantle	0	b Purchase		8
3	J.Aylward	b Freemantle	75	c Harris		0
4	W.Bedster	b Freemantle	63	c Harris		0
5	W.Bowra	c Purchase	50	c Purchase		21
6	W.Brazier	b Freemantle	37	c Taylor		9
7	R.Miller	b Francis	0	c Small		7
8	Hogben	c Small	11	not out		9
9	F.Booker	c Veck	0	run out		8
10	J.Ring	run out	10	b Purchase		4
11	E.Stevens	not out	2	c Harris		5
	Byes		4			
			257			75

FoW (1): 1- , 2- , 3- , 4- , 5- , 6- , 7- , 8- , 9- , 10-257
FoW (2): 1- , 2- , 3- , 4- , 5- , 6- , 7- , 8- , 9- , 10-75

HAMPSHIRE
1	T.Sueter	c Ring	21	b Clifford		12
2	E.Aburrow	b Clifford	6	b Stevens		7
3	J.Small, sen	b Stevens	0	b Stevens		8
4	G.Leer	c Booker	6	b Clifford		8
5	N.Mann	b Clifford	34	b Stevens		8
6	R.A.Veck	c Bedster	19	b Clifford		12
7	T.Taylor	b Stevens	4	b Clifford		4
8	R.Purchase	c Bedster	17	c Clifford		3
9	R.Francis	run out	3	run out		0
10	J.Freemantle	not out	6	not out		2
11	D.Harris	c Bullen	4	b Stevens		2
	Byes		1			
			121			66

FoW (1): 1- , 2- , 3- , 4- , 5- , 6- , 7- , 8- , 9- , 10-121
FoW (2): 1- , 2- , 3- , 4- , 5- , 6- , 7- , 8- , 9- , 10-66

Hampshire Bowling
	O	M	R	W	O	M	R	W
Harris				1				1
Francis				1				
Freemantle				3				
Purchase								2

Kent Bowling
	O	M	R	W	O	M	R	W
Stevens				2				4
Clifford				2				4

Umpires:

Close of Play: 1st day: ; 2nd day: ; 3rd day: .

Kent had Bedster and Stevens as given men.

KENT v HAMPSHIRE

Played at Bourne Paddock, Bishopsbourne, July 25, 26, 1782.

Hampshire won by 9 runs.

HAMPSHIRE

1	D.Harris	b Clifford	1	run out	4
2	R.Purchase	b Clifford	33	c Clifford	2
3	T.Taylor	b Clifford	0	c Aylward	2
4	R.A.Veck	b Clifford	12	c Aylward	4
5	N.Mann	b Bullen	5	b Clifford	21
6	T.Sueter	b Clifford	2	c Clifford	6
7	G.Leer	not out	15	b Bedster	23
8	E.Aburrow	b Clifford	0	b Bullen	32
9	J.Small, sen	b Francis	15	c Bullen	3
10	R.Nyren	b Clifford	0	b Bullen	13
11	E.Stevens	b Bullen	3	not out	6
	Byes		2		12
			88		128

FoW (1): 1- , 2- , 3- , 4- , 5- , 6- , 7- , 8- , 9- , 10-88
FoW (2): 1- , 2- , 3- , 4- , 5- , 6- , 7- , 8- , 9- , 10-128

KENT

1	R.Clifford	c Taylor	28	c Veck	46
2	W.Bullen	c Nyren	11	b Nyren	2
3	W.Bedster	c Sueter	0	c Nyren	0
4	J.Aylward	b Stevens	0	c Veck	4
5	W.Bowra	c Veck	6	b Nyren	0
6	Hogben	c Taylor	1	b Nyren	0
7	F.Booker	not out	11	b Nyren	6
8	W.Brazier	b Stevens	26	run out	23
9	J.Ring	b Nyren	3	c Taylor	7
10	R.Francis	b Stevens	17	b Stevens	1
11	T.Pattenden	b Stevens	1	not out	7
	Byes		4		3
			108		99

FoW (1): 1- , 2- , 3- , 4- , 5- , 6- , 7- , 8- , 9- , 10-108
FoW (2): 1- , 2- , 3- , 4- , 5- , 6- , 7- , 8- , 9- , 10-99

Kent Bowling

	O	M	R	W	O	M	R	W
Clifford				7				1
Bullen				2				2
Francis				1				
Bedster								1

Hampshire Bowling

	O	M	R	W	O	M	R	W
Stevens				4				1
Nyren				1				4

Umpires:

Close of Play: 1st day: .

Hampshire had Stevens as a given man; Kent had Bedster and Francis as given men.

HAMPSHIRE v ENGLAND

Played at Windmill Down, Hambledon, August 8, 9, 10, 1782.

England won by 149 runs.

ENGLAND

1	R.Clifford	c Purchase	1	b Stevens		31
2	R.Francis	b Stevens	21	c Small		4
3	J.Aylward	c Sueter	19	st Sueter		18
4	W.Bedster	c Sueter	11	b Nyren		0
5	W.Bullen	c Sueter	16	c Purchase		28
6	W.Brazier	b Stevens	2	b Stevens		39
7	F.Booker	b Nyren	10	not out		3
8	R.Miller	b Nyren	1	c Harris		25
9	W.Bowra	run out	0	c Stevens		15
10	W.Yalden	not out	24	b Nyren		16
11	J.Ring	c Small	10	b Stevens		9
	Byes					1
			115			189

FoW (1): 1- , 2- , 3- , 4- , 5- , 6- , 7- , 8- , 9- , 10-115
FoW (2): 1- , 2- , 3- , 4- , 5- , 6- , 7- , 8- , 9- , 10-189

HAMPSHIRE

1	R.Purchase	b Clifford	3	c Bedster		23
2	N.Mann	b Bullen	2	run out		42
3	G.Leer	c Bullen	2	b Clifford		6
4	T.Sueter	c Yalden	14	b Bullen		0
5	J.Small, sen	c Bowra	0	c Yalden		8
6	R.A.Veck	b Bullen	4	b Clifford		3
7	E.Aburrow	not out	21	run out		0
8	R.Nyren	b Clifford	3	b Bullen		1
9	T.Taylor	c Aylward	9	b Clifford		0
10	E.Stevens	b Bullen	4	c Francis		2
11	D.Harris	b Clifford	0	not out		2
	Byes		2			4
			64			91

FoW (1): 1- , 2- , 3- , 4- , 5- , 6- , 7- , 8- , 9- , 10-64
FoW (2): 1- , 2- , 3- , 4- , 5- , 6- , 7- , 8- , 9- , 10-91

Hampshire Bowling

	O	M	R	W	O	M	R	W
Stevens				2				3
Nyren				2				2

England Bowling

	O	M	R	W	O	M	R	W
Clifford				3				3
Bullen				3				2

Umpires:

Close of Play: 1st day: ; 2nd day: .

Hampshire had Stevens as a given man. Note that compared to the previous game, Yalden is now playing for the visiting team. This may make it slightly more 'England' than 'Kent', although 'Kent with three given men' would be an equally accurate title. Generally, match titles are very fluid around this time.

WEST KENT v EAST KENT

Played at Sevenoaks Vine Cricket Club Ground, June 25, 26, 1783.

East Kent won by two wickets.

WEST KENT

1	D.Harris	not out	10	c Stanford	6
2	E.Stevens	b Clifford	0	c Clifford	5
3	W.Bedster	c Aylward	14	c Aylward	43
4	W.Bullen	b Martin	0	c Clifford	31
5	W.Brazier	b Martin	5	c W.Pattenden	6
6	F.Booker	b Martin	3	c W.Pattenden	12
7	Townsend	c Martin	9	b Martin	8
8	Couchman	c Amherst	3	b Martin	9
9	G.Louch	b Martin	24	b Clifford	1
10	J.Boorman	c W.Pattenden	0	not out	12
11	W.Bowra	b Martin	28	b Clifford	1
	Byes		1		1
			97		135

FoW (1): 1- , 2- , 3- , 4- , 5- , 6- , 7- , 8- , 9- , 10-97
FoW (2): 1- , 2- , 3- , 4- , 5- , 6- , 7- , 8- , 9- , 10-135

EAST KENT

1	R.Clifford	c Booker	22	c Bowra	17
2	R.Hosmer	c Harris	3	c Boorman	1
3	R.Stanford	b Bedster	9	c Bowra	1
4	J.Aylward	b Boorman	26	b Bullen	25
5	J.Ring	b Bullen	6	b Bullen	1
6	R.Miller	c Boorman	7	c Bowra	11
7	T.Martin	not out	0		
8	B.Rimmington	b Harris	3	not out	1
9	T.Pattenden	b Boorman	52	c Couchman	7
10	W.Pattenden	c Harris	4	not out	18
11	S.Amherst	b Brazier	12	b Bullen	2
	Byes		3		2
			147	(8 wickets)	86

FoW (1): 1- , 2- , 3- , 4- , 5- , 6- , 7- , 8- , 9- , 10-147
FoW (2): 1- , 2- , 3- , 4- , 5- , 6- , 7- , 8-

East Kent Bowling

	O	M	R	W	O	M	R	W
Clifford				1				2
Martin				5				2

West Kent Bowling

	O	M	R	W	O	M	R	W
Harris				1				
Brazier				1				
Bullen				1				3
Bedster				1				
Boorman				2				

Umpires:

Close of Play: 1st day: .

West Kent had Bedster, Harris and Stevens as given men, Stevens not to bowl by agreement. Couchman was possibly from Seal or Ightham. The Kent amateur Stephen Amherst made his first appearance in 'great' matches. There is some doubt about the spelling of his surname: there was a prominent aristocratic family, to which it is assumed he was related, that definitely spelled the name as 'Amherst', and the matter appears to be settled by Haygarth's use of the same spelling in quoting the inscription on the family tablet in West Farleigh church. However, a number of other sources give 'Amhurst'.

HAMPSHIRE v KENT

Played at Windmill Down, Hambledon, July 8, 9, 1783.

Match tied.

KENT

1	R.Clifford	b Harris	5	b Stevens	0
2	W.Bullen	run out	9	c Bayley	11
3	R.Miller	b Stevens	11	c Sueter	11
4	J.Aylward	b Francis	21	hit wkt	27
5	W.Bedster	b Harris	0	c Purchase	0
6	J.Ring	b Stevens	3	c Sueter	1
7	W.Bowra	c Francis	16	b Stevens	11
8	Duke of Dorset	b Francis	8	c Taylor	4
9	W.Brazier	c Sueter	27	c Small	10
10	T.Pattenden	c Small	0	c Francis	14
11	W.Yalden	not out	9	not out	0
	Byes		2		1
			111		90

FoW (1): 1- , 2- , 3- , 4- , 5- , 6- , 7- , 8- , 9- , 10-111
FoW (2): 1- , 2- , 3- , 4- , 5- , 6- , 7- , 8- , 9- , 10-90

HAMPSHIRE

1	J.Bayley	c Dorset	2	c Ring	12
2	D.Harris	b Bullen	10	run out	0
3	R.A.Veck	c Clifford	4	c Yalden	3
4	J.Small, sen	run out	1	b Bullen	8
5	T.Sueter	b Bullen	42	c Yalden	3
6	T.Taylor	b Bullen	51	c Bowra	3
7	N.Mann	b Bullen	9	b Bullen	13
8	R.Francis	c Clifford	0	b Clifford	1
9	R.Purchase	c Bullen	1	c Clifford	4
10	R.Nyren	c Clifford	4	not out	5
11	E.Stevens	not out	2	c Aylward	1
	Byes		14		8
			140		61

FoW (1): 1- , 2- , 3- , 4- , 5- , 6- , 7- , 8- , 9- , 10-140
FoW (2): 1- , 2- , 3- , 4- , 5- , 6- , 7- , 8- , 9-59, 10-61

Hampshire Bowling

	O	M	R	W	O	M	R	W
Stevens				2				2
Harris				2				
Francis				2				

Kent Bowling

	O	M	R	W	O	M	R	W
Bullen				4				2
Clifford								1

Umpires:

Close of Play: 1st day: .

Hampshire had Stevens as a given man; Kent had Bedster and Yalden as given men. This is the first tie in a 'great' match. *Hambledon Cricket Chronicle* notes that 'Lumpy [Stevens] went in last with three needed'. SB quotes a report that 'the game was saved by Clifford's attention', presumably by bowling Francis and catching Purchase near the death.

SB and many other sources have the teams reversed but the quotes above about Stevens and Clifford make sense only if Hampshire batted last. SB also quotes a report that Kent actually won, a run having been missed through a scoring error; but this account is suspect because it is supported by details about tally-sticks, which had long since fallen out of use by this time.

KENT v HAMPSHIRE

Played at Bourne Paddock, Bishopsbourne, August 6, 7, 8, 9, 1783.

Hampshire won by 86 runs.

HAMPSHIRE

1	R.Francis	b Clifford	17	c Brazier		4
2	J.Bayley	b Bullen	25	b Bullen		0
3	J.Small, sen	c Yalden	52	c Bowra		5
4	T.Taylor	c Clifford	5	b Bullen		66
5	N.Mann	b Clifford	11	c Clifford		0
6	T.Sueter	b Clifford	0	c Bedster		36
7	R.A.Veck	b Bullen	9	c Bullen		31
8	R.Nyren	not out	18	b Brazier		25
9	R.Purchase	b Clifford	2	c Clifford		0
10	D.Harris	c Yalden	12	not out		15
11	E.Stevens	b Clifford	0	b Aylward		0
	Byes		9			10
			160			192

FoW (1): 1- , 2- , 3- , 4- , 5- , 6- , 7- , 8- , 9- , 10-160
FoW (2): 1- , 2- , 3- , 4- , 5- , 6- , 7- , 8- , 9- , 10-192

KENT

1	Duke of Dorset	b Stevens	1	c Taylor		4
2	R.Clifford	b Stevens	0	not out		2
3	W.Bullen	b Harris	11	c Taylor		22
4	J.Aylward	b Stevens	5	b Harris		7
5	W.Bowra	b Stevens	5	b Stevens		6
6	W.Brazier	c Purchase	0	run out		1
7	J.Ring	c Francis	82	c Harris		4
8	W.Bedster	c Sueter	61	run out		5
9	W.Yalden	c Small	7	c Stevens		2
10	T.Pattenden	b Stevens	22	b Harris		0
11	R.Miller	not out	2	c Taylor		9
	Byes		8			
			204			62

FoW (1): 1- , 2- , 3- , 4- , 5- , 6- , 7- , 8- , 9- , 10-204
FoW (2): 1- , 2- , 3- , 4- , 5- , 6- , 7- , 8- , 9- , 10-62

Kent Bowling

	O	M	R	W	O	M	R	W
Clifford				5				
Bullen				2				2
Brazier								1
Aylward								1

Hampshire Bowling

	O	M	R	W	O	M	R	W
Stevens				5				1
Harris				1				2

Umpires:

Close of Play: 1st day: ; 2nd day: ; 3rd day: .

Hampshire had Stevens as a given man; Kent had Bedster and Yalden as given men.

HAMPSHIRE v ENGLAND

Played at Windmill Down, Hambledon, August 26, 27, 28, 29, 1783.

Match drawn.

ENGLAND

1	J.Aylward	hit wkt	18	c Taylor	18
2	W.Brazier	c Small	79	b Harris	9
3	J.Ring	b Harris	7	c Taylor	27
4	W.Bedster	b Stevens	15	c Taylor	6
5	R.Clifford	c Nyren	19	c Harris	0
6	Duke of Dorset	b Stevens	3	c Francis	3
7	F.Booker	b Stevens	25	b Stevens	21
8	Townsend	b Francis	14	c Taylor	22
9	J.Wood (Seal)	not out	7	c Small	5
10	W.Yalden	c Stevens	22	not out	11
11	W.Bullen	b Harris	6	b Harris	9
	Byes		3		2
			218		133

FoW (1): 1- , 2- , 3- , 4- , 5- , 6- , 7- , 8- , 9- , 10-218
FoW (2): 1- , 2- , 3- , 4- , 5- , 6- , 7- , 8- , 9- , 10-133

HAMPSHIRE

1	J.Small, sen	run out	78	run out	13
2	N.Mann	c Yalden	18	b Brazier	32
3	T.Taylor	b Brazier	16		
4	R.A.Veck	b Bullen	13	b Bullen	14
5	T.Sueter	c Ring	53		
6	R.Francis	b Bullen	0	b Brazier	0
7	R.Nyren	b Brazier	22		
8	R.Purchase	c Dorset	0	c Bullen	0
9	James Wells	b Brazier	4	not out	2
10	D.Harris	c Bullen	7		
11	E.Stevens	not out	0		
	Byes		6		2
			217	(5 wickets)	63

FoW (1): 1- , 2- , 3- , 4- , 5- , 6- , 7- , 8- , 9- , 10-217
FoW (2): 1- , 2- , 3- , 4- , 5-

Hampshire Bowling

	O	M	R	W	O	M	R	W
Stevens				3				1
Francis				1				
Harris				2				2

England Bowling

	O	M	R	W	O	M	R	W
Brazier				3				2
Bullen				2				1

Umpires:

Close of Play: 1st day: ; 2nd day: ; 3rd day: .

Hampshire had Stevens as a given man. The identity of J.Wood is not certain, but it is assumed to be Wood of Seal in view of the strong Kent flavour of the England team. J.Wells, on debut for Hampshire, must be James: John Wells (b probably 1768) does not appear until 1787. SB reports that 'the match was put off, on account of bad weather, and never resumed': a rare departure from the normal practice of playing to a finish.

ENGLAND v HAMPSHIRE

Played at Sevenoaks Vine Cricket Club Ground, June 1, 2, 1784.

England won by seven wickets.

HAMPSHIRE

1	J.Cole	c Clifford	4	b Bullen	4
2	R.Francis	b Bullen	1	c Aylward	8
3	T.Taylor	b Bullen	12	c Bowra	12
4	J.Small, sen	b Bullen	3	c Bowra	37
5	N.Mann	c Bowra	1	b Clifford	3
6	T.Sueter	not out	36	b Bullen	1
7	R.A.Veck	b Bullen	5	b Clifford	22
8	R.Nyren	b Clifford	0	c Bullen	8
9	R.Purchase	b Clifford	0	c Bedster	17
10	J.Small, jun	b Bullen	6	c Bedster	0
11	E.Stevens	b Bullen	3	not out	1
	Byes				3
			71		116

FoW (1): 1- , 2- , 3- , 4- , 5- , 6- , 7- , 8- , 9- , 10-71
FoW (2): 1- , 2- , 3- , 4- , 5- , 6- , 7- , 8- , 9- , 10-116

ENGLAND

1	J.Aylward	b Francis	37	not out	30
2	J.Ring	b Francis	0	c Taylor	5
3	W.Bedster	c Taylor	0	not out	16
4	R.Hosmer	run out	2	b Francis	11
5	R.Clifford	c Francis	31	b Stevens	0
6	W.Brazier	b Stevens	8		
7	Townsend	c Nyren	7		
8	W.Bowra	c Francis	3		
9	Davidson	b Francis	0		
10	F.Booker	not out	20		
11	W.Bullen	b Francis	14		
	Byes		2		2
			124	(3 wickets)	64

FoW (1): 1- , 2- , 3- , 4- , 5- , 6- , 7- , 8- , 9- , 10-124
FoW (2): 1- , 2- , 3-

England Bowling

	O	M	R	W	O	M	R	W
Bullen				6				2
Clifford				2				2

Hampshire Bowling

	O	M	R	W	O	M	R	W
Stevens				1				1
Francis				4				1

Umpires:

Close of Play: 1st day: .

Hampshire had Stevens as a given man. Davidson in the England team has not been identified. F.S.Ashley-Cooper in his *Register of Kent County Cricketers* suggested a Davison of Hythe, but this is based, at least in part, on Ashley-Cooper's assessment, not followed here, of the home team as Kent rather than England.

WHITE CONDUIT CLUB v KENT

Played at White Conduit Fields, Islington, June 22, 23, 24, 1786.

White Conduit Club won by 5 runs.

WHITE CONDUIT CLUB

1	C.Lennox	c Ring	10	b Clifford		5
2	Earl of Winchilsea	b Bullen	17	c Aylward		13
3	G.H.Monson	c Ring	12	c Clifford		26
4	J.Dampier	c Stanford	3	b Clifford		4
5	G.T.Boult	c Aylward	1	c Aylward		1
6	N.Mann	c Stanford	0	c Bullen		2
7	J.Small, sen	b Bullen	1	b Clifford		49
8	T.Walker	c Aylward	17	c Boorman		13
9	T.Taylor	b Clifford	33	c Bullen		7
10	R.Purchase	b Clifford	1	not out		0
11	E.Stevens	not out	0	b Boorman		2
	Byes		8			1
			103			123

FoW (1): 1- , 2- , 3- , 4- , 5- , 6- , 7- , 8- , 9- , 10-103
FoW (2): 1- , 2- , 3- , 4- , 5- , 6- , 7- , 8- , 9- , 10-123

KENT

1	R.Stanford	c Taylor	14	b Stevens		21
2	R.Hosmer	b Stevens	26	b Stevens		25
3	E.Hussey	c Taylor	0	not out		4
4	S.Amherst	not out	15	b Stevens		11
5	I.Hatch	b Purchase	0	b Stevens		7
6	R.Francis	run out	13	c Small		3
7	J.Aylward	c Stevens	2	c Monson		5
8	J.Ring	c Winchilsea	0	b Purchase		4
9	R.Clifford	b Stevens	12	run out		0
10	W.Bullen	c Boult	26	c Monson		19
11	J.Boorman	c Taylor	11	c Lennox		1
	Byes		2			
			121			100

FoW (1): 1- , 2- , 3- , 4- , 5- , 6- , 7- , 8- , 9- , 10-121
FoW (2): 1- , 2- , 3- , 4- , 5- , 6- , 7- , 8- , 9- , 10-100

Kent Bowling

	O	M	R	W		O	M	R	W
Bullen				2					
Clifford				2					3
Boorman									1

White Conduit Club Bowling

	O	M	R	W		O	M	R	W
Stevens				2					4
Purchase				1					1

Umpires:

Close of Play: 1st day: Kent (1) 113-9; 2nd day: .

This is the first 'great' match involving WCC, forerunner of MCC. WCC had six given men; in other words, it consisted of five amateurs from WCC and six professionals. The Kent side likewise has five amateurs, presumably by arrangement, with five Kent professionals and Francis as a given man. The teams are listed with the amateurs first, not in batting order.

(Variant) CJ gives day 2 close: Kent (2) 37-5 (Hussey 0*) with the men out Amherst 8, Bullen 16, Francis 6, Aylward 4, Ring 3 but this is irreconcilable with the LC version as above, and as CJ is not local to Islington its version is not accepted.

KENT v HAMPSHIRE

Played at Sevenoaks Vine Cricket Club Ground, June 26, 27, 28, 1786.

Kent won by four wickets.

HAMPSHIRE

1	Earl of Winchilsea	run out	6	b Boorman		5
2	Hawkins	b Clifford	0	b Clifford		3
3	J.Small, sen	c Bowra	11	b Boorman		12
4	T.Taylor	b Clifford	2	c Bullen		19
5	N.Mann	run out	0	run out		0
6	R.Purchase	b Bullen	25	c Boorman		3
7	T.Walker	c Bowra	43	b Clifford		10
8	H.Walker	b Clifford	39	b Bullen		24
9	T.Sueter	b Bullen	3	b Bullen		10
10	R.Nyren	c Bullen	10	b Bullen		2
11	E.Stevens	not out	1	not out		1
	Byes		3			
			143			89

FoW (1): 1- , 2- , 3- , 4- , 5- , 6- , 7- , 8- , 9- , 10-143
FoW (2): 1- , 2- , 3- , 4- , 5- , 6- , 7- , 8- , 9- , 10-89

KENT

1	W.Bullen	b Stevens	27	c H.Walker		4
2	J.Aylward	c H.Walker	22	b Stevens		27
3	J.Ring	b Purchase	1	not out		61
4	R.Clifford	run out	4			
5	Townsend	c Small	22	c Taylor		8
6	W.Bowra	c Hawkins	28	not out		3
7	W.Brazier	b Stevens	8	c Small		4
8	J.Boorman	run out	2			
9	R.N.Newman	b Purchase	1	b Stevens		1
10	Couchman	b Stevens	1	b Stevens		2
11	F.Booker	not out	5			
	Byes		2			
			123	(6 wickets)		110

FoW (1): 1- , 2- , 3- , 4- , 5- , 6- , 7- , 8- , 9- , 10-123
FoW (2): 1- , 2- , 3- , 4- , 5- , 6-

Kent Bowling

	O	M	R	W	O	M	R	W
Bullen				2				3
Clifford				3				2
Boorman								2

Hampshire Bowling

	O	M	R	W	O	M	R	W
Stevens				3				3
Purchase				2				

Umpires:

Close of Play: 1st day: ; 2nd day: .

Hampshire had Stevens as a given man. Nyren is assumed to be R.Nyren: see notes to Smith v Winchilsea (16 July 1787) and Hampshires v Kent (3 September 1787). Hawkins of Odiham.

HAMPSHIRE v KENT

Played at Windmill Down, Hambledon, July 13, 14, 15, 1786.

Hampshire won by one wicket.

KENT

1	W.Bullen	b Harris	23	b Mann	29
2	H.Crosoer	b Purchase	7	b Purchase	9
3	J.Aylward	b Harris	19	c Hawkins	53
4	J.Ring	c H.Walker	0	b Harris	14
5	R.Clifford	c H.Walker	9	b Purchase	1
6	W.Bowra	b Harris	6	b Mann	0
7	Townsend	b Mann	4	b Purchase	13
8	Finch	b Harris	0	b Purchase	2
9	W.Pattenden	hit wkt	5	c Mann	0
10	J.Boorman	c H.Walker	5	c Sueter	13
11	F.Booker	not out	5	not out	55
	Byes				
			83		189

FoW (1): 1- , 2- , 3- , 4- , 5- , 6- , 7- , 8- , 9- , 10-83
FoW (2): 1- , 2- , 3- , 4- , 5- , 6- , 7- , 8- , 9- , 10-189

HAMPSHIRE

1	H.Walker	c Bowra	66	c Bullen	7
2	T.Walker	b Bowra	55	run out (Aylward)	26
3	G.T.Boult	b Clifford	3	b Clifford	11
4	J.Small, sen	b Bullen	8	b Boorman	24
5	Earl of Winchilsea	b Clifford	6	b Bullen	0
6	T.Taylor	b Bullen	5	c Aylward	15
7	T.Sueter	hit the ball twice	3	b Bullen	0
8	Hawkins	b Clifford	0	b Clifford	0
9	R.Purchase	c Aylward	4	c Boorman	6
10	N.Mann	c Bowra	4	not out	15
11	D.Harris	not out	1	not out	4
	Byes		8		2
			163	(9 wickets)	110

FoW (1): 1- , 2- , 3- , 4- , 5- , 6- , 7- , 8- , 9- , 10-163
FoW (2): 1- , 2- , 3- , 4- , 5- , 6- , 7- , 8- , 9-98

Hampshire Bowling

	O	M	R	W	O	M	R	W
Harris				4				1
Purchase				1				4
Mann				1				2

Kent Bowling

	O	M	R	W	O	M	R	W
Bowra				1				
Clifford				3				2
Bullen				2				2
Boorman								1

Umpires:

Close of Play: 1st day: ; 2nd day: .

Finch, playing for Kent, is probably the same man as played for XXIII of Kent at Woolwich in 1800 (SB p281); he is assumed not to be the same as J.Finch, who played from 1792 for Oldfield/Berkshire, although it must be observed that the number of Kent players sharing surnames with players appearing elsewhere is far too large to be coincidence (see the Supplementary Notes to Hornchurch v WCC and Moulsey Hurst, 15 May 1787). Some sources have T.Pattenden appearing in this match but he was now aged 44; W.Pattenden, aged 38, seems a likelier candidate but there is no proof either way.

(Variant) KG has minor changes and a different Kent order but the SB version is supported by RM.

A TO C v REST OF THE ALPHABET

Played at Molesey Hurst, August 2, 3, 4, 5, 1786.

Rest of the Alphabet won by 25 runs.

REST OF THE ALPHABET

1	Earl of Winchilsea	b Clifford	6	c Bowra	5
2	E.Hussey	b Brazier	19	c Brazier	28
3	H.Walker	b Clifford	8	c Bullen	21
4	T.Walker	c Bullen	56	b Brazier	6
5	J.Small, sen	c Boorman	6	b Boorman	9
6	T.Taylor	b Bullen	6	b Clifford	10
7	N.Mann	c Amherst	2	b Clifford	8
8	R.Purchase	c Bedster	2	b Brazier	26
9	D.Harris	b Clifford	0	run out	0
10	E.Stevens	c Brazier	0	not out	2
11	W.Fennex	not out	7	b Clifford	22
	Byes		4		7
			116		144

FoW (1): 1- , 2- , 3- , 4- , 5- , 6- , 7- , 8- , 9- , 10-116
FoW (2): 1- , 2- , 3- , 4- , 5- , 6- , 7- , 8- , 9- , 10-144

A TO C

1	J.Aylward	b Stevens	3	c Harris	3
2	W.Bowra	b Purchase	0	b Stevens	10
3	H.Crosoer	c Taylor	0	c Stevens	6
4	R.Clifford	c Taylor	9	c Taylor	3
5	W.Bullen	c Taylor	0	b Stevens	6
6	F.Booker	c Taylor	26	b Harris	39
7	W.Bedster	c H.Walker	15	not out	3
8	W.Brazier	c Fennex	10	b Stevens	1
9	G.T.Boult	c H.Walker	18	c Taylor	7
10	J.Boorman	not out	18	c Small	1
11	S.Amherst	b Stevens	33	b Purchase	8
	Byes		11		5
			143		92

FoW (1): 1- , 2- , 3- , 4- , 5- , 6- , 7- , 8- , 9- , 10-143
FoW (2): 1- , 2- , 3- , 4- , 5- , 6- , 7- , 8- , 9- , 10-92

A to C Bowling

	O	M	R	W	O	M	R	W
Bullen				1				
Clifford				3				3
Brazier				1				2
Boorman								1

Rest of the Alphabet Bowling

	O	M	R	W	O	M	R	W
Stevens				2				3
Purchase				1				1
Harris								1

Umpires:

Close of Play: 1st day: ; 2nd day: ; 3rd day: .

The score is sourced from several newspapers but batting orders from SB seem more convincing and have been retained.

KENT v WHITE CONDUIT CLUB

Played at Bourne Paddock, Bishopsbourne, August 8, 9, 10, 11, 12, 1786.

White Conduit Club won by 164 runs.

WHITE CONDUIT CLUB

1	T.Walker	not out	95	b Bullen		102
2	T.Taylor	b Bullen	8	b Bullen		117
3	J.Small, sen	c Hosmer	22	b Bullen		19
4	Earl of Winchilsea	c Clifford	3	c Boorman		5
5	N.Mann	b Boorman	6	c Bullen		1
6	J.Dampier	b Clifford	3	b Clifford		16
7	G.Louch	b Clifford	3	run out		9
8	G.East	b Clifford	26	run out		7
9	D.Harris	c Hosmer	5	run out		7
10	Hawkins	c Hosmer	0	b Bullen		3
11	E.Stevens	b Clifford	9	not out		3
	Byes		3			7
			183			296

FoW (1): 1- , 2- , 3- , 4- , 5- , 6- , 7- , 8- , 9- , 10-183
FoW (2): 1- , 2- , 3- , 4- , 5- , 6- , 7- , 8- , 9- , 10-296

KENT

1	W.Bullen	b Harris	0	b Harris		3
2	J.Aylward	c Harris	9	b Harris		1
3	J.Ring	b Harris	23	c Louch		0
4	E.Hussey	run out	0	c Taylor		4
5	F.Booker	b Stevens	3	c Louch		0
6	Collier	b Harris	14	b Harris		35
7	R.Hosmer	c Dampier	17	not out		1
8	S.Amherst	b East	39	c Louch		3
9	R.Stanford	b Taylor	73	b Stevens		3
10	R.Clifford	not out	7	b Stevens		41
11	J.Boorman	c Mann	32	c Louch		5
	Byes		1			1
			218			97

FoW (1): 1- , 2- , 3- , 4- , 5- , 6- , 7- , 8- , 9- , 10-218
FoW (2): 1- , 2- , 3- , 4- , 5- , 6- , 7- , 8- , 9- , 10-97

Kent Bowling

	O	M	R	W	O	M	R	W
Bullen				1				4
Boorman				1				
Clifford				4				1

White Conduit Club Bowling

	O	M	R	W	O	M	R	W
Stevens				1				2
Harris				3				3
Taylor				1				
East				1				

Umpires:

Close of Play: 1st day: ; 2nd day: ; 3rd day: ; 4th day: .

This match is famous for T.Walker's scores of 95* and 102, an astonishing double by the standards of the day. WCC had six given men. Collier of Kent is a mystery. The name is otherwise unknown, even in minor matches, yet he made a very respectable 35 in the second innings. *Register of Kent County Cricketers* says he was from Canterbury.

HORNCHURCH v WHITE CONDUIT CLUB AND MOULSEY HURST

Played at Langton Park, Hornchurch, May 15, 16, 1787.

White Conduit Club and Moulsey Hurst won by six wickets.

HORNCHURCH

1	R.N.Newman	c Ingram	2	b Butcher		4
2	R.B.Wyatt	b Stevens	5	b Butcher		3
3	R.Denn	not out	3	c Ingram		4
4	T.Clark	b Stevens	12	b Stevens		13
5	J.Boorman	c Butcher	12	b Butcher		7
6	Murray	c Ingram	2	b Butcher		14
7	M.Rimmington	b Butcher	2	b Stevens		4
8	N.Graham	c Ingram	0	not out		18
9	Davidson	b Stevens	0	b Butcher		0
10	J.Martin	b Stevens	4	b Stevens		7
11	Clements	b Stevens	1	b Stevens		11
	Byes		3			3
			46			88

FoW (1): 1- , 2- , 3- , 4- , 5- , 6- , 7- , 8- , 9- , 10-46
FoW (2): 1- , 2- , 3- , 4- , 5- , 6- , 7- , 8- , 9- , 10-88

WHITE CONDUIT CLUB AND MOULSEY HURST

1	Earl of Winchilsea	b Martin	1	b Boorman		7
2	Lord Strathavon	b Boorman	17	not out		2
3	G.Talbot	not out	9	b Martin		3
4	G.Drummond	b Boorman	1	b Martin		1
5	T.A.Smith	b Boorman	10	b Martin		1
6	G.T.Boult	b Boorman	62			
7	G.Louch	c Clements	2			
8	W.Bedster	c Wyatt	3			
9	Butcher	c Wyatt	3	not out		2
10	E.Stevens	c Clark	0			
11	T.Ingram	b Martin	5			
	Byes		4			2
			117	(4 wickets)		18

FoW (1): 1- , 2- , 3- , 4- , 5- , 6- , 7- , 8- , 9- , 10-117
FoW (2): 1- , 2- , 3- , 4-

White Conduit Club and Moulsey Hurst Bowling

	O	M	R	W		O	M	R	W
Stevens				5					4
Butcher				1					5

Hornchurch Bowling

	O	M	R	W		O	M	R	W
Boorman				4					1
Martin				2					3

Umpires:

Close of Play: 1st day: .

The teams are not in batting order. This match was the first of three between a combined WCC/Moulsey team and Hornchurch. This game probably presents more difficulties than any other single 'great' match. Its venue has been given above as Hornchurch but this is open to considerable doubt: in addition, there are several problems with player identification. These issues are discussed in more detail in the Supplementary Note for this match on page 276.

(Variant) SB gives this and the second match as Moulsey Hurst games but the composition of the team shows that it was WCC and Moulsey Hurst jointly, and this is confirmed by press announcements for the third match at Hornchurch on 2 August (for which the full score has unfortunately not survived).

MIDDLESEX v ESSEX

Played at Lord's Old Ground, Marylebone, May 31, 1787.

Middlesex won by 93 runs.

MIDDLESEX

1	Stanhope	run out	3	b Butcher	1
2	T.Lord	b Butcher	1	c Newman	36
3	J.Boorman	b Butcher	23	b Butcher	37
4	W.White	b Butcher	5	run out	12
5	Z.Boult	st Clark	0	b Butcher	18
6	W.Bedster	b Martin	13	st Clark	14
7	G.Louch	b Martin	0	b Butcher	14
8	G.T.Boult	b Butcher	3	b Martin	36
9	A.Boult	b Martin	3	b Butcher	0
10	C.Slater	b Butcher	0	b Martin	23
11	Oliver	not out	0	not out	1
	Byes		7		11
			58		203

FoW (1): 1- , 2- , 3- , 4- , 5- , 6- , 7- , 8- , 9- , 10-58
FoW (2): 1- , 2- , 3- , 4- , 5- , 6- , 7- , 8- , 9- , 10-203

ESSEX

1	R.N.Newman	c Louch	51	b Boorman	5
2	M.Rimmington	run out	28	c G.T.Boult	0
3	N.Graham	b Bedster	4	run out	0
4	T.Clark	c Louch	13	c Boorman	1
5	R.B.Wyatt	b Boorman	5	c Louch	14
6	Butcher	c Z.Boult	3	c Slater	0
7	Jones	b White	16	c G.T.Boult	1
8	Davidson	b Boorman	1	b Boorman	2
9	R.Denn	not out	4	b White	1
10	J.Martin	b White	0	not out	4
11	Barker	b Boorman	2	b Boorman	9
	Byes		3		1
			130		38

FoW (1): 1- , 2- , 3- , 4- , 5- , 6- , 7- , 8- , 9- , 10-130
FoW (2): 1- , 2- , 3- , 4- , 5- , 6- , 7- , 8- , 9- , 10-38

Essex Bowling

	O	M	R	W	O	M	R	W
Butcher				5				5
Martin				3				2

Middlesex Bowling

	O	M	R	W	O	M	R	W
Bedster				1				
Boorman				3				3
White				2				1

Umpires:

This is the first recorded match played at Thomas Lord's first ground. Middlesex had two of Berkshire and one of Kent as given men; Essex had two given men. Z.Boult (1) and W.Bedster (2) are shown as PO Clark. 'PO', i.e. put out, is taken to mean stumped. Clark has a stumping in 1789 (Hornchurch v MCC, 6 August 1789), so he is known to have kept wicket. SB has 'Davies', otherwise unknown, in the Essex team: this is assumed to be Davidson, who appeared for Hornchurch in the previous match and in the 'lost' match on 2 August. Only one day is given but the scoring suggests that the match must have continued into at least a second day.

WHITE CONDUIT CLUB v MIDDLESEX

Played at Lord's Old Ground, Marylebone, June 14, 15, 1787.

Middlesex won by eight wickets.

WHITE CONDUIT CLUB

1	R.N.Newman	b Boorman	0	c Louch	10
2	M.Rimmington	b Boorman	12	b Weston	12
3	Sir P.Burrell	b Boorman	6	b Boorman	22
4	R.B.Wyatt	b Bedster	3	run out	26
5	Butcher	b Weston	30	b Boorman	0
6	G.East	c Weston	17	c Louch	0
7	Earl of Winchilsea	b Weston	0	c Boorman	0
8	G.Drummond	b Boorman	7	b Bedster	12
9	G.Talbot	c Louch	1	b Bedster	3
10	R.Lawrence	b Weston	0	absent	-
11	J.Martin	not out	2	not out	0
	Byes		2		3
			80		88

FoW (1): 1- , 2- , 3- , 4- , 5- , 6- , 7- , 8- , 9- , 10-80
FoW (2): 1- , 2- , 3-21, 4- , 5- , 6- , 7- , 8- , 9-88

MIDDLESEX

1	Stanhope	c Burrell	1	b East	7
2	N.Graham	b Martin	4	c Wyatt	7
3	W.White	c Newman	13		
4	G.Louch	c East	22	not out	16
5	J.Boorman	b East	1		
6	W.Bedster	c Talbot	6		
7	C.Slater	run out	19		
8	Gibbs	c Burrell	9		
9	W.Allen	b Rimmington	1	not out	14
10	Dean	c Wyatt	23		
11	J.Weston	not out	17		
	Byes		10		1
			126	(2 wickets)	45

FoW (1): 1- , 2- , 3- , 4- , 5- , 6- , 7- , 8- , 9- , 10-126
FoW (2): 1- , 2-

Middlesex Bowling

	O	M	R	W	O	M	R	W
Boorman				4				2
Bedster				1				2
Weston				3				1

White Conduit Club Bowling

	O	M	R	W	O	M	R	W
East				1				1
Martin				1				
Rimmington				1				

Umpires:

Close of Play: 1st day: White Conduit Club (2) 21-3 (Burrell 7*).

Dean is assumed to be the Kent player. The *World* reports, 'On the first day each side played an innings and the Club had scored 21 for 3, Sir P.Burrell being not out 7, when want of light stopped play at 8.30pm. Boorman's bowling won the game. Mr Cumberland, second to none as a bowler and second to few as a fieldsman, was unable to play for the Club owing to an injured ankle.'

In WCC (2) Buckley added Lawrence b 2 but this is based on speculation. He took the scores from the *World* which omits Lawrence from the second innings. It also gives only individual scores and not team totals so Buckley has reasoned that Middlesex had to make 45 to win, therefore WCC must have made 90, but the scores add to only 88 so Lawrence must have contributed 2. But a simpler interpretation of the evidence is that Lawrence was omitted because he was absent, WCC made 88, and Middlesex were set 43 and reached it with a hit of 3 (probably a 'booth ball'), hence the total of 45.

WHITE CONDUIT CLUB v ENGLAND
Played at Lord's Old Ground, Marylebone, June 20, 21, 22, 1787.

England won by 265 runs.

ENGLAND
1	J.Aylward	run out	93	(4) c Taylor		16
2	W.Beldham	b Clifford	17	(1) run out		63
3	R.Hosmer	c H.Walker	43	(10) c H.Walker		2
4	R.Stanford	c H.Walker	0	(8) c H.Walker		0
5	S.Amherst	not out	20	(9) c H.Walker		17
6	N.Mann	b Harris	11	(5) c Hussey		6
7	J.Small, jun	c Clifford	3	(2) c Clifford		42
8	R.Purchase	b Harris	0	(3) c Taylor		3
9	W.Bullen	b Harris	14	(11) b Taylor		0
10	J.Small, sen	b Taylor	30	(6) not out		32
11	John Wells	b Harris	8	(7) c Clifford		12
	Byes		8			4
			247			197

FoW (1): 1- , 2- , 3- , 4- , 5- , 6- , 7- , 8- , 9- , 10-247
FoW (2): 1- , 2- , 3- , 4- , 5- , 6- , 7- , 8- , 9- , 10-197

WHITE CONDUIT CLUB
1	Sir P.Burrell	c Stanford	0	( ) b Mann	10
2	J.Dampier	b Bullen	26	( ) b Bullen	13
3	E.Hussey	b Beldham	21	(5) b Mann	9
4	G.Drummond	c Hosmer	1	( ) c Beldham	1
5	Earl of Winchilsea	b Beldham	3	( ) run out	9
6	T.Taylor	c Bullen	12	(3) c Mann	4
7	J.Ring	c Bullen	18	(2) b Beldham	2
8	H.Walker	run out	0	( ) c Amherst	5
9	R.Clifford	run out	6	(1) b Purchase	0
10	T.Walker	c Bullen	11	(4) b Beldham	12
11	D.Harris	not out	5	( ) not out	2
	Byes		9		
			112		67

FoW (1): 1- , 2- , 3- , 4- , 5- , 6- , 7- , 8- , 9- , 10-112
FoW (2): 1- , 2- , 3- , 4- , 5- , 6- , 7- , 8- , 9- , 10-67

White Conduit Club Bowling
	O	M	R	W	O	M	R	W
Harris				4				
Clifford				1				
Taylor				1				1

England Bowling
	O	M	R	W	O	M	R	W
Beldham				2				2
Bullen				1				1
Mann								2
Purchase								1

Umpires: Hawkins and R.Lawrence.

Close of Play: 1st day: White Conduit Club (1) 24-1 (Dampier 20*, Hussey 1*); 2nd day: England (2) 87-0 (Beldham 52*, J.Small, jun 31*).

All sources give the WCC team with amateurs at the top. The rest of the batting order in WCC (2) is not known. On day 1 Aylward batted from 11am to just after 6pm. Hawkins, the umpire, is probably the Odiham player, nominated by the Hambledon Club as organiser of the England side, so the other umpire is probably R.Lawrence, nominated by WCC.

Other versions differ quite widely, especially in WCC (2), but the above is largely based on the score in the *World*, which is the most complete that has been discovered and is consistent with close of play details from other sources. However, the *World* has England (1) adding up 2 short with Amherst 18; other versions give Amherst 20 and this has been accepted even though it means mixing sources. The *World* also says that England won by 266 runs but if the team totals are correct the margin was 265.

WHITE CONDUIT CLUB AND MOULSEY HURST v HORNCHURCH

Played at Molesey Hurst, July 3, 4, 1787.

White Conduit Club and Moulsey Hurst won by 131 runs.

WHITE CONDUIT CLUB AND MOULSEY HURST

#	Batsman	Dismissal	Runs	Dismissal (2nd)	Runs
1	Earl of Winchilsea	c White	34	c Clark	11
2	Sir P.Burrell	b Butcher	0	b Martin	0
3	J.L.Kaye	b Martin	22	c Graham	12
4	G.East	c Newman	5	c Dupuis	19
5	G.Talbot	hit wkt	3	c Clark	1
6	G.T.Boult	b Butcher	9	not out	56
7	G.Louch	b Martin	26	b Butcher	3
8	C.Slater	c Wyatt	2	c Graham	4
9	Davy	c Butcher	1	c Clark	0
10	E.Stevens	not out	5	b Martin	20
11	W.Bedster	c Wyatt	3	b Martin	2
	Byes		3		9
			113		137

FoW (1): 1- , 2- , 3- , 4- , 5- , 6- , 7- , 8- , 9- , 10-113
FoW (2): 1- , 2- , 3- , 4- , 5- , 6- , 7- , 8- , 9- , 10-137

HORNCHURCH

#	Batsman	Dismissal	Runs	Dismissal (2nd)	Runs
1	R.B.Wyatt	b Stevens	12	b Davy	0
2	R.N.Newman	run out	6	c Slater	3
3	R.Denn	c Burrell	9	not out	0
4	J.Russell	c Davy	0	b Davy	0
5	T.Clark	run out	4	b Davy	3
6	W.White	c Louch	3	c Stevens	13
7	Butcher	c Winchilsea	0	c Winchilsea	10
8	M.Rimmington	b Stevens	6	c Boult	0
9	N.Graham	c Winchilsea	2	b Davy	1
10	G.Dupuis	not out	18	c Stevens	5
11	J.Martin	b Stevens	13	b Davy	0
	Byes		10		1
			83		36

FoW (1): 1- , 2- , 3- , 4- , 5- , 6- , 7- , 8- , 9- , 10-83
FoW (2): 1- , 2- , 3- , 4- , 5- , 6- , 7- , 8- , 9- , 10-36

Hornchurch Bowling

	O	M	R	W	O	M	R	W
Butcher				2				1
Martin				2				3

White Conduit Club and Moulsey Hurst Bowling

	O	M	R	W	O	M	R	W
Stevens				3				
Davy								5

Umpires:

Close of Play: 1st day: .

Hornchurch had Butcher and White as given men. Talbot (1) is recorded as PHO (put himself out), which has been assumed to mean hit wicket.

T.A.SMITH'S XI v EARL OF WINCHILSEA'S XI

Played at Perham Downs, Ludgershall, July 16, 17, 1787.

Earl of Winchilsea's XI won by 69 runs.

EARL OF WINCHILSEA'S XI

1	Earl of Winchilsea	b Purchase	16	b Taylor	0
2	Hawkins	run out	0	b Stevens	3
3	G.Talbot	not out	3	b Stevens	2
4	G.Louch	b Butcher	4	c Stevens	0
5	D.Harris	b Butcher	6	run out	6
6	W.Beldham	run out	30	b Taylor	22
7	J.Small, jun	c Taylor	3	c Purchase	7
8	N.Mann	b Butcher	1	b Taylor	2
9	T.Walker	b Butcher	5	c Stevens	41
10	John Wells	b Purchase	0	b Taylor	28
11	Davy	b Butcher	0	not out	0
	Byes		1		4
			69		115

FoW (1): 1- , 2- , 3- , 4- , 5- , 6- , 7- , 8- , 9- , 10-69
FoW (2): 1- , 2- , 3- , 4- , 5- , 6- , 7- , 8- , 9- , 10-115

T.A.SMITH'S XI

1	T.A.Smith	b Mann	1	b Mann	0
2	G.Drummond	run out	2	b Harris	2
3	E.Stevens	b Mann	0	run out	0
4	J.Small, sen	b Harris	11	run out	30
5	T.Taylor	b Harris	6	b Mann	0
6	R.Purchase	b Harris	10	b Harris	17
7	James Wells	not out	5	b Mann	5
8	H.Walker	b Harris	1	c Beldham	9
9	Butcher	b Mann	1	b Harris	1
10	Butterly	b Mann	3	not out	2
11	J.Nyren	b Harris	2	b Mann	2
	Byes				5
			42		73

FoW (1): 1- , 2- , 3- , 4- , 5- , 6- , 7- , 8- , 9- , 10-42
FoW (2): 1- , 2- , 3- , 4- , 5- , 6- , 7- , 8- , 9- , 10-73

T.A.Smith's XI Bowling

	O	M	R	W		O	M	R	W
Purchase				2					
Butcher				5					
Stevens									2
Taylor									4

Earl of Winchilsea's XI Bowling

	O	M	R	W		O	M	R	W
Harris				5					3
Mann				4					4

Umpires:

Close of Play: 1st day: .

Nyren is assumed to be J. (but see the note to Hampshire v Kent, 3 September 1787). The spelling of the ground has been modernised: in the 18th century it was Perriam Downs, Luggershall. It is treated as a Hampshire ground, although actually just over the border in Wiltshire.

KENT v HAMPSHIRE

Played at Star Inn, Coxheath, August 7, 8, 9, 10, 1787.

Hampshire won by two wickets.

KENT

1	E.Hussey	c J.Small, sen	0	c Taylor		7
2	S.Amherst	c Taylor	18	b Beldham		6
3	R.Hosmer	b Taylor	5	c J.Small, sen		10
4	J.Aylward	run out	3	c Beldham		8
5	J.Ring	b Taylor	16	run out (Purchase)		4
6	R.Clifford	b Taylor	50	c John Wells		23
7	W.Brazier	b Purchase	25	c H.Walker		39
8	H.Crosoer	b Purchase	14	c H.Walker		39
9	R.Stanford	c Winchilsea	1	run out		9
10	J.Pilcher	b Purchase	6	c Beldham		7
11	W.Bullen	not out	1	not out		39
	Byes		1			3
			140			194

FoW (1): 1- , 2- , 3- , 4- , 5- , 6- , 7- , 8- , 9- , 10-140
FoW (2): 1- , 2- , 3- , 4- , 5- , 6- , 7- , 8- , 9-115, 10-194

HAMPSHIRE

1	Earl of Winchilsea	b Brazier	5	run out		5
2	T.Walker	run out	57	run out		1
3	H.Walker	b Bullen	22	b Bullen		23
4	T.Taylor	b Bullen	36	not out		9
5	N.Mann	not out	18			
6	J.Small, sen	b Brazier	15	b Brazier		4
7	J.Small, jun	b Clifford	3	c Hosmer		10
8	James Wells	b Clifford	1	not out		0
9	John Wells	b Clifford	36	b Bullen		3
10	W.Beldham	b Clifford	42	c Clifford		14
11	R.Purchase	run out	14	b Brazier		7
	Byes		7			3
			256	(8 wickets)		79

FoW (1): 1- , 2- , 3- , 4- , 5- , 6- , 7- , 8- , 9- , 10-256
FoW (2): 1- , 2- , 3- , 4- , 5- , 6- , 7- , 8-

Hampshire Bowling

	O	M	R	W		O	M	R	W
Purchase				3					
Taylor				3					
Beldham									1

Kent Bowling

	O	M	R	W		O	M	R	W
Clifford				4					
Bullen				2					2
Brazier				2					2

Umpires:

Close of Play: 1st day: ; 2nd day: ; 3rd day: .

In Kent (2), Ring was stated to be 'put out by Purchase', which has been taken to mean run out. The last pair, Crosoer and Bullen, added 79.

KENT v HAMPSHIRE

Played at Bourne Paddock, Bishopsbourne, August 14, 15, 16, 17, 1787.

Hampshire won by 266 runs.

HAMPSHIRE

1	R.Purchase	b Clifford	6	run out	0
2	J.Small, sen	b Fennex	40	b Boorman	24
3	T.Taylor	b Clifford	8	run out	20
4	T.Walker	c Bullen	65	b Fennex	17
5	H.Walker	b Clifford	2	c Brazier	10
6	N.Mann	b Fennex	6	b Bullen	12
7	John Wells	b Clifford	10	b Fennex	13
8	J.Small, jun	b Clifford	0	not out	10
9	Earl of Winchilsea	b Fennex	12	c Amherst	20
10	W.Beldham	run out	27	b Fennex	42
11	D.Harris	not out	8	b Clifford	3
	Byes		11		3
			195		174

FoW (1): 1- , 2- , 3- , 4- , 5- , 6- , 7- , 8- , 9- , 10-195
FoW (2): 1- , 2- , 3- , 4- , 5- , 6- , 7- , 8- , 9- , 10-174

KENT

1	R.Clifford	c J.Small, jun	5	b Harris	3
2	W.Bullen	c Beldham	0	c Winchilsea	1
3	W.Fennex	b Harris	0	b Harris	9
4	J.Ring	b Harris	24	run out	13
5	W.Brazier	c Beldham	23	c H.Walker	0
6	H.Crosoer	b Harris	0	b Harris	2
7	S.Amherst	c Mann	0	c Wells	3
8	J.Aylward	b Taylor	2	c T.Walker	0
9	J.Boorman	b Harris	1	not out	0
10	G.Louch	c Taylor	4	c Purchase	0
11	F.Booker	not out	0	run out	7
	Byes		3		3
			62		41

FoW (1): 1- , 2- , 3- , 4- , 5- , 6- , 7- , 8- , 9- , 10-62
FoW (2): 1- , 2- , 3- , 4- , 5- , 6- , 7- , 8- , 9- , 10-41

Kent Bowling

	O	M	R	W	O	M	R	W
Clifford				5				1
Fennex				3				3
Bullen								1
Boorman								1

Hampshire Bowling

	O	M	R	W	O	M	R	W
Harris				4				3
Taylor				1				

Umpires:

Close of Play: 1st day: ; 2nd day: ; 3rd day: .

Kent had Fennex as a given man.

A TO M v N TO Z

Played at Bourne Paddock, Bishopsbourne, August 28, 29, 30, 31, 1787.

A to M won by 29 runs.

A TO M

1	W.Bedster	c John Wells	3	c Fennex	1
2	W.Brazier	c Fennex	18	c Fennex	19
3	W.Beldham	run out	1	run out	22
4	W.Bullen	run out	6	b Stevens	29
5	T.Taylor	c John Wells	6	c Fennex	14
6	R.Clifford	c Stevens	4	c Fennex	0
7	F.Booker	b Stevens	10	b Fennex	36
8	G.Louch	b Fennex	1	run out	28
9	T.Lord	b Fennex	11	c Fennex	2
10	N.Mann	c H.Walker	28	b Fennex	4
11	D.Harris	not out	0	not out	0
	Byes		6		
			94		155

FoW (1): 1- , 2- , 3- , 4- , 5- , 6- , 7- , 8- , 9- , 10-94
FoW (2): 1- , 2- , 3- , 4- , 5- , 6- , 7- , 8- , 9- , 10-155

N TO Z

1	T.Walker	run out	4	b Harris	3
2	H.Walker	b Harris	8	c Taylor	5
3	J.Small, sen	b Clifford	8	c Bullen	57
4	J.Ring	hit wkt	7	c Clifford	2
5	W.Fennex	c Louch	8	b Taylor	8
6	J.Small, jun	b Clifford	0	b Taylor	13
7	John Wells	b Taylor	10	b Taylor	0
8	R.Purchase	b Taylor	1	b Taylor	8
9	J.Aylward	b Bullen	28	b Taylor	35
10	James Wells	not out	1	b Harris	1
11	E.Stevens	b Harris	3	not out	2
	Byes		4		4
			82		138

FoW (1): 1- , 2- , 3- , 4- , 5- , 6- , 7- , 8- , 9- , 10-82
FoW (2): 1- , 2- , 3- , 4- , 5- , 6- , 7- , 8- , 9- , 10-138

N to Z Bowling

	O	M	R	W	O	M	R	W
Stevens				1				1
Fennex				2				2

A to M Bowling

	O	M	R	W	O	M	R	W
Harris				2				2
Clifford				2				
Taylor				2				5
Bullen				1				

Umpires:

Close of Play: 1st day: ; 2nd day: ; 3rd day: .

A to M had Taylor as a given man; N to Z had Aylward as a given man. Fennex played for N to Z in this and other matches because his name was understood to be a corruption of 'Phœnix'.

HAMPSHIRE v KENT

Played at Windmill Down, Hambledon, September 3, 4, 5, 1787.

Kent won by 65 runs.

KENT

1	J.Aylward	c Purchase	31	c John Wells	65
2	R.Clifford	b Taylor	3	b Beldham	2
3	J.Ring	c Taylor	14	c H.Walker	2
4	J.Pilcher	c Taylor	0	run out	13
5	W.Brazier	b Harris	3	c John Wells	14
6	W.Fennex	b Harris	2	c Taylor	0
7	F.Booker	c Beldham	1	run out	15
8	G.Louch	not out	21	c Mann	8
9	W.Bullen	c J.Small, sen	2	not out	2
10	J.Boorman	c Beldham	23	b Mann	0
11	J.Nyren	c John Wells	3	c Taylor	1
	Byes		6		1
			109		123

FoW (1): 1- , 2- , 3- , 4- , 5- , 6- , 7- , 8- , 9- , 10-109
FoW (2): 1- , 2- , 3- , 4- , 5- , 6- , 7- , 8- , 9- , 10-123

HAMPSHIRE

1	T.Walker	b Boorman	7	b Boorman	1
2	J.Small, sen	c Aylward	3	b Bullen	7
3	T.Taylor	run out	1	b Bullen	5
4	H.Walker	b Bullen	1	b Bullen	2
5	W.Beldham	c Boorman	0	run out	0
6	John Wells	run out	6	run out	23
7	N.Mann	b Bullen	5	c Bullen	41
8	J.Small, jun	run out	4	b Boorman	4
9	R.Purchase	run out	0	not out	30
10	D.Harris	not out	4	b Bullen	4
11	James Wells	b Bullen	1	run out	5
	Byes		5		8
			37		130

FoW (1): 1- , 2- , 3- , 4- , 5- , 6- , 7- , 8- , 9- , 10-37
FoW (2): 1- , 2- , 3- , 4-17, 5- , 6- , 7- , 8- , 9- , 10-130

Hampshire Bowling

	O	M	R	W	O	M	R	W
Harris				2				
Taylor				1				
Mann								1
Beldham								1

Kent Bowling

	O	M	R	W	O	M	R	W
Bullen				3				4
Boorman				1				2

Umpires:

Close of Play: 1st day: ; 2nd day: Hampshire (2) 17-4 (J.Small, jun not out).

Kent had Fennex as a given man. At the close of day 2, T.Walker, Small, sen, Taylor and Beldham were the men out. Writing in the 1830s, J.Nyren recalled this as his first great match. However, his memory is demonstrably faulty on other points, so an appearance earlier in 1787 has also been attributed to him (Smith v Winchilsea, 16 July). Appearances in previous seasons are assumed to be by R.Nyren.

A TO M v N TO Z

Played at Lord's Old Ground, Marylebone, September 10, 11, 12, 1787.

N to Z won by 94 runs.

N TO Z

#	Batsman	Dismissal (1)	R	Dismissal (2)	R
1	J.Aylward	c Clifford	0	b Boorman	15
2	J.Small, jun	b Bullen	1	c Louch	4
3	J.Small, sen	run out	8	b Clifford	26
4	T.Walker	b Harris	6	b Harris	40
5	H.Walker	b Bullen	44	c Bullen	5
6	J.Ring	b Clifford	26	c Beldham	3
7	John Wells	b Brazier	19	b Harris	11
8	W.Fennex	run out	1	b Harris	1
9	R.Purchase	hit wkt	0	not out	11
10	J.Pilcher	not out	4	c Clifford	0
11	E.Stevens	b Brazier	0	b Brazier	1
	Byes		7		6
			116		123

FoW (1): 1- , 2- , 3- , 4- , 5- , 6- , 7- , 8- , 9- , 10-116
FoW (2): 1- , 2- , 3- , 4- , 5- , 6-105, 7- , 8- , 9- , 10-123

A TO M

#	Batsman	Dismissal (1)	R	Dismissal (2)	R
1	W.Beldham	run out	6	b Purchase	0
2	F.Booker	b Stevens	12	b Stevens	22
3	J.Boorman	c Wells	8	c Aylward	3
4	W.Brazier	b Stevens	3	c J.Small, sen	0
5	G.Louch	c H.Walker	3	c Wells	3
6	T.Taylor	not out	23	b Stevens	6
7	W.Bullen	c J.Small, jun	3	c J.Small, sen	11
8	R.Clifford	c Pilcher	17	b Stevens	8
9	N.Mann	b Stevens	1	c Purchase	5
10	G.T.Boult	run out	1	not out	3
11	D.Harris	c Stevens	0	b Purchase	0
	Byes		7		
			84		61

FoW (1): 1- , 2- , 3- , 4- , 5- , 6- , 7- , 8- , 9- , 10-84
FoW (2): 1- , 2- , 3- , 4- , 5- , 6- , 7- , 8- , 9- , 10-61

A to M Bowling

	O	M	R	W	O	M	R	W
Harris				1				3
Clifford				1				1
Bullen				2				
Brazier				2				1
Boorman								1

N to Z Bowling

	O	M	R	W	O	M	R	W
Stevens				3				3
Purchase								2

Umpires:

Close of Play: 1st day: A to M (1) 51-6; 2nd day: N to Z (2) 105-6 (J.Small, sen 25*).

A to M had Taylor as a given man; N to Z had Aylward as a given man. Fennex played for N to Z because his name was understood to be a corruption of 'Phœnix'.

A TO M v N TO Z

Played at Lord's Old Ground, Marylebone, May 26, 27, 28, 1788.

N to Z won by 105 runs.

N TO Z

1	T.Walker	b Harris	6	(5) b Harris	18
2	H.Walker	c Bullen	12	(4) b Harris	6
3	J.Pilcher	b Clifford	1	(10) b Harris	11
4	J.Aylward	b Clifford	7	(1) b Brazier	20
5	J.Ring	b Harris	4	(2) c Louch	11
6	J.Small, sen	b Harris	19	(3) c Taylor	24
7	Earl of Winchilsea	b Bullen	7	(7) b Harris	7
8	J.Small, jun	c Beldham	3	(8) b Harris	4
9	R.Purchase	b Bullen	24	(6) c Louch	12
10	W.Fennex	b Harris	0	(9) not out	23
11	E.Stevens	not out	5	(11) b Harris	11
	Byes		14		7
			102		154

FoW (1): 1- , 2- , 3- , 4- , 5- , 6- , 7- , 8- , 9- , 10-102
FoW (2): 1- , 2- , 3- , 4- , 5- , 6- , 7- , 8- , 9- , 10-154

A TO M

1	W.Brazier	b Stevens	7	(2) c Fennex	7
2	F.Booker	b Purchase	16	(3) b Stevens	12
3	W.Beldham	c H.Walker	14	( ) b Stevens	3
4	T.Taylor	c Fennex	6	( ) c Winchilsea	1
5	W.Bullen	c H.Walker	8	(1) c J.Small, sen	15
6	N.Mann	run out	0	( ) not out	4
7	G.Louch	c Pilcher	1	( ) b Stevens	15
8	S.Amherst	b Purchase	2	( ) c Ring	7
9	R.Hosmer	b Purchase	1	( ) b Fennex	22
10	R.Clifford	b Purchase	1	( ) c Stevens	5
11	D.Harris	not out	1	( ) run out	1
	Byes				2
			57		94

FoW (1): 1- , 2- , 3- , 4- , 5- , 6- , 7- , 8- , 9- , 10-57
FoW (2): 1- , 2- , 3- , 4- , 5- , 6- , 7- , 8- , 9- , 10-94

A to M Bowling

	O	M	R	W	O	M	R	W
Harris				4				6
Clifford				2				
Bullen				2				
Brazier								1

N to Z Bowling

	O	M	R	W	O	M	R	W
Stevens				1				3
Purchase				4				
Fennex								1

Umpires:

Close of Play: 1st day: A to M (1) 57 all out; 2nd day: A to M (2) 35-3.

A to M had Taylor as a given man; N to Z had Aylward as a given man. Fennex played for N to Z because his name was understood to be a corruption of 'Phœnix'. The score is largely taken from the *General Advertiser*, which gives the fullest account but only to the end of the second day; details for day 3 are taken from other sources. In A to M (2), Booker, Bullen and Brazier were the men out at the end of day 2; the remainder of the batting order is not known.

113

ENGLAND v HAMPSHIRE AND KENT

Played at Lord's Old Ground, Marylebone, June 5, 6, 7, 1788.

Hampshire and Kent won by 25 runs.

HAMPSHIRE AND KENT

1	T.Walker	c Purchase	35	c Louch	2
2	H.Walker	c Ingram	5	c Beldham	13
3	W.Bullen	c Harris	13	not out	1
4	W.Brazier	not out	15	c Beldham	6
5	R.Clifford	c Amherst	1	c Louch	29
6	J.Aylward	b Purchase	8	c Ingram	28
7	J.Ring	c Amherst	7	c Purchase	20
8	W.Bowra	b Harris	3	c Louch	2
9	J.Small, sen	c Purchase	8	c Purchase	3
10	T.Taylor	c Louch	1	c Louch	2
11	N.Mann	c Purchase	7	b Harris	18
	Byes		3		6
			106		130

FoW (1): 1- , 2- , 3- , 4- , 5- , 6- , 7- , 8- , 9- , 10-106
FoW (2): 1- , 2- , 3- , 4- , 5- , 6- , 7- , 8- , 9- , 10-130

ENGLAND

1	G.East	c Aylward	0	c Aylward	0
2	G.Louch	not out	1	c Bowra	1
3	S.Amherst	run out	2	b Clifford	1
4	R.Hosmer	b Clifford	0	b Clifford	9
5	D.Harris	b Clifford	2	b Clifford	8
6	T.Ingram	b Brazier	40	not out	7
7	W.Beldham	b Clifford	5	b Mann	5
8	John Wells	b Brazier	6	st Taylor	11
9	J.Small, jun	b Clifford	12	c Taylor	7
10	F.Booker	b Clifford	11	c Bullen	0
11	R.Purchase	b Brazier	46	c Bullen	18
	Byes		15		4
			140		71

FoW (1): 1- , 2- , 3- , 4- , 5- , 6- , 7- , 8- , 9- , 10-140
FoW (2): 1- , 2- , 3- , 4- , 5- , 6- , 7- , 8- , 9- , 10-71

England Bowling

	O	M	R	W	O	M	R	W
Harris				1				1
Purchase				1				

Hampshire and Kent Bowling

	O	M	R	W	O	M	R	W
Clifford				5				3
Brazier				3				
Mann								1

Umpires: G.Drummond and Horsey.

Close of Play: 1st day: England (1) 82-5; 2nd day: England (2) 20-5 (Wells 5*, Harris 1*).

At the end of day 2, East, Louch, Amherst, Small and Booker were the men out in England (2). England had Harris as a given man. The match arose from a VI-a-side single-wicket match between Hampshire and Kent in August 1787 (see SB p75). The papers explain that 'from the 12 men that played in the single wicket match last year, Harris is withdrawn and Capt East undertook to assemble 10 men who joined with Harris would attack the powerful strength of bats': hence this match (although East's side lost). This accounts for the match title despite the presence of some Kent and Hampshire men on the England side. SB and some other sources call the game G.East's XI v Paulet's XI: 'Paulet' must be Rev C.Powlett, known as a leading Hambledon member (see SB p114 for another instance of the spelling 'Paulet' where 'Powlett' must be meant). The source gives the umpire as Halsey: this is assumed to be Horsey, who makes his playing debut in 'great' matches for Hampshire v Surrey, 2 July 1788.

SURREY v HAMPSHIRE

Played at Molesey Hurst, June 9, 10, 1788.

Surrey won by nine wickets.

HAMPSHIRE

1	G.H.Monson	b Butcher	0	c Wells	4
2	T.A.Smith	c Beldham	0	b Butcher	5
3	G.Drummond	b Butcher	0	c H.Walker	0
4	G.Talbot	not out	6	c Winchilsea	1
5	J.Small, sen	b Stevens	6	c H.Walker	23
6	J.Nyren	b Stevens	3	b Stevens	9
7	J.Small, jun	b Butcher	7	c Wells	1
8	N.Mann	b Butcher	7	b Stevens	11
9	R.Purchase	b Butcher	24	b Butcher	4
10	T.Taylor	c Beldham	3	b Butcher	4
11	D.Harris	b Stevens	0	not out	0
	Byes		3		1
			59		63

FoW (1): 1- , 2- , 3- , 4- , 5- , 6- , 7- , 8- , 9- , 10-59
FoW (2): 1- , 2- , 3- , 4- , 5- , 6- , 7- , 8- , 9- , 10-63

SURREY

1	Earl of Winchilsea	b Purchase	6	b Harris	0
2	Lord Strathavon	c Purchase	2		
3	H.W.Fitzroy	b Mann	0		
4	H.Attfield	c Purchase	22		
5	H.Walker	c Taylor	14	not out	16
6	T.Walker	c Drummond	5	not out	17
7	Butcher	c Smith	11		
8	W.Beldham	c Taylor	10		
9	John Wells	b Harris	14		
10	Davy	c Purchase	0		
11	E.Stevens	not out	0		
	Byes		6		
			90	(1 wicket)	33

FoW (1): 1- , 2- , 3- , 4- , 5- , 6- , 7- , 8- , 9- , 10-90
FoW (2): 1- (1)

Surrey Bowling

	O	M	R	W	O	M	R	W
Stevens				3				2
Butcher				5				3

Hampshire Bowling

	O	M	R	W	O	M	R	W
Harris				1				1
Mann				1				
Purchase				1				

Umpires:

Close of Play: 1st day: .

HAMPSHIRE v ENGLAND

Played at Stoke Down, Alresford, June 17, 18, 1788.

Hampshire won by an innings and 76 runs.

ENGLAND

1	J.Aylward	b Purchase	30	b Purchase	5
2	G.Louch	c Harris	2	c Mann	0
3	W.Bullen	run out	0	b Purchase	7
4	R.Clifford	c James Wells	0	not out	15
5	J.Ring	b Harris	6	b Purchase	6
6	J.Cole	c Mann	1	b Harris	1
7	W.Fennex	b Harris	0	run out	18
8	F.Booker	run out	5	b Harris	2
9	J.Boorman	c Taylor	17	c Taylor	19
10	E.Stevens	not out	1	b Harris	2
11	T.Ingram	b Purchase	1	run out	5
	Byes				1
			63		81

FoW (1): 1- , 2- , 3- , 4- , 5- , 6- , 7- , 8- , 9- , 10-63
FoW (2): 1- , 2- , 3- , 4- , 5- , 6- , 7- , 8- , 9- , 10-81

HAMPSHIRE

1	T.Walker	run out	6
2	H.Walker	b Clifford	23
3	J.Small, sen	run out	3
4	J.Small, jun	b Stevens	5
5	T.Taylor	c Ingram	22
6	W.Beldham	not out	52
7	John Wells	b Bullen	39
8	R.Purchase	b Clifford	3
9	D.Harris	b Fennex	21
10	N.Mann	c Clifford	0
11	James Wells	b Stevens	37
	Byes		9
			220

FoW (1): 1- , 2- , 3- , 4- , 5- , 6- , 7- , 8- , 9- , 10-220

Hampshire Bowling

	O	M	R	W		O	M	R	W
Harris				2					3
Purchase				2					3

England Bowling

	O	M	R	W
Stevens				2
Clifford				2
Bullen				1
Fennex				1

Umpires:

Close of Play: 1st day: .

HAMPSHIRE v SURREY

Played at Perham Downs, Ludgershall, July 2, 3, 4, 1788.

Hampshire won by four wickets.

SURREY

1	T.Walker	b Mann	17	b Harris		0
2	H.Walker	b Taylor	78	run out		10
3	John Wells	b Harris	5	c Mann		3
4	W.Beldham	b Harris	59	c Smith		8
5	H.Attfield	run out	10	b Mann		5
6	Earl of Winchilsea	b Taylor	2	b Taylor		5
7	G.Drummond	b Harris	0	b Mann		6
8	H.W.Fitzroy	b Harris	5	b Mann		0
9	Davy	not out	16	not out		4
10	Butcher	b Mann	6	b Harris		0
11	E.Stevens	b Mann	2	b Mann		0
	Byes		3			3
			203			44

FoW (1): 1- , 2- , 3- , 4- , 5- , 6- , 7- , 8- , 9- , 10-203
FoW (2): 1- , 2- , 3- , 4- , 5- , 6- , 7- , 8- , 9- , 10-44

HAMPSHIRE

1	J.Small, jun	c Beldham	8	c Stevens		21
2	Horsey	b Butcher	1			
3	J.Small, sen	c Wells	4	c Wells		7
4	R.Purchase	b Butcher	14	not out		43
5	T.Taylor	b Butcher	2	c Beldham		22
6	N.Mann	not out	41			
7	T.A.Smith	b Butcher	8	b Butcher		4
8	G.Talbot	b Beldham	28	not out		8
9	H.Stewart	c Beldham	2	c Davy		3
10	Hunt	b Beldham	0	b Stevens		29
11	D.Harris	b Butcher	1			
	Byes		1			1
			110	(6 wickets)		138

FoW (1): 1- , 2- , 3- , 4- , 5- , 6- , 7- , 8- , 9- , 10-110
FoW (2): 1- , 2- , 3- , 4- , 5- , 6-

Hampshire Bowling

	O	M	R	W	O	M	R	W
Harris				4				2
Taylor				2				1
Mann				3				4

Surrey Bowling

	O	M	R	W	O	M	R	W
Butcher				5				1
Beldham				2				
Stevens								1

Umpires:

Close of Play: 1st day: ; 2nd day: .

'Stewart', playing for Hampshire, is assumed to be Henry, nephew of Peter 'Buck' Stewart. Hunt of Odiham.

SURREY v KENT

Played at Molesey Hurst, July 15, 16, 17, 18, 1788.

Surrey won by an innings and 65 runs.

KENT

#	Batsman	Dismissal	Runs	Dismissal (2)	Runs
1	Sir P.Burrell	c Stevens	19	b Stevens	0
2	S.Amherst	c Harris	1	c H.Walker	0
3	R.Hosmer	c H.Walker	1	c H.Walker	1
4	W.Bullen	b Harris	4	run out	5
5	R.Clifford	b Stevens	17	b Stevens	11
6	J.Aylward	not out	17	c John Wells	0
7	R.Francis	b Stevens	1	b Harris	0
8	W.Brazier	b Stevens	0	b Harris	17
9	J.Boorman	b Stevens	0	b Stevens	12
10	F.Booker	b Stevens	20	b Harris	0
11	J.Pilcher	c H.Walker	0	not out	5
	Byes		1		
			81		**51**

FoW (1): 1- , 2- , 3- , 4- , 5- , 6- , 7- , 8- , 9- , 10-81
FoW (2): 1- , 2- , 3- , 4- , 5- , 6- , 7- , 8- , 9- , 10-51

SURREY

#	Batsman	Dismissal	Runs
1	Earl of Winchilsea	b Boorman	0
2	T.Walker	not out	93
3	H.Walker	b Bullen	9
4	W.Beldham	run out	3
5	John Wells	b Brazier	7
6	James Wells	c Pilcher	1
7	T.Sueter	c Clifford	17
8	T.Ingram	c Bullen	0
9	Butcher	c Bullen	14
10	D.Harris	b Boorman	44
11	E.Stevens	c Burrell	3
	Byes		6
			197

FoW (1): 1- , 2- , 3- , 4- , 5- , 6- , 7- , 8- , 9- , 10-197

Surrey Bowling

	O	M	R	W	O	M	R	W
Stevens				5				3
Harris				1				3

Kent Bowling

	O	M	R	W
Boorman				2
Bullen				1
Brazier				1

Umpires:

Close of Play: 1st day: Kent (1) 51-3; 2nd day: ; 3rd day: .

Surrey had Harris as a given man. On the first day rain delayed the start until 6.30pm.

ENGLAND v HAMPSHIRE

Played at Sevenoaks Vine Cricket Club Ground, July 24, 25, 1788.

Hampshire won by 53 runs.

HAMPSHIRE

1	T.Walker	b Stevens	5	c Clifford	9
2	H.Walker	c Louch	8	c Clifford	31
3	J.Small, sen	c Clifford	10	c Clifford	3
4	Earl of Winchilsea	not out	2	c Stevens	4
5	John Wells	c Aylward	0	b Stevens	29
6	James Wells	c Louch	12	b Stevens	0
7	T.Taylor	c Bowra	7	b Fennex	3
8	W.Beldham	c Clifford	7	b Stevens	6
9	R.Purchase	b Clifford	7	not out	8
10	D.Harris	b Clifford	2	b Clifford	0
11	N.Mann	c Bowra	15	b Clifford	5
	Byes				4
			75		102

FoW (1): 1- , 2- , 3- , 4- , 5- , 6- , 7- , 8- , 9- , 10-75
FoW (2): 1- , 2- , 3- , 4- , 5- , 6- , 7- , 8- , 9- , 10-102

ENGLAND

1	G.Louch	b Taylor	35	c John Wells	0
2	J.Aylward	c Beldham	4	b Mann	4
3	R.Clifford	b Purchase	6	run out	10
4	W.Bullen	c Taylor	1	not out	2
5	F.Booker	run out	0	c H.Walker	7
6	W.Brazier	b Harris	2	c Purchase	1
7	W.Fennex	b Taylor	13	c Taylor	2
8	W.Bowra	run out	5	b Mann	1
9	J.Boorman	c H.Walker	9	b Mann	6
10	E.Stevens	not out	3	c Beldham	0
11	J.Crawte	run out	12	b Mann	0
	Byes		1		
			91		33

FoW (1): 1- , 2- , 3- , 4- , 5- , 6- , 7- , 8- , 9- , 10-91
FoW (2): 1- , 2- , 3- , 4- , 5- , 6- , 7- , 8- , 9- , 10-33

England Bowling

	O	M	R	W	O	M	R	W
Stevens				1				3
Clifford				2				2
Fennex								1

Hampshire Bowling

	O	M	R	W	O	M	R	W
Harris				1				
Purchase				1				
Taylor				2				
Mann								4

Umpires:

Close of Play: 1st day: .

KENT v ENGLAND

Played at Star Inn, Coxheath, July 29, 30, 31, 1788.

England won by an innings and 74 runs.

KENT

1	S.Amherst	c Louch	8	b Walker		28
2	R.Hosmer	c Louch	10	b Harris		2
3	R.Clifford	c Louch	10	b Harris		2
4	J.Aylward	c Louch	11	c Fennex		0
5	J.Ring	c J.Small, sen	1	b Harris		16
6	J.Boorman	b Purchase	0	c Louch		0
7	W.Bullen	not out	1	not out		3
8	W.Brazier	b Purchase	7	b Harris		0
9	F.Booker	run out	8	c Hunt		17
10	Small	c Annett	1	c Annett		1
11	Nicholson	b Harris	0	c Louch		2
	Byes		4			
			61			71

FoW (1): 1- , 2- , 3- , 4- , 5- , 6- , 7- , 8- , 9- , 10-61
FoW (2): 1- , 2- , 3- , 4- , 5- , 6- , 7- , 8- , 9- , 10-71

ENGLAND

1	T.Walker	c Small	31
2	G.Louch	b Boorman	10
3	J.Small, sen	c Aylward	27
4	J.Small, jun	b Clifford	11
5	D.Harris	b Clifford	13
6	R.Purchase	c Boorman	44
7	T.Taylor	b Bullen	8
8	W.Fennex	c Small	14
9	N.Mann	not out	39
10	Hunt	c Aylward	7
11	Annett	b Bullen	2
	Byes		
			206

FoW (1): 1- , 2- , 3- , 4- , 5- , 6- , 7- , 8- , 9- , 10-206

England Bowling

	O	M	R	W	O	M	R	W
Harris				1				4
Purchase				2				
Walker								1

Kent Bowling

	O	M	R	W
Clifford				2
Bullen				2
Boorman				1

Umpires:

Close of Play: 1st day: ; 2nd day: .

John Small, sen's son Eli has been suggested as a candidate for 'Small' in the Kent team, but there is no evidence for this.

(Variant) KCM gives the dates as 22-24 July, presumably because the newspaper that carries the match report is dated 29 July. But the newspaper is dated by the first day of the period it covers, not the date of publication; moreover, 22-24 July would create a clash with the previous match. 29-31 July must be correct.

KENT v SURREY

Played at Bourne Paddock, Bishopsbourne, August 5, 6, 7, 1788.

Surrey won by 37 runs.

SURREY

#	Batsman	Dismissal	Score	Dismissal 2	Score 2
1	Earl of Winchilsea	c sub (W.Fennex)	8	b Boorman	0
2	W.Beldham	b Brazier	49	b Clifford	33
3	Butcher	b Boorman	1	not out	9
4	J.Crawte	not out	11	b Clifford	0
5	E.Stevens	c Aylward	9	b Clifford	0
6	T.Sueter	b Clifford	9	b Clifford	0
7	T.Walker	c Amherst	13	b Boorman	0
8	H.Walker	c Bowra	8	b Clifford	16
9	John Wells	b Clifford	18	c Bullen	3
10	James Wells	c Amherst	2	c Brazier	8
11	D.Harris	b Clifford	30	b Brazier	6
	Byes		15		2
			173		77

FoW (1): 1- , 2- , 3- , 4- , 5- , 6- , 7- , 8- , 9- , 10-173
FoW (2): 1- , 2- , 3- , 4- , 5- , 6- , 7- , 8- , 9- , 10-77

KENT

#	Batsman	Dismissal	Score	Dismissal 2	Score 2
1	S.Amherst	c Sueter	11	b Stevens	7
2	J.Aylward	c Crawte	31	c Butcher	2
3	W.Bullen	b Stevens	15	c Butcher	0
4	F.Booker	run out	16	c H.Walker	6
5	W.Brazier	c John Wells	12	not out	31
6	J.Boorman	not out	4	c Stevens	9
7	W.Bowra	run out	0	c Beldham	6
8	R.Clifford	c Beldham	9	c H.Walker	4
9	J.Pilcher	b Harris	15	c John Wells	17
10	J.Ring	c John Wells	9	c T.Walker	4
11	Greenstreet	b Stevens	0	run out	0
	Byes		5		
			127		86

FoW (1): 1- , 2- , 3- , 4- , 5- , 6- , 7- , 8- , 9- , 10-127
FoW (2): 1- , 2- , 3- , 4- , 5- , 6- , 7- , 8- , 9- , 10-86

Kent Bowling

	O	M	R	W	O	M	R	W
Clifford				3				5
Boorman				1				2
Brazier				1				1

Surrey Bowling

	O	M	R	W	O	M	R	W
Stevens				2				1
Harris				1				

Umpires:

Close of Play: 1st day: ; 2nd day: .

Surrey had Harris as a given man. Greenstreet of Wingham.

HAMPSHIRE v SURREY

Played at Windmill Down, Hambledon, August 13, 14, 15, 1788.

Hampshire won by four wickets.

SURREY

1	Earl of Winchilsea	hit wkt	10	c Louch		2
2	Butcher	b Purchase	2	not out		7
3	T.Walker	run out	0	c Neale		12
4	H.Walker	b Taylor	12	c Taylor		4
5	W.Beldham	c Louch	14	b Harris		17
6	John Wells	hit wkt	11	b Harris		6
7	James Wells	c Taylor	7	b Mann		5
8	T.Sueter	b Mann	11	run out		24
9	J.Crawte	b Harris	3	b Taylor		0
10	H.Attfield	not out	2	b Mann		11
11	E.Stevens	b Mann	0	b Mann		0
	Byes		8			7
			80			95

FoW (1): 1- , 2- , 3- , 4- , 5- , 6- , 7- , 8- , 9- , 10-80
FoW (2): 1- , 2- , 3- , 4- , 5- , 6- , 7- , 8- , 9- , 10-95

HAMPSHIRE

1	G.Louch	b Stevens	3	b Beldham		8
2	G.Talbot	b Butcher	7	b Butcher		0
3	J.Small, sen	run out	37	b Stevens		0
4	D.Harris	c John Wells	12			
5	N.Mann	b Stevens	18			
6	R.Purchase	b Butcher	2			
7	J.Neale	c John Wells	0	b Butcher		4
8	J.Small, jun	c Winchilsea	17	b Stevens		22
9	T.Taylor	b Butcher	1	c H.Walker		12
10	Annett	b Stevens	6	not out		2
11	A.Freemantle	not out	5	not out		9
	Byes		6			5
			114	(6 wickets)		62

FoW (1): 1- , 2- , 3- , 4- , 5- , 6- , 7- , 8- , 9- , 10-114
FoW (2): 1- , 2- , 3- , 4- , 5- , 6-

Hampshire Bowling

	O	M	R	W	O	M	R	W
Harris				1				2
Purchase				1				
Taylor				1				1
Mann				2				3

Surrey Bowling

	O	M	R	W	O	M	R	W
Stevens				3				2
Butcher				3				2
Beldham								1

Umpires:

Close of Play: 1st day: ; 2nd day: .

A TO M v N TO Z

Played at Bourne Paddock, Bishopsbourne, August 26, 27, 28, 29, 1788.

A to M won by 75 runs.

A TO M

1	R.Clifford	c Purchase	0	c Purchase	15
2	W.Bullen	run out	7	not out	0
3	W.Brazier	c Fennex	7	c Stevens	11
4	N.Mann	c J.Small, jun	0	c John Wells	28
5	W.Beldham	c Aylward	45	c J.Small, sen	51
6	T.Taylor	b Stevens	0	c H.Walker	0
7	S.Amherst	b Fennex	20	c Purchase	22
8	G.Louch	b Stevens	9	c H.Walker	7
9	F.Booker	b Stevens	0	b Purchase	0
10	D.Harris	b Fennex	3	b Stevens	0
11	J.Crawte	not out	0	c H.Walker	6
	Byes		3		1
			94		141

FoW (1): 1- , 2- , 3- , 4- , 5- , 6- , 7- , 8- , 9- , 10-94
FoW (2): 1- , 2- , 3- , 4- , 5- , 6- , 7- , 8- , 9- , 10-141

N TO Z

1	Windsor	c Beldham	1	c Beldham	0
2	J.Aylward	b Taylor	48	c Bullen	2
3	J.Small, jun	b Harris	0	c Harris	0
4	T.Walker	b Harris	7	c Bullen	17
5	H.Walker	b Harris	0	c Beldham	0
6	John Wells	c Mann	23	b Harris	4
7	James Wells	b Taylor	0	c Clifford	0
8	R.Purchase	c Taylor	4	b Brazier	17
9	W.Fennex	b Bullen	0	not out	3
10	J.Small, sen	b Clifford	12	c Taylor	15
11	E.Stevens	not out	0	c Clifford	1
	Byes		5		1
			100		60

FoW (1): 1- , 2- , 3- , 4- , 5- , 6- , 7- , 8- , 9- , 10-100
FoW (2): 1- , 2- , 3- , 4- , 5- , 6- , 7- , 8- , 9- , 10-60

N to Z Bowling

	O	M	R	W	O	M	R	W
Stevens				3				1
Fennex				2				
Purchase								1

A to M Bowling

	O	M	R	W	O	M	R	W
Harris				3				1
Clifford				1				
Bullen				1				
Taylor				2				
Brazier								1

Umpires:

Close of Play: 1st day: ; 2nd day: ; 3rd day: .

A to M had Taylor as a given man; N to Z had Aylward as a given man. Fennex played for N to Z because his name was understood to be a corruption of 'Phœnix'.

MIDDLESEX v GENTLEMEN OF ENGLAND

Played at Lord's Old Ground, Marylebone, May 18, 19, 1789.

Middlesex won by an innings and 64 runs.

GENTLEMEN OF ENGLAND
1	E.Hussey	50	0
2	W.Bartholomew	1	30
3	C.Lennox	5	32
4	G.Talbot	1	7
5	R.Hosmer	39	3
6	S.Amherst	2	5
7	W.Turner	0	0
8	Vincent	2	0
9	J.Leggate	13	0
10	G.T.Boult	2	4
11	G.Louch	7	3
	Byes	3	1
		125	86

FoW (1): 1- , 2- , 3- , 4- , 5- , 6- , 7- , 8- , 9- , 10-125
FoW (2): 1- , 2- , 3- , 4- , 5- , 6- , 7- , 8- , 9- , 10-86

MIDDLESEX
1	W.White	116
2	R.Turner	6
3	W.Bedster	3
4	T.Shackle	0
5	Stanhope	5
6	N.Graham	26
7	Butler	15
8	Dale	18
9	Matthews	0
10	Cantrell	17
11	T.Lord	61
	Byes	8
		275

FoW (1): 1- , 2- , 3- , 4- , 5- , 6- , 7- , 8- , 9- , 10-275

Umpires: Earl of Winchilsea and ?.

Close of Play: 1st day: Middlesex (1) 115-4.

The dismissal details are not available. Gentlemen of England (2) adds one run short.

A TO M v N TO Z

Played at Lord's Old Ground, Marylebone, June 3, 4, 15, 16, 1789.

N to Z won by 140 runs.

N TO Z

#	Batsman	Dismissal	Runs	2nd innings	Runs
1	H.Walker	b Harris	0	(5) c Beldham	5
2	R.Purchase	b Beldham	40	(3) b Brazier	1
3	Earl of Winchilsea	b Beldham	0	(10) not out	21
4	J.Aylward	b Beldham	0	(2) b Clifford	7
5	T.Walker	b Beldham	29	(4) b Beldham	31
6	J.Ring	b Beldham	0	(1) b Mann	24
7	John Wells	c Clifford	35	(11) c Brazier	48
8	J.Small, sen	c Clifford	44	(6) run out	19
9	J.Small, jun	not out	12	(7) b Mann	13
10	W.Fennex	b Beldham	3	(8) b Mann	7
11	E.Stevens	b Beldham	2	(9) b Beldham	0
	Byes		3		1
			168		177

FoW (1): 1- , 2- , 3- , 4- , 5- , 6- , 7- , 8- , 9- , 10-168
FoW (2): 1- , 2- , 3- , 4- , 5- , 6- , 7- , 8- , 9- , 10-177

A TO M

#	Batsman	Dismissal	Runs	2nd innings	Runs
1	R.Clifford	b Purchase	0	(3) b Fennex	19
2	W.Brazier	c Wells	23	b Purchase	3
3	W.Beldham	c Wells	7	(4) c Wells	44
4	W.Bullen	b Wells	5	(9) b Stevens	11
5	G.Louch	c Wells	5	(7) b Purchase	7
6	C.Lennox	b Purchase	7		
	G.T.Boult			(10) not out	15
7	T.Taylor	b Stevens	2	(8) c Purchase	3
8	N.Mann	c Stevens	0	(5) b Purchase	48
9	T.Ingram	b Purchase	1	(6) c J.Small, sen	0
10	S.Amherst	not out	1	(1) b Stevens	1
11	D.Harris	run out	0	b Purchase	1
	Byes				3
			51		154

FoW (1): 1- , 2- , 3- , 4- , 5- , 6- , 7- , 8- , 9- , 10-51
FoW (2): 1- , 2- , 3- , 4- , 5- , 6- , 7- , 8- , 9- , 10-154

A to M Bowling

	O	M	R	W	O	M	R	W
Harris				1				
Beldham				7				2
Mann								3
Clifford								1
Brazier								1

N to Z Bowling

	O	M	R	W	O	M	R	W
Stevens				1				2
Purchase				3				4
Wells				1				
Fennex								1

Umpires: F.Booker and J.Pilcher.

Close of Play: 1st day: N to Z (1) 150-6 (Wells 34*, J.Small, sen 44*); 2nd day: N to Z (1) 163-8 (J.Small, jun 9*, Fennex 3*); 3rd day: N to Z (2) 177 all out.

G.T.Boult was a full substitute for A to M, replacing C.Lennox (presumably unable to play when the match was resumed on day 3). A to M had Taylor as a given man; N to Z had Aylward as a given man. Fennex played for N to Z because his name was understood to be a corruption of 'Phœnix'. Day 2 was ruined by rain so the match had to be completed some days later. The changes to second-innings batting orders may be in order of dismissal; it is unlikely that Wells batted last in N-Z (2), but he may well have been last out.

SURREY v KENT

Played at Molesey Hurst, June 10, 11, 12, 1789.

Kent won by three wickets.

SURREY

1	Earl of Winchilsea	b Clifford	4	b Brazier	1
2	C.Lennox	b Bullen	13	b Brazier	0
3	H.Walker	c Boorman	7	c Palmer	26
4	T.Walker	b Clifford	50	c Crawte	21
5	J.Walker	b Clifford	7	b Clifford	0
6	W.Beldham	run out	0	b Brazier	19
7	John Wells	b Boxall	15	c Clifford	0
8	E.Stevens	b Boorman	3	not out	3
9	Butcher	not out	13	b Brazier	3
10	T.Sueter	c Boxall	3	b Brazier	13
11	N.Mann	c Bullen	8	b Clifford	0
	Byes				1
			123		87

FoW (1): 1- , 2- , 3- , 4- , 5- , 6- , 7- , 8- , 9- , 10-123
FoW (2): 1- , 2- , 3- , 4- , 5- , 6- , 7- , 8- , 9- , 10-87

KENT

1	S.Amherst	run out	3	b Stevens	1
2	T.Boxall	b Butcher	4		
3	W.Bullen	c Winchilsea	15	not out	1
4	R.Clifford	b T.Walker	11		
5	W.Brazier	b Stevens	6	c Wells	45
6	J.Ring	c Mann	0	b Butcher	15
7	J.Aylward	c J.Walker	10	c Stevens	0
8	J.Boorman	st Wells	0	not out	1
9	J.Crawte	c H.Walker	1	run out	13
10	J.Pilcher	c Wells	24	c J.Walker	10
11	Palmer	not out	43	run out	8
	Byes				
			117	(7 wickets)	94

FoW (1): 1- , 2- , 3- , 4- , 5- , 6- , 7- , 8- , 9- , 10-117
FoW (2): 1- , 2- , 3- , 4- , 5- , 6- , 7-

Kent Bowling

	O	M	R	W	O	M	R	W
Clifford				3				2
Bullen				1				
Boxall				1				
Boorman				1				
Brazier								5

Surrey Bowling

	O	M	R	W	O	M	R	W
Stevens				1				1
Butcher				1				1
T.Walker				1				

Umpires:

Close of Play: 1st day: ; 2nd day: .

Surrey had Lennox and Mann as given men.

ENGLAND v HAMPSHIRE

Played at Lord's Old Ground, Marylebone, June 25, 26, 27, July 2, 1789.

Hampshire won by six wickets.

ENGLAND

1	J.Aylward	b Harris	37	(5) c John Wells	9
2	J.Ring	b Purchase	0	(6) b Purchase	11
3	W.White	b Taylor	17	(10) c John Wells	7
4	W.Bullen	b Harris	12	(13) c Beldham	2
5	R.Clifford	c Beldham	4	(1) b Purchase	0
6	W.Brazier	run out	9	(3) c Beldham	1
7	J.Pilcher	c Beldham	4	(2) b Purchase	7
8	Palmer	b Taylor	2	(4) run out	0
9	W.Fennex	c H.Walker	21	(8) run out	0
10	T.Ingram	b Harris	9	(9) c J.Small, jun	33
11	G.Louch	b Purchase	0	(7) b Harris	2
12	J.Boorman	c Beldham	0	not out	0
13	E.Stevens	not out	0	(11) b Harris	0
	Byes		3		1
			118		73

FoW (1): 1- , 2- , 3- , 4- , 5- , 6- , 7- , 8- , 9- , 10- , 11- , 12-118
FoW (2): 1- , 2- , 3- , 4- , 5- , 6- , 7- , 8- , 9- , 10- , 11- , 12-73

HAMPSHIRE

1	T.Walker	b Clifford	0	c Fennex	0
2	H.Walker	b Boorman	0		
3	W.Beldham	c Brazier	94	not out	16
4	R.Purchase	b Boorman	39		
5	T.Taylor	b Boorman	6	b Boorman	4
6	J.Small, sen	b Boorman	2	not out	6
7	John Wells	b Clifford	4		
8	N.Mann	b Clifford	1	b Fennex	14
9	James Wells	b Clifford	1	b Fennex	0
10	J.Small, jun	c Louch	1		
11	D.Harris	not out	0		
	Byes		2		2
			150	(4 wickets)	42

FoW (1): 1- , 2- , 3- , 4- , 5- , 6- , 7- , 8- , 9- , 10-150
FoW (2): 1- , 2- , 3- , 4-

Hampshire Bowling	O	M	R	W	O	M	R	W
Harris				3				2
Purchase				2				3
Beldham				0				
Taylor				2				

England Bowling	O	M	R	W	O	M	R	W
Clifford				4				
Boorman				4				1
Fennex								2

Umpires:

Close of Play: 1st day: England (1) 19-1 (Aylward 14*, White 5*); 2nd day: Hampshire (1) 54-2 (Beldham 29*, Purchase 23*); 3rd day: England (2) 3-1 (Pilcher 3*).

The teams returned on 2 July to complete the match as many of the players were already committed to appear at Coxheath from 29 June. At the end of day 1, Ring was the man out in England (1); at the end of day 3, Clifford was the man out in England (2). The weather on day 1 was 'showery' according to the *Gentlemen's Magazine*, and the *Times* reports that only 140 balls (i.e. 35 4-ball overs) were bowled, the bowlers being Harris, Purchase, and Beldham.

(Variant) KG gives Hants (2) byes 0, total 40-4 (i.e. 2 short of victory) and says at 7pm England conceded but KG is not local and the *Times* report is fuller so it has been accepted.

EAST KENT v WEST KENT

Played at Star Inn, Coxheath, June 29, 30, 1789.

East Kent won by 8 runs.

EAST KENT

#	Batsman	Dismissal	Runs	Dismissal	Runs
1	R.Purchase	c Beldham	14	c H.Walker	0
2	J.Pilcher	run out	22	run out	0
3	J.Aylward	c Beldham	25	not out	20
4	J.Small, sen	c Wells	28	b Beldham	4
5	J.Ring	c T.Walker	0	b Beldham	1
6	T.Taylor	c Bullen	8	b Beldham	2
7	J.Boorman	c T.Walker	3	b Beldham	2
8	Wood	b Brazier	11	b Clifford	0
9	D.Harris	b Brazier	11	c Wells	1
10	Bates	c Wells	0	run out	1
11	J.Church	not out	2	b Clifford	3
	Byes				2
			124		36

FoW (1): 1- , 2- , 3- , 4- , 5- , 6- , 7- , 8- , 9- , 10-124
FoW (2): 1- , 2- , 3- , 4- , 5- , 6- , 7- , 8- , 9- , 10-36

WEST KENT

#	Batsman	Dismissal	Runs	Dismissal	Runs
1	T.Walker	b Harris	3	c Purchase	0
2	H.Walker	b Harris	0	c Bates	1
3	W.Brazier	c Purchase	9	c Wood	0
4	W.Beldham	b Harris	10	b Harris	6
5	John Wells	c Taylor	20	run out	5
6	Palmer	b Purchase	6	c Aylward	0
7	W.Bullen	b Harris	1	c Ring	5
8	S.Amherst	b Harris	17	b Purchase	9
9	J.Crawte	c Ring	25	c Bates	6
10	R.Hosmer	not out	8	run out	7
11	R.Clifford	b Harris	4	not out	3
	Byes		7		
			110		42

FoW (1): 1- , 2- , 3- , 4- , 5- , 6- , 7- , 8- , 9- , 10-110
FoW (2): 1- , 2- , 3- , 4- , 5- , 6- , 7- , 8- , 9- , 10-42

West Kent Bowling

	O	M	R	W	O	M	R	W
Brazier				2				
Clifford								2
Beldham								4

East Kent Bowling

	O	M	R	W	O	M	R	W
Harris				6				1
Purchase				1				1

Umpires:

Close of Play: 1st day: West Kent (1) 48-4 (Wells 17*, Crawte 4*).

East Kent had Boorman and four of Hampshire as given men; West Kent had four of Surrey as given men.

M.C.C. v ESSEX

Played at Lord's Old Ground, Marylebone, July 8, 9, 1789.

Essex won by 102 runs.

ESSEX

1	Barker	b Butcher	0	c Dehany		8
2	Higgs	c Louch	3	b Lennox		15
3	R.B.Wyatt	c Louch	3	c Louch		33
4	J.Boorman	b Fitzroy	28	b Dehany		23
5	N.Graham	b Fitzroy	18	b Hunt		3
6	Carr	c Louch	1	c Shackle		39
7	J.Goulstone	b Fitzroy	27	b Butcher		2
8	Murray	b Hunt	2	c Butcher		7
9	Clements	b Boult	17	b Hunt		13
10	J.Stevens	run out	11	b Lennox		7
11	J.Martin	not out	8	not out		2
	Byes		5			7
			123			159

FoW (1): 1- , 2- , 3- , 4- , 5- , 6- , 7- , 8- , 9- , 10-123
FoW (2): 1- , 2- , 3- , 4- , 5- , 6- , 7- , 8- , 9- , 10-159

M.C.C.

1	T.Shackle	b Martin	11	not out		24
2	C.Lennox	b Martin	12	b Boorman		10
3	G.Louch	c Boorman	0	b Boorman		0
4	G.T.Boult	b Boorman	25	b Boorman		8
5	Butcher	b Boorman	4	b Martin		0
6	Earl of Winchilsea	b Boorman	35	b Boorman		12
7	H.W.Fitzroy	b Boorman	1	b Boorman		6
8	Hunt	b Barker	11	b Martin		0
9	G.Dehany	b Boorman	7	b Boorman		0
10	C.Anguish	not out	0	b Boorman		3
11	Stanhope	run out	0	c Boorman		11
	Byes					
			106			74

FoW (1): 1- , 2- , 3- , 4- , 5- , 6- , 7- , 8- , 9- , 10-106
FoW (2): 1- , 2- , 3- , 4- , 5- , 6- , 7- , 8- , 9- , 10-74

M.C.C. Bowling

	O	M	R	W	O	M	R	W
Butcher				1				1
Fitzroy				3				
Hunt				1				2
Boult				1				
Lennox								2
Dehany								1

Essex Bowling

	O	M	R	W	O	M	R	W
Boorman				5				7
Martin				2				2
Barker				1				

Umpires:

Close of Play: 1st day: .

HAMPSHIRE v KENT

Played at Windmill Down, Hambledon, July 13, 14, 1789.

Kent won by 56 runs.

KENT

1	J.Pilcher	c Taylor	0	b Mann		8
2	J.Aylward	run out	15	b Harris		15
3	R.Clifford	c J.Small, jun	27	c Purchase		4
4	W.Brazier	b Taylor	13	b Harris		2
5	S.Amherst	c Louch	0	not out		0
6	J.Crawte	b Taylor	1	b Mann		0
7	J.Ring	b Harris	4	b Mann		0
8	G.Talbot	c Louch	1	b Purchase		4
9	Palmer	b Harris	2	b Mann		0
10	W.Bullen	b Purchase	20	b Harris		0
11	J.Boorman	not out	14	b Harris		1
	Byes		1			
			98			34

FoW (1): 1- , 2- , 3- , 4- , 5- , 6- , 7- , 8- , 9- , 10-98
FoW (2): 1- , 2- , 3- , 4- , 5- , 6- , 7- , 8- , 9- , 10-34

HAMPSHIRE

1	R.Purchase	b Clifford	6	c Aylward		1
2	A.Freemantle	run out	11	b Clifford		1
3	J.Small, sen	b Bullen	0	b Clifford		6
4	N.Mann	b Bullen	11	b Clifford		1
5	Earl of Winchilsea	b Bullen	0	b Bullen		0
6	T.A.Smith	b Bullen	0	c Clifford		3
7	J.Small, jun	b Clifford	3	c Amherst		1
8	G.Louch	b Clifford	0	c Clifford		4
9	T.Taylor	b Bullen	3	not out		5
10	G.T.Boult	b Clifford	15	c Amherst		3
11	D.Harris	not out	0	b Bullen		0
	Byes					2
			49			27

FoW (1): 1- , 2- , 3- , 4- , 5- , 6- , 7- , 8- , 9- , 10-49
FoW (2): 1- , 2- , 3- , 4- , 5- , 6- , 7- , 8- , 9- , 10-27

Hampshire Bowling

	O	M	R	W	O	M	R	W
Harris				2				4
Purchase				1				1
Taylor				2				
Mann								4

Kent Bowling

	O	M	R	W	O	M	R	W
Clifford				4				3
Bullen				5				2

Umpires:

Close of Play: 1st day: .

ENGLAND v KENT

Played at W.Fennex's New Ground, Uxbridge, July 23, 24, 25, 1789.

England won by an innings and 10 runs.

KENT

1	J.Pilcher	c Louch	5	c Boult		1
2	J.Aylward	b Harris	7	run out		23
3	R.Clifford	b Harris	13	b Mann		6
4	W.Brazier	b Mann	3	b Harris		2
5	J.Ring	b Mann	6	b Purchase		7
6	S.Amherst	b Purchase	10	b Mann		7
7	G.Talbot	run out	0	b Harris		1
8	W.Bullen	c Louch	1	not out		4
9	J.Boorman	c Beldham	18	run out		2
10	Palmer	b Purchase	4	b Mann		0
11	J.Crawte	not out	19	b Mann		0
	Byes		1			
			87			53

FoW (1): 1- , 2- , 3- , 4- , 5- , 6- , 7- , 8- , 9- , 10-87
FoW (2): 1- , 2- , 3- , 4- , 5- , 6- , 7- , 8- , 9- , 10-53

ENGLAND

1	Earl of Winchilsea	c Boorman	0
2	Vincent	b Clifford	12
3	T.Walker	run out	11
4	John Wells	hit wkt	21
5	G.Louch	b Boorman	3
6	G.T.Boult	b Clifford	13
7	W.Beldham	b Bullen	48
8	R.Purchase	run out	6
9	N.Mann	b Bullen	34
10	T.A.Smith	not out	0
11	D.Harris	run out	0
	Byes		2
			150

FoW (1): 1- , 2- , 3- , 4- , 5- , 6- , 7- , 8- , 9- , 10-150

England Bowling

	O	M	R	W		O	M	R	W
Harris				2					2
Mann				2					4
Purchase				2					1

Kent Bowling

	O	M	R	W
Clifford				2
Boorman				1
Bullen				2

Umpires:

Close of Play: 1st day: ; 2nd day: .

Buckley gives the venue as Fennex's New Ground, which is assumed to be the ground also known as Uxbridge Moor. The question is obscure. Uxbridge Moor is to the south of the town of Uxbridge. The Ordnance Survey 1st series shows only one cricket ground, on Uxbridge Common to the north of the town, but this is dated 1805, i.e. 16 years later. There is also a Cricket Field Road in the town centre, but this apparently refers to a ground used in the 1830s and later.

SURREY v HAMPSHIRE

Played at Molesey Hurst, July 30, 31, August 1, 1789.

Surrey won by 221 runs.

SURREY
1	Earl of Winchilsea	b Taylor	32	c J.Small, jun		1
2	G.Talbot	b Smith	24	b Smith		6
3	Vincent	b Taylor	7	c Smith		29
4	Butcher	b Taylor	28			
5	E.Stevens	b Taylor	0			
6	H.Walker	run out	47	b Flint		47
7	T.Sueter	b Taylor	23	not out		33
8	James Wells	b Neale	80			
9	Bonick	not out	2			
10	T.Ingram	b Smith	20	not out		54
11	J.Walker	c Nyren	13	run out		4
	Byes		9			2
			285	(5 wickets, declared)		176

FoW (1): 1- , 2- , 3- , 4- , 5- , 6- , 7- , 8- , 9- , 10-285
FoW (2): 1- , 2- , 3- , 4- , 5-

HAMPSHIRE
1	T.A.Smith	c Ingram	20	c Ingram		0
2	J.Neale	c H.Walker	12	run out		22
3	E.Hale	c H.Walker	2	c Ingram		9
4	J.Nyren	b Stevens	20	c Ingram		0
5	J.Small, sen	b Bonick	2	b Ingram		48
6	J.Small, jun	c Ingram	30	b Stevens		3
7	Carpenter	c J.Walker	2	c J.Walker		1
8	T.Taylor	b Stevens	0	b Ingram		23
9	Horsey	not out	0	b Ingram		0
10	A.Freemantle	run out	28	c Vincent		2
11	White Flint	b Stevens	4	not out		4
	Byes		6			2
			126			114

FoW (1): 1- , 2- , 3- , 4- , 5- , 6- , 7- , 8- , 9- , 10-126
FoW (2): 1- , 2- , 3- , 4- , 5- , 6- , 7- , 8- , 9- , 10-114

Hampshire Bowling
	O	M	R	W	O	M	R	W
Taylor				5				
Smith				2				1
Neale				1				
Flint								1

Surrey Bowling
	O	M	R	W	O	M	R	W
Stevens				3				1
Bonick				1				
Ingram								3

Umpires:

Close of Play: 1st day: ; 2nd day: .

Flint was a full substitute for Hampshire (in place of whom is not known). Surrey appear to have given up their second innings: this has been treated as a declaration, although the laws of the day did not provide for such an act. All versions of the score have Nyland playing for Hampshire. No player of this name is known, but throughout the career of R.Nyren it is found in reports as a fairly common variant of his surname. Given that R.Nyren was now 55, it has been assumed to be J.Nyren, who appeared in the equivalent match in 1788. White of Andover – assumed not to be the same as W.White. Carpenter of Alresford. See the Supplementary Note on page 277 for more information about this match.

(Variant) One newspaper has T.Walker playing in this match, but two others give J.Walker (who had played for Surrey earlier in 1789) and this is accepted.

EAST KENT v WEST KENT

Played at Star Inn, Coxheath, August 4, 5, 1789.

East Kent won by seven wickets.

WEST KENT

1	J.Crawte	run out	0	run out		0
2	T.Walker	c Harris	5	b Harris		15
3	H.Walker	b Harris	3	c Crosoer		9
4	W.Brazier	b Harris	0	c Crosoer		1
5	W.Beldham	b Harris	0	c Crosoer		9
6	R.Hosmer	c Crosoer	0	b Purchase		0
7	R.Clifford	c Crosoer	4	not out		8
8	S.Amherst	c Crosoer	0	b Harris		2
9	John Wells	b Purchase	7	c Purchase		3
10	W.Bullen	not out	2	c Ring		7
11	Palmer	b Purchase	3	b Purchase		7
	Byes					1
			24			62

FoW (1): 1- , 2- , 3- , 4- , 5- , 6- , 7- , 8- , 9- , 10-24
FoW (2): 1- , 2- , 3- , 4- , 5- , 6- , 7- , 8- , 9- , 10-62

EAST KENT

1	J.Pilcher	b Beldham	7	c Bullen		2
2	R.Purchase	c H.Walker	13	not out		11
3	J.Small, sen	c Wells	13			
4	J.Aylward	b Beldham	0	b Clifford		4
5	J.Small, jun	run out	1			
6	H.Crosoer	c Bullen	0	run out		15
7	J.Boorman	c Bullen	3			
8	J.Ring	run out	12			
9	D.Harris	c Beldham	2			
10	J.Church	not out	2			
11	Kennett	b Clifford	3			
	Byes					-
			56	(3 wickets)		32

FoW (1): 1- , 2- , 3- , 4- , 5- , 6- , 7- , 8- , 9- , 10-56
FoW (2): 1- , 2- , 3-

East Kent Bowling

	O	M	R	W	O	M	R	W
Harris				3				2
Purchase				2				2

West Kent Bowling

	O	M	R	W	O	M	R	W
Clifford				1				1
Beldham				2				

Umpires:

Close of Play: 1st day: .

East Kent had Boorman and four of Hampshire as given men; West Kent had four of Surrey as given men. There must be an unrecorded score of 0* in East Kent (2). East Kent batted on after victory: Purchase b Clifford 11, Small, sen c Bullen 3, Small, jun stumped 17, Boorman c Wells 8, Ring b Clifford 27, Harris b Beldham 0, Church not out 0, Kennett stumped 0, total 87. Remarkably, the game continued with West Kent (3): Crawte c Purchase 23, T.Walker c Aylward 0, H.Walker c Crosoer 2, Wells c Harris 24, Brazier c Purchase 7, Beldham c Harris 0, Hosmer b Purchase 1, Clifford c Crosoer 3, Amherst not out 0, Bullen b Harris 23, Palmer b Purchase 0, byes 1, total 84. This would have left East Kent with 28 to win but time must have run out at this point.

(Variant) The fact that East Kent batted on has caused several sources to reverse the teams, with East Kent batting first, making 87 in (2), and winning by 57 runs. Britcher gives the dates as Tuesday and Wednesday, 3, 4 Aug but these dates were Monday and Tuesday so it is assumed he meant 4, 5 August (as in Epps).

HORNCHURCH v M.C.C.

Played at Langton Park, Hornchurch, August 6, 7, 1789.

Hornchurch won by six wickets.

M.C.C.
1	Hunt	b Boorman	2	c Boorman		11
2	Butcher	c Wyatt	1	not out		17
3	T.Shackle	run out	13	b Martin		1
4	G.T.Boult	b Boorman	14	c Wyatt		38
5	Earl of Winchilsea	b Martin	3	b Martin		1
6	Stanhope	b Martin	2	c Clements		5
7	E.Bligh	b Martin	0	c Wyatt		1
8	G.Louch	b Martin	11	b Martin		46
9	C.Anguish	run out	0	st Clark		5
10	G.Dehany	c Clements	4	c Barker		9
11	Earl of Darnley	not out	2	b Boorman		21
	Byes					3
			52			158

FoW (1): 1- , 2- , 3- , 4- , 5- , 6- , 7- , 8- , 9- , 10-52
FoW (2): 1- , 2- , 3- , 4- , 5- , 6- , 7- , 8- , 9- , 10-158

HORNCHURCH
1	N.Graham	b Butcher	34			
2	Barker	c Hunt	24	c sub (T.Lloyd)		17
3	Clements	b Winchilsea	3			
4	J.Boorman	b Butcher	17			
5	J.Goulstone	c Butcher	0			
6	Murray	b Shackle	33	not out		0
7	T.Clark	c sub (T.Lloyd)	26	b Butcher		8
8	Higgs	b Stanhope	5	not out		3
9	R.B.Wyatt	not out	0	st Butcher		6
10	R.Denn	b Butcher	2	c Louch		8
11	J.Martin	b Butcher	0			
	Byes		23			2
			167	(4 wickets)		44

FoW (1): 1- , 2- , 3- , 4- , 5- , 6- , 7- , 8- , 9- , 10-167
FoW (2): 1- , 2- , 3- , 4-

Hornchurch Bowling

	O	M	R	W	O	M	R	W
Boorman				2				1
Martin				4				3

M.C.C. Bowling

	O	M	R	W	O	M	R	W
Butcher				4				1
Winchilsea				1				
Shackle				1				
Stanhope				1				

Umpires:

Close of Play: 1st day: .

KENT v SURREY

Played at Bourne Paddock, Bishopsbourne, August 11, 12, 13, 14, 1789.

Surrey won by nine wickets.

KENT
1	Sir P. Burrell	c T.Walker	20	run out		27
2	W.Bullen	b Beldham	4	b Stevens		0
3	W.Brazier	b Ingram	37	b Mann		1
4	J.Aylward	b Stevens	6	c Ingram		10
5	J.Ring	c Beldham	3	c Beldham		14
6	J.Pilcher	c Beldham	7	c John Wells		6
7	J.Boorman	b Stevens	4	not out		1
8	J.Crawte	b Stevens	0	c Mann		39
9	H.Crosoer	not out	38	b Mann		5
10	R.Clifford	b Stevens	6	c Beldham		8
11	Dean	c Ingram	16	b Mann		9
	Byes					
			141			120

FoW (1): 1- , 2- , 3- , 4- , 5- , 6- , 7- , 8- , 9- , 10-141
FoW (2): 1- , 2- , 3- , 4- , 5- , 6- , 7- , 8- , 9- , 10-120

SURREY
1	Earl of Winchilsea	b Clifford	5	not out		2
2	T.Walker	c Crawte	27			
3	H.Walker	run out	67			
4	W.Beldham	c Clifford	20	c Clifford		0
5	John Wells	c Crosoer	29	not out		3
6	James Wells	not out	7			
7	T.Sueter	c Boorman	59			
8	E.Stevens	b Clifford	0			
9	Butcher	st Clifford	5			
10	N.Mann	b Boorman	20			
11	T.Ingram	c Boorman	13			
	Byes		4			1
			256	(1 wicket)		6

FoW (1): 1- , 2- , 3- , 4- , 5- , 6- , 7- , 8- , 9- , 10-256
FoW (2): 1-

Surrey Bowling
	O	M	R	W	O	M	R	W
Stevens				4				1
Ingram				1				
Beldham				1				
Mann								3

Kent Bowling
	O	M	R	W	O	M	R	W
Clifford				2				
Boorman				1				

Umpires:

Close of Play: 1st day: ; 2nd day: ; 3rd day: Kent (2) 110-8.

Surrey had Mann as a given man.

KENT v HAMPSHIRE

Played at Bourne Paddock, Bishopsbourne, August 18, 19, 20, 21, 1789.

Hampshire won by 29 runs.

HAMPSHIRE

1	Earl of Winchilsea	b Clifford	3	run out		2
2	G.Louch	not out	4	b Bullen		20
3	D.Harris	c Crosoer	1	not out		7
4	N.Mann	run out	26	c Crosoer		5
5	R.Purchase	b Clifford	59	c Bullen		3
6	J.Small, sen	b Bullen	7	b Boorman		23
7	J.Small, jun	c Boorman	8	c Clifford		29
8	A.Freemantle	b Clifford	2	c Dean		0
9	T.Taylor	b Bullen	10	run out		6
10	T.Scott	run out	9	run out		8
11	H.Stewart	c Clifford	4	b Clifford		0
	Byes		2			3
			135			106

FoW (1): 1- , 2- , 3- , 4- , 5- , 6- , 7- , 8- , 9- , 10-135
FoW (2): 1- , 2- , 3- , 4- , 5- , 6- , 7- , 8- , 9- , 10-106

KENT

1	W.Bullen	b Mann	13	b Purchase		1
2	W.Brazier	c Scott	1	b Purchase		13
3	J.Aylward	b Purchase	37	c Taylor		16
4	J.Ring	c Harris	0	c Scott		7
5	J.Pilcher	b Harris	0	b Harris		2
6	J.Boorman	c Purchase	1	not out		4
7	J.Crawte	b Taylor	35	c Taylor		4
8	H.Crosoer	c Harris	17	b Purchase		8
9	R.Clifford	c Scott	12	b Harris		0
10	Dean	b Harris	8	b Harris		14
11	Palmer	not out	9	b Harris		5
	Byes		4			1
			137			75

FoW (1): 1- , 2- , 3- , 4- , 5- , 6- , 7- , 8- , 9- , 10-137
FoW (2): 1- , 2- , 3- , 4- , 5- , 6- , 7- , 8- , 9- , 10-75

Kent Bowling

	O	M	R	W		O	M	R	W
Clifford				3					1
Bullen				2					1
Boorman									1

Hampshire Bowling

	O	M	R	W		O	M	R	W
Harris				2					4
Purchase				1					3
Mann				1					
Taylor				1					

Umpires:

Close of Play: 1st day: ; 2nd day: ; 3rd day: Kent (2) 32-4.

ENGLAND v HAMPSHIRE

Played at Sevenoaks Vine Cricket Club Ground, September 2, 3, 4, 5, 1789.

Hampshire won by 15 runs.

HAMPSHIRE

1	J.Aylward	b Bullen	7	run out		13
2	J.Ring	c H.Walker	2	b Clifford		38
3	D.Harris	b Clifford	1	c Crawte		0
4	N.Mann	b Bullen	4	c Beldham		4
5	R.Purchase	b Bullen	19	c Crawte		12
6	J.Small, sen	b Clifford	13	b Clifford		4
7	J.Small, jun	c H.Walker	10	b Clifford		16
8	A.Freemantle	not out	3	b Clifford		23
9	T.Taylor	b Bullen	1	b Clifford		0
10	T.Scott	b Bullen	0	c Clifford		13
11	F.Foster	b Bullen	3	not out		7
	Byes		5			1
			68			131

FoW (1): 1- , 2- , 3- , 4- , 5- , 6- , 7- , 8- , 9- , 10-68
FoW (2): 1- , 2- , 3- , 4- , 5- , 6- , 7- , 8- , 9- , 10-131

ENGLAND

1	Earl of Winchilsea	b Mann	2	b Taylor		0
2	W.Beldham	not out	19	c Scott		14
3	R.Clifford	b Purchase	5	b Harris		3
4	W.Bullen	c Scott	1	not out		8
5	W.Brazier	c Harris	4	c Taylor		5
6	John Wells	b Purchase	11	c Scott		39
7	J.Crawte	c Taylor	6	c Harris		7
8	T.Sueter	b Harris	7	c J.Small, sen		17
9	T.Walker	b Harris	0	c Aylward		16
10	H.Walker	hit wkt	6	c Taylor		10
11	E.Stevens	b Purchase	3	b Harris		0
	Byes		1			
			65			119

FoW (1): 1- , 2- , 3- , 4- , 5- , 6- , 7- , 8- , 9- , 10-65
FoW (2): 1- , 2- , 3- , 4- , 5- , 6- , 7- , 8- , 9- , 10-119

England Bowling

	O	M	R	W	O	M	R	W
Clifford				2				5
Bullen				6				

Hampshire Bowling

	O	M	R	W	O	M	R	W
Harris				2				2
Purchase				3				
Mann				1				
Taylor								1

Umpires:

Close of Play: 1st day: ; 2nd day: ; 3rd day: .

Hampshire had Aylward and Ring as given men.

137

LEFT-HANDED v RIGHT-HANDED

Played at Lord's Old Ground, Marylebone, May 10, 11, 12, 1790.

Left-Handed won by 39 runs.

LEFT-HANDED

1	R.Clifford	c Beldham	4	b Walker	0
2	J.Crawte	run out	1	c Ring	8
3	J.Aylward	b Beldham	30	b Beldham	7
4	T.Sueter	b Purchase	39	c Louch	0
5	W.Brazier	c Wells	5	c Louch	0
6	H.Walker	c Bullen	15	b Beldham	15
7	A.Freemantle	not out	23	c Fennex	0
8	T.Ingram	b Purchase	4	b Beldham	4
9	D.Harris	c Ring	4	b Beldham	0
10	F.Booker	c Taylor	3	c Purchase	10
11	N.Graham	run out	1	not out	2
	Byes		2		1
			131		47

FoW (1): 1- , 2- , 3- , 4- , 5- , 6- , 7- , 8- , 9- , 10-131
FoW (2): 1- , 2- , 3- , 4- , 5- , 6- , 7- , 8- , 9- , 10-47

RIGHT-HANDED

1	John Wells	c Walker	4	b Brazier	13
2	W.Beldham	c Ingram	4	b Harris	18
3	J.Small, sen	c Ingram	0	b Harris	4
4	T.Walker	b Clifford	14	run out	1
5	R.Purchase	b Harris	3	b Clifford	2
6	J.Small, jun	b Harris	9	run out	19
7	W.Fennex	c Walker	3	b Harris	0
8	G.Louch	b Brazier	8	c Clifford	1
9	T.Taylor	b Brazier	1	not out	8
10	J.Ring	run out	21	b Harris	4
11	W.Bullen	not out	1	run out	0
	Byes		1		
			69		70

FoW (1): 1- , 2- , 3- , 4- , 5- , 6- , 7- , 8- , 9- , 10-69
FoW (2): 1- , 2- , 3- , 4- , 5- , 6- , 7- , 8- , 9- , 10-70

Right-Handed Bowling

	O	M	R	W	O	M	R	W
Purchase				2				
Beldham				1				4
Walker								1

Left-Handed Bowling

	O	M	R	W	O	M	R	W
Harris				2				4
Clifford				1				1
Brazier				2				1

Umpires:

Close of Play: 1st day: ; 2nd day: .

According to Epps, Crawte batted right but threw with his left hand.

M.C.C. v HORNCHURCH

Played at Lord's Old Ground, Marylebone, May 20, 21, 1790.

M.C.C. won by eight wickets.

HORNCHURCH

#	Player	Dismissal	Score	Dismissal (2)	Score (2)
1	R.B.Wyatt	b Darnley	12	b Hussey	11
2	J.Russell	b Hussey	11	not out	7
3	R.Denn	c Louch	6	c Louch	1
4	T.Clark	run out	13	c Hussey	11
5	J.Goulstone	b Fitzroy	1	b Grover	11
6	Higgs	b Hussey	1	b Fitzroy	13
7	Simmons	b Fitzroy	5	run out	19
8	J.Stevens	not out	10	b Hussey	7
9	Carr	b Hussey	20	b Grover	0
10	Clements	c Leycester	5	b Grover	5
11	J.Martin	c Hussey	29	b Fitzroy	10
	Byes		3		1
			116		96

FoW (1): 1- , 2- , 3- , 4- , 5- , 6- , 7- , 8- , 9- , 10-116
FoW (2): 1- , 2- , 3- , 4- , 5- , 6- , 7- , 8- , 9- , 10-96

M.C.C.

#	Player	Dismissal	Score	Dismissal (2)	Score (2)
1	Earl of Winchilsea	b Martin	6		
2	Earl of Darnley	st Clark	7	c Wyatt	3
3	T.A.Smith	c Wyatt	24		
4	C.Lennox	b Martin	0	c Denn	4
5	E.Hussey	c Clements	3		
6	G.Louch	c Clements	43		
7	E.Bligh	c Wyatt	18		
8	C.Anguish	c Wyatt	12		
9	G.Leycester	c Goulstone	19	not out	11
10	J.S.Grover	c Simmons	3	not out	18
11	H.W.Fitzroy	not out	36		
	Byes		6		
			177	(2 wickets)	36

FoW (1): 1- , 2- , 3- , 4- , 5- , 6- , 7- , 8- , 9- , 10-177
FoW (2): 1- , 2-

M.C.C. Bowling

	O	M	R	W	O	M	R	W
Hussey				3				2
Fitzroy				2				2
Darnley				1				
Grover								3

Hornchurch Bowling

	O	M	R	W	O	M	R	W
Martin				2				

Umpires:

Close of Play: 1st day: .

Note that George Leycester has no middle initial. George Hamer Leycester, his cousin, did not play in 'great' matches. Grover has been tentatively identified as John Septimus Grover.

HAMPSHIRE v KENT

Played at Lord's Old Ground, Marylebone, June 10, 11, 12, 1790.

Hampshire won by eight wickets.

KENT

#	Batsman	Dismissal	Score		2nd Dismissal	2nd Score
1	R.Clifford	c Purchase	0		b Harris	8
2	S.Amherst	b Harris	2		c Harris	0
3	J.Ring	b Purchase	4		b Harris	7
4	J.Crawte	c Taylor	0		b Harris	8
5	J.Aylward	c J.Small, jun	20		run out	0
6	W.Brazier	c J.Small, jun	2		b Taylor	32
7	E.Bligh	b Harris	4		c Taylor	17
8	J.Boorman	c J.Small, jun	3		not out	0
9	Earl of Darnley	c J.Small, sen	3		b Purchase	2
10	R.Stone	not out	2		c Taylor	0
11	W.Bullen	b Purchase	11		b Harris	8
	Byes		1			3
			52			**85**

FoW (1): 1- , 2- , 3- , 4- , 5- , 6- , 7- , 8- , 9- , 10-52
FoW (2): 1- , 2- , 3- , 4- , 5- , 6- , 7- , 8- , 9- , 10-85

HAMPSHIRE

#	Batsman	Dismissal	Score		2nd Dismissal	2nd Score
1	D.Harris	c Bullen	5			
2	T.Walker	c Bullen	6		not out	12
3	R.Purchase	run out	1			
4	G.Louch	c Amherst	6			
5	J.Small, jun	b Clifford	0			
6	C.Lennox	b Brazier	17		not out	2
7	T.Taylor	b Brazier	1			
8	J.Small, sen	b Bullen	33			
9	Earl of Winchilsea	b Boorman	23		b Boorman	2
10	T.A.Smith	c Ring	12			
11	H.W.Fitzroy	not out	10		c Amherst	3
	Byes		5			
			119		**(2 wickets)**	**19**

FoW (1): 1- , 2- , 3- , 4- , 5- , 6- , 7- , 8- , 9- , 10-119
FoW (2): 1- , 2-

Hampshire Bowling

	O	M	R	W		O	M	R	W
Harris				2					4
Purchase				2					1
Taylor									1

Kent Bowling

	O	M	R	W		O	M	R	W
Boorman				1					1
Brazier				2					
Bullen				1					
Clifford				1					

Umpires:

Close of Play: 1st day: ; 2nd day: .

Hampshire had Walker as a given man. The batting orders may be in order of dismissal.

HORNCHURCH v M.C.C.

Played at Langton Park, Hornchurch, July 5, 6, 1790.

M.C.C. won by 67 runs.

M.C.C.

1	Earl of Winchilsea	b Goulstone	22	b Clements	11
2	Earl of Darnley	b Clements	6	b Goulstone	11
3	T.A.Smith	b Clements	9	c Russell	1
4	C.Lennox	c Goulstone	69	b Martin	27
5	G.Louch	b Wyatt	31	c Clark	17
6	Butcher	b Martin	8	b Clements	0
7	C.Anguish	b Clements	26	b Goulstone	0
8	H.W.Fitzroy	c Simmons	23	c Stevens	4
9	R.Stone	c Oxley	0	b Goulstone	0
10	T.E.Capel	not out	2	not out	4
11	R.Brudenell	c Denn	2	c Russell	0
	Byes		11		3
			209		78

FoW (1): 1- , 2- , 3- , 4- , 5- , 6- , 7- , 8- , 9- , 10-209
FoW (2): 1- , 2- , 3- , 4- , 5- , 6- , 7- , 8- , 9- , 10-78

HORNCHURCH

1	R.B.Wyatt	b Fitzroy	0	c Capel	39
2	J.Russell	b Fitzroy	0	b Fitzroy	1
3	R.Denn	not out	5	c Lennox	4
4	J.Goulstone	c Capel	42	c Winchilsea	41
5	W.Oxley	b Darnley	9	b Capel	4
6	Carr	b Darnley	0	c Stone	6
7	T.Clark	b Fitzroy	1	not out	6
8	J.Stevens	run out	10	b Lennox	2
9	Simmons	b Darnley	26	c Darnley	0
10	Clements	b Fitzroy	0	b Fitzroy	0
11	J.Martin	run out	2	run out	1
	Byes		5		10
			106		114

FoW (1): 1- , 2- , 3- , 4- , 5- , 6- , 7- , 8- , 9- , 10-106
FoW (2): 1- , 2- , 3- , 4- , 5- , 6- , 7- , 8- , 9- , 10-114

Hornchurch Bowling

	O	M	R	W	O	M	R	W
Clements				3				2
Goulstone				1				3
Wyatt				1				
Martin				1				1

M.C.C. Bowling

	O	M	R	W	O	M	R	W
Fitzroy				4				2
Darnley				3				
Lennox								1
Capel								1

Umpires:

Close of Play: 1st day: .

ENGLAND v HAMPSHIRE

Played at Sevenoaks Vine Cricket Club Ground, July 12, 13, 14, 15, 16, 1790.

Hampshire won by 44 runs.

HAMPSHIRE

1	T.Scott	c Beldham	7	b Bullen	28
2	J.Small, jun	c Burrell	20	b Beldham	27
3	R.Purchase	c Clifford	0	b Clifford	18
4	J.Ring	b Clifford	4	b Clifford	15
5	J.Small, sen	b Clifford	24	c Wells	16
6	J.Aylward	c Wells	55	c Sueter	10
7	A.Freemantle	c Sueter	3	not out	25
8	C.Lennox	b Brazier	15	c Clifford	0
9	Annett	c Burrell	18	b Bullen	4
10	T.Taylor	b Boorman	7	b Clifford	8
11	D.Harris	not out	0	b Clifford	1
	Byes		5		1
			158		153

FoW (1): 1- , 2- , 3- , 4- , 5- , 6- , 7- , 8- , 9- , 10-158
FoW (2): 1- , 2- , 3- , 4- , 5- , 6- , 7- , 8- , 9- , 10-153

ENGLAND

1	T.Walker	run out	6	c Taylor	20
2	John Wells	b Taylor	33	run out	1
3	W.Beldham	run out	11	c Taylor	35
4	T.Sueter	c Taylor	11	c Scott	17
5	Sir P.Burrell	b Purchase	1	c Lennox	3
6	H.Walker	b Purchase	21	run out	41
7	W.Bullen	b Purchase	2	c Lennox	4
8	W.Brazier	c Freemantle	5	c Purchase	20
9	R.Clifford	b Harris	4	c Harris	1
10	J.Boorman	c Ring	6	b Harris	3
11	F.Booker	not out	5	not out	14
	Byes		1		2
			106		161

FoW (1): 1- , 2- , 3- , 4- , 5- , 6- , 7- , 8- , 9- , 10-106
FoW (2): 1- , 2- , 3- , 4- , 5- , 6- , 7- , 8- , 9- , 10-161

England Bowling

	O	M	R	W	O	M	R	W
Clifford				2				4
Boorman				1				
Brazier				1				
Beldham								1
Bullen								2

Hampshire Bowling

	O	M	R	W	O	M	R	W
Harris				1				1
Purchase				3				
Taylor				1				

Umpires:

Close of Play: 1st day: ; 2nd day: ; 3rd day: ; 4th day: .

Hampshire had Aylward and Ring as given men.

(Variant) Britcher has Hampshire (1) Aylward 35, total 158; margin 24 runs. He also calls the home team Kent and Surrey (and in terms of composition it has to be said that it makes little difference). KG supports the version in Epps and SB, which is accepted.

ENGLAND v HAMPSHIRE

Played at The Park, Burley-on-the-Hill, July 19, 20, 21, 1790.

Hampshire won by seven wickets.

ENGLAND

1	Earl of Winchilsea	c Clifford	23	b Taylor		1
2	Earl of Darnley	c Purchase	4	st		10
3	G.Louch	c Butcher	8	c Butcher		17
4	H.Walker	c Taylor	0	c Taylor		1
5	T.Walker	c Taylor	31	b Purchase		16
6	John Wells	b Purchase	8	c J.Small, jun		21
7	W.Beldham	hit wkt	0	c J.Small, jun		0
8	T.Sueter	run out	8	b Purchase		19
9	W.Bullen	not out	6	b Purchase		8
10	W.Brazier	b Clifford	4	b Purchase		1
11	J.Boorman	c J.Small, sen	0	not out		6
	Byes					3
			92			103

FoW (1): 1- , 2- , 3- , 4- , 5- , 6- , 7- , 8- , 9- , 10-92
FoW (2): 1- , 2- , 3- , 4- , 5- , 6- , 7- , 8- , 9- , 10-103

HAMPSHIRE

1	T.A.Smith	not out	15			
2	Butcher	b Brazier	1	b Bullen		1
3	C.Anguish	c Boorman	0			
4	J.Small, sen	b Brazier	0			
5	J.Small, jun	b Beldham	9	not out		30
6	R.Purchase	c Beldham	3			
7	T.Taylor	run out	36			
8	R.Clifford	c Louch	4			
9	A.Freemantle	run out	0	b Bullen		1
10	J.Aylward	c Wells	36	c Wells		5
11	J.Ring	c Beldham	24	not out		24
	Byes		7			
			135	(3 wickets)		61

FoW (1): 1- , 2- , 3- , 4- , 5- , 6- , 7- , 8- , 9- , 10-135
FoW (2): 1- , 2- , 3-

Hampshire Bowling

	O	M	R	W	O	M	R	W
Clifford				1				
Purchase				1				4
Taylor								1

England Bowling

	O	M	R	W	O	M	R	W
Brazier				2				
Beldham				1				
Bullen								2

Umpires:

Close of Play: 1st day: ; 2nd day: .

The newspapers all call this England v Hampshire. Hampshire is stated to have had Aylward and Ring as given men, although it should be noted that the team also includes Butcher and Clifford. Possibly they stood in for unavailable Hampshire players. This was the first 'great' match at Lord Winchilsea's house at Burley-on-the-Hill, near Oakham. In the ACS book *Country House Cricket Grounds of Leicestershire*, E.E.Snow remarks: 'Undoubtedly the most historic and important cricket venue in Leicestershire and Rutland, Burley-on-the-Hill (this is the correct name of the house as the village is just called Burley) has been largely ignored and has often been confused with Burghley House, Stamford.'

(Variant) SB gives the match as Winchilsea v Smith: it also spells the venue incorrectly as Burghley.

HAMPSHIRE AND SURREY v KENT

Played at Perham Downs, Ludgershall, July 27, 28, 29, 1790.

Hampshire and Surrey won by six wickets.

KENT

1	J.Ring	c Beldham	9	b Beldham	8
2	J.Aylward	c Taylor	0	b Taylor	29
3	A.Freemantle	c Beldham	26	b Beldham	0
4	J.Crawte	c Wells	0	c T.Walker	31
5	Earl of Darnley	b Purchase	5	b Taylor	3
6	White	b Purchase	6	b T.Walker	0
7	S.Amherst	b Beldham	18	c Beldham	11
8	Butcher	c H.Walker	1	not out	13
9	R.Clifford	b Beldham	10	b Taylor	1
10	W.Bullen	b Purchase	10	b T.Walker	0
11	T.Boxall	not out	6	c Wells	0
	Byes				
			91		96

FoW (1): 1- , 2- , 3- , 4- , 5- , 6- , 7- , 8- , 9- , 10-91
FoW (2): 1- , 2- , 3- , 4- , 5- , 6- , 7- , 8- , 9- , 10-96

HAMPSHIRE AND SURREY

1	R.Purchase	run out	0	not out	19
2	T.Walker	b Clifford	2	not out	1
3	John Wells	b Clifford	11		
4	H.Walker	b Clifford	15		
5	J.Small, jun	b Bullen	4		
6	Earl of Winchilsea	b Bullen	0	c Amherst	9
7	T.Taylor	c Amherst	26		
8	W.Beldham	b Darnley	60		
9	T.A.Smith	b Clifford	0	b Bullen	4
10	C.Anguish	run out	9	c Amherst	2
11	G.Louch	not out	25	b Clifford	0
	Byes				1
			152	(4 wickets)	36

FoW (1): 1- , 2- , 3- , 4- , 5- , 6- , 7- , 8- , 9- , 10-152
FoW (2): 1- , 2- , 3- , 4-

Hampshire and Surrey Bowling

	O	M	R	W	O	M	R	W
Purchase				3				
Beldham				2				2
Taylor								3
T.Walker								2

Kent Bowling

	O	M	R	W	O	M	R	W
Clifford				4				1
Bullen				2				1
Darnley				1				

Umpires:

Close of Play: 1st day: ; 2nd day: .

Kent had Freemantle as a given man. No Kentish White is known. In view of the venue, it is assumed that this is the local man, White of Andover, making up the eleven.

(Variant) SB gives the match as Smith v Mann.

EARL OF DARNLEY'S XI v EARL OF WINCHILSEA'S XI
Played at Windmill Down, Hambledon, August 4, 5, 6, 7, 1790.

Earl of Darnley's XI won by 184 runs.

EARL OF DARNLEY'S XI

1	J.Aylward	b Beldham	9	b Beldham	6
2	J.Small, jun	c Brazier	39	c H.Walker	5
3	J.Ring	b Bullen	68	b Beldham	13
4	R.Purchase	b Brazier	73	b Bullen	13
5	R.Clifford	c Brazier	34	c Wells	5
6	Earl of Darnley	c Sueter	7	b Bullen	0
7	French	b Bullen	0	not out	1
8	T.Taylor	b Bullen	14	b Beldham	6
9	J.Small, sen	b Beldham	12	run out	19
10	T.A.Smith	b Beldham	2	b Beldham	6
11	A.Freemantle	not out	13	c H.Walker	32
	Byes		7		2
			278		108

FoW (1): 1- , 2- , 3- , 4- , 5- , 6- , 7- , 8- , 9- , 10-278
FoW (2): 1- , 2- , 3- , 4- , 5- , 6- , 7- , 8- , 9- , 10-108

EARL OF WINCHILSEA'S XI

1	John Wells	c Taylor	5	c J.Small, jun	3
2	T.Walker	b Purchase	0	b Clifford	5
3	H.Walker	run out	9	b Clifford	0
4	T.Sueter	b Clifford	0	c J.Small, sen	12
5	Earl of Winchilsea	c Aylward	19	b Clifford	19
6	J.Crawte	b Darnley	22	c French	3
7	G.Louch	b Darnley	1	b Purchase	8
8	W.Beldham	c Smith	54	b Purchase	11
9	W.Brazier	b Darnley	1	not out	19
10	Butcher	not out	0	c J.Small, sen	4
11	W.Bullen	b Taylor	0	c J.Small, sen	1
	Byes		5		1
			116		86

FoW (1): 1- , 2- , 3- , 4- , 5- , 6- , 7- , 8- , 9- , 10-116
FoW (2): 1- , 2- , 3- , 4- , 5- , 6- , 7- , 8- , 9- , 10-86

Earl of Winchilsea's XI Bowling

	O	M	R	W		O	M	R	W
Bullen				3					2
Beldham				3					4
Brazier				1					

Earl of Darnley's XI Bowling

	O	M	R	W		O	M	R	W
Clifford				1					3
Purchase				1					2
Taylor				1					
Darnley				3					

Umpires:

Close of Play: 1st day: ; 2nd day: ; 3rd day: .

M.C.C. v MIDDLESEX

Played at Lord's Old Ground, Marylebone, August 16, 1790.

M.C.C. won by two wickets.

MIDDLESEX

1	W.White	b Clifford	14	b Beldham	2
2	W.Bedster	b Clifford	13	c Wyatt	11
3	T.Shackle	b Beldham	24	c Beldham	12
4	G.T.Boult	b Beldham	11	b Beldham	3
5	T.Webb	b Clifford	4	c Lennox	35
6	W.Fennex	c Clifford	16	c Wyatt	3
7	T.V.R.Nicoll	b Clifford	1	not out	0
8	Butler	c Burrell	1	c Beldham	11
9	T.Lord	c Beldham	11	c Beldham	56
10	Clarke	not out	0	b Beldham	5
11	Grange	c Winchilsea	9	c Smith	30
	Byes				14
			104		182

FoW (1): 1- , 2- , 3- , 4- , 5- , 6- , 7- , 8- , 9- , 10-104
FoW (2): 1- , 2- , 3- , 4- , 5- , 6- , 7- , 8- , 9- , 10-182

M.C.C.

1	Sir P.Burrell	b Fennex	14	b Lord	1
2	R.Clifford	c Bedster	42	c Webb	29
3	C.Lennox	b Fennex	1	b Lord	3
4	G.Louch	b Lord	2	run out	20
5	W.Beldham	c Bedster	24	c Webb	16
6	Earl of Darnley	b Fennex	5		
7	R.B.Wyatt	run out	5	c Webb	8
8	H.W.Fitzroy	b Fennex	2	not out	15
9	T.A.Smith	c Bedster	5	not out	30
10	Earl of Winchilsea	c Webb	18	b Lord	0
11	C.Anguish	not out	20	b Fennex	4
	Byes		7		16
			145	(8 wickets)	142

FoW (1): 1- , 2- , 3- , 4- , 5- , 6- , 7- , 8- , 9- , 10-145
FoW (2): 1- , 2- , 3- , 4- , 5- , 6- , 7- , 8-

M.C.C. Bowling

	O	M	R	W		O	M	R	W
Clifford				4					
Beldham				2					3

Middlesex Bowling

	O	M	R	W		O	M	R	W
Fennex				4					1
Lord				1					3

Umpires:

Close of Play: 1st day: .

MCC had Beldham and Clifford as given men. Only one day is given for the match in Britcher and SB but it must have lasted longer. 17 and 18 August would appear to have been available before the teams met at Uxbridge for the return on 19 August. Clarke in the Middlesex team is assumed not to be T.Clark of Hornchurch.

MIDDLESEX v M.C.C.

Played at W.Fennex's New Ground, Uxbridge, August 19, 20, 1790.

M.C.C. won by 56 runs.

M.C.C.

1	W.Beldham	b Fennex	3	b Fennex		46
2	R.Clifford	c Bedster	4	b Fennex		4
3	H.W.Fitzroy	b Lord	7	not out		6
4	Earl of Winchilsea	c Bedster	15	b Grange		17
5	G.Louch	b Lord	38	c Grange		8
6	T.A.Smith	b Lord	2	c Webb		1
7	C.Anguish	b Fennex	0	c Packer		4
8	Earl of Darnley	c Lord	8	b Fennex		0
9	C.Lennox	b Fennex	28	b Lord		6
10	T.E.Capel	b Bedster	0	c Webb		2
11	Tyson	not out	0	c Grange		0
	Byes		5			7
			110			101

FoW (1): 1- , 2- , 3- , 4- , 5- , 6- , 7- , 8- , 9- , 10-110
FoW (2): 1- , 2- , 3- , 4- , 5- , 6- , 7- , 8- , 9- , 10-101

MIDDLESEX

1	T.Shackle	c Clifford	2	c Tyson		10
2	T.Webb	run out	5	b Beldham		7
3	W.White	b Beldham	0	c Beldham		1
4	Grange	c Lennox	0	b Beldham		0
5	T.Lord	c Fitzroy	8	hit wkt		4
6	W.Bedster	c Louch	17	not out		7
7	W.Fennex	hit wkt	41	run out		4
8	W.Beeston	b Clifford	0	b Clifford		3
9	R.Beeston	b Clifford	11	b Beldham		21
10	Talmege	c Tyson	3	b Clifford		8
11	Packer	not out	0	c Louch		0
	Byes		2			1
			89			66

FoW (1): 1- , 2- , 3- , 4- , 5- , 6- , 7- , 8- , 9- , 10-89
FoW (2): 1- , 2- , 3- , 4- , 5- , 6- , 7- , 8- , 9- , 10-66

Middlesex Bowling

	O	M	R	W	O	M	R	W
Fennex				3				3
Lord				3				1
Bedster				1				
Grange								1

M.C.C. Bowling

	O	M	R	W	O	M	R	W
Clifford				2				2
Beldham				1				3

Umpires:

Close of Play: 1st day: .

MCC had Beldham and Clifford as given men. Talmege in the Middlesex team is one of two brothers, Charles or William. The MCC batting order is taken from Britcher but the Middlesex order from SB.

ENGLAND v HAMPSHIRE AND M.C.C.

Played at Lord's Old Ground, Marylebone, August 30, 31, September 1, 2, 1790.

Hampshire and M.C.C. won by ten wickets.

ENGLAND
1	John Wells	c Taylor	9	c Taylor	0
2	H.Walker	c Winchilsea	20	b Harris	3
3	J.Aylward	b Harris	14	b Taylor	27
4	W.Beldham	b Purchase	31	b Harris	3
5	C.Lennox	c Taylor	0	b Harris	0
6	R.Clifford	c J.Small, sen	7	c Purchase	0
7	T.Walker	b Harris	60	b Harris	0
8	C.Anguish	b Harris	0	b Harris	11
9	W.Bullen	b Harris	11	b Harris	15
10	T.E.Capel	c Louch	19	c Purchase	0
11	N.Graham	not out	5	not out	3
	Byes		1		4
			177		66

FoW (1): 1- , 2- , 3- , 4- , 5- , 6- , 7- , 8- , 9- , 10-177
FoW (2): 1- , 2- , 3- , 4- , 5- , 6- , 7- , 8- , 9- , 10-66

HAMPSHIRE AND M.C.C.
1	T.Scott	c Wells	43	not out	44
2	A.Freemantle	b Clifford	5		
3	G.Louch	b T.Walker	6		
4	J.Small, jun	c H.Walker	51	not out	32
5	T.Taylor	b Clifford	31		
6	R.Purchase	run out	0		
7	J.Small, sen	run out	1		
8	G.Dehany	b Beldham	0		
9	Earl of Darnley	b Beldham	1		
10	Earl of Winchilsea	st Clifford	15		
11	D.Harris	not out	10		
	Byes		2		3
			165	(no wicket)	79

FoW (1): 1- , 2- , 3- , 4- , 5- , 6- , 7- , 8- , 9- , 10-165

Hampshire and M.C.C. Bowling

	O	M	R	W		O	M	R	W
Harris				4					6
Purchase				1					
Taylor									1

England Bowling

	O	M	R	W		O	M	R	W
Clifford				2					
Beldham				2					
T.Walker				1					

Umpires:

Close of Play: 1st day: ; 2nd day: ; 3rd day: .

EAST KENT v WEST KENT

Played at Bourne Paddock, Bishopsbourne, September 7, 8, 9, 10, 11, 1790.

West Kent won by 128 runs.

WEST KENT
1	W.Bullen	c Ring	6	b Fitzroy		3
2	J.Crawte	b Pilcher	1	b Fitzroy		23
3	R.Clifford	c Venner	30	c Crosoer		6
4	S.Amherst	c Purchase	4	not out		17
5	W.Brazier	run out	13	c Hammond		58
6	T.Selby	b Walker	8	b Pilcher		12
7	R.Fielder	b Purchase	15	b Fitzroy		0
8	F.Booker	c Ring	29	b Pilcher		3
9	Dean	b Aylward	12	c Crosoer		20
10	T.Boxall	not out	0	b Fitzroy		0
11	J.Boorman	run out	1	b Pilcher		1
	Byes					3
			119			146

FoW (1): 1- , 2- , 3- , 4- , 5- , 6- , 7- , 8- , 9- , 10-119
FoW (2): 1- , 2- , 3- , 4- , 5- , 6- , 7- , 8- , 9- , 10-146

EAST KENT
1	J.Hammond	b Bullen	2	b Bullen		2
2	R.Purchase	b Clifford	1	c Dean		6
3	J.Pilcher	b Boxall	17	c Amherst		0
4	J.Aylward	b Boxall	9	c Amherst		0
5	Earl of Winchilsea	c Booker	0	b Clifford		9
6	J.Ring	c Brazier	16	c Bullen		14
7	H.W.Fitzroy	b Clifford	34	c Amherst		0
8	H.Crosoer	b Boxall	13	b Bullen		6
9	Venner	c Selby	0	not out		0
10	Wood	c Amherst	4	b Boxall		2
11	Walker	not out	0	b Boxall		0
	Byes		1			1
			97			40

FoW (1): 1- , 2- , 3- , 4- , 5- , 6- , 7- , 8- , 9- , 10-97
FoW (2): 1- , 2- , 3- , 4- , 5- , 6- , 7- , 8- , 9- , 10-40

East Kent Bowling
	O	M	R	W	O	M	R	W
Pilcher				1				3
Purchase				1				
Aylward				1				
Walker				1				
Fitzroy								4

West Kent Bowling
	O	M	R	W	O	M	R	W
Clifford				2				1
Bullen				1				2
Boxall				3				2

Umpires:

Close of Play: 1st day: ; 2nd day: ; 3rd day: ; 4th day: .

East Kent had Purchase as a given man. Walker, appearing for East Kent, is not one of the famous Walker brothers from Surrey. He was probably from Aldington, near Ashford. Bad weather extended the game to five days.

M.C.C. v MIDDLESEX

Played at Lord's Old Ground, Marylebone, May 16, 17, 18, 1791.

Middlesex won by 30 runs.

MIDDLESEX

#	Batsman	Dismissal	Score	Dismissal	Score
1	W.White	not out	39	c Fitzroy	7
2	Grange	c Bligh	4	c Beldham	30
3	W.Fennex	b Beldham	1	b Bligh	41
4	T.Shackle	b Beldham	0	run out	17
5	T.Lord	run out	21	c Winchilsea	21
6	W.Wells	c Bligh	6	c Bligh	0
7	W.Bedster	b Beldham	3	b Purchase	27
8	Cantrell	b Beldham	0	c Bligh	6
9	Dale	c Hussey	8	not out	3
10	J.T.White	b Beldham	11	c Wyatt	2
11	R.Turner	c Hussey	7	b Beldham	1
	Byes		10		11
			110		166

FoW (1): 1- , 2- , 3- , 4- , 5- , 6- , 7- , 8- , 9- , 10-110
FoW (2): 1- , 2- , 3- , 4- , 5- , 6- , 7- , 8- , 9- , 10-166

M.C.C.

#	Batsman	Dismissal	Score	Dismissal	Score
1	T.A.Smith	b Fennex	1	run out	8
2	R.B.Wyatt	b Fennex	9	b Fennex	7
3	R.Purchase	b Turner	10	c Cantrell	44
4	E.Hussey	c Lord	0	run out	16
5	G.Louch	b Turner	36	b Turner	1
6	E.Bligh	b Fennex	1	b Fennex	4
7	C.Anguish	c Bedster	13	b Turner	0
8	H.W.Fitzroy	b Fennex	6	not out	1
9	Earl of Winchilsea	b Fennex	4	c Cantrell	10
10	J.L.Kaye	b Grange	4	b Grange	4
11	W.Beldham	not out	44	b Fennex	1
	Byes		17		5
			145		101

FoW (1): 1- , 2- , 3- , 4- , 5- , 6- , 7- , 8- , 9- , 10-145
FoW (2): 1- , 2- , 3- , 4- , 5- , 6- , 7- , 8- , 9- , 10-101

M.C.C. Bowling

	O	M	R	W	O	M	R	W
Beldham				5				1
Purchase								1
Bligh								1

Middlesex Bowling

	O	M	R	W	O	M	R	W
Fennex				5				3
Turner				2				2
Grange				1				1

Umpires:

Close of Play: 1st day: ; 2nd day: .

MCC batting order appears to be by dismissal: Beldham obviously came in much higher.

(Variant) Buckley's unpublished manuscript notes at Lord's state that this and the following match are Middlesex (i.e. Thursday) Club matches, but it is believed that Thursday Club matches do not commence until 1794. In any case, the composition of the team suggests a Middlesex county side, as does the employment of Beldham and Purchase as given men by MCC.

M.C.C. v MIDDLESEX

Played at Lord's Old Ground, Marylebone, May 23, 24, 25, 1791.

Middlesex won by six wickets.

M.C.C.

1	C.Anguish	run out	2	c Fennex	17
2	R.Purchase	c Cantrell	15	b Fennex	9
3	H.W.Fitzroy	b Fennex	27	not out	11
4	G.Louch	b Lord	11	c Grange	12
5	W.Beldham	b Fennex	62	c Bedster	43
6	Earl of Winchilsea	b Fennex	7	b Fennex	5
7	E.Hussey	b Fennex	35	run out	4
8	T.A.Smith	c White	11	b Grange	1
9	E.Bligh	c Fennex	3	c Grange	24
10	A.Pitcairn	not out	1	run out	6
11	G.Talbot	b Fennex	1	c Cantrell	5
	Byes		15		13
			190		150

FoW (1): 1- , 2- , 3- , 4- , 5- , 6- , 7- , 8- , 9- , 10-190
FoW (2): 1- , 2- , 3- , 4- , 5- , 6- , 7- , 8- , 9- , 10-150

MIDDLESEX

1	T.Webb	c Hussey	1		
2	R.Turner	c Louch	3		
3	T.Shackle	b Purchase	5	c Bligh	6
4	Grange	run out	0	c Beldham	13
5	T.Lord	b Beldham	3	not out	5
6	W.Fennex	st Hussey	61	not out	3
7	G.T.Boult	c Louch	89		
8	W.Bedster	c Louch	53		
9	Dale	c Pitcairn	23	c Winchilsea	24
10	Cantrell	b Beldham	26	c Beldham	5
11	W.White	not out	9		
	Byes		11		1
			284	(4 wickets)	57

FoW (1): 1- , 2- , 3- , 4- , 5- , 6- , 7- , 8- , 9- , 10-284
FoW (2): 1- , 2- , 3- , 4-

Middlesex Bowling

	O	M	R	W	O	M	R	W
Fennex				5				2
Lord				1				
Grange								1

M.C.C. Bowling

	O	M	R	W	O	M	R	W
Beldham				2				
Purchase				1				

Umpires:

Close of Play: 1st day: ; 2nd day: .

MCC had Beldham and Purchase as given men.

151

GENTLEMEN OF ENGLAND v OLD ETONIANS

Played at Lord's Old Ground, Marylebone, May 30, 31, June 1, 2, 1791.

Gentlemen of England won by six wickets.

OLD ETONIANS

1	Earl of Winchilsea	b Cumberland	54	b Cumberland	8
2	H.W.Fitzroy	c Louch	6	not out	41
3	E.Bligh	b Cumberland	25	c Louch	21
4	T.A.Smith	b Grange	1	c Talbot	4
5	Earl of Darnley	b Cumberland	3	b Cumberland	7
6	R.B.Wyatt	b Cumberland	13	st Lennox	32
7	G.Leycester	b Cumberland	0	st Lennox	6
8	G.Dupuis	b Grange	6	b Cumberland	28
9	Miller	run out	0	b Cumberland	9
10	C.Anguish	c Thanet	1	b Cumberland	0
11	T.Lord	not out	4	c Louch	5
	Byes		3		6
			116		167

FoW (1): 1- , 2- , 3- , 4- , 5- , 6- , 7- , 8- , 9- , 10-116
FoW (2): 1- , 2- , 3- , 4- , 5- , 6- , 7- , 8- , 9- , 10-167

GENTLEMEN OF ENGLAND

1	C.Cumberland	run out	12	b Lord	2
2	T.V.R.Nicoll	b Lord	8	not out	7
3	J.L.Kaye	b Darnley	57		
4	G.Louch	b Fitzroy	10		
5	Earl of Thanet	c Darnley	17	b Darnley	10
6	C.Lennox	b Fitzroy	61		
7	R.Stewart	c Smith	17	not out	3
8	A.Pitcairn	b Dupuis	34	b Darnley	8
9	G.Talbot	b Lord	1	b Darnley	0
10	G.Dehany	not out	8		
11	Grange	b Lord	6		
	Byes		20		3
			251	(4 wickets)	33

FoW (1): 1- , 2- , 3- , 4- , 5- , 6- , 7- , 8- , 9- , 10-251
FoW (2): 1- , 2- , 3- , 4-

Gentlemen of England Bowling

	O	M	R	W	O	M	R	W
Cumberland				5				5
Grange				2				

Old Etonians Bowling

	O	M	R	W	O	M	R	W
Lord				3				1
Darnley				1				3
Dupuis				1				
Fitzroy				2				

Umpires:

Close of Play: 1st day: ; 2nd day: ; 3rd day: .

Old Etonians had Lord as a given man; Gentlemen of England had Grange as a given man. *The Star* gives what may be a dismissal order for the Old Etonians with Winchilsea at 10, so he may have been last out.

(Variant) Britcher calls the Gentlemen the Old Westminsters but a number of them did not attend this school. SB has T.Mellish appearing in place of Anguish.

M.C.C. v GENTLEMEN OF KENT

Played at Lord's Old Ground, Marylebone, June 2, 3, 1791.

M.C.C. won by an innings and 113 runs.

GENTLEMEN OF KENT

1	S.Amherst	b Fennex	2	b Beauclerk		3
2	J.Aylward	b Beauclerk	1	b Fennex		21
3	E.Bligh	b Fennex	6	c Beauclerk		0
4	W.Browning	b Fennex	2	c Louch		5
5	Butcher	c Louch	1	not out		15
6	Earl of Thanet	b Fennex	0	c Fennex		1
7	Earl of Darnley	b Beauclerk	5	b Fennex		0
8	C.Cumberland	b Fennex	0	c Fennex		24
9	R.Hosmer	run out	11	c Beldham		12
10	W.Bullen	not out	2	b Fennex		1
11	A.Pitcairn	b Fennex	9	b Beldham		0
	Byes					6
			39			88

FoW (1): 1- , 2- , 3- , 4- , 5- , 6- , 7- , 8- , 9- , 10-39
FoW (2): 1- , 2- , 3- , 4- , 5- , 6- , 7- , 8- , 9- , 10-88

M.C.C.

1	G.Leycester	b Bullen	17
2	W.Beldham	run out	57
3	Earl of Winchilsea	c Amherst	42
4	T.A.Smith	b Cumberland	7
5	C.Anguish	b Cumberland	11
6	G.Dupuis	c Amherst	3
7	Lord F.Beauclerk	b Bullen	0
8	G.Louch	b Butcher	24
9	W.Fennex	b Butcher	53
10	H.W.Fitzroy	not out	9
11	G.Talbot	b Cumberland	1
	Byes		16
			240

FoW (1): 1- , 2- , 3- , 4- , 5- , 6- , 7- , 8- , 9- , 10-240

M.C.C. Bowling

	O	M	R	W	O	M	R	W
Fennex				6				3
Beauclerk				2				1
Beldham								1

Gentlemen of Kent Bowling

	O	M	R	W
Bullen				2
Butcher				2
Cumberland				3

Umpires:

Close of Play: 1st day: .

Gentlemen of Kent had Aylward and Bullen as given men; MCC had Beldham and Fennex as given men. Britcher supplies the initial for 'Brown', appearing for Kent in this match. This is likely to be the player of this name who appears for East Malling around this time, who has been identified as W.Browning. Cambridge alumni gives Beauclerk's full name as Frederick de Vere Beauclerk, but this is not confirmed by other sources. The match began the same day the previous one ended.

M.C.C. v HORNCHURCH

Played at Lord's Old Ground, Marylebone, June 13, 14, 1791.

Hornchurch won by 45 runs.

HORNCHURCH

1	R.B.Wyatt	c Cumberland	9	b Darnley	4
2	J.Martin	run out	2	b Beauclerk	7
3	J.Goulstone	c Cumberland	33	b Darnley	2
4	T.Ingram	b Beauclerk	0	c Leycester	80
5	R.Denn	b Beauclerk	5	not out	13
6	M.Rimmington	not out	8	c Louch	23
7	T.Clark	c Leycester	3	b Darnley	4
8	J.Russell	run out	3	c Cumberland	12
9	J.Boorman	c Leycester	7	c Winchilsea	38
10	Simmons	b Cumberland	4	b Beauclerk	11
11	J.Stevens	b Cumberland	2	b Cumberland	4
	Byes		8		10
			84		208

FoW (1): 1- , 2- , 3- , 4- , 5- , 6- , 7- , 8- , 9- , 10-84
FoW (2): 1- , 2- , 3- , 4- , 5- , 6- , 7- , 8- , 9- , 10-208

M.C.C.

1	Earl of Winchilsea	b Boorman	6	b Ingram	22
2	Lord F.Beauclerk	c Russell	0	not out	6
3	H.W.Fitzroy	b Boorman	25	b Boorman	6
4	E.Bligh	b Ingram	5	c Simmons	12
5	G.Talbot	c Ingram	1	b Ingram	5
6	C.Lennox	c Wyatt	3	run out	5
7	G.Louch	c Stevens	28	b Martin	0
8	C.Cumberland	b Boorman	0	c Russell	43
9	G.Leycester	c Clark	24	c Wyatt	47
10	C.Anguish	c Wyatt	6	c Ingram	0
11	Earl of Darnley	not out	2	b Martin	0
	Byes				1
			100		147

FoW (1): 1- , 2- , 3- , 4- , 5- , 6- , 7- , 8- , 9- , 10-100
FoW (2): 1- , 2- , 3- , 4- , 5- , 6- , 7- , 8- , 9- , 10-147

M.C.C. Bowling

	O	M	R	W	O	M	R	W
Beauclerk				2				2
Cumberland				2				1
Darnley								3

Hornchurch Bowling

	O	M	R	W	O	M	R	W
Boorman				3				1
Ingram				1				2
Martin								2

Umpires:

Close of Play: 1st day: .

ENGLAND v HAMPSHIRE

Played at The Park, Burley-on-the-Hill, June 20, 21, 22, 1791.

England won by 54 runs.

ENGLAND

1	T.Walker	b Taylor	13	c Taylor		1
2	W.Fennex	c Purchase	0	c J.Small, sen		18
3	W.Beldham	c Harris	7	c Taylor		63
4	J.Aylward	c Taylor	13	c Purchase		1
5	T.A.Smith	b Harris	1	c Taylor		0
6	John Wells	run out	23	b Taylor		3
7	E.Bligh	c Taylor	28	b Harris		14
8	G.Louch	c Taylor	9	b Harris		0
9	Earl of Darnley	b Harris	3	c J.Small, sen		0
10	C.Anguish	not out	1	not out		4
11	W.Bullen	run out	3	b Harris		8
	Byes		2			2
			103			114

FoW (1): 1- , 2- , 3- , 4- , 5- , 6- , 7- , 8- , 9- , 10-103
FoW (2): 1- , 2- , 3- , 4- , 5- , 6- , 7- , 8- , 9- , 10-114

HAMPSHIRE

1	A.Freemantle	c Walker	1	not out		6
2	R.Purchase	c Beldham	5	b Fennex		7
3	J.Small, jun	c Beldham	10	run out		15
4	C.Lennox	b Bullen	7	c Wells		36
5	Earl of Winchilsea	c Beldham	24	b Fennex		2
6	J.Small, sen	c Wells	14	c Louch		7
7	H.W.Fitzroy	b Walker	9	c Beldham		0
8	T.Taylor	c Bullen	0	c Beldham		4
9	C.Cumberland	b Fennex	1	b Fennex		6
10	G.Talbot	run out	0	c Fennex		1
11	D.Harris	not out	1	c Beldham		0
	Byes		5			2
			77			86

FoW (1): 1- , 2- , 3- , 4- , 5- , 6- , 7- , 8- , 9- , 10-77
FoW (2): 1- , 2- , 3- , 4- , 5- , 6- , 7- , 8- , 9- , 10-86

Hampshire Bowling

	O	M	R	W	O	M	R	W
Harris				2				3
Taylor				1				1

England Bowling

	O	M	R	W	O	M	R	W
Fennex				1				3
Bullen				1				
Walker				1				

Umpires:

Close of Play: 1st day: ; 2nd day: .

Britcher says 'with five pick'd Gentlemen on each Side'.

OLD ETONIANS v M.C.C.

Played at The Park, Burley-on-the-Hill, June 23, 24, 1791.

M.C.C. won by six wickets.

OLD ETONIANS

1	C.Anguish	b Walker	14	run out		6
2	H.W.Fitzroy	c Louch	6	b Cumberland		4
3	Earl of Darnley	c Lennox	0	c Talbot		1
4	Sale	b Walker	0	b Taylor		5
5	T.A.Smith	b Cumberland	1	b Cumberland		0
6	E.Bligh	c Lennox	2	b Taylor		15
7	Earl of Winchilsea	b Cumberland	20	c Talbot		76
8	W.Beeston	b Cumberland	7	run out		1
9	N.Graham	b Cumberland	0	c Lennox		0
10	R.Purchase	not out	7	b Cumberland		0
11	W.Bullen	b Cumberland	0	not out		4
	Byes		2			2
			59			114

FoW (1): 1- , 2- , 3- , 4- , 5- , 6- , 7- , 8- , 9- , 10-59
FoW (2): 1- , 2- , 3- , 4- , 5- , 6- , 7- , 8- , 9- , 10-114

M.C.C.

1	C.Cumberland	c Bullen	2	b Bullen		0
2	R.Welch	b Purchase	9	b Bullen		5
3	W.A.Harbord	b Purchase	1	c Purchase		10
4	G.Talbot	run out	3	b Bullen		17
5	C.Lennox	b Fitzroy	8	not out		4
6	G.Louch	c Bullen	29	not out		2
7	J.Maddox	b Fitzroy	0			
8	C.Towell	b Purchase	2			
9	J.Goldham	b Bullen	24			
10	T.Walker	not out	31			
11	T.Taylor	b Fitzroy	18			
	Byes		7			2
			134	(4 wickets)		40

FoW (1): 1- , 2- , 3- , 4- , 5- , 6- , 7- , 8- , 9- , 10-134
FoW (2): 1- , 2- , 3- , 4-

M.C.C. Bowling

	O	M	R	W	O	M	R	W
Cumberland				5				3
Walker				2				
Taylor								2

Old Etonians Bowling

	O	M	R	W	O	M	R	W
Purchase				3				
Bullen				1				3
Fitzroy				3				

Umpires:

Close of Play: 1st day: .

Old Etonians had 'Brown', Bullen, Graham and Purchase as given men; MCC had Goldham, Taylor, Towell and Walker. Obviously the given men would not have batted last, as shown, but no source gives a more convincing order. The identity of 'Brown' is uncertain. W.Browning of East Malling appears sometimes as Brown but does not seem a likely candidate to have been engaged as a given man and the appearance has therefore been assigned to W.Beeston, who is known to have used Brown as an alias.

ENGLAND v HAMPSHIRE

Played at Sevenoaks Vine Cricket Club Ground, July 6, 7, 8, 1791.

England won by one wicket.

HAMPSHIRE

1	J.Walker	c Beldham	10	b Clifford	25
2	J.Small, jun	b Clifford	11	b T.Walker	37
3	T.Scott	b Clifford	0	c Aylward	39
4	James Wells	b T.Walker	1	b Clifford	11
5	Annett	b T.Walker	9	run out	1
6	R.Purchase	b T.Walker	0	c Beldham	5
7	J.Small, sen	b T.Walker	0	c T.Walker	0
8	A.Freemantle	b T.Walker	5	st Clifford	1
9	T.Taylor	not out	1	c Bullen	0
10	Collins	b T.Walker	1	c T.Walker	4
11	D.Harris	c Clifford	0	not out	0
	Byes				
			38		123

FoW (1): 1- , 2- , 3- , 4- , 5- , 6- , 7- , 8- , 9- , 10-38
FoW (2): 1- , 2- , 3- , 4- , 5- , 6- , 7- , 8- , 9- , 10-123

ENGLAND

1	John Wells	c Taylor	5	c Taylor	2
2	H.Walker	b Harris	0	b Harris	7
3	T.Walker	c Scott	9	c Scott	0
4	W.Beldham	c Taylor	0	b Purchase	0
5	J.Pilcher	c Taylor	2	c Taylor	1
6	J.Aylward	c J.Small, sen	6	c Wells	37
7	W.Fennex	b Purchase	7	c Walker	0
8	J.Ring	b Harris	3	c Scott	2
9	J.Crawte	b Harris	7	not out	46
10	R.Clifford	run out	1	not out	8
11	W.Bullen	not out	4	b Harris	9
	Byes		1		5
			45	(9 wickets)	117

FoW (1): 1- , 2- , 3- , 4- , 5- , 6- , 7- , 8- , 9- , 10-45
FoW (2): 1- , 2- , 3- , 4- , 5- , 6- , 7- , 8- , 9-102

England Bowling

	O	M	R	W	O	M	R	W
Clifford				2				2
T.Walker				6				1

Hampshire Bowling

	O	M	R	W	O	M	R	W
Harris				3				2
Purchase				1				1

Umpires:

Close of Play: 1st day: ; 2nd day: .

Hampshire had J.Walker and James Wells as given men. Collins is probably the player that appeared for Hambledon Town in 1791 (SB p125); he is likely the same Collins as appeared for Over 38 as far as on July 1810. The batting order in England (2) is not known, except that the *World* reports that Clifford came in last and was dropped by Taylor, H.Walker (assumed to be an error for J.Walker) and James Wells whilst adding 15 with Crawte to win the match.

(Variant) Some sources give the match as Surrey and Kent v Hampshire and Sussex but there are no Sussex men on the losing side. The above title is as in Britcher and SB.

HAMPSHIRE v ENGLAND

Played at Windmill Down, Hambledon, July 13, 14, 15, 1791.

England won by 60 runs.

ENGLAND

1	T.Walker	run out	22	b Purchase		21
2	J.Crawte	c Ring	10	b Purchase		0
3	H.Walker	b Taylor	9	c Purchase		0
4	J.Pilcher	c J.Small, jun	26	b Taylor		25
5	W.Beldham	run out	5	b Collins		38
6	G.Louch	b Collins	39	c Taylor		0
7	John Wells	c J.Small, sen	3	c Annett		28
8	W.Fennex	run out	5	not out		16
9	J.Walker	c Purchase	3	b Purchase		2
10	W.Bullen	not out	3	b Purchase		2
11	T.Boxall	b Taylor	11	b Taylor		11
	Byes		1			
			137			143

FoW (1): 1- , 2- , 3- , 4- , 5- , 6- , 7- , 8- , 9- , 10-137
FoW (2): 1- , 2- , 3- , 4- , 5- , 6- , 7- , 8- , 9- , 10-143

HAMPSHIRE

1	J.Small, jun	b Boxall	0	c Beldham		0
2	J.Ring	c Fennex	20	c H.Walker		4
3	J.Aylward	b Boxall	1	b T.Walker		0
4	C.Lennox	b Boxall	12	b T.Walker		22
5	T.Scott	b Boxall	3	run out		13
6	J.Small, sen	b Boxall	36	c Wells		0
7	R.Purchase	run out	19	b Boxall		3
8	T.Taylor	c Wells	1	c Wells		0
9	Annett	run out	20	not out		13
10	A.Freemantle	not out	30	run out		13
11	Collins	b Boxall	0	b Boxall		9
	Byes		1			
			143			77

FoW (1): 1- , 2- , 3- , 4- , 5- , 6- , 7- , 8- , 9- , 10-143
FoW (2): 1- , 2- , 3- , 4- , 5- , 6- , 7- , 8- , 9- , 10-77

Hampshire Bowling

	O	M	R	W	O	M	R	W
Taylor				2				2
Collins				1				1
Purchase								4

England Bowling

	O	M	R	W	O	M	R	W
Boxall				6				2
T.Walker								2

Umpires:

Close of Play: 1st day: ; 2nd day: .

Hampshire had Aylward and Ring as given men.

HAMPSHIRE v ENGLAND

Played at Perham Downs, Ludgershall, July 25, 26, 27, 28, 1791.

England won by an innings and 67 runs.

HAMPSHIRE

1	G.Leycester	c Wells	12	c Wells		7
2	J.Small, sen	c Boxall	0	run out		1
3	J.Small, jun	c Aylward	21	c H.Walker		13
4	T.Scott	b T.Walker	20	b T.Walker		37
5	R.Purchase	c Wells	6	not out		0
6	G.Louch	c Beldham	8	c Beldham		35
7	A.Freemantle	not out	5	b Fennex		28
8	T.A.Smith	b Boxall	0	b Boxall		0
9	G.Talbot	b Boxall	0	b Boxall		6
10	T.Taylor	c Beldham	5	b Boxall		0
11	W.Bullen	c H.Walker	1	c Fennex		1
	Byes		1			1
			79			129

FoW (1): 1- , 2- , 3- , 4- , 5- , 6- , 7- , 8- , 9- , 10-79
FoW (2): 1- , 2- , 3- , 4- , 5- , 6- , 7- , 8- , 9- , 10-129

ENGLAND

1	John Wells	b Purchase	11
2	H.Walker	b Bullen	37
3	W.Beldham	c Leycester	91
4	J.Aylward	c Freemantle	28
5	Earl of Winchilsea	b Purchase	15
6	C.Lennox	c Leycester	42
7	C.Anguish	b Purchase	10
8	T.Walker	run out	34
9	E.Bligh	c Taylor	4
10	W.Fennex	run out	1
11	T.Boxall	not out	0
	Byes		2
			275

FoW (1): 1- , 2- , 3- , 4- , 5- , 6- , 7- , 8- , 9- , 10-275

England Bowling

	O	M	R	W		O	M	R	W
Boxall				2					3
T.Walker				1					1
Fennex									1

Hampshire Bowling

	O	M	R	W
Bullen				1
Purchase				3

Umpires:

Close of Play: 1st day: ; 2nd day: ; 3rd day: .

Buckley notes a report in the *Salisbury Journal* that Bullen (a Kent man) replaced D.Harris in the Hampshire team.

HORNCHURCH v M.C.C.

Played at Langton Park, Hornchurch, August 11, 12, 13, 1791.

M.C.C. won by 166 runs.

M.C.C.

1	Earl of Winchilsea	c Boorman	13	c Wyatt	0
2	E.Bligh	c Wyatt	32	b Boorman	3
3	H.W.Fitzroy	run out	21	b Wyatt	89
4	C.Lennox	c Allen	28	b Ingram	40
5	T.A.Smith	b Wyatt	7	c Ingram	29
6	C.Anguish	c Littler	8	b Wyatt	0
7	W.A.Harbord	c Ingram	3	c Carr	1
8	G.Louch	b Littler	1	c Ingram	16
9	C.Cumberland	c Littler	15	c Russell	0
10	G.Talbot	not out	11	not out	7
11	T.Walker	b Wyatt	5	b Boorman	9
	Byes		3		2
			147		196

FoW (1): 1- , 2- , 3- , 4- , 5- , 6- , 7- , 8- , 9- , 10-147
FoW (2): 1- , 2- , 3- , 4- , 5- , 6- , 7- , 8- , 9- , 10-196

HORNCHURCH

1	R.B.Wyatt	b Cumberland	0	c Lennox	2
2	J.Russell	c Winchilsea	4	b Cumberland	12
3	R.Denn	c Louch	3	b Walker	0
4	W.Oxley	c Smith	5	not out	3
5	Carr	c Lennox	31	c Bligh	0
6	J.Stevens	b Cumberland	45	c Smith	0
7	W.Allen	b Cumberland	4	run out	0
8	T.Ingram	c Winchilsea	11	b Walker	2
9	J.Boorman	c Louch	4	b Walker	9
10	J.Goulstone	b Walker	13	c Smith	12
11	J.Littler	not out	0	b Cumberland	2
	Byes		4		11
			124		53

FoW (1): 1- , 2- , 3- , 4- , 5- , 6- , 7- , 8- , 9- , 10-124
FoW (2): 1- , 2- , 3- , 4- , 5- , 6- , 7- , 8- , 9- , 10-53

Hornchurch Bowling

	O	M	R	W	O	M	R	W
Wyatt				2				2
Littler				1				
Boorman								2
Ingram								1

M.C.C. Bowling

	O	M	R	W	O	M	R	W
Cumberland				3				2
Walker				1				3

Umpires:

Close of Play: 1st day: ; 2nd day: .

Littler is assumed to be J.Littler, although there was a T.Littler also associated with Hornchurch.

M.C.C. v KENT

Played at Lord's Old Ground, Marylebone, August 15, 16, 17, 18, 1791.

Kent won by five wickets.

M.C.C.
1	W.Beldham	c Amherst	36	b Boxall	59
2	J.Small, jun	b Clifford	5	run out	15
3	T.Walker	b Boxall	3	c Bullen	32
4	T.Scott	b Crawte	13	c Amherst	5
5	C.Lennox	c Bullen	4	b Clifford	5
6	Earl of Winchilsea	b Boxall	2	b Ring	0
7	H.W.Fitzroy	c Pilcher	12	c Crawte	6
8	R.Purchase	b Clifford	7	c Clifford	19
9	G.Louch	run out	25	b Boxall	1
10	C.Cumberland	not out	2	not out	0
11	T.A.Smith	b Clifford	6	c Freemantle	3
	Byes		2		2
			117		147

FoW (1): 1- , 2- , 3- , 4- , 5- , 6- , 7- , 8- , 9- , 10-117
FoW (2): 1- , 2- , 3- , 4- , 5- , 6- , 7-138, 8- , 9- , 10-147

KENT
1	A.Freemantle	b Beldham	39	b Beldham	17
2	J.Ring	run out	1	not out	61
3	J.Crawte	c Purchase	2	c Scott	5
4	J.Pilcher	c Beldham	34	b Purchase	3
5	Goodhew	b Walker	1	b Purchase	15
6	J.Aylward	c Scott	13	run out	17
7	S.Amherst	c Beldham	18		
8	E.Bligh	c Small	7	not out	14
9	T.Boxall	c Scott	1		
10	W.Bullen	not out	10		
11	R.Clifford	b Walker	0		
	Byes		1		6
			127	(5 wickets)	138

FoW (1): 1- , 2- , 3- , 4- , 5- , 6- , 7- , 8- , 9- , 10-127
FoW (2): 1- , 2- , 3- , 4- , 5-

Kent Bowling
	O	M	R	W	O	M	R	W
Clifford				3				1
Boxall				2				2
Crawte				1				
Ring								1

M.C.C. Bowling
	O	M	R	W	O	M	R	W
Beldham				1				1
Walker				2				
Purchase								2

Umpires:

Close of Play: 1st day: ; 2nd day: ; 3rd day: M.C.C. (2) 138-7 (Purchase 16*).

MCC had Beldham, Purchase, Scott, Small and Walker as given men; Kent had Freemantle as a given man. In MCC (2), Winchilsea, Fitzroy and Cumberland were the players yet to bat at the close of day 3.

161

SURREY v HAMPSHIRE

Played at Holt Pound Cricket Ground, Wrecclesham, August 23, 24, 25, 1791.

Surrey won by 17 runs.

SURREY

1	Earl of Winchilsea	hit wkt		4	run out	0
2	C.Anguish	c Lennox		0	b Collins	7
3	W.A.Harbord	b Collins		0	not out	0
4	G.Louch	b Collins		9	c Collins	6
5	G.Leycester	not out		20	run out	6
6	T.Walker	c Scott		0	c Bligh	16
7	H.Walker	b Taylor		2	c Taylor	32
8	J.Walker	b Taylor		14	c Lennox	1
9	John Wells	b Purchase		19	c Taylor	11
10	James Wells	c Small		2	b Purchase	12
11	W.Beldham	b Purchase		9	c Smith	17
	Byes			10		4
				89		112

FoW (1): 1- , 2- , 3- , 4- , 5- , 6- , 7- , 8- , 9- , 10-89
FoW (2): 1- , 2- , 3- , 4- , 5- , 6- , 7- , 8- , 9- , 10-112

HAMPSHIRE

1	E.Bligh	c John Wells		19	c Beldham	3
2	C.Lennox	c Louch		3	b John Wells	8
3	H.W.Fitzroy	b John Wells		1	b John Wells	11
4	T.A.Smith	b John Wells		5	b T.Walker	8
5	T.Scott	b John Wells		3	b T.Walker	9
6	G.Talbot	c H.Walker		0	not out	14
7	A.Freemantle	c Louch		11	b T.Walker	2
8	J.Small, jun	c Leycester		47	c Beldham	7
9	R.Purchase	b John Wells		8	c James Wells	7
10	T.Taylor	c John Wells		2	run out	4
11	Collins	not out		0	c Louch	2
	Byes			7		3
				106		78

FoW (1): 1- , 2- , 3- , 4- , 5- , 6- , 7- , 8- , 9- , 10-106
FoW (2): 1- , 2- , 3- , 4- , 5- , 6- , 7- , 8- , 9- , 10-78

Hampshire Bowling

	O	M	R	W		O	M	R	W
Purchase				2					1
Collins				2					1
Taylor				2					

Surrey Bowling

	O	M	R	W		O	M	R	W
John Wells				4					2
T.Walker									3

Umpires:

Close of Play: 1st day: ; 2nd day: .

BRIGHTON v MIDDLESEX

Played at Prince of Wales Ground, Brighton, September 19, 20, 21, 22, 1791.

Middlesex won by 21 runs.

MIDDLESEX

1	E.Bligh	run out	9	b Hammond		3
2	J.Goldham	b Hammond	8	b Hammond		3
3	W.Bedster	c Hammond	0	b Streeter		5
4	W.Fennex	b Hammond	90	c Hammond		0
5	T.Lord	b Hammond	6	c Hammond		17
6	G.Louch	b Hammond	6	b Streeter		6
7	Butler	c Jutten	50	b Hammond		13
8	H.W.Fitzroy	run out	10	not out		11
9	H.H.Aston	b Streeter	3	c Jutten		4
10	Cantrell	b Hammond	2	b Hammond		20
11	R.Turner	not out	3	b Hammond		6
	Byes		10			
			197			88

FoW (1): 1- , 2- , 3- , 4- , 5- , 6- , 7- , 8- , 9- , 10-197
FoW (2): 1- , 2- , 3- , 4- , 5- , 6- , 7- , 8- , 9- , 10-88

BRIGHTON

1	T.Liffen	b Fennex	9	c Aston		4
2	Hyde	run out	9	b Lord		5
3	Lord Barrymore	c Fennex	0	c Louch		0
4	W.Bowra	not out	12	run out		20
5	J.Marchant	b Fennex	36	c Fennex		20
6	E.Streeter	c Bligh	3	b Lord		1
7	P.Vallance	b Fennex	39	c Butler		5
8	J.Hammond	b Fennex	0	c Butler		50
9	Gregory	b Lord	0	run out		1
10	T.Jutten	b Lord	0	c Louch		23
11	J.Vallance	b Fennex	3	not out		10
	Byes		5			9
			116			148

FoW (1): 1- , 2- , 3- , 4- , 5- , 6- , 7- , 8- , 9- , 10-116
FoW (2): 1- , 2- , 3- , 4- , 5- , 6- , 7- , 8- , 9- , 10-148

Brighton Bowling

	O	M	R	W	O	M	R	W
Hammond				5				5
Streeter				1				2

Middlesex Bowling

	O	M	R	W	O	M	R	W
Fennex				5				
Lord				2				2

Umpires:

Close of Play: 1st day: ; 2nd day: ; 3rd day: .

W.Bowra retired hurt in the Brighton first innings having scored 1 and later returned (bruised left hand).

M.C.C. v MIDDLESEX

Played at Lord's Old Ground, Marylebone, May 7, 8, 9, 1792.

M.C.C. won by 274 runs.

M.C.C.

1	E.Bligh	b Fennex	0	st Amherst		40
2	W.Beldham	c Goldham	13	b Bedster		144
3	Earl of Winchilsea	c Cantrell	11	b Lord		28
4	T.Ingram	b Turner	3	b Bedster		4
5	G.Louch	b Fennex	11	c Turner		40
6	J.L.Kaye	b Turner	3	b Fennex		1
7	T.A.Smith	b Lord	15	c Boult		0
8	T.Walker	c Bedster	107	b Bedster		0
9	R.Brudenell	b Fennex	0	not out		0
10	G.Dehany	b Fennex	0	c Lord		30
11	A.Pitcairn	not out	18	c Amherst		9
	Byes		12			10
			193			306

FoW (1): 1- , 2- , 3- , 4- , 5- , 6- , 7- , 8- , 9- , 10-193
FoW (2): 1- , 2- , 3- , 4- , 5- , 6- , 7- , 8- , 9- , 10-306

MIDDLESEX

1	N.Graham	b Walker	6	st Bligh		5
2	Butler	b Walker	6	c Brudenell		8
3	W.Bedster	b Walker	3	c Beldham		3
4	W.Fennex	not out	60	c Bligh		6
5	T.Lord	b Beldham	1	b Beldham		12
6	G.T.Boult	c Louch	14	st Bligh		13
7	S.Amherst	b Beldham	0	hit wkt		16
8	Dale	c Kaye	4	not out		8
9	J.Goldham	run out	1	c Bligh		13
10	Cantrell	c Bligh	5	b Walker		10
11	R.Turner	c Kaye	10	c Kaye		16
	Byes		1			4
			111			114

FoW (1): 1- , 2- , 3- , 4- , 5- , 6- , 7- , 8- , 9- , 10-111
FoW (2): 1- , 2- , 3- , 4- , 5- , 6- , 7- , 8- , 9- , 10-114

Middlesex Bowling

	O	M	R	W	O	M	R	W
Fennex				4				1
Lord				1				1
Turner				2				
Bedster								3

M.C.C. Bowling

	O	M	R	W	O	M	R	W
Beldham				2				1
Walker				3				1

Umpires:

Close of Play: 1st day: ; 2nd day: .

MCC had Beldham and Walker as given men. The score is from the *Gazetteer & New Daily Advertiser*, signed 'S Britcher'. The batting order it gives for MCC is in order of first-innings dismissal and shows Walker at 8 although he scored 107 of a total of 193. Since he was known as a slow scorer, this very strongly suggests that he opened. At any rate, the order above is a great improvement on the version in SB, which has century-makers Beldham and Walker listed last because they were given men.

(Variant) SB and Bentley indicate one of the MCC team by a dash but other soutces confirm the missing name as T.Ingram. Also, SB has the Earl of Darnley in place of Brudenell.

M.C.C. v MIDDLESEX

Played at Lord's Old Ground, Marylebone, May 15, 16, 17, 1792.

Middlesex won by 5 runs.

MIDDLESEX

1	T.Lord	run out		49	b Walker	2
2	J.Goldham	b Beldham		1	b Walker	41
3	W.Fennex	st Bligh		3	st Bligh	15
4	W.White	c Dehany		0	c Winchilsea	9
5	Grange	b Beldham		4	b Walker	11
6	W.Bedster	c Louch		14	st Bligh	5
7	R.Turner	b Walker		1	b Beldham	3
8	Butler	c Winchilsea		4	b Beldham	3
9	N.Graham	b Beldham		2	b Beldham	1
10	Dale	not out		15	not out	13
11	Cantrell	run out		7	b Walker	44
	Byes			1		1
				101		148

FoW (1): 1- , 2- , 3- , 4- , 5- , 6- , 7- , 8- , 9- , 10-101
FoW (2): 1- , 2- , 3- , 4- , 5- , 6- , 7- , 8- , 9- , 10-148

M.C.C.

1	Earl of Winchilsea	b Lord		14	b Bedster	12
2	Lord Strathavon	not out		0	not out	12
3	E.Bligh	b Lord		14	b Bedster	64
4	T.A.Smith	b Lord		2	c Cantrell	2
5	E.Husscy	b Lord		4	b Lord	19
6	G.Dehany	c Fennex		9	b Lord	9
7	G.Louch	c Lord		4	b Fennex	4
8	R.Welch	b Fennex		0	run out	5
9	R.Stewart	b Lord		3	b Fennex	0
10	W.Beldham	b Lord		11	b Bedster	11
11	T.Walker	run out		35	run out	5
	Byes					5
				96		148

FoW (1): 1- , 2- , 3- , 4- , 5- , 6- , 7- , 8- , 9- , 10-96
FoW (2): 1- , 2- , 3- , 4- , 5- , 6- , 7- , 8- , 9- , 10-148

M.C.C. Bowling

	O	M	R	W		O	M	R	W
Beldham				3					3
Walker				1					4

Middlesex Bowling

	O	M	R	W		O	M	R	W
Lord				6					2
Fennex				1					2
Bedster									3

Umpires:

Close of Play: 1st day: ; 2nd day: .

MCC had Beldham and Walker as given men. As such, they are listed last in the order in all sources.

(Variant) SB has Granger appearing in place of Grange.

E.BLIGH'S XI v EARL OF WINCHILSEA'S XI

Played at Lord's Old Ground, Marylebone, May 21, 22, 1792.

Earl of Winchilsea's XI won by eight wickets.

E.BLIGH'S XI

1	E.Bligh	c Bedster	0	b Walker	2
2	T.A.Smith	c Wells	9	b Walker	3
3	W.Beldham	b Harris	20	b Harris	18
4	W.Fennex	c Walker	17	b Harris	4
5	T.Boxall	b Walker	16	c Fitzroy	16
6	G.Louch	run out	25	c Bedster	2
7	Butler	c Graham	2	b Harris	6
8	H.H.Aston	c Walker	5	b Walker	0
9	R.Turner	b Harris	2	not out	2
10	J.Boorman	b Walker	11	b Harris	2
11	Sylvester	not out	2	b Harris	0
	Byes		1		
			110		55

FoW (1): 1- , 2- , 3- , 4- , 5- , 6- , 7- , 8- , 9- , 10-110
FoW (2): 1- , 2- , 3- , 4- , 5- , 6- , 7- , 8- , 9- , 10-55

EARL OF WINCHILSEA'S XI

1	Earl of Winchilsea	c Boxall	16	b Boxall	10
2	E.Hussey	b Beldham	8	run out	7
3	John Wells	b Boxall	34	not out	7
4	H.W.Fitzroy	b Boxall	1		
5	T.Walker	run out	13	not out	23
6	W.Bedster	b Fennex	20		
7	N.Graham	b Boxall	0		
8	R.Welch	b Fennex	0		
9	R.Brudenell	b Boxall	0		
10	T.Lord	not out	22		
11	D.Harris	b Boxall	0		
	Byes		1		4
			115	(2 wickets)	51

FoW (1): 1- , 2- , 3- , 4- , 5- , 6- , 7- , 8- , 9- , 10-115
FoW (2): 1- , 2-

Earl of Winchilsea's XI Bowling

	O	M	R	W		O	M	R	W
Harris				2					5
Walker				2					3

E.Bligh's XI Bowling

	O	M	R	W		O	M	R	W
Boxall				5					1
Beldham				1					
Fennex				2					

Umpires:

Close of Play: 1st day: .

M.C.C. v BRIGHTON
Played at Lord's Old Ground, Marylebone, May 28, 29, 30, 1792.

Brighton won by nine wickets.

M.C.C.

1	W.Bedster	c J.Vallance	10	not out	36
2	W.Fennex	run out	38	run out	2
3	E.Bligh	c Marchant	43	b Hammond	16
4	G.Louch	b Hammond	8	c Liffen	20
5	T.Lord	b Jutten	11	c Hammond	1
6	Butler	b Jutten	0	c Marchant	0
7	T.A.Smith	run out	1	b Hammond	1
8	Earl of Winchilsea	b Liffen	39	b Hammond	10
9	A.Pitcairn	run out	14	b Hammond	13
10	H.H.Aston	not out	5	b Hammond	0
11	H.W.Fitzroy	b Hammond	9	b Hammond	4
	Byes		2		2
			180		105

FoW (1): 1- , 2- , 3- , 4- , 5- , 6- , 7- , 8- , 9- , 10-180
FoW (2): 1- , 2- , 3- , 4- , 5- , 6- , 7- , 8- , 9- , 10-105

BRIGHTON

1	T.Jutten	b Lord	4		
2	P.Vallance	b Lord	0	not out	68
3	Gregory	b Bedster	24		
4	J.Hammond	b Lord	34		
5	W.Bowra	b Bedster	17	not out	60
6	J.Marchant	b Bedster	16	b Lord	1
7	T.Liffen	b Bedster	15		
8	J.Vallance	c Lord	17		
9	E.Streeter	b Lord	0		
10	Lord Barrymore	not out	1		
11	Hart	c Aston	26		
	Byes		1		2
			155	(1 wicket)	131

FoW (1): 1- , 2- , 3- , 4- , 5- , 6- , 7- , 8- , 9- , 10-155
FoW (2): 1- (1)

Brighton Bowling

	O	M	R	W	O	M	R	W
Hammond				2				6
Jutten				2				
Liffen				1				

M.C.C. Bowling

	O	M	R	W	O	M	R	W
Lord				4				1
Bedster				4				

Umpires:

Close of Play: 1st day: ; 2nd day: .

MCC had four given men from Middlesex.

M.C.C. v BERKSHIRE

Played at Lord's Old Ground, Marylebone, May 31, June 1, 1792.

M.C.C. won by 7 runs.

M.C.C.
1	Earl of Winchilsea	c Thompson	1	b Monk		5
2	E.Bligh	b Thompson	27	c East		38
3	H.W.Fitzroy	run out	20	c East		8
4	H.H.Aston	b Monk	1	not out		8
5	T.A.Smith	b Monk	19	c Sale		0
6	G.Louch	b Thompson	1	b Monk		10
7	A.Pitcairn	run out	10	b Quarme		20
8	J.L.Kaye	c Lawrence	0	b Monk		5
9	Sir G.Wombwell	not out	0	run out		19
10	Blunt	b Monk	0	c East		0
11	T.Lord	c Quarme	5	c Thompson		7
	Byes					3
			84			123

FoW (1): 1- , 2- , 3- , 4- , 5- , 6- , 7- , 8- , 9- , 10-84
FoW (2): 1- , 2- , 3- , 4- , 5- , 6- , 7- , 8- , 9- , 10-123

BERKSHIRE
1	G.East	c Lord	12	b Fitzroy		1
2	R.Quarme	b Lord	0	c Aston		1
3	Sale	b Lord	6	c Kaye		3
4	T.Ray	b Lord	3	c Winchilsea		10
5	S.Gill	st Bligh	0	b Fitzroy		3
6	J.Finch	b Lord	13	b Lord		11
7	Thompson	b Lord	7	run out		8
8	N.Graham	b Winchilsea	0	b Fitzroy		3
9	R.Lawrence	b Lord	31	c Louch		25
10	Monk	b Winchilsea	19	b Lord		31
11	Timber	not out	3	not out		5
	Byes		2			3
			96			104

FoW (1): 1- , 2- , 3- , 4- , 5- , 6- , 7- , 8- , 9- , 10-96
FoW (2): 1- , 2- , 3- , 4- , 5- , 6- , 7- , 8- , 9- , 10-104

Berkshire Bowling

	O	M	R	W	O	M	R	W
Thompson				2				
Monk				3				3
Quarme								1

M.C.C. Bowling

	O	M	R	W	O	M	R	W
Lord				6				2
Winchilsea				2				
Fitzroy								3

Umpires:

Close of Play: 1st day: .

M.C.C. v ENGLAND

Played at Lord's Old Ground, Marylebone, June 6, 7, 8, 1792.

M.C.C. won by an innings and 10 runs.

ENGLAND

1	W.Fennex	run out	15	c Wells		0
2	H.Walker	hit wkt	17	hit wkt		35
3	J.Aylward	b Harris	1	c Beldham		16
4	J.Pilcher	c Beldham	0	b Harris		1
5	A.Freemantle	b Harris	7	not out		35
6	R.Purchase	c Winchilsea	7	c Winchilsea		12
7	J.Crawte	c Beldham	4	c Wells		4
8	W.Bedster	b Walker	1	c Beldham		2
9	T.Boxall	not out	3	b Walker		0
10	T.Taylor	c Louch	0	c Goldham		23
11	R.Clifford	run out	2	c Walker		6
	Byes					3
			57			137

FoW (1): 1- , 2- , 3- , 4- , 5- , 6- , 7- , 8- , 9- , 10-57
FoW (2): 1- , 2- , 3- , 4- , 5- , 6- , 7- , 8- , 9- , 10-137

M.C.C.

1	Earl of Winchilsea	c Walker	54
2	E.Bligh	b Boxall	0
3	H.W.Fitzroy	b Clifford	15
4	T.A.Smith	c Aylward	0
5	G.Louch	c Purchase	2
6	J.Goldham	run out	2
7	D.Harris	not out	11
8	W.Beldham	b Boxall	29
9	T.Walker	c Bedster	22
10	John Wells	b Boxall	63
11	J.Small, jun	c Taylor	0
	Byes		6
			204

FoW (1): 1- , 2- , 3- , 4- , 5- , 6- , 7- , 8- , 9- , 10-204

M.C.C. Bowling

	O	M	R	W	O	M	R	W
Harris				2				1
Walker				1				1

England Bowling

	O	M	R	W
Boxall				3
Clifford				1

Umpires:

Close of Play: 1st day: ; 2nd day: .

MCC had Beldham, Harris, Small, Walker and Wells as given men. They are listed last in the order.

ENGLAND v KENT

Played at Lord's Old Ground, Marylebone, June 21, 22, 23, 1792.

England won by 10 runs.

ENGLAND
1	T.Walker	c Beldham	3	c Beldham		10
2	W.Fennex	c Beldham	2	c Beldham		6
3	John Wells	c Beldham	6	c Bligh		9
4	H.Walker	b Harris	46	b Harris		1
5	A.Freemantle	b Harris	6	not out		15
6	Earl of Winchilsea	c Ring	16	b Boxall		15
7	R.Purchase	b Harris	0	c Louch		1
8	J.Hammond	b Beldham	1	c Beldham		0
9	H.W.Fitzroy	b Beldham	0	c Louch		0
10	J.Small, jun	not out	22	c Beldham		0
11	H.H.Aston	c Boxall	0	b Boxall		9
	Byes		1			2
			103			68

FoW (1): 1- , 2- , 3- , 4- , 5- , 6- , 7- , 8- , 9- , 10-103
FoW (2): 1- , 2- , 3- , 4- , 5- , 6- , 7- , 8- , 9- , 10-68

KENT
1	R.Fielder	run out	0	c Wells		9
2	J.Crawte	b T.Walker	3	run out		0
3	W.Beldham	c Fennex	16	b Hammond		14
4	E.Bligh	c Wells	5	c T.Walker		17
5	J.Ring	c Wells	0	c Fitzroy		9
6	J.Aylward	c Wells	9	c Fennex		22
7	S.Amherst	c T.Walker	1	not out		8
8	Earl of Darnley	b T.Walker	0	b Hammond		0
9	G.Louch	c Aston	23	b T.Walker		5
10	T.Boxall	not out	6	c Fennex		7
11	D.Harris	b T.Walker	2	b T.Walker		4
	Byes					1
			65			96

FoW (1): 1- , 2- , 3- , 4- , 5- , 6- , 7- , 8- , 9- , 10-65
FoW (2): 1- , 2- , 3- , 4- , 5- , 6- , 7- , 8- , 9- , 10-96

Kent Bowling
	O	M	R	W	O	M	R	W
Harris				3				1
Beldham				2				
Boxall								2

England Bowling
	O	M	R	W	O	M	R	W
T.Walker				3				2
Hammond								2

Umpires:

Close of Play: 1st day: ; 2nd day: .

Kent had Beldham and Harris as given men.

EARL OF WINCHILSEA'S XI v T.A.SMITH'S XI

Played at The Park, Burley-on-the-Hill, July 2, 3, 4, 1792.

T.A.Smith's XI won by 75 runs.

T.A.SMITH'S XI

1	W.Fennex	c Graham	0	c Bligh	55
2	R.Purchase	c Beldham	4	b Wells	61
3	J.Small, sen	c Beldham	3	b T.Walker	3
4	A.Freemantle	b T.Walker	21	c Beldham	5
5	T.Taylor	c Wells	2	not out	3
6	G.Louch	b Wells	1	c Beldham	17
7	A.Pitcairn	hit wkt	4	b Wells	0
8	T.A.Smith	c Beldham	12	c Monson	12
9	T.Boxall	c Beldham	0	c T.Walker	9
10	Viscount Milsington	run out	1	b Wells	0
11	J.Small, jun	not out	37	run out	35
	Byes		2		4
			87		204

FoW (1): 1- , 2- , 3- , 4- , 5- , 6- , 7- , 8- , 9- , 10-87
FoW (2): 1- , 2- , 3- , 4- , 5- , 6- , 7- , 8- , 9- , 10-204

EARL OF WINCHILSEA'S XI

1	E.Bligh	c Purchase	2	b Purchase	17
2	W.Beldham	b Purchase	11	b Boxall	51
3	H.Walker	run out	0	c Louch	0
4	John Wells	c Boxall	11	c J.Small, sen	12
5	T.Walker	c Boxall	27	b Taylor	30
6	W.Bedster	c Taylor	0	not out	2
7	Earl of Winchilsea	b Boxall	25	run out	4
8	J.Goldham	b Boxall	0	b Purchase	1
9	G.H.Monson	c Taylor	9	run out	7
10	N.Graham	not out	0	c Purchase	1
11	H.W.Fitzroy	b Boxall	3	b Purchase	1
	Byes				3
			88		128

FoW (1): 1- , 2- , 3- , 4- , 5- , 6- , 7- , 8- , 9- , 10-88
FoW (2): 1- , 2- , 3- , 4- , 5- , 6- , 7- , 8- , 9- , 10-128

Earl of Winchilsea's XI Bowling

	O	M	R	W	O	M	R	W
Wells				1				3
T.Walker				1				1

T.A.Smith's XI Bowling

	O	M	R	W	O	M	R	W
Boxall				3				1
Purchase				1				3
Taylor								1

Umpires:

Close of Play: 1st day: ; 2nd day: .

The teams are listed in dismissal order: obviously Small, jun came in much higher than 11. Other sources call the match 'Smith with 4 of Hants v Winchilsea with 4 of Surrey' (Britcher) or 'England (bar Kent) v Hants' (*Lincolnshire, Rutland and Stamford Mercury*, the local newspaper). Both are reasonable descriptions and indicate how fluid and uncertain match titles can be. In view of the lack of consensus the title has been left as above.

HAMPSHIRE v SURREY

Played at Windmill Down, Hambledon, July 16, 17, 18, 1792.

Hampshire won by 127 runs.

HAMPSHIRE

1	E.Bligh	c Monson	1	c J.Walker	15
2	T.A.Smith	not out	2	not out	4
3	E.Hale	c John Wells	2	c Louch	8
4	J.Neale	b Beldham	13	b Beldham	17
5	Collins	b John Wells	6	b T.Walker	0
6	J.Small, jun	c John Wells	42	c Louch	35
7	A.Freemantle	hit wkt	37	b Beldham	58
8	T.Scott	b T.Walker	12	b T.Walker	1
9	R.Purchase	b T.Walker	14	b T.Walker	1
10	J.Small, sen	c John Wells	3	b T.Walker	8
11	T.Taylor	c Beldham	6	c John Wells	8
	Byes		2		3
			140		158

FoW (1): 1- , 2- , 3- , 4- , 5- , 6- , 7- , 8- , 9- , 10-140
FoW (2): 1- , 2- , 3- , 4- , 5- , 6- , 7- , 8- , 9- , 10-158

SURREY

1	G.H.Monson	c Purchase	19	b Taylor	4
2	G.Louch	b Collins	0	c Taylor	18
3	J.Walker	b Purchase	3	b Purchase	7
4	H.Walker	b Collins	1	b Taylor	6
5	John Wells	c Scott	13	b Purchase	10
6	W.Beldham	c Purchase	0	b Taylor	3
7	T.Walker	b Purchase	28	c Scott	13
8	Annett	c Taylor	4	b Purchase	1
9	James Wells	b Purchase	8	b Purchase	10
10	J.Goldsmith	not out	3	b Taylor	8
11	J.Harding	b Taylor	7	not out	0
	Byes		1		4
			87		84

FoW (1): 1- , 2- , 3- , 4- , 5- , 6- , 7- , 8- , 9- , 10-87
FoW (2): 1- , 2- , 3- , 4- , 5- , 6- , 7- , 8- , 9- , 10-84

Surrey Bowling

	O	M	R	W	O	M	R	W
Beldham				1				2
T.Walker				2				4
John Wells				1				

Hampshire Bowling

	O	M	R	W	O	M	R	W
Purchase				3				4
Taylor				1				4
Collins				2				

Umpires:

Close of Play: 1st day: ; 2nd day: .

J.Goldsmith is not a Surrey man but is local to Hambledon; presumably Surrey arrived a man short.

HAMPSHIRE v SURREY

Played at Perham Downs, Ludgershall, July 23, 24, 25, 26, 1792.

Surrey won by 109 runs.

SURREY
1	Earl of Winchilsea	c Fennex	7	c Taylor		22
2	E.Bligh	c Harris	9	b Harris		10
3	H.W.Fitzroy	run out	0	run out		0
4	G.H.Monson	not out	40	b Fennex		20
5	T.Walker	c Harris	58	run out		48
6	H.Walker	b Harris	10	b Purchase		9
7	John Wells	b Purchase	9	b Harris		4
8	W.Beldham	b Taylor	15	b Purchase		11
9	W.Bedster	b Harris	0	c Fennex		11
10	T.Ingram	b Harris	17	not out		3
11	T.Boxall	b Harris	0	b Harris		2
	Byes		4			
			169			140

FoW (1): 1- , 2- , 3- , 4- , 5- , 6- , 7- , 8- , 9- , 10-169
FoW (2): 1- , 2- , 3- , 4- , 5- , 6- , 7- , 8- , 9- , 10-140

HAMPSHIRE
1	T.A.Smith	run out	0	c Beldham		0
2	H.H.Aston	b T.Walker	0	b Boxall		5
3	A.Pitcairn	b Boxall	2	b Boxall		2
4	J.Small, jun	c Monson	27	b Boxall		2
5	W.Fennex	c Boxall	17	c Boxall		55
6	A.Freemantle	c Beldham	8	b Boxall		20
7	J.Small, sen	not out	10	not out		16
8	R.Purchase	run out	0	run out		10
9	T.Taylor	c Monson	3	b Boxall		4
10	Mundy	b T.Walker	0	c Fitzroy		4
11	D.Harris	c Monson	0	b T.Walker		12
	Byes					3
			67			133

FoW (1): 1- , 2- , 3- , 4- , 5- , 6- , 7- , 8- , 9- , 10-67
FoW (2): 1- , 2- , 3- , 4- , 5- , 6- , 7- , 8- , 9- , 10-133

Hampshire Bowling
	O	M	R	W	O	M	R	W
Harris				4				3
Purchase				1				2
Taylor				1				
Fennex								1

Surrey Bowling
	O	M	R	W	O	M	R	W
Boxall				1				5
T.Walker				2				1

Umpires:

Close of Play: 1st day: ; 2nd day: ; 3rd day: .

Mundy of Andover.

BERKSHIRE v M.C.C.

Played at Old Field, Bray, August 2, 3, 4, 1792.

Berkshire won by 10 runs.

BERKSHIRE

1	G.East	b Lord	7	b Dupuis		4
2	R.Quarme	c Monson	4	b Dupuis		2
3	Sale	c Monson	4	not out		0
4	S.Gill	b Lord	0	b Lord		20
5	Monk	c Fitzroy	0	b Dupuis		6
6	J.Finch	b Nicoll	59	b Lord		13
7	T.Shackle	c Leycester	15	c Monson		23
8	R.Lawrence	b Lord	2	c Winchilsea		14
9	Thompson	b Lord	1	c Lord		6
10	T.Ray	b Dupuis	20	b Dupuis		40
11	T.Lloyd	not out	1	b Lord		9
	Byes		3			9
			116			146

FoW (1): 1- , 2- , 3- , 4- , 5- , 6- , 7- , 8- , 9- , 10-116
FoW (2): 1- , 2- , 3- , 4- , 5- , 6- , 7- , 8- , 9- , 10-146

M.C.C.

1	E.Bligh	c Gill	5	b Monk		6
2	G.Leycester	b Monk	2	c Gill		15
3	T.A.Smith	b Thompson	9	not out		16
4	G.H.Monson	c Monk	14	b Monk		55
5	A.Pitcairn	c Monk	1	hit wkt		1
6	G.Dupuis	c East	4	b Thompson		0
7	T.V.R.Nicoll	run out	2	run out		5
8	H.H.Aston	b East	14	run out		2
9	Earl of Winchilsea	not out	3	b Monk		9
10	H.W.Fitzroy	b East	3	c Gill		6
11	T.Lord	run out	31	b Thompson		36
	Byes		9			4
			97			155

FoW (1): 1- , 2- , 3- , 4- , 5- , 6- , 7- , 8- , 9- , 10-97
FoW (2): 1- , 2- , 3- , 4- , 5- , 6- , 7- , 8- , 9- , 10-155

M.C.C. Bowling

	O	M	R	W	O	M	R	W
Lord				4				3
Dupuis				1				4
Nicoll				1				

Berkshire Bowling

	O	M	R	W	O	M	R	W
Monk				1				3
East				2				
Thompson				1				2

Umpires:

Close of Play: 1st day: ; 2nd day: .

The batting order is from the *Star* and is preferable to that in SB, although both have Lord, as the professional, implausibly listed last. SB and many other sources give the venue as Oldfield Bray, as if 'Bray' were part of the name of the ground. John Goulstone has established that it was Old Field, Bray. That is, the ground was located in the parish of Bray, which in the 18th century included the southern half of the town of Maidenhead, where the Oldfield Club was based. Not until 1894 was Maidenhead created as a separate parish.

KENT v HAMPSHIRE

Played at Cobham Park, August 15, 16, 17, 1792.

Hampshire won by eight wickets.

KENT

1	T.Walker	b Harris	0	b Purchase		16
2	John Wells	b Harris	4	c Taylor		1
3	W.Beldham	b Purchase	25	b Harris		14
4	E.Bligh	b Purchase	2	b Harris		0
5	R.Fielder	b Harris	5	b Harris		6
6	J.Crawte	b Harris	10	c Monson		5
7	Earl of Darnley	b Harris	0	c Purchase		5
8	T.Boxall	b Harris	3	not out		3
9	J.Ring	b Harris	16	run out		3
10	G.Louch	not out	15	c Purchase		3
11	S.Amherst	b Harris	0	run out		0
	Byes					1
			80			57

FoW (1): 1- , 2- , 3- , 4- , 5- , 6- , 7- , 8- , 9- , 10-80
FoW (2): 1- , 2- , 3- , 4- , 5- , 6- , 7- , 8- , 9- , 10-57

HAMPSHIRE

1	G.H.Monson	c Walker	0	b Walker		10
2	H.Walker	b Boxall	0			
3	H.W.Fitzroy	c Louch	19			
4	T.Taylor	c Beldham	10			
5	J.Small, jun	c Wells	6			
6	T.Scott	c Louch	10			
7	A.Freemantle	c Fielder	21	not out		7
8	Earl of Winchilsea	b Beldham	8	run out		5
9	R.Purchase	c Beldham	26			
10	H.H.Aston	b Boxall	0	not out		15
11	D.Harris	not out	0			
	Byes					1
			100	(2 wickets)		38

FoW (1): 1- , 2- , 3- , 4- , 5- , 6- , 7- , 8- , 9- , 10-100
FoW (2): 1- , 2-

Hampshire Bowling

	O	M	R	W	O	M	R	W
Harris				8				3
Purchase				2				1

Kent Bowling

	O	M	R	W	O	M	R	W
Boxall				2				
Beldham				1				
Walker								1

Umpires:

Close of Play: 1st day: ; 2nd day: .

Britcher calls the match 'Darnley v Winchilsea with 3 gentlemen and 7 picked men on each side', but the above title seems a reasonable reflection of the teams. On this basis, Beldham, T.Walker and Wells will have been given men for Kent and H.Walker for Hampshire.

BRIGHTON v M.C.C.

Played at Prince of Wales Ground, Brighton, August 20, 21, 22, 23, 1792.

Brighton won by three wickets.

M.C.C.
1	G.H.Monson	b Boxall	0	b Boxall		4
2	H.H.Aston	b Hammond	0	not out		2
3	E.Hussey	c Hammond	0	b Hammond		4
4	G.Leycester	b Hammond	0	b Hammond		15
5	R.Purchase	not out	38	c Boxall		7
6	Earl of Winchilsea	b Boxall	4	run out		8
7	E.Bligh	c Hammond	4	b Boxall		0
8	G.Louch	b Boxall	8	c P.Vallance		8
9	H.W.Fitzroy	b Hammond	2	c Boxall		0
10	J.Goldham	c Capron	0	run out		6
11	Collins	b Boxall	11	run out		6
	Byes		1			2
			68			62

FoW (1): 1- , 2- , 3- , 4- , 5- , 6- , 7- , 8- , 9- , 10-68
FoW (2): 1- , 2- , 3- , 4- , 5- , 6- , 7- , 8- , 9- , 10-62

BRIGHTON
1	Capron	c Purchase	1	not out		21
2	T.Jutten	run out	2			
3	T.Liffen	b Purchase	2	b Purchase		1
4	T.Boxall	b Purchase	3	not out		10
5	J.Hammond	b Purchase	11	c Monson		24
6	J.Marchant	b Collins	4	b Collins		4
7	W.Bowra	c Monson	0	c Monson		13
8	Sir J.Shelley	c Bligh	8			
9	P.Vallance	c Winchilsea	14	c Monson		1
10	Gregory	b Collins	2	b Collins		1
11	J.Vallance	not out	4	b Purchase		2
	Byes					3
			51	(7 wickets)		80

FoW (1): 1- , 2- , 3- , 4- , 5- , 6- , 7- , 8- , 9- , 10-51
FoW (2): 1- , 2- , 3- , 4- , 5- , 6- , 7-

Brighton Bowling
	O	M	R	W	O	M	R	W
Boxall				4				2
Hammond				3				2

M.C.C. Bowling
	O	M	R	W	O	M	R	W
Purchase				3				2
Collins				2				2

Umpires:

Close of Play: 1st day: No play; 2nd day: ; 3rd day: .

Brighton had Boxall as a given man; MCC had Collins and Purchase as given men. The *Morning Herald* reports that rain prevented any play on 20 August.

BRIGHTON v HAMPSHIRE AND M.C.C.

Played at Prince of Wales Ground, Brighton, August 23, 24, 25, 1792.

Brighton won by an innings and 44 runs.

HAMPSHIRE AND M.C.C.

1	Earl of Winchilsea	c Wells	1	c Aston	2
2	G.Louch	b Walker	2	c Hammond	0
3	R.Purchase	b Boxall	3	b Boxall	18
4	G.Leycester	c Beldham	3	st Hammond	11
5	T.Taylor	c Beldham	0	c Vallance	3
6	A.Freemantle	run out	6	st Hammond	18
7	E.Bligh	b Boxall	0	run out	0
8	G.H.Monson	b Walker	0	run out	21
9	J.Small, jun	b Boxall	4	c Aston	3
10	E.Hussey	b Walker	1	b Boxall	7
11	D.Harris	not out	1	not out	6
	Byes				
			21		89

FoW (1): 1- , 2- , 3- , 4- , 5- , 6- , 7- , 8- , 9- , 10-21
FoW (2): 1- , 2- , 3- , 4- , 5- , 6- , 7- , 8- , 9- , 10-89

BRIGHTON

1	J.Marchant	b Purchase	0
2	John Wells	b Taylor	24
3	T.Walker	b Hussey	53
4	H.H.Aston	b Hussey	0
5	J.Hammond	b Hussey	20
6	W.Beldham	b Harris	6
7	P.Vallance	b Taylor	3
8	W.Bowra	c Bligh	13
9	Capron	c Taylor	21
10	H.W.Fitzroy	not out	0
11	T.Boxall	c Taylor	14
	Byes		
			154

FoW (1): 1- , 2- , 3- , 4- , 5- , 6- , 7- , 8- , 9- , 10-154

Brighton Bowling

	O	M	R	W		O	M	R	W
Boxall				3					2
Walker				3					

Hampshire and M.C.C. Bowling

	O	M	R	W
Harris				1
Purchase				1
Taylor				2
Hussey				3

Umpires:

Close of Play: 1st day: ; 2nd day: .

Brighton had Beldham, Boxall, Walker and Wells as given men. It is not entirely clear when this match started. Some reports say 24 August, but the balance of evidence suggests that it began on 23 August after the previous match ended. Oddly, there appear to have been no byes in this match.

KENT v ESSEX

Played at Dartford Brent, August 29, 30, 31, 1792.

Kent won by 81 runs.

KENT

1	T.Boxall	c Wyatt	0	not out		8
2	R.Fielder	run out	6	b Littler		1
3	W.Beldham	st Ingram	18	c Ingram		15
4	J.Ring	hit wkt	26	c Scott		18
5	E.Bligh	c Ingram	30	b Boorman		3
6	Earl of Winchilsea	b Boorman	1	st Ingram		30
7	G.H.Monson	c Littler	10	c Fennex		17
8	Earl of Darnley	c Boult	3	st Ingram		3
9	S.Amherst	c Ingram	5	c Boorman		9
10	R.Clifford	c Ingram	6	c Ingram		5
11	J.Crawte	not out	13	c Wyatt		1
	Byes		3			3
			121			113

FoW (1): 1- , 2- , 3- , 4- , 5- , 6- , 7- , 8- , 9- , 10-121
FoW (2): 1- , 2- , 3- , 4- , 5- , 6- , 7- , 8- , 9- , 10-113

ESSEX

1	J.Boorman	b Clifford	0	c Fielder		13
2	R.B.Wyatt	b Clifford	4	not out		6
3	W.Oxley	c Ring	6	c Beldham		0
4	W.Fennex	c Ring	5	st Monson		26
5	T.Scott	b Beldham	17	run out		0
6	T.Ingram	c Monson	20	c Clifford		7
7	J.Goulstone	run out	4	b Boxall		9
8	G.T.Boult	c Beldham	2	b Boxall		2
9	J.Stevens	not out	8	b Darnley		18
10	R.Denn	c Beldham	0	run out		1
11	J.Littler	c Fielder	3	c Fielder		1
	Byes					1
			69			84

FoW (1): 1- , 2- , 3- , 4- , 5- , 6- , 7- , 8- , 9- , 10-69
FoW (2): 1- , 2- , 3- , 4- , 5- , 6- , 7- , 8- , 9- , 10-84

Essex Bowling

	O	M	R	W	O	M	R	W
Boorman				1				1
Littler								1

Kent Bowling

	O	M	R	W	O	M	R	W
Clifford				2				
Beldham				1				
Boxall								2
Darnley								1

Umpires:

Close of Play: 1st day: ; 2nd day: .

Kent had Beldham as a given man; Essex had Fennex and Scott as given men.

(Variant) KC calls the match 'West Kent with Beldham & Ring v Essex with Fennex & Scott'.

BRIGHTON v MIDDLESEX

Played at Prince of Wales Ground, Brighton, September 5, 6, 7, 1792.

Brighton won by five wickets.

MIDDLESEX

#	Batsman	Dismissal	Score	2nd Innings	Score
1	Earl of Winchilsea	hit wkt	6	b Hammond	8
2	E.Bligh	c J.Vallance	2	b Purchase	0
3	H.H.Aston	b Hammond	0	run out	3
4	H.W.Fitzroy	c Jutten	1	not out	4
5	G.Louch	c J.Vallance	31	b Purchase	3
6	T.Walker	not out	24	c Liffen	5
7	Grange	c Hammond	5	b Hammond	12
8	W.Fennex	b Purchase	2	b Hammond	6
9	T.Shackle	c Purchase	1	b Hammond	0
10	T.Lord	b Purchase	0	b Hammond	0
11	T.Ray	b Hammond	2	b Purchase	4
	Byes				
			74		**45**

FoW (1): 1- , 2- , 3- , 4- , 5- , 6- , 7- , 8- , 9- , 10-74
FoW (2): 1- , 2- , 3- , 4- , 5- , 6- , 7- , 8- , 9- , 10-45

BRIGHTON

#	Batsman	Dismissal	Score	2nd Innings	Score
1	Sir J.Shelley	c Grange	2	c Fennex	8
2	J.Vallance	c Shackle	0	not out	11
3	T.Jutten	b Lord	3		
4	T.Liffen	c Walker	6	b Walker	8
5	W.Bowra	run out	0	c Lord	8
6	P.Vallance	run out	1	c Fennex	18
7	R.Purchase	run out	2	not out	24
8	J.Hammond	not out	11	b Lord	10
9	W.Bedster	c Shackle	8		
10	Gregory	c Winchilsea	0		
11	Hudson	b Walker	0		
	Byes		1		
			34	(5 wickets)	**87**

FoW (1): 1- , 2- , 3- , 4- , 5- , 6- , 7- , 8- , 9- , 10-34
FoW (2): 1- , 2- , 3- , 4- , 5-

Brighton Bowling

	O	M	R	W	O	M	R	W
Purchase				2				3
Hammond				2				5

Middlesex Bowling

	O	M	R	W	O	M	R	W
Lord				1				1
Walker				1				1

Umpires:

Close of Play: 1st day: ; 2nd day: .

Brighton had Purchase as a given man; Middlesex had Walker as a given man.

(Variant) SB says the second innings took place on 27 May 1793 but this is a misreading of the date set aside to resume the return match, which began on 20 September.

KENT v HAMPSHIRE

Played at Dartford Brent, September 17, 18, 19, 1792.

Hampshire won by an innings and 23 runs.

KENT

1	J.Ring	c Scott	0	c Scott		6
2	T.Walker	c J.Small, sen	13	c Stewart		6
3	W.Beldham	b Harris	6	c J.Small, sen		7
4	W.Fennex	b Purchase	3	c Purchase		32
5	J.Pilcher	run out	2	b Harris		6
6	R.Fielder	run out	11	c Scott		28
7	J.Crawte	b Collins	12	c Walker		22
8	R.Clifford	c Walker	3	b Collins		10
9	T.Boxall	c Scott	2	b Harris		0
10	J.Smith	not out	4	run out		4
11	W.Bullen	c Purchase	4	not out		2
	Byes		1			
			61			123

FoW (1): 1- , 2- , 3- , 4- , 5- , 6- , 7- , 8- , 9- , 10-61
FoW (2): 1- , 2- , 3- , 4- , 5- , 6- , 7- , 8- , 9- , 10-123

HAMPSHIRE

1	G.Louch	b Boxall	1
2	R.Purchase	b Walker	4
3	J.Small, jun	b Boxall	45
4	A.Freemantle	c Bullen	2
5	T.Scott	run out	21
6	H.Walker	c Beldham	3
7	R.Robinson	c Bullen	107
8	J.Stewart	b Clifford	3
9	J.Small, sen	not out	16
10	Collins	c Walker	0
11	D.Harris	b Boxall	4
	Byes		1
			207

FoW (1): 1- , 2- , 3- , 4- , 5- , 6- , 7- , 8- , 9- , 10-207

Hampshire Bowling

	O	M	R	W	O	M	R	W
Harris				1				2
Collins				1				1
Purchase				1				

Kent Bowling

	O	M	R	W
Boxall				3
Clifford				1
Walker				1

Umpires:

Close of Play: 1st day: Hampshire (1) ?-? (Robinson not out); 2nd day: Hampshire (1) ?-? (Robinson not out).

Hampshire had Robinson and H.Walker as given men; Kent had Beldham, Fennex and T.Walker as given men. Robinson batted all three days in scoring a century on his debut in 'great' matches.

MIDDLESEX v BRIGHTON

Played at Lord's Old Ground, Marylebone, September 20, 21, 22, 24, 1792.

Match drawn.

MIDDLESEX

1	H.H.Aston	b Hammond	0
2	G.Louch	c Capron	8
3	T.Walker	c Sharpe	3
4	Grange	c Capron	0
5	T.Lord	run out	5
6	W.Fennex	b Hammond	13
7	T.Shackle	b Hammond	30
8	T.Webb	b Hammond	0
9	Cantrell	b Hammond	2
10	T.Ray	c P.Vallance	18
11	R.Turner	not out	0
	Byes		1
			80

FoW (1): 1- , 2- , 3- , 4- , 5- , 6- , 7- , 8- , 9- , 10-80

BRIGHTON

1	Priest	b Fennex	18
2	R.Purchase	c Shackle	6
3	D.Sharpe	b Walker	9
4	Capron	c Grange	0
5	J.Hammond	hit wkt	5
6	J.Marchant	st Fennex	0
7	T.Liffen	run out	0
8	J.Vallance	not out	12
9	P.Vallance	c Louch	4
10	T.Jutten	c Louch	5
11	Gregory	b Walker	0
	Byes		5
			64

FoW (1): 1- , 2- , 3- , 4- , 5- , 6- , 7- , 8- , 9- , 10-64

Brighton Bowling

	O	M	R	W
Hammond				5

Middlesex Bowling

	O	M	R	W
Fennex				1
Walker				2

Umpires:

Close of Play: 1st day: ; 2nd day: ; 3rd day: Brighton (1) 35-5.

Brighton had Purchase as a given man; Middlesex had Walker as a given man. Play was postponed because of rain and it was announced that the match would continue on 20 May 1793 (Whit Monday) but there is no evidence that such a resumption took place or was attempted.

ESSEX v KENT

Played at Langton Park, Hornchurch, September 27, 28, 1792.

Kent won by 158 runs.

KENT

1	S.Amherst	c Harvey	2	run out		3
2	R.Clifford	b Boorman	5	c Fennex		18
3	J.Smith	c Ingram	0	c Boult		1
4	J.Ring	st Ingram	11	b Fennex		27
5	W.Beldham	b Boorman	15	c Scott		30
6	R.Fielder	b Boorman	12	run out		1
7	J.Crawte	c Oxley	12	not out		49
8	T.Boxall	b Boorman	6	c Boorman		4
9	W.Bedster	run out	2	b Littler		5
10	N.Graham	c Scott	2	c Goulstone		4
11	W.Bullen	not out	2	c Fennex		8
	Byes		1			10
			70			160

FoW (1): 1- , 2- , 3- , 4- , 5- , 6- , 7- , 8- , 9- , 10-70
FoW (2): 1- , 2- , 3- , 4- , 5- , 6- , 7- , 8- , 9- , 10-160

ESSEX

1	R.B.Wyatt	run out	0	c Amherst		4
2	G.T.Boult	c Beldham	0	run out		0
3	J.Goulstone	b Boxall	7	b Boxall		6
4	W.Fennex	c Beldham	1	c Boxall		5
5	T.Ingram	c Smith	5	b Boxall		0
6	W.Oxley	c Clifford	11	c Amherst		0
7	T.Scott	b Boxall	1	c Beldham		1
8	Harvey	b Boxall	0	b Boxall		13
9	J.Stevens	run out	7	b Clifford		0
10	J.Boorman	c Bedster	2	not out		3
11	J.Littler	not out	0	c Ring		1
	Byes		1			4
			35			37

FoW (1): 1- , 2- , 3- , 4- , 5- , 6- , 7- , 8- , 9- , 10-35
FoW (2): 1- , 2- , 3- , 4- , 5- , 6- , 7- , 8- , 9- , 10-37

Essex Bowling

	O	M	R	W	O	M	R	W
Boorman				4				
Fennex								1
Littler								1

Kent Bowling

	O	M	R	W	O	M	R	W
Boxall				3				3
Clifford								1

Umpires:

Close of Play: 1st day: .

Essex had Fennex and Scott as given men; Kent had Bedster and Beldham.

OLD ETONIANS v OLD WESTMINSTERS

Played at Lord's Old Ground, Marylebone, May 13, 14, 1793.

Old Etonians won by 34 runs.

OLD ETONIANS

1	Earl of Winchilsea	b Nicoll	9	c Ray	13
2	T.A.Smith	c Louch	21	b Fennex	2
3	T.Mellish	b Fennex	3	b Cumberland	0
4	R.Walpole	b Cumberland	1	c Nicoll	0
5	Tyson	run out	14	c Goldham	3
6	Sale	c Dehany	2	b Cumberland	0
7	W.Bullen	c Nicoll	21	c Welch	27
8	T.Lord	run out	18	c Sylvester	5
9	R.Turner	b Cumberland	2	b Sylvester	0
10	W.Bedster	not out	15	b Fennex	7
11	N.Graham	b Cumberland	25	not out	0
	Byes		6		1
			137		58

FoW (1): 1- , 2- , 3- , 4- , 5- , 6- , 7- , 8- , 9- , 10-137
FoW (2): 1- , 2- , 3- , 4- , 5- , 6- , 7- , 8- , 9- , 10-58

OLD WESTMINSTERS

1	T.V.R.Nicoll	b Lord	17	run out	0
2	G.Dehany	c Bedster	5	b Lord	22
3	A.Freemantle	b Lord	1	c Lord	1
4	C.Cumberland	b Bullen	9	b Winchilsea	15
5	G.Louch	b Lord	1	b Lord	30
6	R.Welch	run out	7	c Walpole	4
7	Z.Button	b Bullen	8	c Bedster	9
8	J.Goldham	b Bullen	0	not out	10
9	T.Ray	b Lord	0	b Bullen	0
10	Sylvester	c Bedster	0	b Lord	11
11	W.Fennex	not out	1	b Bullen	3
	Byes		1		6
			50		111

FoW (1): 1- , 2- , 3- , 4- , 5- , 6- , 7- , 8- , 9- , 10-50
FoW (2): 1- , 2- , 3- , 4- , 5- , 6- , 7- , 8- , 9- , 10-111

Old Westminsters Bowling

	O	M	R	W	O	M	R	W
Cumberland				3				2
Fennex				1				2
Nicoll				1				
Sylvester								1

Old Etonians Bowling

	O	M	R	W	O	M	R	W
Lord				4				3
Bullen				3				2
Winchilsea								1

Umpires:

Close of Play: 1st day: .

Each side had five given men. Freemantle is A.Freemantle; Bentley's suggestion of a Capt Freemantle is not supported by other sources and would leave Old Westminsters very light on professional support compared with Old Etonians.

M.C.C. v MIDDLESEX

Played at Lord's Old Ground, Marylebone, May 22, 23, 1793.

M.C.C. won by 54 runs.

M.C.C.

1	T.Walker	c Fennex	10	b Lord	20
2	T.Boxall	b Lord	14	b Fennex	11
3	R.Robinson	hit wkt	9	not out	32
4	C.Cumberland	not out	30	c Bedster	1
5	Earl of Winchilsea	b Fennex	0	c Turner	0
6	T.V.R.Nicoll	b Lord	0	b Turner	3
7	T.A.Smith	b Lord	3	b Turner	1
8	G.Louch	b Lord	3	b Turner	15
9	G.Dehany	b Lord	0	c Turner	6
10	R.Welch	b Lord	3	run out	0
11	Scott	b Lord	4	b Turner	5
	Byes		4		4
			80		98

FoW (1): 1- , 2- , 3- , 4- , 5- , 6- , 7- , 8- , 9- , 10-80
FoW (2): 1- , 2- , 3- , 4- , 5- , 6- , 7- , 8- , 9- , 10-98

MIDDLESEX

1	W.Bedster	run out	13	c Nicoll	4
2	N.Graham	b Walker	17	c Smith	0
3	T.Ray	b Walker	2	not out	3
4	W.Fennex	c Nicoll	5	c Walker	3
5	Butler	b Walker	5	b Boxall	0
6	T.Lord	c Smith	3	c Walker	2
7	J.Goldham	run out	3	b Boxall	36
8	Dale	b Boxall	0	b Walker	3
9	R.Turner	b Boxall	2	b Boxall	0
10	J.Martin	c Walker	5	c Walker	11
11	Sylvester	not out	4	b Boxall	0
	Byes		2		1
			61		63

FoW (1): 1- , 2- , 3- , 4- , 5- , 6- , 7- , 8- , 9- , 10-61
FoW (2): 1- , 2- , 3- , 4- , 5- , 6- , 7- , 8- , 9- , 10-63

Middlesex Bowling

	O	M	R	W	O	M	R	W
Lord				7				1
Fennex				1				1
Turner								4

M.C.C. Bowling

	O	M	R	W	O	M	R	W
Boxall				2				4
Walker				3				1

Umpires:

Close of Play: 1st day: .

MCC had Boxall, Robinson and Walker as given men. Scott in the MCC team is an amateur cricketer, not to be confused with the Hampshire professional T.Scott.

HORNCHURCH v M.C.C.

Played at Langton Park, Hornchurch, May 30, 31, 1793.

M.C.C. won by an innings and 10 runs.

HORNCHURCH

1	R.B.Wyatt	b Walker	9	run out	8
2	R.N.Newman	c Walker	0	not out	0
3	J.Littler	b Cumberland	0	run out	10
4	Harvey	c Walker	4	b Walker	7
5	J.Boorman	c Louch	15	c Fitzroy	10
6	J.Goulstone	c Smith	1	b Cumberland	6
7	T.Ingram	b Cumberland	7	c Walker	0
8	J.Stevens	b Cumberland	10	st Winchilsea	2
9	W.Oxley	not out	8	b Cumberland	0
10	R.Francis	b Cumberland	4	c Aston	11
11	Spencer	run out	2	c Louch	0
	Byes				2
			60		56

FoW (1): 1- , 2- , 3- , 4- , 5- , 6- , 7- , 8- , 9- , 10-60
FoW (2): 1- , 2- , 3- , 4- , 5- , 6- , 7- , 8- , 9- , 10-56

M.C.C.

1	Earl of Winchilsea	not out	25
2	Earl of Darnley	run out	0
3	T.A.Smith	b Littler	2
4	G.Louch	b Littler	40
5	T.V.R.Nicoll	b Littler	0
6	T.Mellish	b Littler	4
7	Tyson	c Stevens	5
8	H.H.Aston	run out	0
9	H.W.Fitzroy	c Wyatt	3
10	C.Cumberland	c Ingram	13
11	T.Walker	run out	34
	Byes		
			126

FoW (1): 1- , 2- , 3- , 4- , 5- , 6- , 7- , 8- , 9- , 10-126

M.C.C. Bowling

	O	M	R	W	O	M	R	W
Cumberland				4				2
Walker				1				1

Hornchurch Bowling

	O	M	R	W
Littler				4

Umpires:

Close of Play: 1st day: .

MCC had Walker as a given man.

(Variant) SM and the *Sun* give Hornchurch (1) byes 2, total 62; they also give the following MCC order - Winchilsea, Darnley, Fitzroy, Smith, Louch, Nicoll, Mellish, Tyson, Cumberland, Walker, Aston - but it seems hardly better than the order in Britcher, above.

M.C.C. v HORNCHURCH

Played at Lord's Old Ground, Marylebone, June 6, 7, 1793.

Hornchurch won by two wickets.

M.C.C.

1	T.A.Smith	c Newman	17	c Ingram		5
2	T.Walker	b Littler	16	b Boorman		1
3	G.Louch	b Littler	0	c Newman		1
4	H.W.Fitzroy	c Wyatt	9	c Francis		4
5	Earl of Winchilsea	b Littler	2	b Littler		1
6	G.Dehany	b Boorman	2	not out		14
7	T.V.R.Nicoll	b Littler	0	b Boorman		11
8	T.Mellish	not out	4	b Boorman		2
9	Tyson	b Boorman	1	b Boorman		6
10	Scott	c Goulstone	3	run out		9
11	C.Cumberland	run out	2	c Wyatt		13
	Byes					1
			56			68

FoW (1): 1- , 2- , 3- , 4- , 5- , 6- , 7- , 8- , 9- , 10-56
FoW (2): 1- , 2- , 3- , 4- , 5- , 6- , 7- , 8- , 9- , 10-68

HORNCHURCH

1	W.Oxley	c Smith	8	c Tyson		5
2	Groombridge	b Walker	0	not out		6
3	J.Boorman	b Walker	3	run out		1
4	J.Stevens	c Winchilsea	2	b Cumberland		11
5	R.B.Wyatt	b Cumberland	7	b Walker		8
6	R.N.Newman	run out	15	c Walker		2
7	T.Ingram	c Tyson	0	c Walker		19
8	J.Goulstone	c Winchilsea	17	not out		13
9	R.Francis	c Fitzroy	0	c Fitzroy		0
10	Harvey	not out	2	b Cumberland		4
11	J.Littler	st Winchilsea	0			
	Byes					2
			54	(8 wickets)		71

FoW (1): 1- , 2- , 3- , 4- , 5- , 6- , 7- , 8- , 9- , 10-54
FoW (2): 1- , 2- , 3- , 4- , 5- , 6- , 7- , 8-

Hornchurch Bowling

	O	M	R	W	O	M	R	W
Boorman				2				4
Littler				4				1

M.C.C. Bowling

	O	M	R	W	O	M	R	W
Walker				2				1
Cumberland				1				2

Umpires:

Close of Play: 1st day: .

MCC had Walker as a given man.

(Variant) Britcher and Bentley have Turner playing instead of Cumberland, but it is believed that Turner was an alias for Cumberland.

ENGLAND v SURREY AND SUSSEX

Played at Lord's Old Ground, Marylebone, June 12, 13, 14, 1793.

Surrey and Sussex won by an innings and 299 runs.

ENGLAND

1	C.Cumberland	b Hammond	0	c Tufton	1
2	T.Scott	c Hammond	3	run out	35
3	R.Purchase	c Wells	24	c Hammond	19
4	W.Fennex	c Beldham	8	b Beldham	12
5	A.Freemantle	b T.Walker	8	not out	13
6	J.Ring	b Wells	1	c Hammond	0
7	G.Louch	c Beldham	0	b Beldham	1
8	R.Fielder	c Wells	8	b T.Walker	3
9	T.Taylor	c Hammond	6	b Beldham	2
10	R.Welch	c H.Walker	4	b Hammond	1
11	T.Boxall	not out	1	c H.Walker	1
	Byes		3		
			66		88

FoW (1): 1- , 2- , 3- , 4- , 5- , 6- , 7- , 8- , 9- , 10-66
FoW (2): 1- , 2- , 3- , 4- , 5- , 6- , 7- , 8- , 9- , 10-88

SURREY AND SUSSEX

1	T.Walker	b Boxall	138
2	Earl of Winchilsea	b Fennex	56
3	John Wells	b Purchase	51
4	G.Dehany	b Boxall	1
5	H.J.Tutton	c Fennex	0
6	T.V.R.Nicoll	b Boxall	2
7	J.Walker	b Purchase	24
8	J.Crawte	b Purchase	11
9	W.Beldham	hit wkt b Purchase	77
10	H.Walker	b Cumberland	51
11	J.Hammond	not out	37
	Byes		5
			453

FoW (1): 1- , 2- , 3- , 4- , 5- , 6- , 7- , 8- , 9- , 10-453

Surrey and Sussex Bowling

	O	M	R	W	O	M	R	W
Hammond				1				1
T.Walker				1				1
Wells				1				
Beldham								3

England Bowling

	O	M	R	W
Fennex				1
Boxall				3
Purchase				4
Cumberland				1

Umpires:

Close of Play: 1st day: ; 2nd day: .

The batting order for the England team is from *Sporting Magazine* as this seems likely to represent the first-innings batting order. The batting order for the Surrey and Sussex team has been reconstructed from a range of contemporary sources. For more details, see the Supplementary Note on page 277.

(Variant) SB gives the date as 1792 but advance notice of the match was given in the *World* on 10 June 1793, thus conclusively establishing the year as above.

M.C.C. v ESSEX

Played at Lord's Old Ground, Marylebone, June 17, 18, 1793.

Essex won by three wickets.

M.C.C.

1	Earl of Winchilsea	c Ingram	0	b Boorman		7
2	T.Lord	b Boorman	3	c Harvey		0
3	T.V.R.Nicoll	b Littler	0	run out		8
4	W.Fennex	b Boorman	4	b Boorman		1
5	H.W.Fitzroy	c Stevens	64	b Boorman		0
6	G.Louch	b Boorman	27	c Oxley		24
7	H.J.Tufton	c Francis	3	st Ingram		7
8	T.Mellish	c Stevens	6	b Boorman		4
9	R.Brudenell	not out	16	run out		1
10	R.Welch	c Ingram	4	not out		12
11	R.Walpole	b Littler	4	c Ingram		14
	Byes		2			
			133			78

FoW (1): 1- , 2- , 3- , 4- , 5- , 6- , 7- , 8- , 9- , 10-133
FoW (2): 1- , 2- , 3- , 4- , 5- , 6- , 7- , 8- , 9- , 10-78

ESSEX

1	W.Oxley	run out	9	b Lord	6
2	Harvey	c Walpole	9	c Louch	0
3	T.Ingram	b Fitzroy	19	b Fitzroy	10
4	J.Goulstone	c Winchilsea	1	b Fitzroy	6
5	J.Stevens	run out	15	b Lord	2
6	Groombridge	c Tufton	22	st Winchilsea	8
7	R.Francis	b Lord	4	not out	22
8	W.Allen	not out	15	b Fitzroy	25
9	J.Littler	b Lord	0		
10	Miles	b Lord	11		
11	J.Boorman	st Fitzroy	4	not out	13
	Byes		9		3
			118	(7 wickets)	95

FoW (1): 1- , 2- , 3- , 4- , 5- , 6- , 7- , 8- , 9- , 10-118
FoW (2): 1- , 2- , 3- , 4- , 5- , 6- , 7-

Essex Bowling

	O	M	R	W	O	M	R	W
Boorman				3				4
Littler				2				

M.C.C. Bowling

	O	M	R	W	O	M	R	W
Lord				3				2
Fitzroy				1				3

Umpires:

Close of Play: 1st day: .

MCC had Fennex as a given man.

M.C.C. v KENT

Played at Lord's Old Ground, Marylebone, June 20, 21, 1793.

M.C.C. won by ten wickets.

KENT

1	J.Smith	c Wells	1	b Beldham		9
2	J.Pilcher	run out	5	c Beldham		3
3	T.Boxall	c Newman	3	b Walker		10
4	J.Aylward	b Beldham	5	b Beldham		2
5	Luck	c Wells	0	c Beldham		0
6	R.Fielder	run out	12	c Fitzroy		5
7	C.Cumberland	st Wells	2	c Newman		3
8	Earl of Darnley	c Wells	4	c Newman		0
9	James Wells	hit wkt	0	c Dehany		0
10	W.Bullen	b Walker	11	b Beldham		2
11	J.Ring	not out	45	not out		26
	Byes					
			88			**60**

FoW (1): 1- , 2- , 3- , 4- , 5- , 6- , 7- , 8- , 9- , 10-88
FoW (2): 1- , 2- , 3- , 4- , 5- , 6- , 7- , 8- , 9- , 10-60

M.C.C.

1	John Wells	c Ring	5			
2	H.W.Fitzroy	b Boxall	27			
3	T.Walker	b Boxall	3	not out		23
4	Earl of Winchilsea	c Cumberland	28	not out		30
5	G.Louch	b Boxall	0			
6	R.N.Newman	b Boxall	0			
7	W.Beldham	c Ring	25			
8	T.V.R.Nicoll	run out	0			
9	R.B.Wyatt	b Boxall	5			
10	G.Dehany	b Boxall	2			
11	T.Mellish	not out	1			
	Byes					
			96	(no wicket)		**53**

FoW (1): 1- , 2- , 3- , 4- , 5- , 6- , 7- , 8- , 9- , 10-96

M.C.C. Bowling

	O	M	R	W	O	M	R	W
Beldham				1				3
Walker				1				1

Kent Bowling

	O	M	R	W	O	M	R	W
Boxall				6				

Umpires:

Close of Play: 1st day: .

MCC had Beldham, Walker and John Wells as given men. It is not known on what basis James Wells appeared for Kent. The teams are listed in dismissal order: Beldham will have batted higher for MCC and Ring much higher for Kent, probably in the top three. Oddly, there appear to have been no byes in this match. Luck of Strood.

M.C.C. v BERKSHIRE

Played at Lord's Old Ground, Marylebone, June 24, 25, 26, 1793.

Berkshire won by 118 runs.

BERKSHIRE

1	J.Finch	b Littler	7	run out	46
2	T.Shackle	c Newman	0	b Bedster	0
3	Monk	b Littler	20	c Newman	32
4	S.Gill	st Winchilsea	3	c Tufton	11
5	G.East	c Littler	8	b Hussey	18
6	R.Quarme	c Louch	0	b Fitzroy	7
7	T.Ray	b Cumberland	7	hit wkt	2
8	Carter	run out	2	not out	34
9	Thompson	b Hussey	5	c Newman	6
10	R.Lawrence	b Bedster	69	c Tufton	11
11	Timber	not out	10	c Hussey	15
	Byes		9		3
			140		185

FoW (1): 1- , 2- , 3- , 4- , 5- , 6- , 7- , 8- , 9- , 10-140
FoW (2): 1- , 2- , 3- , 4- , 5- , 6- , 7- , 8- , 9- , 10-185

M.C.C.

1	G.Louch	b Timber	0	st Monk	11
2	W.Bedster	c Ray	2	c Ray	0
3	R.N.Newman	b Timber	0	b Thompson	9
4	G.Dehany	b Timber	4	b Timber	0
5	E.Hussey	b Timber	6	b Timber	8
6	C.Cumberland	c Monk	8	b Monk	21
7	Earl of Winchilsea	c Quarme	23	c Shackle	17
8	T.V.R.Nicoll	c Ray	5	run out	5
9	H.J.Tufton	c Ray	8	c East	23
10	H.W.Fitzroy	not out	13	c Ray	24
11	J.Littler	c Finch	4	not out	5
	Byes		2		9
			75		132

FoW (1): 1- , 2- , 3- , 4- , 5- , 6- , 7- , 8- , 9- , 10-75
FoW (2): 1- , 2- , 3- , 4- , 5- , 6- , 7- , 8- , 9- , 10-132

M.C.C. Bowling

	O	M	R	W	O	M	R	W
Cumberland				1				
Bedster				1				1
Littler				2				
Hussey				1				1
Fitzroy								1

Berkshire Bowling

	O	M	R	W	O	M	R	W
Timber				4				2
Monk								1
Thompson								1

Umpires:

Close of Play: 1st day: ; 2nd day: .

MCC had Bedster and Littler as given men. The teams are listed in dismissal order. Lawrence will have come in much higher before being last out.

KENT v M.C.C.
Played at Dartford Brent, June 27, 28, 1793.

Kent won by eight wickets.

M.C.C.
1	T.Walker	c Fielder	1	c Boxall		29
2	John Wells	hit wkt	0	b Purchase		1
3	W.Beldham	c Boxall	3	st Ring		8
4	Earl of Winchilsea	b Boxall	3	c Bullen		2
5	J.Tufton	c Purchase	1	c Bullen		0
6	G.Louch	b Boxall	0	c Ring		0
7	R.B.Wyatt	b Boxall	0	not out		0
8	R.N.Newman	run out	0	b Boxall		1
9	R.Brudenell	b Boxall	7	c Ring		0
10	H.W.Fitzroy	b Boxall	27	st Ring		0
11	H.J.Tufton	not out	3	run out		0
	Byes		2			
			47			41

FoW (1): 1- , 2- , 3- , 4- , 5- , 6- , 7- , 8- , 9- , 10-47
FoW (2): 1- , 2- , 3- , 4- , 5- , 6- , 7- , 8- , 9- , 10-41

KENT
1	J.Pilcher	c Walker	12			
2	J.Ring	st Walker	18	b Wells		0
3	R.Purchase	c Newman	3			
4	A.Freemantle	c Beldham	1	not out		14
5	J.Aylward	c Beldham	3	not out		13
6	R.Fielder	c Beldham	0			
7	Luck	b Wells	1			
8	T.Boxall	b Wells	4			
9	W.Bullen	c Beldham	0			
10	Butcher	not out	9			
11	Earl of Darnley	b Wells	4	c Newman		4
	Byes					3
			55	(2 wickets)		34

FoW (1): 1- , 2- , 3- , 4- , 5- , 6- , 7- , 8- , 9- , 10-55
FoW (2): 1- , 2-

Kent Bowling
	O	M	R	W	O	M	R	W
Boxall				5				1
Purchase								1

M.C.C. Bowling
	O	M	R	W	O	M	R	W
Wells				3				1

Umpires:

Close of Play: 1st day: .

Kent had Freemantle and Purchase as given men; MCC had Beldham, Walker and Wells as given men. The teams are in dismissal order: Fitzroy clearly came in much higher.

KENT v M.C.C.
Played at Dartford Brent, June 28, 29, 1793.

M.C.C. won by 73 runs.

M.C.C.
1	J.Hampton	c Purchase	0	c Ring		0
2	John Wells	c Ring	10	b Bullen		3
3	Earl of Winchilsea	b Butcher	30	c Purchase		1
4	T.Walker	c Purchase	5	c Bullen		20
5	W.Fennex	b Purchase	4	c Ring		28
6	R.N.Newman	c Fielder	2	b Bullen		3
7	R.Brudenell	c Bullen	1	b Bullen		0
8	H.J.Tufton	b Fielder	8	not out		3
9	J.Tufton	b Purchase	0	run out		1
10	H.W.Fitzroy	not out	8	c Smith		1
11	W.Beldham	run out	69	c Ring		5
	Byes		3			9
			140			74

FoW (1): 1- , 2- , 3- , 4- , 5- , 6- , 7- , 8- , 9- , 10-140
FoW (2): 1- , 2- , 3- , 4- , 5- , 6- , 7- , 8- , 9- , 10-74

KENT
1	J.Pilcher	c Newman	20	run out		0
2	R.Purchase	c Beldham	0	c Beldham		0
3	A.Freemantle	c Beldham	3	c Wells		0
4	J.Ring	c Beldham	29	c Newman		5
5	R.Fielder	b Walker	0	c Beldham		0
6	J.Aylward	c Beldham	10	not out		28
7	Butcher	b Walker	11	c H.J.Tufton		3
8	J.Smith	b Hampton	8	run out		1
9	Luck	c Walker	0	c Beldham		3
10	W.Bullen	c Wells	6	st Wells		10
11	T.Boxall	not out	4	c J.Tufton		0
	Byes					
			91			50

FoW (1): 1- , 2- , 3- , 4- , 5- , 6- , 7- , 8- , 9- , 10-91
FoW (2): 1- , 2- , 3- , 4- , 5- , 6- , 7- , 8- , 9- , 10-50

Kent Bowling
	O	M	R	W	O	M	R	W
Purchase				2				
Butcher				1				
Fielder				1				
Bullen								3

M.C.C. Bowling
	O	M	R	W	O	M	R	W
Walker				2				
Hampton				1				

Umpires:

Close of Play: 1st day: .

Kent had Freemantle and Purchase as given men; MCC had Beldham, Fennex, Hampton, Walker and Wells as given men. The teams are in dismissal order: Beldham clearly came in much higher, probably in the first four. This match began the same day the previous one ended.

(Variant) Britcher gives Boxall c H.J.Tufton in Kent (2).

EARL OF WINCHILSEA'S XI v G.LOUCH'S XI

Played at Lord's Old Ground, Marylebone, July 1, 2, 3, 1793.

Earl of Winchilsea's XI won by 3 runs.

EARL OF WINCHILSEA'S XI

1	J.Walker	c Newman	10	b Boxall	1
2	J.Ring	c Freemantle	0	c Fennex	7
3	H.Walker	b Boxall	0	c Boxall	12
4	Earl of Winchilsea	b Boxall	0	b Boxall	0
5	J.Smith	b Purchase	11	b Lord	30
6	J.Tufton	c Fennex	4	b Boxall	0
7	G.Dehany	c Newman	3	b Boxall	0
8	H.J.Tufton	b Boxall	2	b Boxall	0
9	W.Bullen	b Lord	2	c Fennex	7
10	J.Hampton	b Lord	0	not out	11
11	T.Walker	not out	53	c Fennex	24
	Byes		5		3
			90		95

FoW (1): 1- , 2- , 3- , 4- , 5- , 6- , 7- , 8- , 9- , 10-90
FoW (2): 1- , 2- , 3- , 4- , 5- , 6- , 7- , 8- , 9- , 10-95

G.LOUCH'S XI

1	J.Goldham	c Bullen	0	c J.Tufton	12
2	R.Purchase	b Hampton	1	b Hampton	6
3	J.Aylward	run out	5	b T.Walker	67
4	W.Fennex	b Hampton	3	c Ring	1
5	G.Louch	b T.Walker	4	st Ring	1
6	Butcher	c Ring	3	b Hampton	8
7	T.Boxall	b Hampton	1	c Hampton	3
8	R.N.Newman	c Ring	1	c Ring	0
9	A.Freemantle	b Hampton	9	c Bullen	8
10	N.Graham	not out	2	c J.Tufton	14
11	T.Lord	c Smith	7	not out	20
	Byes		2		4
			38		144

FoW (1): 1- , 2- , 3- , 4- , 5- , 6- , 7- , 8- , 9- , 10-38
FoW (2): 1- , 2- , 3- , 4- , 5- , 6- , 7- , 8- , 9- , 10-144

G.Louch's XI Bowling

	O	M	R	W	O	M	R	W
Boxall				3				5
Lord				2				1
Purchase				1				

Earl of Winchilsea's XI Bowling

	O	M	R	W	O	M	R	W
T.Walker				1				1
Hampton				4				2

Umpires:

Close of Play: 1st day: ; 2nd day: .

The teams are listed in what appears to be order of dismissal. T.Walker came in much higher; he may even have carried his bat, but no source says so.

ENGLAND v SURREY

Played at Windmill Down, Hambledon, July 12, 13, 15, 1793.

Surrey won by 15 runs.

SURREY

#	Batsman	Dismissal (1)	Score	Dismissal (2)	Score
1	T.Walker	b Harris	16	c Hammond	26
2	J.Crawte	b Hammond	2	b Littler	33
3	J.Walker	run out	25	b Boxall	8
4	Earl of Winchilsea	b Hammond	14	b Hammond	1
5	H.Walker	c Scott	3	not out	3
6	W.Beldham	b Harris	0	c J.Small, jun	9
7	J.Aylward	c Scott	9	c Scott	2
8	John Wells	c Hammond	8	c Harris	14
9	H.W.Fitzroy	c Hammond	1	c Hammond	3
10	G.Louch	c Newman	15	c Littler	0
11	J.Hampton	not out	5	b Boxall	1
	Byes		1		1
			99		101

FoW (1): 1- , 2- , 3- , 4- , 5- , 6- , 7- , 8- , 9- , 10-99
FoW (2): 1- , 2- , 3- , 4- , 5- , 6- , 7- , 8- , 9- , 10-101

ENGLAND

#	Batsman	Dismissal (1)	Score	Dismissal (2)	Score
1	J.Ring	c Aylward	5	run out	27
2	J.Small, jun	hit wkt	2	c Beldham	9
3	J.Hammond	c T.Walker	11	b T.Walker	22
4	T.Scott	c J.Walker	13	c Fitzroy	5
5	J.Small, sen	st Wells	2	c H.Walker	21
6	A.Freemantle	c Beldham	17	c Wells	11
7	R.N.Newman	b T.Walker	0	b Hampton	16
8	R.Brudenell	b Hampton	3	c Wells	0
9	T.Boxall	b Hampton	7	not out	4
10	D.Harris	c Beldham	1	c Crawte	6
11	J.Littler	not out	0	b T.Walker	2
	Byes		1		
			62		123

FoW (1): 1- , 2- , 3- , 4- , 5- , 6- , 7- , 8- , 9- , 10-62
FoW (2): 1- , 2- , 3- , 4- , 5- , 6- , 7- , 8- , 9- , 10-123

England Bowling

	O	M	R	W	O	M	R	W
Harris				2				
Hammond				2				1
Boxall								2
Littler								1

Surrey Bowling

	O	M	R	W	O	M	R	W
Hampton				2				1
T.Walker				1				2

Umpires:

Close of Play: 1st day: ; 2nd day: .

Surrey had Aylward as a given man. The *Sporting Magazine* gives much better batting orders than Britcher so its version of the score is accepted.

(Variant) Britcher gives Boxall b Beldham in England (1); J.Walker c Harris in Surrey (2).

ENGLAND v SURREY

Played at Dartford Brent, July 22, 23, 24, 1793.

Surrey won by 53 runs.

SURREY

1	W.Beldham	not out	106	b Boxall		5
2	H.Walker	run out	18	c Ring		9
3	John Wells	c Scott	0	b Harris		9
4	T.Walker	run out	10	run out		11
5	J.Walker	b Purchase	10	c Newman		8
6	J.Crawte	b Harris	2	c Ring		0
7	J.Hammond	c Newman	2	run out		12
8	Earl of Winchilsea	b Boxall	5	not out		19
9	H.W.Fitzroy	b Boxall	6	b Boxall		7
10	G.Louch	c Scott	7	b Boxall		0
11	J.Hampton	b Purchase	1	b Harris		2
	Byes		4			1
			171			83

FoW (1): 1- , 2- , 3- , 4- , 5- , 6- , 7- , 8- , 9- , 10-171
FoW (2): 1- , 2- , 3- , 4- , 5- , 6- , 7- , 8- , 9- , 10-83

ENGLAND

1	R.N.Newman	st Hammond	15	st Hammond		2
2	W.Fennex	c Beldham	17	c Beldham		3
3	J.Ring	c Hammond	34	b T.Walker		34
4	A.Freemantle	c T.Walker	11	b Hampton		6
5	J.Aylward	b Hampton	1	c Hammond		8
6	J.Small, jun	run out	4	b Hampton		4
7	R.Purchase	run out	4	b T.Walker		8
8	J.Small, sen	not out	8	st Hammond		4
9	T.Scott	run out	0	c Beldham		0
10	T.Boxall	b Wells	17	not out		13
11	D.Harris	c Beldham	2	c Crawte		0
	Byes					6
			113			88

FoW (1): 1- , 2- , 3- , 4- , 5- , 6- , 7- , 8- , 9- , 10-113
FoW (2): 1- , 2- , 3- , 4- , 5- , 6- , 7- , 8- , 9- , 10-88

England Bowling

	O	M	R	W	O	M	R	W
Harris				1				2
Boxall				2				3
Purchase				2				

Surrey Bowling

	O	M	R	W	O	M	R	W
Hampton				1				2
Wells				1				
T.Walker								2

Umpires:

Close of Play: 1st day: ; 2nd day: .

The batting order above, confirmed by two newspapers, means that Beldham carried his bat. The *Kentish Gazette* reports that Hammond was originally selected for England but when R.Robinson dropped out of the Surrey team, Hammond switched sides and was replaced in the England team by Newman.

(Variant) SB incorrectly gives the venue as Lord's.

OLDFIELD v M.C.C.

Played at Old Field, Bray, July 25, 26, 1793.

Oldfield won by 85 runs.

OLDFIELD

1	J.Finch	b Cumberland	12	b Cumberland	52
2	Monk	b Lord	10	b Cumberland	5
3	Timber	b Lord	0	b Cumberland	0
4	Carter	b Cumberland	1	not out	2
5	R.Lawrence	b Lord	2	c Smith	57
6	T.Ray	b Lord	0	b Turner	30
7	T.Shackle	c Graham	3	b Cumberland	7
8	S.Gill	b Cumberland	4	b Turner	18
9	Thompson	b Cumberland	0	b Turner	1
10	G.East	not out	2	c Winchilsea	11
11	R.Quarme	b Cumberland	0	b Cumberland	1
	Byes		3		7
			37		191

FoW (1): 1- , 2- , 3- , 4- , 5- , 6- , 7- , 8- , 9- , 10-37
FoW (2): 1- , 2- , 3- , 4- , 5- , 6- , 7- , 8- , 9- , 10-191

M.C.C.

1	G.Louch	c Finch	15	c Finch	0
2	R.N.Newman	b Timber	7	b Timber	0
3	T.A.Smith	c East	3	c Ray	4
4	Earl of Winchilsea	b Timber	1	b Timber	21
5	C.Cumberland	c Finch	1	b Timber	29
6	N.Graham	b Timber	0	not out	0
7	G.Dehany	c Ray	0	b Timber	8
8	T.Lord	b Thompson	12	c Lawrence	0
9	R.Turner	run out	15	b Thompson	5
10	W.Bedster	c Ray	18	c Shackle	2
11	H.J.Tufton	not out	0	b Thompson	0
	Byes		1		1
			73		70

FoW (1): 1- , 2- , 3- , 4- , 5- , 6- , 7- , 8- , 9- , 10-73
FoW (2): 1- , 2- , 3- , 4- , 5- , 6- , 7- , 8- , 9- , 10-70

M.C.C. Bowling

	O	M	R	W	O	M	R	W
Cumberland				5				5
Lord				4				
Turner								3

Oldfield Bowling

	O	M	R	W	O	M	R	W
Thompson				1				2
Timber				3				4

Umpires:

Close of Play: 1st day: .

ENGLAND v SURREY

Played at The Park, Burley-on-the-Hill, August 5, 6, 7, 1793.

England won by seven wickets.

SURREY
1	Earl of Winchilsea	c Hammond	1	run out		0
2	Viscount Milsington	c Ring	0	c Purchase		0
3	H.J.Tufton	c Hammond	0	b Purchase		4
4	G.Louch	c Dehany	7	b Harris		1
5	T.Walker	c Hammond	0	c Small		6
6	H.Walker	c Hammond	26	b Purchase		4
7	W.Beldham	c Hammond	17	b Boxall		26
8	John Wells	c Hammond	20	b Purchase		3
9	J.Crawte	run out	1	b Purchase		0
10	J.Walker	not out	7	c Bullen		0
11	J.Hampton	b Boxall	0	not out		27
	Byes		2			1
			81			72

FoW (1): 1- , 2- , 3- , 4- , 5- , 6- , 7- , 8- , 9- , 10-81
FoW (2): 1- , 2- , 3- , 4- , 5- , 6- , 7- , 8- , 9- , 10-72

ENGLAND
1	G.Dehany	b Wells	5	c J.Walker		0
2	J.Small, jun	c H.Walker	10	c Beldham		2
3	J.Ring	c Beldham	2	c Hampton		22
4	A.Freemantle	b Wells	1	not out		43
5	W.Bullen	c H.Walker	22	not out		20
6	R.Brudenell	c Hampton	3			
7	C.Cumberland	c Beldham	0			
8	J.Hammond	b Wells	16			
9	R.Purchase	b Hampton	3			
10	T.Boxall	b Hampton	0			
11	D.Harris	not out	3			
	Byes		2			
			67	(3 wickets)		87

FoW (1): 1- , 2- , 3- , 4- , 5- , 6- , 7- , 8- , 9- , 10-67
FoW (2): 1- , 2- , 3-

England Bowling
	O	M	R	W	O	M	R	W
Boxall				1				1
Harris								1
Purchase								4

Surrey Bowling
	O	M	R	W	O	M	R	W
Wells				3				
Hampton				2				

Umpires:

Close of Play: 1st day: ; 2nd day: .

197

EARL OF WINCHILSEA'S XI v R.LEIGH'S XI

Played at The Park, Burley-on-the-Hill, August 7, 8, 9, 10, 1793.

Earl of Winchilsea's XI won by five wickets.

R.LEIGH'S XI

1	W.Fennex	c Beldham	0	b Hampton		0
2	A.Freemantle	b Harris	5	run out		1
3	T.Walker	b Hampton	0	c Wells		24
4	J.Ring	c Wells	10	not out		5
5	R.Purchase	c Jones	5	b Hampton		4
6	J.Small, jun	c Jones	13	c H.Walker		0
7	T.Boxall	b Hampton	1	c Beldham		0
8	G.Louch	run out	3	c Winchilsea		5
9	G.Dehany	b Hampton	9	run out		7
10	Viscount Milsington	b Harris	3	c Harris		3
11	E.G.Morant	not out	0	b Harris		0
	Byes					5
			49			54

FoW (1): 1- , 2- , 3- , 4- , 5- , 6- , 7- , 8- , 9- , 10-49
FoW (2): 1- , 2- , 3- , 4- , 5- , 6- , 7- , 8- , 9- , 10-54

EARL OF WINCHILSEA'S XI

1	H.Walker	c Purchase	31			
2	J.Walker	c Louch	0	st Morant		3
3	W.Beldham	b Boxall	7	not out		0
4	Earl of Winchilsea	c Purchase	0	c Morant		7
5	John Wells	c sub (W.Bullen)	11	not out		17
6	J.Hampton	b Boxall	4			
7	H.J.Tufton	b Boxall	3	c Small		0
8	R.Brudenell	c Small	3	c Walker		3
9	C.Cumberland	run out	8			
10	D.Harris	not out	0			
11	E.Jones	b Walker	0	run out		5
	Byes		2			
			69	(5 wickets)		35

FoW (1): 1- , 2- , 3- , 4- , 5- , 6- , 7- , 8- , 9- , 10-69
FoW (2): 1- , 2- , 3- , 4- , 5-

Earl of Winchilsea's XI Bowling

	O	M	R	W		O	M	R	W
Harris				2					1
Hampton				3					2

R.Leigh's XI Bowling

	O	M	R	W		O	M	R	W
Boxall				3					
Walker				1					

Umpires:

Close of Play: 1st day: ; 2nd day: ; 3rd day: .

Jones was formerly thought to be an alias for H.Bridger, but he has now been identified as Rev E.Jones, Vicar of Greetham, Rutland. This match began the same day the previous one ended.

R.N.NEWMAN'S XI v R.LEIGH'S XI

Played at The Green Man, Navestock, August 19, 20, 1793.

R.N.Newman's XI won by 37 runs.

R.N.NEWMAN'S XI

1	J.Small, jun	c Oxley	4	b Harris	2
2	J.Hammond	c Walker	6	b Purchase	0
3	T.Walker	c Wells	2	c Beldham	24
4	A.Freemantle	c Walker	17	b Harris	8
5	W.Fennex	b Harris	1	b Purchase	21
6	J.Stevens	b Purchase	0	run out	3
7	W.Bullen	b Purchase	2	not out	16
8	T.Boxall	c Barker	2	run out	14
9	R.N.Newman	c Walker	2	c Purchase	0
10	R.Denn	not out	0	c Walker	3
11	J.Boorman	b Harris	0	c Wells	0
	Byes		3		2
			39		93

FoW (1): 1- , 2- , 3- , 4- , 5- , 6- , 7- , 8- , 9- , 10-39
FoW (2): 1- , 2- , 3- , 4- , 5- , 6- , 7- , 8- , 9- , 10-93

R.LEIGH'S XI

1	R.Robinson	st Hammond	15	run out	6
2	H.Walker	c Hammond	5	hit wkt	3
3	John Wells	c Hammond	2	c Newman	1
4	W.Beldham	b Hammond	11	c Walker	15
5	R.Purchase	c Hammond	6	run out	7
6	J.Goulstone	c Newman	6	st Hammond	2
7	W.Oxley	c Bullen	3	c Bullen	11
8	D.Harris	c Bullen	0	b Boxall	0
9	J.Russell	b Walker	0	c Walker	2
10	Sadler	b Boxall	0	not out	0
11	Barker	not out	0	c Newman	0
	Byes				
			48		47

FoW (1): 1- , 2- , 3- , 4- , 5- , 6- , 7- , 8- , 9- , 10-48
FoW (2): 1- , 2- , 3- , 4- , 5- , 6- , 7- , 8- , 9- , 10-47

R.Leigh's XI Bowling

	O	M	R	W	O	M	R	W
Harris				2				2
Purchase				2				2

R.N.Newman's XI Bowling

	O	M	R	W	O	M	R	W
Boxall				1				1
Walker				1				
Hammond				1				

Umpires:

Close of Play: 1st day: .

SB gives the venue as Knavestock but this appears to be an error: contemporary maps spell the name as Navestock, which is also the modern spelling.

M.C.C. v MIDDLESEX

Played at Lord's Old Ground, Marylebone, May 26, 27, 28, 29, 1794.

M.C.C. won by 100 runs.

M.C.C.

1	T.Walker	b Lord	32	c Finch		44
2	J.Hammond	hit wkt	0	b Fennex		3
3	W.Beldham	b Fennex	11	c Turner		0
4	Earl of Winchilsea	b Fennex	16	b Lord		1
5	C.Anguish	b Turner	0	not out		12
6	T.A.Smith	b Fennex	0	b Fennex		19
7	G.Louch	b Fennex	17	b Lord		1
8	H.J.Tufton	b Lord	27	b Lord		6
9	T.Mellish	not out	41	c Wheeler		17
10	T.J.Twistleton	run out	11	b Rubegall		4
11	T.V.R.Nicoll	b Lord	2	c Ray		13
	Byes		12			7
			169			127

FoW (1): 1- , 2- , 3- , 4- , 5- , 6- , 7- , 8- , 9- , 10-169
FoW (2): 1- , 2- , 3- , 4- , 5- , 6- , 7- , 8- , 9- , 10-127

MIDDLESEX

1	N.Graham	b Beldham	30	c Walker		4
2	J.Finch	c Tufton	7	c Louch		6
3	T.Ray	c Beldham	1	c Beldham		8
4	W.Fennex	st Hammond	5	b Hammond		62
5	J.Goldham	c Walker	17	run out		0
6	T.Lord	c Louch	0	b Beldham		18
7	Dale	c Walker	1	not out		2
8	R.Turner	c Walker	6	b Beldham		0
9	J.Beeston	b Walker	3	b Walker		3
10	Rubegall	not out	3	b Hammond		2
11	J.Wheeler	st Hammond	11	b Walker		3
	Byes					4
			84			112

FoW (1): 1- , 2- , 3- , 4- , 5- , 6- , 7- , 8- , 9- , 10-84
FoW (2): 1- , 2- , 3- , 4- , 5- , 6- , 7- , 8- , 9- , 10-112

Middlesex Bowling

	O	M	R	W	O	M	R	W
Lord				3				3
Fennex				4				2
Turner				1				
Rubegall								1

M.C.C. Bowling

	O	M	R	W	O	M	R	W
Walker				1				2
Beldham				1				2
Hammond								2

Umpires:

Close of Play: 1st day: ; 2nd day: ; 3rd day: .

MCC had Beldham, Hammond and Walker as given men. Wheeler in the Middlesex side, identified by Britcher as an amateur, is believed to be Mr J.Wheeler of Highgate since R.Wheeler, also of Highgate, was a professional.

ENGLAND v SURREY

Played at Lord's Old Ground, Marylebone, June 9, 10, 11, 1794.

Surrey won by 197 runs.

SURREY

1	John Wells	c Hammond	8		
2	W.Beldham	c Fennex	72	b Fennex	102
3	T.Walker	b Harris	6	run out	5
4	H.Walker	c Hammond	23	not out	115
5	R.Robinson	b Boxall	38	run out	12
6	J.Walker	c Smith	6		
7	Earl of Winchilsea	b Boxall	12	c Fennex	1
8	J.Hampton	b Harris	4		
9	G.Louch	b Harris	41	not out	9
10	T.Mellish	not out	9	c Scott	8
11	T.J.Twistleton	b Hammond	0		
	Byes		4		7
			223	(5 wickets, declared)	259

FoW (1): 1- , 2- , 3- , 4- , 5- , 6- , 7- , 8- , 9- , 10-223
FoW (2): 1- , 2- , 3- , 4- , 5-

ENGLAND

1	W.Fennex	b T.Walker	44	b T.Walker	9
2	J.Small, jun	b T.Walker	0	b Hampton	0
3	C.Anguish	b Beldham	5	b Beldham	10
4	J.Ring	b T.Walker	0	not out	75
5	T.Scott	c Robinson	15	c T.Walker	43
6	A.Freemantle	b Beldham	1	c Beldham	26
7	J.Hammond	c T.Walker	9	b T.Walker	6
8	T.A.Smith	b Hampton	0	b T.Walker	11
9	H.J.Tufton	c Beldham	4	b T.Walker	6
10	T.Boxall	run out	1	b T.Walker	8
11	D.Harris	not out	7	b T.Walker	0
	Byes		2		3
			88		197

FoW (1): 1- , 2- , 3- , 4- , 5- , 6- , 7- , 8- , 9- , 10-88
FoW (2): 1- , 2- , 3- , 4- , 5- , 6- , 7- , 8- , 9- , 10-197

England Bowling

	O	M	R	W	O	M	R	W
Harris				3				
Boxall				2				
Hammond				1				
Fennex								1

Surrey Bowling

	O	M	R	W	O	M	R	W
T.Walker				3				6
Beldham				2				1
Hampton				1				1

Umpires:

Close of Play: 1st day: ; 2nd day: .

Surrey appears to have given up its second innings; this has been treated as a declaration.

R.LEIGH'S XI v E.G.MORANT'S XI
Played at Old Field, Bray, June 18, 19, 20, 1794.

R.Leigh's XI won by 89 runs.

R.LEIGH'S XI

1	T.Walker	run out	5	not out		62
2	H.Walker	run out	0	b Fennex		5
3	R.Robinson	b Boxall	0	b Fennex		19
4	John Wells	c Boxall	22	b Fennex		0
5	T.A.Smith	b Boxall	0	run out		10
6	J.Ring	c Finch	40	c Scott		13
7	J.Crawte	b Harris	3	c Scott		2
8	R.Purchase	b Harris	10	run out		5
9	J.Hammond	b Fennex	4	b Harris		20
10	R.Fielder	not out	5	b Fennex		7
11	W.Bullen	b Boxall	6	b Beldham		1
	Byes		2			2
			97			146

FoW (1): 1- , 2- , 3- , 4- , 5- , 6- , 7- , 8- , 9- , 10-97
FoW (2): 1- , 2- , 3- , 4- , 5- , 6- , 7- , 8- , 9- , 10-146

E.G.MORANT'S XI

1	W.Fennex	st Hammond	2	run out		3
2	J.Walker	c Hammond	0	not out		6
3	W.Beldham	st Hammond	7	c H.Walker		60
4	J.Small, jun	run out	0	c T.Walker		6
5	A.Freemantle	c Hammond	2	st Hammond		7
6	J.Finch	c Smith	6	c Wells		9
7	T.Scott	c Robinson	0	b Wells		7
8	T.Ray	c Fielder	5	c Bullen		10
9	J.Harding	not out	14	b T.Walker		2
10	T.Boxall	c H.Walker	0	b Purchase		0
11	D.Harris	b Wells	5	c Bullen		1
	Byes					2
			41			113

FoW (1): 1- , 2- , 3- , 4- , 5- , 6- , 7- , 8- , 9- , 10-41
FoW (2): 1- , 2- , 3- , 4- , 5- , 6- , 7- , 8- , 9- , 10-113

E.G.Morant's XI Bowling

	O	M	R	W	O	M	R	W
Harris				2				1
Boxall				3				
Fennex				1				4
Beldham								1

R.Leigh's XI Bowling

	O	M	R	W	O	M	R	W
Wells				1				1
Purchase								1
T.Walker								1

Umpires:

Close of Play: 1st day: ; 2nd day: .

R.LEIGH'S XI v G.LOUCH'S XI

Played at Lord's Old Ground, Marylebone, June 30, July 1, 2, 1794.

R.Leigh's XI won by 132 runs.

R.LEIGH'S XI

1	A.Freemantle	c Wells	4	b Hampton	25
2	T.Walker	c Beldham	102	b Purchase	14
3	H.Walker	run out	70	b Wells	8
4	J.Small, jun	c Beldham	12	hit wkt	11
5	T.Scott	b Wells	4	run out	16
6	J.Hammond	b Wells	1	c Boxall	54
7	J.Goldham	b Wells	0	b Hampton	1
8	H.J.Tufton	b Wells	12	c Beldham	0
9	T.Ray	not out	6	c Louch	0
10	T.J.Twistleton	b Boxall	0	c Louch	7
11	D.Harris	c Fennex	1	not out	1
	Byes		7		1
			219		138

FoW (1): 1- , 2- , 3- , 4- , 5- , 6- , 7- , 8- , 9- , 10-219
FoW (2): 1- , 2- , 3- , 4- , 5- , 6- , 7- , 8- , 9- , 10-138

G.LOUCH'S XI

1	R.Robinson	b Harris	0	c H.Walker	0
2	J.Ring	st Hammond	37	b Harris	19
3	John Wells	b T.Walker	54	c Ray	18
4	W.Beldham	b T.Walker	4	c Ray	6
5	W.Fennex	st Hammond	4	c Hammond	15
6	R.Purchase	b Harris	5	c T.Walker	5
7	G.Louch	c T.Walker	0	c H.Walker	9
8	C.Anguish	c Hammond	17	c Hammond	4
9	N.Graham	c Hammond	4	c Scott	1
10	T.Boxall	b T.Walker	10	c Twistleton	6
11	J.Hampton	not out	0	not out	0
	Byes		3		4
			138		87

FoW (1): 1- , 2- , 3- , 4- , 5- , 6- , 7- , 8- , 9- , 10-138
FoW (2): 1- , 2- , 3- , 4- , 5- , 6- , 7- , 8- , 9- , 10-87

G.Louch's XI Bowling

	O	M	R	W		O	M	R	W
Boxall				1					
Wells				4					1
Purchase									1
Hampton									2

R.Leigh's XI Bowling

	O	M	R	W		O	M	R	W
Harris				2					1
T.Walker				3					

Umpires:

Close of Play: 1st day: ; 2nd day: .

OLDFIELD v MIDDLESEX AND M.C.C.

Played at Old Field, Bray, July 7, 8, 1794.

Middlesex and M.C.C. won by three wickets.

OLDFIELD

1	Thompson	b Hampton	1	c Graham		5
2	Timber	c Louch	2	b Hampton		9
3	West	c Lord	4	c Louch		0
4	G.East	c Turner	5	b Lord		19
5	J.Finch	b Hampton	34	c Hampton		1
6	R.Lawrence	b Hampton	19	c Graham		1
7	Monk	b Lord	1	c Winchilsea		6
8	E.Winter	not out	13	c Winchilsea		8
9	S.Gill	run out	1	b Lord		5
10	T.Shackle	b Lord	3	c Hampton		3
11	Bexley	b Hampton	3	not out		2
	Byes		4			
			90			**59**

FoW (1): 1- , 2- , 3- , 4- , 5- , 6- , 7- , 8- , 9- , 10-90
FoW (2): 1- , 2- , 3- , 4- , 5- , 6- , 7- , 8- , 9- , 10-59

MIDDLESEX AND M.C.C.

1	G.Louch	c Timber	10	b Thompson	3
2	J.Wheeler	st Thompson	0	c Gill	1
3	C.Anguish	run out	12	run out	18
4	H.J.Tufton	c Monk	14	hit wkt	0
5	J.Goldham	c Finch	0	run out	6
6	Earl of Winchilsea	c Monk	14	b Thompson	19
7	T.Lord	c Monk	3	not out	1
8	N.Graham	b Monk	7	not out	14
9	R.Turner	run out	8		
10	J.Hampton	b Timber	1		
11	W.Bedster	not out	0	run out	19
	Byes				
			69	(7 wickets)	**81**

FoW (1): 1- , 2- , 3- , 4- , 5- , 6- , 7- , 8- , 9- , 10-69
FoW (2): 1- , 2- , 3- , 4- , 5- , 6- , 7-

Middlesex and M.C.C. Bowling

	O	M	R	W	O	M	R	W
Lord				2				2
Hampton				4				1

Oldfield Bowling

	O	M	R	W	O	M	R	W
Monk				1				
Timber				1				
Thompson								2

Umpires:

Close of Play: 1st day: .

The visiting team was seven of Middlesex with four gentlemen of MCC.

R.LEIGH'S XI v E.G.MORANT'S XI

Played at Dartford Brent, July 21, 22, 1794.

E.G.Morant's XI won by 33 runs.

E.G.MORANT'S XI

1	J.Walker	c Hammond	3	b T.Walker	0
2	W.Fennex	c H.Walker	5	c Hammond	10
3	W.Beldham	c H.Walker	24	run out	2
4	J.Small, jun	c Hammond	21	c H.Walker	2
5	A.Freemantle	b Wells	3	c Purchase	9
6	T.Scott	c Tufton	8	c Robinson	1
7	G.Louch	b Wells	5	c Wells	3
8	T.Ray	b Wells	39	c Purchase	0
9	T.Taylor	run out	4	c Wells	0
10	T.Boxall	b Bullen	12	not out	5
11	D.Harris	not out	0	b Wells	3
	Byes		4		
			128		35

FoW (1): 1- , 2- , 3- , 4- , 5- , 6- , 7- , 8- , 9- , 10-128
FoW (2): 1- , 2- , 3- , 4- , 5- , 6- , 7- , 8- , 9- , 10-35

R.LEIGH'S XI

1	H.Walker	b Boxall	1	b Beldham	2
2	John Wells	c Ray	18	b Boxall	11
3	T.Walker	c Beldham	6	c Fennex	3
4	J.Ring	c Taylor	17	b Harris	0
5	R.Robinson	b Harris	3	b Boxall	1
6	J.Crawte	c Beldham	0	c Louch	7
7	J.Hammond	c Taylor	12	b Harris	3
8	R.Purchase	b Harris	3	b Boxall	1
9	H.J.Tufton	not out	8	b Boxall	0
10	J.Smith	c Fennex	1	b Harris	4
11	W.Bullen	b Boxall	1	not out	8
	Byes		15		5
			85		45

FoW (1): 1- , 2- , 3- , 4- , 5- , 6- , 7- , 8- , 9- , 10-85
FoW (2): 1- , 2- , 3- , 4- , 5- , 6- , 7- , 8- , 9- , 10-45

R.Leigh's XI Bowling

	O	M	R	W	O	M	R	W
Wells				3				1
Bullen				1				
T.Walker								1

E.G.Morant's XI Bowling

	O	M	R	W	O	M	R	W
Harris				2				3
Boxall				2				4
Beldham								1

Umpires:

Close of Play: 1st day: .

D.HARRIS' XI v T.WALKER'S XI

Played at Dartford Brent, July 23, 24, 1794.

T.Walker's XI won by 53 runs.

T.WALKER'S XI

1	H.Walker	b Purchase	1	c Taylor		2
2	John Wells	b Harris	37	b Purchase		3
3	J.Ring	c Scott	17	b Purchase		0
4	T.Walker	run out	2	b Harris		32
5	J.Hammond	c Harris	22	run out		8
6	J.Crawte	c Taylor	14	c Taylor		2
7	H.J.Tufton	b Harris	22	b Harris		1
8	J.Walker	b Lord	0	c Beldham		8
9	C.Anguish	b Purchase	1	c Purchase		1
10	W.Bullen	run out	6	b Lord		0
11	T.Boxall	not out	3	not out		2
	Byes		5			
			130			59

FoW (1): 1- , 2- , 3- , 4- , 5- , 6- , 7- , 8- , 9- , 10-130
FoW (2): 1- , 2- , 3- , 4- , 5- , 6- , 7- , 8- , 9- , 10-59

D.HARRIS' XI

1	A.Freemantle	b Boxall	2	c H.Walker	4
2	J.Small, jun	b Boxall	11	st Hammond	2
3	R.Robinson	b T.Walker	6	b Boxall	3
4	W.Beldham	not out	27	c J.Walker	2
5	W.Fennex	c Hammond	0	b Boxall	6
6	G.Louch	run out	0	c Ring	4
7	T.Scott	b T.Walker	2	c Hammond	4
8	R.Purchase	c Bullen	0	c H.Walker	20
9	T.Taylor	c Bullen	20	c Bullen	2
10	T.Lord	run out	0	not out	3
11	D.Harris	run out	2	c H.Walker	9
	Byes		6		1
			76		60

FoW (1): 1- , 2- , 3- , 4- , 5- , 6- , 7- , 8- , 9- , 10-76
FoW (2): 1- , 2- , 3- , 4- , 5- , 6- , 7- , 8- , 9- , 10-60

D.Harris' XI Bowling

	O	M	R	W	O	M	R	W
Harris				2				2
Purchase				2				2
Lord				1				1

T.Walker's XI Bowling

	O	M	R	W	O	M	R	W
Boxall				2				2
T.Walker				2				

Umpires:

Close of Play: 1st day: .

M.C.C. v OLDFIELD

Played at Lord's Old Ground, Marylebone, July 29, 30, 1794.

M.C.C. won by 56 runs.

M.C.C.

1	C.Anguish	b Timber	5	b Thompson	9
2	Sir J.Shelley	b Gates	23	b Thompson	1
3	N.Graham	b Timber	2	c Finch	1
4	G.Louch	c East	1	c Finch	14
5	Earl of Winchilsea	b Timber	5	b Gates	15
6	H.J.Tufton	b Gates	17	b East	49
7	T.Lord	c Gates	0	b East	23
8	Earl of Thanet	c Gill	6	b Timber	0
9	R.Turner	b Gates	3	b Timber	10
10	J.Hampton	not out	5	b Gates	5
11	J.Lambert	c Monk	1	not out	0
	Byes		3		5
			71		132

FoW (1): 1- , 2- , 3- , 4- , 5- , 6- , 7- , 8- , 9- , 10-71
FoW (2): 1- , 2- , 3- , 4- , 5- , 6- , 7- , 8- , 9- , 10-132

OLDFIELD

1	T.Shackle	b Lord	20	b Lord	1
2	S.Gill	c Louch	0	b Hampton	10
3	G.East	c Lambert	9	b Hampton	1
4	J.Finch	b Hampton	10	c Tufton	38
5	Timber	c Winchilsea	0	b Hampton	1
6	Gates	b Hampton	6	b Lord	0
7	R.Lawrence	c Hampton	3	b Lord	3
8	Monk	b Lord	7	c Louch	13
9	E.Winter	run out	0	c Winchilsea	0
10	Thompson	c Turner	0	not out	13
11	E.G.Morant	not out	3	b Hampton	3
	Byes				6
			58		89

FoW (1): 1- , 2- , 3- , 4- , 5- , 6- , 7- , 8- , 9- , 10-58
FoW (2): 1- , 2- , 3- , 4- , 5- , 6- , 7- , 8- , 9- , 10-89

Oldfield Bowling

	O	M	R	W	O	M	R	W
Timber				3				2
Gates				3				2
Thompson								2
East								2

M.C.C. Bowling

	O	M	R	W	O	M	R	W
Lord				2				3
Hampton				2				4

Umpires:

Close of Play: 1st day: .

M.C.C. v HAMPSHIRE AND KENT

Played at Lord's Old Ground, Marylebone, August 7, 8, 9, 11, 1794.

M.C.C. won by 59 runs.

M.C.C.

1	T.Walker	b Harris	9	st Hammond		13
2	John Wells	run out	30	not out		54
3	H.Walker	c Hammond	44	run out		4
4	W.Beldham	c Hammond	0	run out		51
5	Earl of Winchilsea	b Boxall	6	b Hammond		0
6	G.Louch	c Boxall	1	c Bullen		6
7	H.J.Tufton	c Pilcher	8	b Boxall		0
8	C.Anguish	b Harris	25	c Bullen		0
9	Sir J.Shelley	c Scott	1	c Harris		3
10	R.Turner	c Bullen	5	c Ring		14
11	J.Lambert	not out	0	b Hammond		2
	Byes		5			4
			134			151

FoW (1): 1- , 2- , 3- , 4- , 5- , 6- , 7- , 8- , 9- , 10-134
FoW (2): 1- , 2- , 3- , 4- , 5- , 6- , 7- , 8- , 9- , 10-151

HAMPSHIRE AND KENT

1	J.Pilcher	run out	0	b T.Walker		1
2	T.Scott	st Wells	10	c T.Walker		2
3	J.Small, jun	b Beldham	27	b Wells		32
4	J.Ring	c Beldham	20	c Wells		18
5	J.Hammond	b T.Walker	6	b T.Walker		2
6	A.Freemantle	b Beldham	19	run out		15
7	T.Taylor	b Beldham	0	c Beldham		9
8	R.Purchase	b Beldham	12	run out		6
9	W.Bullen	b Beldham	3	not out		9
10	T.Boxall	b T.Walker	10	c T.Walker		6
11	D.Harris	not out	0	c Beldham		13
	Byes		3			3
			110			116

FoW (1): 1- , 2- , 3- , 4- , 5- , 6- , 7- , 8- , 9- , 10-110
FoW (2): 1- , 2- , 3- , 4- , 5- , 6- , 7- , 8- , 9- , 10-116

Hampshire and Kent Bowling

	O	M	R	W	O	M	R	W
Harris				2				
Boxall				1				1
Hammond								2

M.C.C. Bowling

	O	M	R	W	O	M	R	W
Beldham				5				
T.Walker				2				2
Wells								1

Umpires:

Close of Play: 1st day: ; 2nd day: ; 3rd day: .

MCC had Beldham, H.Walker, T.Walker and Wells as given men.

M.C.C. v OLDFIELD

Played at Lord's Old Ground, Marylebone, August 12, 13, 1794.

Oldfield won by 6 runs.

OLDFIELD

1	G.East	b Hampton	2	b Hampton	10
2	Monk	b Lord	1	c Winchilsea	9
3	S.Gill	c Louch	3	b Lord	0
4	Gates	c Louch	10	b Lord	13
5	Timber	hit wkt	1	not out	8
6	J.Finch	c Hampton	5	b Hampton	6
7	R.Lawrence	c Louch	1	b Lord	0
8	E.Winter	b Hampton	34	b Hampton	0
9	T.Shackle	b Lord	21	c Lord	1
10	Thompson	c Lord	2	b Lord	18
11	West	not out	6	c Louch	9
	Byes		6		4
			92		78

FoW (1): 1- , 2- , 3- , 4- , 5- , 6- , 7- , 8- , 9- , 10-92
FoW (2): 1- , 2- , 3- , 4- , 5- , 6- , 7- , 8- , 9- , 10-78

M.C.C.

1	Sir J.Shelley	b Monk	0	b Gates	1
2	W.Bedster	c East	15	run out	0
3	H.J.Tufton	c Finch	10	b Gates	3
4	C.Anguish	c West	29	b Timber	0
5	Earl of Winchilsea	b Thompson	15	b Timber	0
6	G.Louch	b Monk	6	not out	25
7	T.Lord	not out	13	b Timber	0
8	R.Turner	b Timber	17	c Monk	3
9	Earl of Thanet	b Timber	10	b Gates	0
10	J.Hampton	b Gates	12	b Gates	1
11	J.Lambert	c West	0	b Timber	0
	Byes		3		1
			130		34

FoW (1): 1- , 2- , 3- , 4- , 5- , 6- , 7- , 8- , 9- , 10-130
FoW (2): 1- , 2- , 3- , 4- , 5- , 6- , 7- , 8- , 9- , 10-34

M.C.C. Bowling

	O	M	R	W	O	M	R	W
Lord				2				4
Hampton				2				3

Oldfield Bowling

	O	M	R	W	O	M	R	W
Monk				2				
Thompson				1				
Gates				1				4
Timber				2				4

Umpires:

Close of Play: 1st day: .

M.C.C. v OLDFIELD

Played at Lord's Old Ground, Marylebone, August 13, 14, 1794.

Oldfield won by six wickets.

M.C.C.

1	H.J.Tufton	c Finch	6	b Gates		1
2	W.Bedster	c Timber	1	b Timber		4
3	Earl of Winchilsea	b Ingram	17	b Gates		0
4	Sir J.Shelley	b Timber	31	b Gates		11
5	C.Anguish	c Thompson	14	b Gates		1
6	G.Louch	c Timber	11	b Gates		5
7	Earl of Thanet	c Lawrence	1	b Gates		3
8	T.Lord	b Ingram	3	b Gates		2
9	R.Turner	c Finch	11	b Timber		8
10	J.Hampton	not out	5	run out		4
11	J.Lambert	b Ingram	0	not out		0
	Byes		2			4
			102			43

FoW (1): 1- , 2- , 3- , 4- , 5- , 6- , 7- , 8- , 9- , 10-102
FoW (2): 1- , 2- , 3- , 4- , 5- , 6- , 7- , 8- , 9- , 10-43

OLDFIELD

1	T.Shackle	c Louch	18	run out		1
2	R.Lawrence	b Lord	0	c Louch		5
3	E.Winter	c Hampton	11	not out		12
4	J.Finch	run out	19	not out		14
5	Gates	c Lord	15			
6	G.East	b Lord	13	b Hampton		0
7	T.Ingram	b Turner	0			
8	Monk	b Hampton	4			
9	Timber	c Anguish	6			
10	Thompson	not out	13	b Hampton		11
11	S.Gill	b Hampton	0			
	Byes		4			
			103	(4 wickets)		43

FoW (1): 1- , 2- , 3- , 4- , 5- , 6- , 7- , 8- , 9- , 10-103
FoW (2): 1- , 2- , 3- , 4-

Oldfield Bowling

	O	M	R	W	O	M	R	W
Ingram				3				
Timber				1				2
Gates								7

M.C.C. Bowling

	O	M	R	W	O	M	R	W
Hampton				2				2
Lord				2				
Turner				1				

Umpires:

Close of Play: 1st day: .

This match began the same day the previous one ended.

HAMPSHIRE v SURREY AND KENT

Played at Stoke Down, Alresford, August 19, 20, 1794.

Surrey and Kent won by six wickets.

HAMPSHIRE

1	John Wells	c T.Walker	19	c T.Walker	4
2	J.Small, jun	c J.Walker	4	b T.Walker	26
3	W.Beldham	b Hammond	23	c J.Walker	20
4	A.Freemantle	b T.Walker	9	b Hammond	2
5	T.Scott	run out	1	b T.Walker	2
6	Earl of Winchilsea	b T.Walker	2	b T.Walker	2
7	G.Louch	b Hammond	2	c Tufton	5
8	R.Purchase	b T.Walker	2	st Ring	4
9	J.Small, sen	b T.Walker	1	b T.Walker	6
10	T.Taylor	b Hammond	1	b T.Walker	0
11	D.Harris	not out	1	not out	0
	Byes				
			65		71

FoW (1): 1- , 2- , 3- , 4- , 5- , 6- , 7- , 8- , 9- , 10-65
FoW (2): 1- , 2- , 3- , 4- , 5- , 6- , 7- , 8- , 9- , 10-71

SURREY AND KENT

1	J.Harding	hit wkt	1		
2	J.Walker	b Purchase	22	b Harris	9
3	H.Walker	b Harris	4	c Wells	9
4	T.Walker	c Beldham	9	not out	20
5	J.Ring	run out	0	not out	26
6	R.Robinson	not out	27	run out	1
7	J.Crawte	b Harris	1		
8	J.Hammond	b Purchase	4		
9	C.Anguish	c Beldham	0		
10	H.J.Tufton	b Purchase	0	b Harris	1
11	T.Boxall	c Louch	1		
	Byes		1		1
			70	(4 wickets)	67

FoW (1): 1- , 2- , 3- , 4- , 5- , 6- , 7- , 8- , 9- , 10-70
FoW (2): 1- , 2- , 3- , 4-

Surrey and Kent Bowling

	O	M	R	W		O	M	R	W
T.Walker				4					5
Hammond				3					1

Hampshire Bowling

	O	M	R	W		O	M	R	W
Harris				2					2
Purchase				3					

Umpires:

Close of Play: 1st day: .

Hampshire had Beldham and Wells as given men.

(Variant) SB incorrectly gives the date as 9 August.

HAMPSHIRE v SURREY AND KENT

Played at Stoke Down, Alresford, August 21, 22, 23, 1794.

Hampshire won by six wickets.

SURREY AND KENT

1	J.Harding	run out	19	b Harris	21
2	J.Walker	c Wells	9	b Harris	5
3	R.Robinson	b Purchase	2	run out	15
4	T.Walker	b Beldham	2	c Scott	27
5	H.Walker	c Wells	4	b Harris	19
6	J.Ring	not out	66	b Purchase	5
7	J.Hammond	b Beldham	6	b Harris	2
8	J.Crawte	c Taylor	0	c Harris	0
9	C.Anguish	b Beldham	3	b Harris	0
10	H.J.Tufton	run out	7	b Purchase	1
11	T.Boxall	hit wkt	0	not out	0
	Byes				
			118		95

FoW (1): 1- , 2- , 3- , 4- , 5- , 6- , 7- , 8- , 9- , 10-118
FoW (2): 1- , 2- , 3- , 4- , 5- , 6- , 7- , 8- , 9- , 10-95

HAMPSHIRE

1	John Wells	run out	75	not out	1
2	T.Scott	c Harding	2		
3	A.Freemantle	run out	4	not out	10
4	J.Small, jun	c J.Walker	9	run out	12
5	W.Beldham	st Hammond	46		
6	G.Louch	b T.Walker	0	b T.Walker	4
7	R.Purchase	b Hammond	3	b T.Walker	2
8	J.Small, sen	b T.Walker	2		
9	Earl of Winchilsea	c H.Walker	15	b Boxall	1
10	T.Taylor	not out	24		
11	D.Harris	b Boxall	1		
	Byes		3		
			184	(4 wickets)	30

FoW (1): 1- , 2- , 3- , 4- , 5- , 6- , 7- , 8- , 9- , 10-184
FoW (2): 1- , 2- , 3- , 4-

Hampshire Bowling

	O	M	R	W		O	M	R	W
Purchase				1					2
Beldham				3					
Harris									5

Surrey and Kent Bowling

	O	M	R	W		O	M	R	W
Boxall				1					1
T.Walker				2					2
Hammond				1					

Umpires:

Close of Play: 1st day: ; 2nd day: .

Hampshire had Beldham and Wells as given men.

(Variant) SB has James Wells playing instead of J.Walker.

OLDFIELD v KENT

Played at Lord's Old Ground, Marylebone, August 27, 28, 29, 30, 1794.

Oldfield won by 49 runs.

OLDFIELD
1	T.Ray	run out	6	b Boxall	12
2	J.Harding	b Hammond	13	b Boxall	2
3	T.Shackle	c Goodhew	12	c Ring	37
4	W.Fennex	c Boxall	51	c Fielder	2
5	J.Finch	b Hammond	24	run out	1
6	E.Winter	not out	24	c Hammond	6
7	Gates	c Brazier	0	c Bullen	23
8	R.Lawrence	c Boxall	0	b Boxall	12
9	Thompson	c Boxall	13	c Hammond	2
10	Timber	c Ring	0	not out	0
11	S.Gill	b Hammond	0	b Boxall	32
	Byes		3		4
			146		133

FoW (1): 1- , 2- , 3- , 4- , 5- , 6- , 7- , 8- , 9- , 10-146
FoW (2): 1- , 2- , 3- , 4- , 5- , 6- , 7- , 8- , 9- , 10-133

KENT
1	J.Pilcher	st Gates	2	b Fennex	0
2	T.Boxall	c Timber	38	b Fennex	8
3	J.Ring	b Fennex	10	c Ray	8
4	R.Fielder	c Finch	35	c Harding	3
5	J.Hammond	c Fennex	5	b Ray	22
6	Earl of Winchilsea	c Ray	15	b Timber	12
7	Goodhew	run out	0	b Timber	1
8	W.Brazier	b Fennex	3	not out	10
9	H.J.Tufton	c Finch	15	b Fennex	4
10	J.Burgess	b Fennex	8	c Harding	13
11	W.Bullen	not out	5	b Timber	2
	Byes		8		3
			144		86

FoW (1): 1- , 2- , 3- , 4- , 5- , 6- , 7- , 8- , 9- , 10-144
FoW (2): 1- , 2- , 3- , 4- , 5- , 6- , 7- , 8- , 9- , 10-86

Kent Bowling
	O	M	R	W	O	M	R	W
Hammond				3				
Boxall								4

Oldfield Bowling
	O	M	R	W	O	M	R	W
Fennex				3				3
Timber								3
Ray								1

Umpires:

Close of Play: 1st day: ; 2nd day: ; 3rd day: .

Oldfield had Fennex, Harding and Ray as given men.

ENGLAND v SURREY

Played at Lord's Old Ground, Marylebone, September 10, 11, 12, 13, 15, 1794.

England won by 3 runs.

ENGLAND

1	J.Ring	b T.Walker	5	b W.Beldham		22
2	J.Small, jun	c H.Walker	23	c Harding		22
3	J.Hammond	c W.Beldham	7	b W.Beldham		3
4	T.Ray	c H.Walker	22	b John Wells		2
5	T.Shackle	b John Wells	1	run out		2
6	T.Boxall	c John Wells	14	b John Wells		2
7	A.Freemantle	b W.Beldham	7	b T.Walker		19
8	W.Fennex	b T.Walker	4	b W.Beldham		6
9	R.Fielder	c W.Beldham	6	b Robinson		27
10	T.Scott	c T.Walker	14	c Harding		15
11	T.Taylor	b W.Beldham	5	b John Wells		13
12	T.Lord	not out	0	c James Wells		2
13	D.Harris	b T.Walker	1	not out		0
	Byes					1
			109			136

FoW (1): 1- , 2- , 3- , 4- , 5- , 6- , 7- , 8- , 9- , 10- , 11- , 12-109
FoW (2): 1- , 2- , 3- , 4- , 5- , 6- , 7- , 8- , 9- , 10- , 11- , 12-136

SURREY

1	John Wells	b Boxall	6	b Fennex		0
2	J.Harding	run out	13	b Harris		4
3	T.Walker	run out	11	b Fennex		46
4	W.Beldham	b Fennex	7	c Ray		1
5	H.Walker	c Fennex	40	run out		18
6	R.Robinson	b Harris	8	hit wkt		0
7	J.Walker	b Boxall	0	b Harris		12
8	J.Crawte	b Boxall	7	not out		33
9	James Wells	b Boxall	9	b Harris		4
10	J.Beldham	not out	6	run out		1
11	J.Hampton	b Boxall	1	run out		1
	Byes		3			11
			111			131

FoW (1): 1- , 2- , 3- , 4- , 5- , 6- , 7- , 8- , 9- , 10-111
FoW (2): 1- , 2- , 3- , 4- , 5- , 6- , 7- , 8- , 9- , 10-131

Surrey Bowling

	O	M	R	W	O	M	R	W
W.Beldham				2				3
John Wells				1				3
T.Walker				3				1
Robinson								1

England Bowling

	O	M	R	W	O	M	R	W
Boxall				5				
Harris				1				3
Fennex				1				2

Umpires:

Close of Play: 1st day: ; 2nd day: ; 3rd day: ; 4th day: .

ENGLAND v SURREY

Played at Dartford Brent, September 16, 17, 18, 19, 1794.

England won by 150 runs.

ENGLAND

1	J.Hammond	c John Wells	26	c H.Walker	5
2	J.Small, jun	run out	63	run out	2
3	J.Ring	c W.Beldham	18	c W.Beldham	1
4	R.Fielder	b T.Walker	8	st John Wells	1
5	A.Freemantle	c W.Beldham	4	c John Wells	21
6	T.Boxall	hit wkt	1	run out	1
7	T.Ray	c W.Beldham	48	b John Wells	41
8	W.Fennex	c John Wells	6	b John Wells	0
9	T.Scott	c Harding	8	c J.Beldham	1
10	R.Purchase	c H.Walker	13	c W.Beldham	0
11	T.Taylor	b John Wells	7	b John Wells	0
12	T.Shackle	c Harding	2	c Hampton	3
13	D.Harris	not out	0	not out	0
	Byes		1		1
			205		77

FoW (1): 1- , 2- , 3- , 4- , 5- , 6- , 7- , 8- , 9- , 10- , 11- , 12-205
FoW (2): 1- , 2- , 3- , 4- , 5- , 6- , 7- , 8- , 9- , 10- , 11- , 12-77

SURREY

1	J.Walker	c Taylor	0	c Scott	1
2	H.Walker	b Harris	11	b Taylor	13
3	T.Walker	b Harris	12	c Taylor	0
4	John Wells	hit wkt	16	b Boxall	3
5	W.Beldham	c Ray	10	b Harris	4
6	R.Robinson	c Small	0	not out	25
7	J.Crawte	not out	7	c Ray	0
8	J.Harding	b Boxall	3	c Taylor	5
9	James Wells	c Hammond	4	run out	2
10	J.Beldham	c Ray	0	b Harris	11
11	J.Hampton	b Harris	1	c Hammond	0
	Byes		4		
			68		64

FoW (1): 1- , 2- , 3- , 4- , 5- , 6- , 7- , 8- , 9- , 10-68
FoW (2): 1- , 2- , 3- , 4- , 5- , 6- , 7- , 8- , 9- , 10-64

Surrey Bowling

	O	M	R	W		O	M	R	W
T.Walker				1					
John Wells				1					3

England Bowling

	O	M	R	W		O	M	R	W
Harris				3					2
Boxall				1					1
Taylor									1

Umpires:

Close of Play: 1st day: ; 2nd day: ; 3rd day: .

M.C.C. v MIDDLESEX

Played at Lord's Old Ground, Marylebone, May 25, 26, 27, 1795.

M.C.C. won by 94 runs.

M.C.C.

1	Lord F.Beauclerk	b Turner	1	b Turner	15
2	C.Lennox	b Lord	23	b Ray	21
3	W.Beldham	b Turner	7	b Sylvester	41
4	G.Louch	b Turner	11	c Warren	15
5	J.Tufton	b Turner	0	b Lord	46
6	Earl of Winchilsea	b Turner	0	b Ray	0
7	H.J.Tufton	c Ray	16	b Ray	71
8	Sir J.Shelley	b Lord	1	b Sylvester	7
9	C.Anguish	b Sylvester	4	run out	0
10	J.L.Kaye	b Lord	13	not out	16
11	C.Cumberland	not out	0	run out	8
	Byes		4		9
			80		249

FoW (1): 1- , 2- , 3- , 4- , 5- , 6- , 7- , 8- , 9- , 10-80
FoW (2): 1- , 2- , 3- , 4- , 5- , 6- , 7- , 8- , 9- , 10-249

MIDDLESEX

1	J.Rice	b Beauclerk	4	run out	1
2	W.Barton	b Cumberland	11	b Cumberland	0
3	J.Goldham	c Beldham	8	b Beauclerk	6
4	T.Ray	b Cumberland	8	c Lennox	12
5	N.Graham	b Beauclerk	1	c Lennox	1
6	G.T.Boult	b Beldham	76	b Beauclerk	11
7	T.Lord	b Beauclerk	5	b Cumberland	2
8	C.Warren	b Cumberland	0	b Cumberland	1
9	J.Beeston	c Kaye	49	st Beldham	4
10	R.Turner	b Beldham	6	c Lennox	11
11	Sylvester	not out	3	not out	8
	Byes		5		2
			176		59

FoW (1): 1- , 2- , 3- , 4- , 5- , 6- , 7- , 8- , 9- , 10-176
FoW (2): 1- , 2- , 3- , 4- , 5- , 6- , 7- , 8- , 9- , 10-59

Middlesex Bowling

	O	M	R	W	O	M	R	W
Turner				5				1
Lord				3				1
Sylvester				1				2
Ray								3

M.C.C. Bowling

	O	M	R	W	O	M	R	W
Cumberland				3				3
Beauclerk				3				2
Beldham				2				

Umpires:

Close of Play: 1st day: ; 2nd day: .

MCC had Beldham as a given man.

C.LENNOX'S XI v EARL OF WINCHILSEA'S XI

Played at Lord's Old Ground, Marylebone, June 1, 2, 3, 1795.

C.Lennox's XI won by 48 runs.

C.LENNOX'S XI

1	C.Lennox	run out	0	run out		29
2	R.Robinson	b T.Walker	61	not out		32
3	J.Small, jun	b Boxall	2	c H.Walker		13
4	W.Beldham	b T.Walker	6	b Wells		9
5	J.Hammond	c T.Walker	27	c Freemantle		2
6	Sir J.Shelley	c Wells	1	c T.Walker		0
7	T.Taylor	c H.Walker	9	c Wells		8
8	G.Louch	st Wells	10	c H.Walker		7
9	Lord F.Beauclerk	b Wells	5	b T.Walker		5
10	G.Drummond	not out	3	b T.Walker		0
11	D.Harris	b Wells	0	b Boxall		1
	Byes		2			4
			126			110

FoW (1): 1- , 2- , 3- , 4- , 5- , 6- , 7- , 8- , 9- , 10-126
FoW (2): 1- , 2- , 3- , 4- , 5- , 6- , 7- , 8- , 9- , 10-110

EARL OF WINCHILSEA'S XI

1	T.Boxall	b Harris	0	c Taylor		6
2	A.Freemantle	b Harris	20	b Harris		4
3	T.Walker	b Beauclerk	11	c Small		47
4	H.Walker	c Hammond	11	c Taylor		28
5	John Wells	c Hammond	1	b Harris		18
6	Earl of Winchilsea	b Beauclerk	11	c Hammond		8
7	J.Tufton	b Harris	0	b Harris		6
8	H.J.Tufton	b Harris	0	c Beldham		0
9	R.Purchase	c Beauclerk	9	c Small		2
10	C.Anguish	c Shelley	1	b Harris		0
11	T.Mellish	not out	0	not out		2
	Byes		2			1
			66			122

FoW (1): 1- , 2- , 3- , 4- , 5- , 6- , 7- , 8- , 9- , 10-66
FoW (2): 1- , 2- , 3- , 4- , 5- , 6- , 7- , 8- , 9- , 10-122

Earl of Winchilsea's XI Bowling

	O	M	R	W		O	M	R	W
Boxall				1					1
Wells				2					1
T.Walker				2					2

C.Lennox's XI Bowling

	O	M	R	W		O	M	R	W
Harris				4					4
Beauclerk				2					

Umpires:

Close of Play: 1st day: ; 2nd day: .

217

C.LENNOX'S XI v EARL OF WINCHILSEA'S XI
Played at Lord's Old Ground, Marylebone, June 9, 10, 11, 1795.

C.Lennox's XI won by ten wickets.

EARL OF WINCHILSEA'S XI

1	Earl of Winchilsea	b Harris	0	b Beldham		10
2	T.Walker	b Harris	1	c Beldham		31
3	H.Walker	c Hammond	5	b Harris		2
4	John Wells	b Harris	16	run out		23
5	A.Freemantle	b Harris	1	c Louch		50
6	T.Ray	run out	2	c Hammond		0
7	T.Boxall	c Beldham	22	c Upton		6
8	R.Purchase	b Beldham	4	b Beldham		4
9	H.J.Tufton	b Beldham	0	c Hammond		21
10	J.Tufton	b Beldham	10	not out		19
11	T.Mellish	not out	0	b Hammond		0
	Byes		1			2
			62			168

FoW (1): 1- , 2- , 3- , 4- , 5- , 6- , 7- , 8- , 9- , 10-62
FoW (2): 1- , 2- , 3- , 4- , 5- , 6- , 7- , 8- , 9- , 10-168

C.LENNOX'S XI

1	C.Lennox	c H.Walker	15			
2	J.Small, jun	b Boxall	13	not out		20
3	W.Beldham	b Wells	4	not out		8
4	R.Robinson	c Wells	67			
5	J.Hammond	b Wells	58			
6	N.Graham	c Freemantle	3			
7	G.Louch	c Freemantle	3			
8	T.Lord	b Boxall	0			
9	A.P.Upton	run out	16			
10	Sylvester	run out	15			
11	D.Harris	not out	0			
	Byes		9			
			203	(no wicket)		28

FoW (1): 1- , 2- , 3- , 4- , 5- , 6- , 7- , 8- , 9- , 10-203

C.Lennox's XI Bowling

	O	M	R	W		O	M	R	W
Harris				4					1
Beldham				3					2
Hammond									1

Earl of Winchilsea's XI Bowling

	O	M	R	W		O	M	R	W
Boxall				2					
Wells				2					

Umpires:

Close of Play: 1st day: ; 2nd day: .

SURREY AND M.C.C. v ENGLAND

Played at Lord's Old Ground, Marylebone, June 22, 23, 24, 25, 26, 1795.

Surrey and M.C.C. won by 15 runs.

SURREY AND M.C.C.

1	C.Lennox	c Hammond	2	b Boxall		4
2	H.Walker	run out	8	b Harris		40
3	T.Walker	b Harris	21	b Harris		73
4	R.Robinson	b Harris	12	b Harris		44
5	John Wells	b Harris	1	run out		7
6	W.Beldham	b Harris	6	c Boxall		6
7	Earl of Winchilsea	b Harris	15	b Boxall		0
8	J.Tufton	not out	12	not out		1
9	H.J.Tufton	b Boxall	2	b Harris		0
10	G.Louch	c Ray	4	c Ring		1
11	C.Cumberland	c Ray	2	b Harris		0
	Byes					
			85			176

FoW (1): 1- , 2- , 3- , 4- , 5- , 6- , 7- , 8- , 9- , 10-85
FoW (2): 1- , 2- , 3- , 4- , 5- , 6- , 7- , 8- , 9- , 10-176

ENGLAND

1	R.Fielder	c Wells	7	c Beldham		10
2	T.Boxall	b T.Walker	3	c T.Walker		7
3	J.Ring	b Wells	1	b Beldham		69
4	J.Small, jun	b Wells	2	b Wells		4
5	J.Hammond	b T.Walker	2	c H.Walker		53
6	A.Freemantle	run out	7	run out		2
7	T.Ray	c Lennox	4	c T.Walker		3
8	J.Walker	c Louch	7	c H.Walker		35
9	R.Purchase	c Louch	8	b T.Walker		0
10	J.Crawte	not out	3	b T.Walker		13
11	D.Harris	c J.Tufton	0	not out		5
	Byes		1			
			45			201

FoW (1): 1- , 2- , 3- , 4- , 5- , 6- , 7- , 8- , 9- , 10-45
FoW (2): 1- , 2- , 3- , 4- , 5- , 6- , 7- , 8- , 9- , 10-201

England Bowling

	O	M	R	W	O	M	R	W
Harris				5				5
Boxall				1				2

Surrey and M.C.C. Bowling

	O	M	R	W	O	M	R	W
T.Walker				2				2
Wells				2				1
Beldham								1

Umpires:

Close of Play: 1st day: ; 2nd day: ; 3rd day: ; 4th day: .

M.C.C. v MIDDLESEX

Played at Lord's Old Ground, Marylebone, June 26, 27, 29, 1795.

Middlesex won by three wickets.

M.C.C.

1	C.Lennox	b Turner	16	b Turner		4
2	R.Purchase	b Lord	36	b Turner		0
3	J.Hammond	b Lord	7	c Graham		7
4	J.Tufton	c Carter	0	b Turner		0
5	H.J.Tufton	b Lord	19	c Wheeler		4
6	A.P.Upton	b Lord	2	b Turner		4
7	C.Cumberland	not out	37	b Turner		3
8	Earl of Winchilsea	b Turner	6	b Lord		0
9	G.Louch	run out	0	c Lord		4
10	J.Church	b Lord	1	b Lord		1
11	Park	b Lord	0	not out		1
	Byes					
			124			28

FoW (1): 1- , 2- , 3- , 4- , 5- , 6- , 7- , 8- , 9- , 10-124
FoW (2): 1- , 2- , 3- , 4- , 5- , 6- , 7- , 8- , 9- , 10-28

MIDDLESEX

1	J.Rice	c Louch	12			
2	T.Ray	c Louch	33	b Purchase		0
3	T.Shackle	b Hammond	1	c Hammond		22
4	N.Graham	b Hammond	6	not out		13
5	R.Whitehead	c Lennox	1	b Purchase		0
6	H.Bridger	b Hammond	5	b Purchase		2
7	T.Lord	b Purchase	0	b Hammond		1
8	J.Wheeler	b Purchase	2	b Purchase		9
9	Sylvester	b Hammond	0			
10	Carter	not out	0	c Lennox		24
11	R.Turner	b Purchase	7	not out		11
	Byes		1			3
			68	(7 wickets)		85

FoW (1): 1- , 2- , 3- , 4- , 5- , 6- , 7- , 8- , 9- , 10-68
FoW (2): 1- , 2- , 3- , 4- , 5- , 6- , 7-

Middlesex Bowling

	O	M	R	W	O	M	R	W
Lord				6				2
Turner				2				5

M.C.C. Bowling

	O	M	R	W	O	M	R	W
Purchase				3				4
Hammond				4				1

Umpires:

Close of Play: 1st day: ; 2nd day: .

MCC had Hammond and Purchase as given men. This match began the same day the previous one ended.

SURREY v ENGLAND

Played at Molesey Hurst, July 6, 7, 8, 1795.

Surrey won by 76 runs.

SURREY

1	T.Walker	b Harris	70	b Taylor	20
2	J.Walker	c Hammond	3	c Lennox	9
3	R.Robinson	run out	20	b Boxall	1
4	H.Walker	b Harris	4	c Boxall	36
5	J.Beldham	c Hammond	0	not out	3
6	W.Beldham	c Hammond	2	b Boxall	4
7	John Wells	c Harris	14	c Hammond	3
8	J.Crawte	c J.Small, jun	6	b Boxall	2
9	Earl of Winchilsea	run out	0	c Hammond	1
10	Gates	not out	3	c Taylor	0
11	T.Payne	b Harris	0	b Boxall	2
	Byes		2		2
			124		83

FoW (1): 1- , 2- , 3- , 4- , 5- , 6- , 7- , 8- , 9- , 10-124
FoW (2): 1- , 2- , 3- , 4- , 5- , 6- , 7- , 8- , 9- , 10-83

ENGLAND

1	J.Small, sen	c W.Beldham	1	b T.Walker	6
2	J.Hammond	c H.Walker	1	b Wells	5
3	J.Ring	c Wells	21	b Wells	11
4	J.Small, jun	c W.Beldham	20	b Wells	2
5	C.Lennox	c Gates	5	c H.Walker	2
6	A.Freemantle	run out	0	b Wells	1
7	T.Taylor	b T.Walker	0	c T.Walker	0
8	J.Tufton	b Wells	10	b T.Walker	12
9	Soane	c H.Walker	1	c Gates	1
10	R.Purchase	run out	15	c W.Beldham	0
11	T.Boxall	c H.Walker	0	b Wells	6
12	H.J.Tufton	not out	5	b Wells	6
13	D.Harris	b Wells	0	not out	0
	Byes				
			79		52

FoW (1): 1- , 2- , 3- , 4- , 5- , 6- , 7- , 8- , 9- , 10-79, 11- , 12-79
FoW (2): 1- , 2- , 3- , 4- , 5- , 6- , 7- , 8- , 9- , 10-52, 11- , 12-52

England Bowling

	O	M	R	W	O	M	R	W
Harris				3				
Boxall								4
Taylor								1

Surrey Bowling

	O	M	R	W	O	M	R	W
T.Walker				1				2
Wells				2				6

Umpires:

Close of Play: 1st day: ; 2nd day: .

C.LENNOX'S XI v EARL OF WINCHILSEA'S XI

Played at Molesey Hurst, July 8, 9, 10, 1795.

C.Lennox's XI won by 129 runs.

C.LENNOX'S XI

1	H.J.Tufton	c Crawte	4	c Beldham		2
2	J.Hammond	b Walker	12	c Beldham		37
3	John Wells	c Beldham	3	c Taylor		0
4	H.Walker	run out	15	c Walker		13
5	J.Ring	b Boxall	11	c J.Small, sen		0
6	C.Lennox	b Walker	6	c Beldham		1
7	A.Freemantle	not out	34	c J.Small, sen		22
8	T.Ray	b Boxall	3	b Taylor		5
9	R.Purchase	b Boxall	13	c J.Small, jun		7
10	Soane	b Beldham	11	c Beldham		9
11	D.Harris	b Taylor	4	not out		3
	Byes		1			7
			117			106

FoW (1): 1- , 2- , 3- , 4- , 5- , 6- , 7- , 8- , 9- , 10-117
FoW (2): 1- , 2- , 3- , 4- , 5- , 6- , 7- , 8- , 9- , 10-106

EARL OF WINCHILSEA'S XI

1	R.Robinson	b Harris	5	c Hammond		7
2	J.Tufton	b Harris	3	c Ray		1
3	Earl of Winchilsea	c Hammond	17	b Wells		2
4	T.Walker	b Harris	0	c Hammond		18
5	J.Small, jun	b Wells	9	c Freemantle		0
6	W.Beldham	b Wells	6	c Lennox		9
7	J.Crawte	c Harris	1	c Walker		8
8	J.Small, sen	c Ray	2	c Hammond		0
9	G.Louch	c Ray	3	b Wells		2
10	T.Taylor	b Harris	0	b Wells		0
11	T.Boxall	not out	0	not out		0
	Byes		1			
			47			47

FoW (1): 1- , 2- , 3- , 4- , 5- , 6- , 7- , 8- , 9- , 10-47
FoW (2): 1- , 2- , 3- , 4- , 5- , 6- , 7- , 8- , 9- , 10-47

Earl of Winchilsea's XI Bowling

	O	M	R	W	O	M	R	W
Boxall				3				
Walker				2				
Taylor				1				1
Beldham				1				

C.Lennox's XI Bowling

	O	M	R	W	O	M	R	W
Harris				4				
Wells				2				3

Umpires:

Close of Play: 1st day: ; 2nd day: .

This match began the same day the previous one ended.

MIDDLESEX v OLDFIELD

Played at Lord's Old Ground, Marylebone, July 16, 17, 18, 1795.

Middlesex won by 233 runs.

MIDDLESEX

1	T.Lord	run out	68	b Ray	21
2	C.Cumberland	st Gates	4	c Shackle	0
3	J.Hammond	b Timber	55	c Ray	89
4	H.J.Tufton	b Timber	11	b Timber	17
5	G.T.Boult	b Monk	14	b Monk	0
6	Earl of Winchilsea	b Timber	1	c Monk	24
7	G.Louch	b Timber	23	b Timber	12
8	N.Graham	c Gill	9	c Gill	3
9	W.Turner	c Ray	2	b Ray	11
10	R.Turner	not out	3	not out	4
11	J.Tufton	c Ray	8	c Timber	13
	Byes		1		7
			199		201

FoW (1): 1- , 2- , 3- , 4- , 5- , 6- , 7- , 8- , 9- , 10-199
FoW (2): 1- , 2- , 3- , 4- , 5- , 6- , 7- , 8- , 9- , 10-201

OLDFIELD

1	T.Ray	c Winchilsea	0	c H.J.Tufton	13
2	Timber	c Hammond	5	b Hammond	6
3	E.Winter	c Cumberland	1	b Cumberland	4
4	J.Finch	c H.J.Tufton	12	c H.J.Tufton	33
5	T.Shackle	b Lord	12	c Winchilsea	1
6	Carter	b Lord	3	run out	20
7	Gates	b Lord	0	b Cumberland	0
8	S.Gill	c Graham	11	b Cumberland	1
9	E.G.Morant	not out	6	b Hammond	1
10	Monk	b Hammond	19	c R.Turner	1
11	R.Lawrence	run out	2	not out	14
	Byes		1		1
			72		95

FoW (1): 1- , 2- , 3- , 4- , 5- , 6- , 7- , 8- , 9- , 10-72
FoW (2): 1- , 2- , 3- , 4- , 5- , 6- , 7- , 8- , 9- , 10-95

Oldfield Bowling

	O	M	R	W	O	M	R	W
Timber				4				2
Monk				1				1
Ray								2

Middlesex Bowling

	O	M	R	W	O	M	R	W
Lord				3				
Hammond				1				2
Cumberland								3

Umpires:

Close of Play: 1st day: ; 2nd day: .

Middlesex had Hammond as a given man.

EARL OF WINCHILSEA'S XI v R.LEIGH'S XI

Played at Windmill Down, Hambledon, July 20, 21, 22, 1795.

Earl of Winchilsea's XI won by 113 runs.

EARL OF WINCHILSEA'S XI

1	Earl of Winchilsea	b Boxall	3	b Boxall		6
2	T.Walker	b Harris	2	c H.Walker		1
3	R.Robinson	c Beldham	78	c H.Walker		71
4	John Wells	b Boxall	12	c Tufton		3
5	J.Hammond	c H.Walker	15	b Harris		31
6	C.Lennox	run out	3	b Boxall		1
7	J.Tufton	b Harris	12	c Beldham		10
8	T.Scott	c Beldham	7	run out		3
9	J.Crawte	c Beldham	6	b Boxall		3
10	T.Ray	b Harris	0	not out		11
11	T.Taylor	not out	3	b Boxall		3
	Byes		4			3
			145			146

FoW (1): 1- , 2- , 3- , 4- , 5- , 6- , 7- , 8- , 9- , 10-145
FoW (2): 1- , 2- , 3- , 4- , 5- , 6- , 7- , 8- , 9- , 10-146

R.LEIGH'S XI

1	H.Walker	b Wells	2	run out		16
2	J.Walker	c Hammond	1	c Walker		1
3	J.Ring	st Hammond	2	b Walker		15
4	A.Freemantle	c Hammond	0	run out		14
5	T.Boxall	b Walker	5	b Hammond		2
6	W.Beldham	c Ray	2	b Walker		3
7	J.Small, jun	b Hammond	34	b Wells		3
8	H.J.Tufton	c Crawte	5	c Ray		8
9	R.Purchase	c Winchilsea	11	c Wells		10
10	G.Louch	b Walker	18	b Walker		23
11	D.Harris	not out	0	not out		0
	Byes		2			1
			82			96

FoW (1): 1- , 2- , 3- , 4- , 5- , 6- , 7- , 8- , 9- , 10-82
FoW (2): 1- , 2- , 3- , 4- , 5- , 6- , 7- , 8- , 9- , 10-96

R.Leigh's XI Bowling

	O	M	R	W	O	M	R	W
Harris				3				1
Boxall				2				4

Earl of Winchilsea's XI Bowling

	O	M	R	W	O	M	R	W
Walker				2				3
Hammond				1				1
Wells				1				1

Umpires:

Close of Play: 1st day: ; 2nd day: .

EARL OF WINCHILSEA'S XI v R.LEIGH'S XI

Played at Stoke Down, Alresford, July 23, 24, 25, 1795, June 28, 1796.

R.Leigh's XI won by three wickets.

EARL OF WINCHILSEA'S XI

1	J.Hammond	b Wells	52	b Harris	7
2	J.Small, jun	b Harris	0	b Wells	4
3	R.Robinson	c Ray	13	run out	0
4	T.Walker	b Beldham	12	run out	10
5	J.Ring	b Harris	15	not out	58
6	J.Tufton	c Beldham	13	b Harris	4
7	F.Reynolds	b Harris	3	run out	0
8	R.Purchase	c Tufton	7	c H.Walker	5
9	J.Small, sen	b Beldham	6	b Harris	7
10	T.Boxall	not out	3	run out	0
11	T.Taylor	run out	1	run out	14
	Byes				5
			125		114

FoW (1): 1- , 2- , 3- , 4- , 5- , 6- , 7- , 8- , 9- , 10-125
FoW (2): 1- , 2- , 3- , 4- , 5- , 6- , 7- , 8- , 9- , 10-114

R.LEIGH'S XI

				25 Jul 1795		28 Jun 1796	
1	John Wells	b Walker	25	b Boxall	10		
2	A.Freemantle	c J.Small, sen	4			st Hammond	7
3	J.Walker	c Tufton	13	c Hammond	3		
4	H.Walker	b Hammond	7	not out	19	b Boxall	20
5	W.Beldham	b Purchase	56	not out	10	c Hammond	18
6	J.Crawte	b Boxall	11			b Boxall	0
7	T.Ray	not out	32			not out	11
8	G.Louch	b Boxall	7			not out	8
9	H.J.Tufton	b Boxall	0	c Taylor	0		
10	W.Bullen	b Walker	4				
11	D.Harris	b Walker	0				
	Byes		3				1
			162	(3 wickets)	42	(7 wickets)	78

FoW (1): 1- , 2- , 3- , 4- , 5- , 6- , 7- , 8- , 9- , 10-162
FoW (2): 1- , 2- , 3- , 4- , 5- , 6- , 7-

R.Leigh's XI Bowling

	O	M	R	W	O	M	R	W
Harris				3				3
Wells				1				1
Beldham				2				

Earl of Winchilsea's XI Bowling

					25 Jul 1795			28 Jun 1796		
	O	M	R	W	O	M	R	W	O	M	R	W
Boxall				3				1				3
Purchase				1								
Walker				3								
Hammond				1								

Umpires:

Close of Play: 1st day: ; 2nd day: ; 3rd day: R.Leigh's XI (2) 42-3 (H.Walker 19*, Beldham 10*).

At close of play on 25 July (a Saturday), Leigh's XI, with seven wickets in hand, required an additional 36 runs to win. Normal practice at the time would have been to continue at the earliest opportunity, and it was announced that the game would resume on 17 August. In the event, this did not take place and it was not until eleven months later, on 28 June 1796, that the match was brought to a conclusion. In these unique circumstances the batting and bowling in Leigh (2) are presented so as to show the position both at the close of play on 25 July 1795 and at the conclusion of the match in 1796. See also the Supplementary Note on page 277.

M.C.C. v OLDFIELD

Played at Lord's Old Ground, Marylebone, August 6, 7, 1795.

M.C.C. won by two wickets.

OLDFIELD

1	T.Ray	b Walker	7	hit wkt		13
2	T.Shackle	c Graham	18	run out		4
3	J.Ring	hit wkt	12	st Hammond		21
4	Brades	c H.J.Tufton	3	c Winchilsea		0
5	J.Finch	b Lord	15	c H.J.Tufton		14
6	Timber	b Lord	10	not out		10
7	Monk	b Lord	22	st Hammond		2
8	Gates	b Lord	1	b Lord		6
9	S.Gill	b Lord	0	b Lord		8
10	R.Lawrence	c H.J.Tufton	0	b Hammond		13
11	D.Harris	not out	0	b Hammond		3
	Byes		1			6
			89			100

FoW (1): 1- , 2- , 3- , 4- , 5- , 6- , 7- , 8- , 9- , 10-89
FoW (2): 1- , 2- , 3- , 4- , 5- , 6- , 7- , 8- , 9- , 10-100

M.C.C.

1	N.Graham	b Harris	5	not out		20
2	J.Tufton	b Harris	10	b Harris		4
3	Butler	c Brades	1			
4	T.Walker	c Ring	17	b Monk		18
5	J.Hammond	c Finch	6	b Harris		0
6	H.J.Tufton	b Harris	2	c Timber		1
7	T.Lord	c Ray	3	not out		18
8	Earl of Winchilsea	b Timber	4	run out		7
9	G.Louch	b Timber	0	c Brades		13
10	G.Leycester	b Harris	14	b Monk		7
11	J.Goldham	not out	21	c Ring		7
	Byes		4			8
			87	(8 wickets)		103

FoW (1): 1- , 2- , 3- , 4- , 5- , 6- , 7- , 8- , 9- , 10-87
FoW (2): 1- , 2- , 3- , 4- , 5- , 6- , 7- , 8-

M.C.C. Bowling

	O	M	R	W	O	M	R	W
Lord				5				2
Walker				1				
Hammond								2

Oldfield Bowling

	O	M	R	W	O	M	R	W
Harris				4				2
Timber				2				
Monk								2

Umpires:

Close of Play: 1st day: .

MCC had Hammond and Walker as given men; Oldfield had Harris and Ring as given men.

SURREY v ENGLAND

Played at Molesey Hurst, August 10, 11, 12, 1795.

England won by 38 runs.

ENGLAND

1	J.Tufton	c H.Walker	8	b Wells		6
2	J.Hammond	c Harding	49	run out		17
3	A.Freemantle	c Beldham	0	b Wells		1
4	J.Ring	run out	9	c Leycester		5
5	J.Small, jun	c H.Walker	7	c Beldham		10
6	J.Goldham	c Beldham	0	b T.Walker		0
7	C.Lennox	c Wells	27	c Leycester		0
8	T.Ray	c J.Walker	8	c Leycester		2
9	R.Fielder	c T.Walker	7	run out		9
10	H.J.Tufton	c Bliss	8	b Wells		1
11	T.Lord	c Beldham	0	c H.Walker		0
12	T.Boxall	hit wkt	12	c Beldham		2
13	D.Harris	not out	0	not out		1
	Byes		2			1
			137			55

FoW (1): 1- , 2- , 3- , 4- , 5- , 6- , 7- , 8- , 9- , 10- , 11- , 12-137
FoW (2): 1- , 2- , 3- , 4- , 5- , 6- , 7- , 8- , 9- , 10- , 11- , 12-55

SURREY

1	H.Walker	b Boxall	0	b Boxall		0
2	J.Walker	c Ray	0	c Ray		0
3	R.Robinson	c Small	14	b Lord		22
4	J.Harding	b Boxall	6	b Harris		4
5	W.Beldham	b Harris	3	c H.J.Tufton		3
6	T.Walker	c Ray	19	c Hammond		31
7	John Wells	run out	0	c Hammond		15
8	Earl of Winchilsea	c Boxall	2	b Boxall		1
9	G.Leycester	b Boxall	0	not out		18
10	J.Crawte	c Fielder	0	c Hammond		7
11	Bliss	not out	0	c Lord		0
	Byes					9
			44			110

FoW (1): 1- , 2- , 3- , 4- , 5- , 6- , 7- , 8- , 9- , 10-44
FoW (2): 1- , 2- , 3- , 4- , 5- , 6- , 7- , 8- , 9- , 10-110

Bowling

	O	M	R	W	O	M	R	W
Wells								3
T.Walker								1

England Bowling

	O	M	R	W	O	M	R	W
Boxall				3				2
Harris				1				1
Lord								1

Umpires:

Close of Play: 1st day: ; 2nd day: .

Bliss of Ripley.

SURREY v ENGLAND

Played at Molesey Hurst, August 12, 13, 14, 15, 1795.

England won by 27 runs.

ENGLAND
1	J.Hammond	c T.Walker	39	run out		0
2	A.Freemantle	c T.Walker	4	b Wells		10
3	J.Tufton	lbw b Wells	3	b Wells		14
4	R.Fielder	c J.Walker	1	b Wells		1
5	T.Ray	c Wells	26	b T.Walker		13
6	J.Small, jun	c Wells	15	c Beldham		31
7	J.Ring	c H.Walker	3	c J.Walker		21
8	C.Lennox	b Beldham	0	b T.Walker		8
9	H.J.Tufton	b T.Walker	6	not out		51
10	J.Goldham	c Wells	1	b T.Walker		2
11	T.Lord	c H.Walker	1	b Wells		4
12	T.Boxall	b Wells	1	b T.Walker		13
13	D.Harris	not out	5	b Wells		5
	Byes		2			1
			107			174

FoW (1): 1- , 2- , 3- , 4- , 5- , 6- , 7- , 8- , 9- , 10- , 11- , 12-107
FoW (2): 1- , 2- , 3- , 4- , 5- , 6- , 7- , 8- , 9- , 10- , 11- , 12-174

SURREY
1	H.Walker	b Boxall	0	b Harris		14
2	W.Beldham	b Hammond	47	c Ray		10
3	R.Robinson	b Boxall	0	st Hammond		47
4	T.Walker	b Harris	6	c Ray		23
5	John Wells	c Ray	32	c Ray		8
6	G.Leycester	hit wkt	14	b Harris		12
7	Earl of Winchilsea	b Hammond	0	b Harris		5
8	J.Harding	c Hammond	12	b Harris		0
9	G.Louch	c Ray	2	not out		3
10	J.Crawte	c J.Tufton	18	b Boxall		0
11	J.Walker	not out	0	c Ray		1
	Byes					
			131			123

FoW (1): 1- , 2- , 3- , 4- , 5- , 6- , 7- , 8- , 9- , 10-131
FoW (2): 1- , 2- , 3- , 4- , 5- , 6- , 7- , 8- , 9- , 10-123

Surrey Bowling
	O	M	R	W	O	M	R	W
Wells				2				5
T.Walker				1				4
Beldham				1				

England Bowling
	O	M	R	W	O	M	R	W
Harris				1				4
Boxall				2				1
Hammond				2				

Umpires:

Close of Play: 1st day: ; 2nd day: ; 3rd day: .

This match began the same day the previous one ended.

(Variant) SM and KG offer accounts that differ from Britcher, and from each other, at various points. In view of the lack of consensus Britcher has been accepted.

ENGLAND v HAMPSHIRE

Played at Dartford Heath, August 24, 25, 26, 1795.

England won by 16 runs.

ENGLAND

1	J.Tufton	lbw	28	c Hammond	11
2	John Wells	c Hammond	28	b T.Walker	7
3	R.Robinson	st Hammond	11	st Hammond	20
4	W.Beldham	c J.Small, sen	38	b Purchase	19
5	J.Ring	c H.Walker	15	b T.Walker	0
6	H.J.Tufton	b Hammond	8	c T.Walker	3
7	T.Ray	c H.Walker	1	b T.Walker	0
8	J.Crawte	c J.Small, jun	0	c H.Walker	0
9	N.Graham	c T.Walker	13	c Freemantle	13
10	T.Boxall	run out	14	run out	0
11	W.Bullen	not out	0	not out	0
	Byes				1
			156		74

FoW (1): 1- , 2- , 3- , 4- , 5- , 6- , 7- , 8- , 9- , 10-156
FoW (2): 1- , 2- , 3- , 4- , 5- , 6- , 7- , 8- , 9- , 10-74

HAMPSHIRE

1	J.Small, sen	c Ray	16	c Boxall	8
2	T.Walker	run out	0	c H.J.Tufton	10
3	J.Hammond	c Wells	32	c Wells	3
4	J.Small, jun	b Wells	8	not out	15
5	H.Walker	c Ring	29	c Graham	24
6	G.Leycester	run out	16	c Wells	1
7	A.Freemantle	b Bullen	5	b Wells	3
8	R.Purchase	not out	13	b Boxall	4
9	J.Walker	b Boxall	6	c Wells	9
10	G.Louch	b Boxall	0	b Wells	3
11	T.Lord	b Boxall	8	b Wells	1
	Byes				
			133		81

FoW (1): 1- , 2- , 3- , 4- , 5- , 6- , 7- , 8- , 9- , 10-133
FoW (2): 1- , 2- , 3- , 4- , 5- , 6- , 7- , 8- , 9- , 10-81

Hampshire Bowling

	O	M	R	W	O	M	R	W
Hammond				1				
Purchase								1
T.Walker								3

England Bowling

	O	M	R	W	O	M	R	W
Wells				1				3
Bullen				1				
Boxall				3				1

Umpires:

Close of Play: 1st day: ; 2nd day: .

Hampshire was stated to have three (unnamed) given men but SB suggests it should be five (Hammond, Lord and the Walkers). Britcher confirms that the match was played at Dartford Heath, not Dartford Brent. These were separate grounds. See the ACS *Guide to Kent Cricket Grounds* for further details.

ENGLAND v HAMPSHIRE

Played at Dartford Heath, August 27, 28, 29, 1795.

Hampshire won by four wickets.

ENGLAND

#	Batsman	Dismissal		Score	Dismissal	Score
1	John Wells	hit wkt		43	c T.Walker	3
2	W.Beldham	c J.Small, sen		6	lbw	35
3	R.Robinson	c H.Walker		64	b Purchase	4
4	H.J.Tufton	c Freemantle		0	b Purchase	1
5	J.Ring	run out		3	run out	7
6	J.Tufton	c Hammond		7	c J.Small, jun	7
7	T.Ray	b Purchase		16	b Purchase	10
8	J.Crawte	c J.Small, sen		62	st Hammond	6
9	N.Graham	c Turner		8	c J.Small, sen	8
10	T.Boxall	b T.Walker		17	c J.Small, jun	1
11	W.Bullen	not out		0	not out	1
	Byes					2
				226		85

FoW (1): 1- , 2- , 3- , 4- , 5- , 6- , 7- , 8- , 9- , 10-226
FoW (2): 1- , 2- , 3- , 4- , 5- , 6- , 7- , 8- , 9- , 10-85

HAMPSHIRE

#	Batsman	Dismissal		Score	Dismissal	Score
1	J.Small, sen	b Wells		13	b Boxall	1
2	T.Walker	run out		46	b Wells	3
3	H.Walker	c Beldham		27	c Beldham	32
4	J.Hammond	b Boxall		5	c Ray	28
5	J.Small, jun	c Wells		13	c Beldham	26
6	A.Freemantle	run out		9	not out	28
7	T.Shackle	c Wells		20	not out	18
8	R.Purchase	b Wells		18		
9	J.Walker	b Wells		8	c Boxall	2
10	T.Lord	not out		5		
11	W.Turner	b Boxall		5		
	Byes			2		3
				171	(6 wickets)	141

FoW (1): 1- , 2- , 3- , 4- , 5- , 6- , 7- , 8- , 9- , 10-171
FoW (2): 1- , 2- , 3- , 4- , 5- , 6-

Hampshire Bowling

	O	M	R	W		O	M	R	W
Purchase				1					3
T.Walker				1					

England Bowling

	O	M	R	W		O	M	R	W
Boxall				2					1
Wells				3					1

Umpires:

Close of Play: 1st day: ; 2nd day: .

Hampshire was stated to have three (unnamed) given men but SB suggests it should be five (Hammond, Lord and the Walkers). Britcher confirms that the match was played at Dartford Heath, not Dartford Brent.

KENT v ENGLAND

Played at Penenden Heath, Maidstone, August 31, September 1, 2, 1795.

England won by five wickets.

KENT

1	R.Fielder	b T.Walker	0	absent hurt	-
2	J.Small, jun	b Purchase	15	c H.Walker	8
3	R.Robinson	c J.Tufton	12	c H.Walker	42
4	W.Beldham	st Hammond	2	c Freemantle	43
5	T.Browning	c J.Tufton	3	c H.Walker	0
6	T.Boxall	b T.Walker	18	c H.Walker	0
7	Hooker	st Hammond	12	c Hammond	1
8	W.Browning	c Hammond	3	c H.Walker	0
9	Goodhew	b Hammond	10	c Hammond	0
10	S.Amherst	b Purchase	4	not out	3
11	W.Bullen	not out	16	b Purchase	2
	Byes				
			95		99

FoW (1): 1- , 2- , 3- , 4- , 5- , 6- , 7- , 8- , 9- , 10-95
FoW (2): 1- , 2- , 3- , 4- , 5- , 6- , 7- , 8- , 9-99

ENGLAND

1	A.Freemantle	c Amherst	13	not out	5
2	J.Tufton	hit wkt	6	b Boxall	0
3	R.Purchase	b Boxall	0		
4	T.Walker	b Boxall	12	c Amherst	8
5	J.Hammond	not out	53		
6	H.Walker	st Amherst	6	b Boxall	27
7	J.Ring	c Beldham	15	c Beldham	13
8	H.J.Tufton	b Bullen	22	b Beldham	1
9	C.Russell	b Boxall	0	not out	8
10	J.Crawte	c Goodhew	1		
11	G.Louch	c Bullen	0		
	Byes		2		3
			130	(5 wickets)	65

FoW (1): 1- , 2- , 3- , 4- , 5- , 6- , 7- , 8- , 9- , 10-130
FoW (2): 1- , 2- , 3- , 4- , 5-

England Bowling

	O	M	R	W	O	M	R	W
Purchase				2				1
Hammond				1				
T.Walker				2				

Kent Bowling

	O	M	R	W	O	M	R	W
Boxall				3				2
Bullen				1				
Beldham								1

Umpires:

Close of Play: 1st day: ; 2nd day: .

The match was advertised in the *Kentish Gazette* as East Malling (with Amherst, Boxall, Robinson, Tufton, H.Walker and J.Walker) v Kent (with Beldham, Harris, Louch, Small and Tufton) but not all these players appeared. Britcher calls it Kent (with Beldham, Robinson and Small) v England, as does SB. This has been accepted, although two Kent men, Ring and Russell (of Rochester) appear on the England side.

SIR H.MANN'S XI v R.LEIGH'S XI

Played at Dandelion Paddock, Margate, September 7, 8, 9, 10, 1795.

Sir H.Mann's XI won by 37 runs.

SIR H.MANN'S XI

1	A.Freemantle	c Walker	1	st Hammond		1
2	J.Small, jun	b Beldham	22	b Bullen		20
3	J.Walker	c Bullen	26	c Beldham		0
4	R.Robinson	c Beldham	31	b Bullen		24
5	J.Ring	c Hooker	1	lbw		5
6	T.Ray	c Beldham	16	run out		8
7	R.Purchase	c Louch	0	c Tufton		1
8	H.J.Tufton	c Hammond	6	not out		44
9	T.Lord	c Bullen	5	c Walker		6
10	T.Boxall	not out	2	c Beldham		11
11	W.Turner	c Graham	1	c Louch		1
	Byes		2			7
			113			128

FoW (1): 1- , 2- , 3- , 4- , 5- , 6- , 7- , 8- , 9- , 10-113
FoW (2): 1- , 2- , 3- , 4- , 5- , 6- , 7- , 8- , 9- , 10-128

R.LEIGH'S XI

1	Hooker	b Boxall	0	lbw		0
2	N.Graham	b Lord	25	b Purchase		0
3	J.Tufton	b Lord	32	c Tufton		1
4	J.Hammond	b Purchase	9	c Freemantle		6
5	T.Walker	c Freemantle	0	c Ray		27
6	W.Beldham	b Boxall	41	b Boxall		26
7	E.Bligh	st Tufton	6	b Boxall		4
8	J.Goldham	b Boxall	11	b Boxall		0
9	G.Louch	c Freemantle	2	b Boxall		0
10	J.Rice	c Freemantle	2	not out		0
11	W.Bullen	not out	0	c Ray		8
	Byes		3			1
			131			73

FoW (1): 1- , 2- , 3- , 4- , 5- , 6- , 7- , 8- , 9- , 10-131
FoW (2): 1- , 2- , 3- , 4- , 5- , 6- , 7- , 8- , 9- , 10-73

R.Leigh's XI Bowling

	O	M	R	W	O	M	R	W
Beldham				1				
Bullen								2

Sir H.Mann's XI Bowling

	O	M	R	W	O	M	R	W
Boxall				3				4
Purchase				1				1
Lord				2				

Umpires:

Close of Play: 1st day: ; 2nd day: ; 3rd day: .

Some accounts call the match Small v Walker, and they may have been the captains.

(Variant) A number of sources (KC, KG, SM, the *Star*) disagree with Britcher, but also with each other, on various points. In view of the lack of consensus Britcher is accepted. DC incorrectly has this match dated 1796.

SIR H.MANN'S XI v EARL OF DARNLEY'S XI

Played at Dandelion Paddock, Margate, September 10, 11, 12, 1795.

Earl of Darnley's XI won by 242 runs.

EARL OF DARNLEY'S XI

1	N.Graham	b Purchase	11	c Purchase		18
2	T.Walker	b Boxall	13	c Purchase		85
3	W.Beldham	c Boxall	35	c Ray		31
4	J.Hammond	c Tufton	19	b Robinson		60
5	J.Tufton	b Boxall	4	b Boxall		0
6	E.Bligh	c Freemantle	0	run out		5
7	W.Bullen	c Small	0	b Boxall		12
8	G.Louch	b Boxall	4	b Boxall		4
9	W.Barton	c Tufton	0	not out		28
10	Earl of Darnley	b Purchase	10	c Tufton		2
11	Hooker	not out	15	run out		7
	Byes		2			9
			113			261

FoW (1): 1- , 2- , 3- , 4- , 5- , 6- , 7- , 8- , 9- , 10-113
FoW (2): 1- , 2- , 3- , 4- , 5- , 6- , 7- , 8- , 9- , 10-261

SIR H.MANN'S XI

1	J.Walker	c Hammond	11	b Beldham		0
2	J.Ring	c Hammond	18	b Beldham		9
3	R.Robinson	c Tufton	6	c Louch		14
4	J.Small, jun	b Beldham	16	c Graham		0
5	A.Freemantle	run out	21	st Hammond		0
6	T.Ray	b Beldham	5	run out		0
7	H.J.Tufton	c Barton	0	c Tufton		0
8	R.Purchase	b Walker	4	c Bullen		0
9	T.Boxall	not out	22	not out		1
10	T.Lord	run out	2	c Tufton		0
11	J.Drew	b Hammond	2	c Walker		0
	Byes		1			
			108			24

FoW (1): 1- , 2- , 3- , 4- , 5- , 6- , 7- , 8- , 9- , 10-108
FoW (2): 1- , 2- , 3- , 4- , 5- , 6- , 7- , 8- , 9- , 10-24

Sir H.Mann's XI Bowling

	O	M	R	W	O	M	R	W
Boxall				3				3
Purchase				2				
Robinson								1

Earl of Darnley's XI Bowling

	O	M	R	W	O	M	R	W
Beldham				2				2
Walker				1				
Hammond				1				

Umpires:

Close of Play: 1st day: ; 2nd day: .

Some accounts call the match Hammond v Boxall, and they may have been the captains. This match began the same day the previous one ended.

SIR H.MANN'S XI v R.LEIGH'S XI

Played at Dandelion Paddock, Margate, September 14, 15, 16, 1795.

R.Leigh's XI won by an innings and 98 runs.

SIR H.MANN'S XI

1	J.Tufton	c Boxall	11	c Tufton	11
2	J.Walker	c Ray	16	c Small	1
3	T.Walker	c Bullen	24	c Small	3
4	J.Hammond	b Bullen	11	c Boxall	3
5	J.Ring	b Purchase	4	b Purchase	0
6	J.Pilcher	b Bullen	0	c Boxall	13
7	J.Burgess	not out	14	c Tufton	0
8	J.Goldham	c Boxall	2	c Tufton	1
9	T.Lord	c Freemantle	4	not out	2
10	J.Drew	b Boxall	0	c Purchase	0
11	Marclew	c Downham	2	c Robinson	9
	Byes		3		
			91		43

FoW (1): 1- , 2- , 3- , 4- , 5- , 6- , 7- , 8- , 9- , 10-91
FoW (2): 1- , 2- , 3- , 4- , 5- , 6- , 7- , 8- , 9- , 10-43

R.LEIGH'S XI

1	T.Boxall	c J.Walker	0
2	N.Graham	c Tufton	11
3	J.Small, jun	c Burgess	95
4	A.Freemantle	c Tufton	0
5	T.Ray	c Hammond	15
6	W.Bullen	c Pilcher	9
7	R.Robinson	c Tufton	46
8	H.J.Tufton	c Tufton	4
9	W.Barton	b T.Walker	27
10	Downham	c Tufton	10
11	R.Purchase	not out	13
	Byes		2
			232

FoW (1): 1- , 2- , 3- , 4- , 5- , 6- , 7- , 8- , 9- , 10-232

R.Leigh's XI Bowling

	O	M	R	W		O	M	R	W
Boxall				1					
Purchase				1					1
Bullen				2					

Sir H.Mann's XI Bowling

	O	M	R	W
T.Walker				1

Umpires:

Close of Play: 1st day: ; 2nd day: .

The *Sporting Magazine* gives a different batting order for Leigh's XI with Small at 10, which may mean he was last out. Marclew appears in some sources as Marklin.

MIDDLESEX v KENT

Played at Lord's Old Ground, Marylebone, May 16, 17, 1796.

Kent won by 51 runs.

KENT

1	J.Tufton	hit wkt	16	b Walker		0
2	J.Hammond	b Walker	1	c Wells		39
3	J.Pilcher	c Shackle	8	c Wells		11
4	J.Ring	c Ray	1	c Graham		14
5	E.Bligh	b Beauclerk	6	c Walker		3
6	H.J.Tufton	c Wells	10	run out		10
7	W.Barton	b Walker	9	c Ray		5
8	T.Boxall	c Ray	0	c Shackle		1
9	E.Hussey	c Ray	0	b Walker		0
10	R.Ayling	b Walker	11	not out		6
11	W.Bullen	not out	0	c Graham		0
	Byes					2
			62			91

FoW (1): 1- , 2- , 3- , 4- , 5- , 6- , 7- , 8- , 9- , 10-62
FoW (2): 1- , 2- , 3- , 4- , 5- , 6- , 7- , 8- , 9- , 10-91

MIDDLESEX

1	Earl of Winchilsea	b Boxall	0	b Boxall		6
2	Lord F Beauclerk	b Bullen	10	b Pilcher		14
3	A.P.Upton	b Boxall	0	b Boxall		0
4	G.Louch	not out	0	c Pilcher		0
5	T.Mellish	b Boxall	2	b Boxall		1
6	John Wells	c Hammond	2	b Bullen		0
7	N.Graham	c Ring	5	c Ring		0
8	T.Walker	run out	13	b Boxall		3
9	T.Shackle	run out	2	c Hammond		24
10	T.Ray	c Boxall	2	not out		9
11	T.Lord	c Pilcher	6	b Boxall		2
	Byes					1
			42			60

FoW (1): 1- , 2- , 3- , 4- , 5- , 6- , 7- , 8- , 9- , 10-42
FoW (2): 1- , 2- , 3- , 4- , 5- , 6- , 7- , 8- , 9- , 10-60

Middlesex Bowling

	O	M	R	W	O	M	R	W
Beauclerk				1				
Walker				3				2

Kent Bowling

	O	M	R	W	O	M	R	W
Boxall				3				5
Bullen				1				1
Pilcher								1

Umpires:

Close of Play: 1st day: .

Walker played for Middlesex in 1796 without being mentioned as a given man, so he was probably residing in the county. Middlesex had Wells as a given man. SB questions whether this was John Wells, but it seems likely that Middlesex (even with T.Walker) would have needed reinforcement by a 'crack' player against Kent. W.Beldham was the given man in the return match (if it can be called that - both games were at Lord's).

EARL OF WINCHILSEA'S XI v EARL OF DARNLEY'S XI

Played at Lord's Old Ground, Marylebone, June 13, 14, 15, 1796.

Earl of Darnley's XI won by 4 runs.

EARL OF DARNLEY'S XI

1	J.Ring	hit wkt	8	b Beauclerk		4
2	J.Pilcher	b Walker	12	b Walker		2
3	J.Tufton	b Beauclerk	2	b Beauclerk		0
4	J.Hammond	b Walker	21	c Walker		28
5	E.Bligh	run out	2	not out		8
6	T.Ray	c J.Small, jun	50	b Walker		14
7	E.Winter	c Beauclerk	6	b Walker		3
8	T.Boxall	b Beauclerk	20	b Walker		6
9	Earl of Darnley	c Walker	0	c Louch		8
10	W.Bullen	b Walker	2	b Beauclerk		4
11	D.Onslow	not out	0	b Beauclerk		3
	Byes					1
			123			81

FoW (1): 1- , 2- , 3- , 4- , 5- , 6- , 7- , 8- , 9- , 10-123
FoW (2): 1- , 2- , 3- , 4- , 5- , 6- , 7- , 8- , 9- , 10-81

EARL OF WINCHILSEA'S XI

1	Earl of Winchilsea	run out	11	c Pilcher		0
2	T.Walker	b Boxall	0	run out		9
3	J.Small, jun	c Pilcher	2	b Bullen		48
4	J.Small, sen	c Pilcher	1	c Pilcher		9
5	Lord F Beauclerk	b Bullen	11	run out		4
6	J.Harding	run out	21	b Bullen		9
7	G.Louch	b Boxall	2	b Hammond		18
8	E.Small	b Boxall	0	not out		0
9	T.Mellish	b Darnley	4	b Boxall		4
10	A.P.Upton	not out	2	b Boxall		0
11	A.Freemantle	c Ray	35	b Bullen		1
	Byes		4			5
			93			107

FoW (1): 1- , 2- , 3- , 4- , 5- , 6- , 7- , 8- , 9- , 10-93
FoW (2): 1- , 2- , 3- , 4- , 5- , 6- , 7- , 8- , 9- , 10-107

Earl of Winchilsea's XI Bowling

	O	M	R	W	O	M	R	W
Walker				3				4
Beauclerk				2				4

Earl of Darnley's XI Bowling

	O	M	R	W	O	M	R	W
Boxall				3				2
Bullen				1				3
Darnley				1				
Hammond								1

Umpires:

Close of Play: 1st day: ; 2nd day: .

Britcher's full title is 'Five Gentlemen of the Mary-le-bone Club and Six Players from Hants, against Four Gentlemen of the Mary-le-bone Club and Seven Players of Kent'. Freemantle must have batted higher in Winchilsea (1).

MIDDLESEX v KENT

Played at Lord's Old Ground, Marylebone, June 20, 21, 22, 1796.

Middlesex won by three wickets.

KENT

1	Earl of Darnley	c Butler	1	b Walker		0
2	E.Bligh	c Ray	7	c Beauclerk		19
3	J.Tufton	b Beauclerk	26	st Walker		10
4	H.J.Tufton	c Shackle	2	b Walker		0
5	J.Pilcher	run out	3	c Beldham		9
6	R.Fielder	c Ray	0	b Beauclerk		24
7	J.Hammond	st Beldham	13	c Walker		42
8	J.Ring	b Beldham	30	c Ray		9
9	R.Ayling	b Walker	3	run out		2
10	T.Boxall	not out	10	c Beauclerk		18
11	W.Bullen	b Beauclerk	9	not out		0
	Byes					1
			104			**134**

FoW (1): 1- , 2- , 3- , 4- , 5- , 6- , 7- , 8- , 9- , 10-104
FoW (2): 1- , 2- , 3- , 4- , 5- , 6- , 7- , 8- , 9- , 10-134

MIDDLESEX

1	Earl of Winchilsea	b Boxall	20	c Hammond		0
2	Lord F.Beauclerk	b Boxall	4	run out		25
3	G.Louch	c Fielder	1	b Darnley		30
4	T.Mellish	not out	0	c H.J.Tufton		2
5	T.Walker	b Boxall	15	c Boxall		37
6	W.Beldham	c Fielder	8	not out		17
7	N.Graham	b Boxall	6			
8	T.Ray	b Boxall	16	run out		2
9	T.Shackle	run out	4	not out		2
10	T.Lord	c Pilcher	22			
11	Butler	c Boxall	21	b Bullen		0
	Byes		7			
			124	(7 wickets)		**115**

FoW (1): 1- , 2- , 3- , 4- , 5- , 6- , 7- , 8- , 9- , 10-124
FoW (2): 1- , 2- , 3- , 4- , 5- , 6- , 7-

Middlesex Bowling

	O	M	R	W	O	M	R	W
Beauclerk				2				1
Walker				1				2
Beldham				1				

Kent Bowling

	O	M	R	W	O	M	R	W
Boxall				5				
Bullen								1
Darnley								1

Umpires:

Close of Play: 1st day: ; 2nd day: .

Middlesex had Beldham as a given man.

ENGLAND v SURREY AND KENT

Played at Stoke Down, Alresford, June 28, 29, 30, 1796.

England won by three wickets.

SURREY AND KENT

1	J.Tufton	c Beauclerk	2	b Bullen		11
2	H.J.Tufton	not out	12	b Bullen		8
3	T.J.Twistleton	c Hammond	2	st Hammond		0
4	G.Louch	b Walker	13	b Beauclerk		5
5	J.Walker	c Walker	0	c Beauclerk		0
6	T.Boxall	c Beauclerk	9	c Hammond		19
7	W.Beldham	b Beauclerk	23	c Walker		0
8	H.Walker	st Hammond	2	b Bullen		58
9	R.Robinson	run out	52	c Beauclerk		11
10	J.Ring	c Bullen	0	c Small		0
11	John Wells	c Beauclerk	12	not out		17
	Byes					
			127			129

FoW (1): 1- , 2- , 3- , 4- , 5- , 6- , 7- , 8- , 9- , 10-127
FoW (2): 1- , 2- , 3- , 4- , 5- , 6- , 7- , 8- , 9- , 10-129

ENGLAND

1	Earl of Winchilsea	b Wells	12	b Wells		0
2	Lord F.Beauclerk	b Wells	0	c Louch		34
3	E.Bligh	b Beldham	5	not out		8
4	T.Mellish	b Wells	0			
5	T.Walker	b Wells	3	hit wkt		10
6	A.Freemantle	b Wells	13	not out		57
7	J.Hammond	b Boxall	8	b Boxall		4
8	J.Small, jun	c H.J.Tufton	60	b Wells		1
9	T.Ray	b Boxall	18	c Wells		15
10	J.Harding	c H.J.Tufton	4	b Wells		0
11	W.Bullen	not out	1			
	Byes		2			2
			126	(7 wickets)		131

FoW (1): 1- , 2- , 3- , 4- , 5- , 6- , 7- , 8- , 9- , 10-126
FoW (2): 1- , 2- , 3- , 4- , 5- , 6- , 7-

England Bowling

	O	M	R	W	O	M	R	W
Walker				1				
Beauclerk				1				1
Bullen								3

Surrey and Kent Bowling

	O	M	R	W	O	M	R	W
Boxall				2				1
Wells				5				3
Beldham				1				

Umpires:

Close of Play: 1st day: ; 2nd day: .

The *Hampshire Chronicle* calls this match England v Surrey (with two given men). This seems less accurate than Britcher's title, as above, although it would account for the presence of Bullen on the England side. The teams are listed by social status. Before the commencement of this match, the Winchilsea v Leigh game from the previous season was concluded.

MIDDLESEX v SURREY

Played at Lord's Old Ground, Marylebone, August 15, 16, 1796.

Surrey won by eight wickets.

MIDDLESEX

#	Batsman	Dismissal	Runs	Dismissal	Runs
1	T.Boxall	b Hampton	2	b Wells	10
2	N.Graham	c Beldham	0	b Wells	13
3	T.Ray	b Wells	13	b Wells	1
4	T.Walker	b Wells	7	b Wells	10
5	J.Hammond	b Beldham	16	c Fennex	0
6	T.Shackle	c Beldham	3	b Wells	26
7	W.Barton	b Beldham	13	b Wells	11
8	J.Goldham	c Robinson	14	c Wells	3
9	J.Beeston	c Fennex	5	b Wells	0
10	T.Lord	b Wells	9	run out	0
11	Sylvester	not out	0	not out	8
	Byes		1		3
			83		85

FoW (1): 1- , 2- , 3- , 4- , 5- , 6- , 7- , 8- , 9- , 10-83
FoW (2): 1- , 2- , 3- , 4- , 5- , 6- , 7- , 8- , 9- , 10-85

SURREY

#	Batsman	Dismissal	Runs	Dismissal	Runs
1	Earl of Winchilsea	b Boxall	2	not out	10
2	E.Bligh	c Walker	2	st Hammond	2
3	R.Robinson	not out	76		
4	W.Beldham	lbw	4	not out	14
5	W.Fennex	c Hammond	10		
6	John Wells	c Hammond	4		
7	J.Crawte	st Hammond	27		
8	G.Louch	st Hammond	6		
9	J.Walker	b Walker	6	b Boxall	5
10	G.Shepheard	b Boxall	1		
11	J.Hampton	st Hammond	0		
	Byes				
			138	(2 wickets)	31

FoW (1): 1- , 2- , 3- , 4- , 5- , 6- , 7- , 8- , 9- , 10-138
FoW (2): 1- , 2-

Surrey Bowling

	O	M	R	W	O	M	R	W
Wells				3				7
Beldham				2				
Hampton				1				

Middlesex Bowling

	O	M	R	W	O	M	R	W
Boxall				2				1
Walker				1				

Umpires:

Close of Play: 1st day: .

Middlesex had Boxall and Hammond as given men. The artist G.Shepheard made his sole appearance in a 'great' match. This was the last 'great' or 'important' match in which two counties opposed each other until Sussex played Kent in June 1825.

(Variant) DC incorrectly gives the dates as 1, 2 August.

ENGLAND v SURREY

Played at Dandelion Paddock, Margate, August 22, 23, 1796.

Surrey won by an innings and 16 runs.

ENGLAND

1	A.Freemantle	run out	2	b Wells	1
2	J.Pilcher	run out	7	c Beldham	18
3	J.Tufton	c Beauclerk	2	run out	2
4	T.Walker	run out	0	st Tufton	3
5	J.Hammond	b Beldham	9	c Beldham	20
6	J.Small, jun	c Beauclerk	14	b Wells	15
7	J.Ring	c Wells	7	st Tufton	0
8	R.Purchase	b Beauclerk	0	c Beldham	5
9	T.Boxall	c Tufton	1	b Beauclerk	2
10	G.Ring	b Beldham	0	not out	2
11	F.Reynolds	not out	0	c Beauclerk	1
	Byes				7
			42		76

FoW (1): 1- , 2- , 3- , 4- , 5- , 6- , 7- , 8- , 9- , 10-42
FoW (2): 1- , 2- , 3- , 4- , 5- , 6- , 7- , 8- , 9- , 10-76

SURREY

1	Lord F.Beauclerk	c Boxall	9
2	J.Walker	c G.Ring	10
3	R.Robinson	c Hammond	34
4	W.Beldham	b Purchase	46
5	John Wells	c Small	3
6	J.Crawte	c Pilcher	16
7	H.Walker	st Hammond	12
8	T.Ray	c G.Ring	3
9	H.J.Tufton	c Small	1
10	C.Redett	c Tufton	0
11	Turnbull	not out	0
	Byes		
			134

FoW (1): 1- , 2- , 3- , 4- , 5- , 6- , 7- , 8- , 9- , 10-134

Surrey Bowling

	O	M	R	W		O	M	R	W
Beldham				2					
Beauclerk				1					1
Wells									2

England Bowling

	O	M	R	W
Purchase				1

Umpires:

Close of Play: 1st day: .

ENGLAND v SURREY

Played at Dandelion Paddock, Margate, August 24, 25, 26, 1796.

England won by five wickets.

SURREY

1	H.Walker	c Walker	1	b Purchase	8
2	J.Walker	c Boxall	12	c Walker	4
3	R.Robinson	b Fennex	36	run out	41
4	W.Beldham	b Fennex	24	b Boxall	2
5	John Wells	b Purchase	0	run out	1
6	Lord F.Beauclerk	b Boxall	20	b Boxall	1
7	T.Ray	b Boxall	2	b Purchase	2
8	J.Crawte	c Walker	0	st Hammond	23
9	H.J.Tufton	b Fennex	0	not out	8
10	Turnbull	st Hammond	1	b Purchase	0
11	Heneage	not out	3	b Walker	0
	Byes		6		4
			105		94

FoW (1): 1- , 2- , 3- , 4- , 5- , 6- , 7- , 8- , 9- , 10-105
FoW (2): 1- , 2- , 3- , 4- , 5- , 6- , 7- , 8- , 9- , 10-94

ENGLAND

1	J.Tufton	b Beauclerk	21	c Heneage	5
2	J.Ring	b Beldham	6		
3	J.Pilcher	st Tufton	5	c Ray	14
4	J.Small, jun	b Beauclerk	8	not out	12
5	T.Boxall	c Ray	2		
6	T.Walker	c Robinson	8	c Tufton	0
7	J.Hammond	c Beldham	17	b Beldham	2
8	A.Freemantle	b Wells	12	st Tufton	4
9	W.Fennex	c Tufton	0	not out	72
10	R.Purchase	st Tufton	5		
11	G.Ring	not out	5		
	Byes		2		
			91	(5 wickets)	109

FoW (1): 1- , 2- , 3- , 4- , 5- , 6- , 7- , 8- , 9- , 10-91
FoW (2): 1- , 2- , 3- , 4- , 5-

England Bowling

	O	M	R	W	O	M	R	W
Boxall				2				2
Purchase				1				3
Fennex				3				
Walker								1

Surrey Bowling

	O	M	R	W	O	M	R	W
Wells				1				
Beauclerk				2				
Beldham				1				1

Umpires:

Close of Play: 1st day: ; 2nd day: .

Britcher has Pilcher st Hammond in England (1) but this must be an error because Hammond is on the England side. Bentley gives st Tufton and this has been accepted.

C.LENNOX'S XI v EARL OF WINCHILSEA'S XI

Played at Lord's Old Ground, Marylebone, May 15, 16, 1797.

C.Lennox's XI won by 132 runs.

C.LENNOX'S XI

1	E.Bligh	st H.J.Tufton	15	run out	3
2	T.Boxall	c Mellish	1	c Sylvester	0
3	Lord F.Beauclerk	c Sylvester	104	b Sylvester	14
4	Earl of Dalkeith	b Walker	10	c Walker	1
5	T.Lord	b Walker	9	c Ray	3
6	C.Lennox	b J.Tufton	18	not out	6
7	G.Louch	b J.Tufton	1	b Sylvester	1
8	C.Douglas	b Sylvester	26	b Sylvester	2
9	N.Graham	c Sylvester	11	c Sylvester	1
10	J.Lambert	not out	7	c Walker	1
11	C.B.Codrington	c Ray	0	b Sylvester	1
	Byes		2		2
			204		35

FoW (1): 1- , 2- , 3- , 4- , 5- , 6- , 7- , 8- , 9- , 10-204
FoW (2): 1- , 2- , 3- , 4- , 5- , 6- , 7- , 8- , 9- , 10-35

EARL OF WINCHILSEA'S XI

1	J.Tufton	c Beauclerk	10	b Beauclerk	0
2	T.Walker	b Beauclerk	7	c Lord	10
3	Earl of Winchilsea	c Louch	0	c Bligh	0
4	H.J.Tufton	run out	8	b Beauclerk	3
5	T.Ray	b Beauclerk	2	b Boxall	4
6	T.Mellish	c Louch	7	c Lennox	12
7	A.P.Upton	b Beauclerk	2	not out	24
8	Sir H.W.Marten	b Lord	4	b Beauclerk	0
9	Sanderson	b Boxall	1	b Douglas	1
10	Sylvester	st Lennox	1	run out	0
11	D.Onslow	not out	4	b Douglas	6
	Byes		1		
			47		60

FoW (1): 1- , 2- , 3- , 4- , 5- , 6- , 7- , 8- , 9- , 10-47
FoW (2): 1- , 2- , 3- , 4- , 5- , 6- , 7- , 8- , 9- , 10-60

Earl of Winchilsea's XI Bowling

	O	M	R	W		O	M	R	W
Sylvester				1					4
Walker				2					
J.Tufton				2					

C.Lennox's XI Bowling

	O	M	R	W		O	M	R	W
Boxall				1					1
Beauclerk				3					3
Lord				1					
Douglas									2

Umpires:

Close of Play: 1st day: .

C.LENNOX'S XI v EARL OF WINCHILSEA'S XI
Played at Lord's Old Ground, Marylebone, May 19, 20, 1797.

Earl of Winchilsea's XI won by an innings and 94 runs.

C.LENNOX'S XI

1	E.Bligh	c J.Tufton	30	b Sylvester		13
2	T.Boxall	c Ray	4	run out		0
3	Earl of Dalkeith	b Lord	5	b Lord		4
4	Lord F.Beauclerk	lbw	32	c Upton		17
5	G.Louch	b Lord	1	b Sylvester		2
6	J.Lambert	c Sylvester	2	st H.J.Tufton		0
7	N.Graham	b Lord	0	c J.Tufton		4
8	J.Gibbons	run out	1	run out		3
9	C.Lennox	b Lord	22	b Lord		2
10	C.B.Codrington	not out	10	not out		3
11	A.Buller	c Ray	0	b Lord		0
	Byes					1
			107			49

FoW (1): 1- , 2- , 3- , 4- , 5- , 6- , 7- , 8- , 9- , 10-107
FoW (2): 1- , 2- , 3- , 4- , 5- , 6- , 7- , 8- , 9- , 10-49

EARL OF WINCHILSEA'S XI

1	T.Walker	c Bligh	125
2	A.P.Upton	run out	5
3	J Tufton	b Boxall	1
4	H.J.Tufton	c Beauclerk	8
5	Earl of Winchilsea	c Graham	10
6	T.Lord	c Boxall	20
7	T.Ray	c Bligh	53
8	Sir H.W.Marten	run out	0
9	D.Onslow	b Boxall	5
10	Sylvester	not out	17
11	Knowles	run out	3
	Byes		3
			250

FoW (1): 1- , 2- , 3- , 4- , 5- , 6- , 7- , 8- , 9- , 10-250

Earl of Winchilsea's XI Bowling

	O	M	R	W		O	M	R	W
Lord				4					3
Sylvester									2

C.Lennox's XI Bowling

	O	M	R	W
Boxall				2

Umpires:

Close of Play: 1st day: .

(Variant) DC incorrectly gives the dates as 10, 11 May.

ENGLAND v SURREY

Played at Lord's Old Ground, Marylebone, June 6, 7, 8, 9, 1797.

England won by six wickets.

SURREY

1	T.Walker	run out	101	c Lennox		0
2	H.Walker	b Boxall	56	c Tufton		13
3	R.Robinson	b Beauclerk	17	st Hammond		2
4	W.Beldham	b Boxall	0	b Beauclerk		0
5	John Wells	b Beauclerk	3	c Harding		9
6	E.Bligh	b Beauclerk	15	c Lennox		4
7	J.Walker	c Hammond	1	b Boxall		4
8	G.Louch	c Beauclerk	9	c Beauclerk		2
9	H.J.Tufton	b Boxall	3	not out		4
10	Earl of Winchilsea	not out	6	b Boxall		5
11	T.Mellish	c Fennex	0	run out		2
	Byes		4			
			215			45

FoW (1): 1- , 2- , 3- , 4- , 5- , 6- , 7- , 8- , 9- , 10-215
FoW (2): 1- , 2- , 3- , 4- , 5- , 6- , 7- , 8- , 9- , 10-45

ENGLAND

1	J.Small, jun	c Bligh	1	b Wells		12
2	J.Harding	c H.Walker	2			
3	J.Tufton	b Wells	2	not out		7
4	J.Hammond	b Robinson	82	c Tufton		22
5	Lord F.Beauclerk	c Bligh	53	b Wells		1
6	W.Fennex	st Tufton	11			
7	T.Boxall	not out	41			
8	A.Freemantle	c Tufton	20			
9	A.P.Upton	st Tufton	0	not out		4
10	C.Lennox	st Tufton	0	b Wells		0
11	E.Hussey	b Wells	2			
	Byes		1			
			215	(4 wickets)		46

FoW (1): 1- , 2- , 3- , 4- , 5- , 6- , 7- , 8- , 9- , 10-215
FoW (2): 1- , 2- , 3- , 4-

England Bowling

	O	M	R	W		O	M	R	W
Boxall				3					2
Beauclerk				3					1

Surrey Bowling

	O	M	R	W		O	M	R	W
Wells				2					3
Robinson				1					

Umpires:

Close of Play: 1st day: ; 2nd day: ; 3rd day: .

ENGLAND v SURREY

Played at Lord's Old Ground, Marylebone, June 19, 20, 21, 22, 23, 24, July 3, 1797.

England won by 23 runs.

ENGLAND

1	A.Freemantle	b Wells	7	run out	6
2	J.Small, jun	c Beldham	5	run out	12
3	J.Tufton	not out	36	b T.Walker	0
4	J.Hammond	b Wells	2	run out	65
5	Lord F.Beauclerk	b Wells	0	not out	47
6	W.Fennex	c T.Walker	12	b Beldham	74
7	T.Ray	c Beldham	28	run out	7
8	C.Lennox	b T.Walker	15	b Wells	29
9	T.Boxall	c Bligh	18	b Beldham	0
10	J.Lambert	b Wells	3	run out	0
11	N.Graham	b Wells	0	c Bligh	0
	Byes				2
			126		242

FoW (1): 1- , 2- , 3- , 4- , 5- , 6- , 7- , 8- , 9- , 10-126
FoW (2): 1- , 2- , 3- , 4- , 5- , 6- , 7- , 8- , 9- , 10-242

SURREY

1	W.Beldham	c Freemantle	43	c Small	2
2	Earl of Winchilsea	c Graham	3	c Small	0
3	R.Robinson	b Fennex	81	b Boxall	15
4	T.Walker	c Graham	25	b Beauclerk	15
5	H.Walker	run out	4	c Lennox	48
6	John Wells	c Ray	11	not out	11
7	E.Bligh	c Lambert	20	c Lennox	0
8	H.J.Tufton	c Ray	0	b Boxall	17
9	J.Walker	b Hammond	11	c Small	33
10	G.Louch	b Hammond	4	b Boxall	1
11	T.Mellish	not out	0	c Hammond	0
	Byes				1
			202		143

FoW (1): 1- , 2- , 3- , 4- , 5- , 6- , 7- , 8- , 9- , 10-202
FoW (2): 1- , 2- , 3- , 4- , 5- , 6- , 7- , 8- , 9- , 10-143

Surrey Bowling

	O	M	R	W	O	M	R	W
T.Walker				1				1
Wells				5				1
Beldham								2

England Bowling

	O	M	R	W	O	M	R	W
Fennex				1				
Hammond				2				
Boxall								3
Beauclerk								1

Umpires:

Close of Play: 1st day: ; 2nd day: ; 3rd day: ; 4th day: ; 5th day: England (2) 208-7; 6th day: No play.

When Saturday 24 June was wet the match was postponed until 3 July.

C.LENNOX'S XI v EARL OF WINCHILSEA'S XI
Played at Lord's Old Ground, Marylebone, July 4, 5, 6, 1797.

Earl of Winchilsea's XI won by four wickets.

C.LENNOX'S XI
1	T.Boxall	b T.Walker	6	b Bullen		0
2	H.Walker	b Wells	6	b Wells		6
3	W.Beldham	b Wells	3	c J.Tufton		62
4	W.Fennex	b Bullen	4	c H.J.Tufton		9
5	A.Freemantle	c T.Walker	12	c Ray		12
6	J.Hammond	run out	19	c Ray		32
7	E.Bligh	not out	8	c J.Tufton		0
8	C.Lennox	c T.Walker	6	c Ray		6
9	T.Mellish	b T.Walker	0	c Small		11
10	N.Graham	hit wkt	0	st H.J.Tufton		11
11	Hall	b T.Walker	0	not out		11
	Byes		1			
			65			160

FoW (1): 1- , 2- , 3- , 4- , 5- , 6- , 7- , 8- , 9- , 10-65
FoW (2): 1- , 2- , 3- , 4- , 5- , 6- , 7- , 8- , 9- , 10-160

EARL OF WINCHILSEA'S XI
1	J.Small, jun	b Fennex	0	b Boxall	8
2	J.Walker	b Fennex	4	not out	8
3	T.Ray	c Hammond	7	not out	5
4	T.Walker	b Fennex	31	lbw	31
5	R.Robinson	b Beldham	52	c Freemantle	25
6	J.Tufton	b Fennex	0	c Beldham	9
7	John Wells	c Hammond	0	b Boxall	12
8	Earl of Winchilsea	b Beldham	9	b Hammond	0
9	H.J.Tufton	b Boxall	15		
10	G.Louch	c Freemantle	4		
11	W.Bullen	not out	0		
	Byes		3		3
			125	(6 wickets)	101

FoW (1): 1- , 2- , 3- , 4- , 5- , 6- , 7- , 8- , 9- , 10-125
FoW (2): 1- , 2- , 3- , 4- , 5- , 6-

Earl of Winchilsea's XI Bowling
	O	M	R	W		O	M	R	W
Bullen				1					1
Wells				2					1
T.Walker				3					

C.Lennox's XI Bowling
	O	M	R	W		O	M	R	W
Boxall				1					2
Fennex				4					
Beldham				2					
Hammond									1

Umpires:

Close of Play: 1st day: ; 2nd day: .

The *Hampshire Chronicle* reports that 'the Earl of Winchilsea has made an improvement in the game of cricket, by having four stumps instead of three, and the wickets two inches higher'. SB quotes this report but says that four stumps can have been used only in practice games. However, contemporary press reports suggest, although not unambiguously, that four stumps may have been used in this game. At any rate, the size of the wicket was clearly a live issue at the time. The new code of laws adopted in 1798 retained three stumps, but increased their height from 22 inches to 24, and the length of the bail from 6 inches to 7.

M.C.C. v LONDON

Played at Lord's Old Ground, Marylebone, July 10, 11, 12, 1797.

M.C.C. won by 109 runs.

M.C.C.

1	E.Bligh	b Turner	1	b Sylvester	1
2	A.P.Upton	b Turner	0	b Beeston	4
3	J.Tufton	b Sylvester	48	b Beeston	59
4	Lord F.Beauclerk	b Ray	24	b Ray	11
5	C.Lennox	b Ray	1	b Beeston	28
6	Earl of Winchilsea	b Sylvester	11	b Beeston	4
7	H.J.Tufton	b Turner	9	b Beeston	17
8	C.Douglas	c Turner	27	run out	20
9	G.Louch	c Aylward	20	not out	39
10	C.Cumberland	b Sylvester	6	c Butler	9
11	T.Mellish	not out	8	b Sylvester	0
	Byes				3
			155		195

FoW (1): 1- , 2- , 3- , 4- , 5- , 6- , 7- , 8- , 9- , 10-155
FoW (2): 1- , 2- , 3- , 4- , 5- , 6- , 7- , 8- , 9- , 10-195

LONDON

1	J.Beeston	c Lennox	0	run out	6
2	Butler	b Beauclerk	16	b J.Tufton	6
3	J.Aylward	b Cumberland	82	c Beauclerk	48
4	R.Turner	c Douglas	1	c Beauclerk	2
5	T.Lord	st H.J.Tufton	12	b Beauclerk	0
6	T.Ray	b Beauclerk	0	lbw	0
7	T.Ingram	c Winchilsea	1	b Beauclerk	0
8	N.Graham	b Beauclerk	22	c Louch	1
9	J.Goldham	b Beauclerk	12	b Beauclerk	0
10	T.J.Burgoyne	not out	0	not out	21
11	Sylvester	b Cumberland	0	st H.J.Tufton	10
	Byes		1		
			147		94

FoW (1): 1- , 2- , 3- , 4- , 5- , 6- , 7- , 8- , 9- , 10-147
FoW (2): 1- , 2- , 3- , 4- , 5- , 6- , 7- , 8- , 9- , 10-94

London Bowling

	O	M	R	W	O	M	R	W
Sylvester				3				2
Ray				2				1
Turner				3				
Beeston								5

M.C.C. Bowling

	O	M	R	W	O	M	R	W
Beauclerk				4				3
Cumberland				2				
J.Tufton								1

Umpires:

Close of Play: 1st day: ; 2nd day: .

247

SURREY AND MIDDLESEX v ENGLAND

Played at Aram's New Ground, Montpelier Gardens, Walworth, July 12, 13, 1797.

Surrey and Middlesex won by four wickets.

ENGLAND

1	A.Freemantle	c Ingram	4	c H.Walker		26
2	J.Small, jun	c Ingram	18	b Wells		9
3	W.Wells	c Robinson	13	c Butler		6
4	J.Hammond	b Beldham	81	c Wells		3
5	W.Fennex	run out	17	b Beldham		35
6	T.Ray	b Wells	2	b Wells		0
7	J.Aylward	run out	10	c J.Walker		3
8	T.Boxall	b T.Walker	0	b Beldham		2
9	W.Gunnell	b T.Walker	3	run out		1
10	J.Tanner	not out	3	b Beldham		8
11	T.Taylor	b T.Walker	0	not out		0
	Byes					
			151			93

FoW (1): 1- , 2- , 3- , 4- , 5- , 6- , 7- , 8- , 9- , 10-151
FoW (2): 1- , 2- , 3- , 4- , 5- , 6- , 7- , 8- , 9- , 10-93

SURREY AND MIDDLESEX

1	T.Walker	b Boxall	1	b Fennex	4
2	J.Walker	b Tanner	0	b Taylor	2
3	John Wells	c Taylor	6	run out	4
4	R.Robinson	st Hammond	6	run out	7
5	W.Beldham	b Boxall	46	not out	65
6	H.Walker	b Taylor	48	not out	3
7	Butler	c Ray	9	b Boxall	12
8	T.Ingram	b Taylor	0		
9	J.Goldham	b Taylor	0		
10	J.Beeston	not out	6	run out	0
11	N.Graham	c Taylor	5		
	Byes		16		5
			143	(6 wickets)	102

FoW (1): 1- , 2- , 3- , 4- , 5- , 6- , 7- , 8- , 9- , 10-143
FoW (2): 1- , 2- , 3- , 4- , 5- , 6-

Surrey and Middlesex Bowling

	O	M	R	W	O	M	R	W
Wells				1				2
T.Walker				3				
Beldham				1				3

England Bowling

	O	M	R	W	O	M	R	W
Boxall				2				1
Taylor				3				1
Tanner				1				
Fennex								1

Umpires:

Close of Play: 1st day: .

The sources are unanimous that this game began the same day as the previous match ended, meaning that Aylward, Goldham, Graham and Ray must have hurried across London from Lord's. Gunnell is assumed to be the senior of the two Mitcham players of this name, i.e. W.Gunnell, rather than J.Gunnell who was to make a single appearance in an important match in 1810.

(Variant) SB has W.Bullen playing instead of Taylor, but no contemporary source has been found for this. Buckley in *Fresh Light on Pre-Victorian Cricket* notes 'Bullen vice Taylor' but the *Morning Herald*, which he cites, does not appear to contain any such statement. It is possible that Buckley was attempting to account for the presence of Bullen in the SB version when the list in MH of those due to play gives Taylor instead. Britcher, SM and Bentley all give Taylor and this is accepted.

EARL OF WINCHILSEA'S XI v C.LENNOX'S XI

Played at Racecourse Ground, Swaffham, July 20, 21, 1797.

Earl of Winchilsea's XI won by 27 runs.

EARL OF WINCHILSEA'S XI

1	John Wells	c Fennex	6	c Lennox	26
2	J.Tufton	c Hammond	13	c Upton	15
3	T.Walker	b Hammond	24	b Fennex	4
4	T.Ray	b Hammond	17	c Hammond	2
5	Earl of Dalkeith	b Hammond	0	b Beauclerk	0
6	Earl of Winchilsea	st Hammond	6	c Hammond	4
7	W.Beldham	st Hammond	75	st Hammond	18
8	Wilson	c Lennox	0	not out	0
9	J.Rice	c Lennox	1	b Fennex	0
10	T.Mellish	c Fennex	4	run out	0
11	Sylvester	not out	0	c Fennex	4
	Byes		3		3
			149		76

FoW (1): 1- , 2- , 3- , 4- , 5- , 6- , 7- , 8- , 9- , 10-149
FoW (2): 1- , 2- , 3- , 4- , 5- , 6- , 7- , 8- , 9- , 10-76

C.LENNOX'S XI

1	J.Small, jun	b Walker	4	c Ray	9
2	J.Hammond	run out	21	c Beldham	13
3	Lord F.Beauclerk	c Ray	37	b Wells	0
4	W.Fennex	b Wells	12	b Walker	40
5	N.Graham	c Wells	15	c Wells	6
6	A.P.Upton	b Beldham	4	c Beldham	1
7	T.Lord	run out	0	not out	1
8	Brown	b Wells	1	c Beldham	0
9	W.Courtenay	lbw	1	b Walker	0
10	G.Cooper	not out	0	c Ray	0
11	C.Lennox	c Ray	25	b Beldham	4
	Byes		2		2
			122		76

FoW (1): 1- , 2- , 3- , 4- , 5- , 6- , 7- , 8- , 9- , 10-122
FoW (2): 1- , 2- , 3- , 4- , 5- , 6- , 7- , 8- , 9- , 10-76

C.Lennox's XI Bowling

	O	M	R	W	O	M	R	W
Hammond				3				
Fennex								2
Beauclerk								1

Earl of Winchilsea's XI Bowling

	O	M	R	W	O	M	R	W
Wells				2				1
Beldham				1				1
Walker				1				2

Umpires:

Close of Play: 1st day: .

This game immediately followed a match between England and XXXIII of Norfolk at the same venue. The identity of 'Brown', appearing for Lennox's XI, is uncertain; it may be the player of that name appearing in the Norfolk XXXIII, although J.Beeston has also been suggested since it is known that the Beestons used 'Brown' as an alias. G.Booth has also been put forward since he is known to have been present at Swaffham during the Norfolk match, but his unpublished diaries confirm that he left for Norwich on 19 July, proceeding thence to Yarmouth the following day. 'Wilson', in Winchilsea's XI, is likewise not known.

HAMPSHIRE v M.C.C.

Played at Stoke Down, Alresford, August 7, 8, 9, 10, 1797.

M.C.C. won by 113 runs.

M.C.C.

1	G.Leycester	c Freemantle	0	lbw		24
2	C.Lennox	run out	0	b Purchase		4
3	J.Tufton	c Hale	22	b Purchase		61
4	Lord F.Beauclerk	not out	75	run out		43
5	E.Bligh	b Clair	4	b Purchase		21
6	H.J.Tufton	b Clair	14	b Purchase		19
7	G.Louch	b Bennett	1	b Purchase		3
8	Earl of Winchilsea	c May	11	c Freemantle		0
9	T.Mellish	c Freemantle	6	c Hale		9
10	C.Cumberland	b Taylor	0	c Bennett		0
11	Scott	c May	7	not out		2
	Byes		7			6
			147			192

FoW (1): 1- , 2- , 3- , 4- , 5- , 6- , 7- , 8- , 9- , 10-147
FoW (2): 1- , 2- , 3- , 4- , 5- , 6- , 7- , 8- , 9- , 10-192

HAMPSHIRE

1	J.Small, sen	c H.J.Tufton	4	b Beauclerk		2
2	John Bennett	b Beauclerk	1	c Winchilsea		26
3	R.Purchase	b Cumberland	4	not out		26
4	J.Small, jun	c Leycester	12	c H.J.Tufton		53
5	T.Taylor	st H.J.Tufton	16	st H.J.Tufton		0
6	May	run out	12	c H.J.Tufton		36
7	J.Stewart	b Cumberland	3	b Cumberland		4
8	A.Freemantle	b Beauclerk	17	b Beauclerk		0
9	E.Hale	c J.Tufton	2	b Beauclerk		0
10	Clair	run out	5	b Cumberland		0
11	Mundy	not out	0	st H.J.Tufton		1
	Byes		2			
			78			148

FoW (1): 1- , 2- , 3- , 4- , 5- , 6- , 7- , 8- , 9- , 10-78
FoW (2): 1- , 2- , 3- , 4- , 5- , 6- , 7- , 8- , 9- , 10-148

Hampshire Bowling

	O	M	R	W	O	M	R	W
Clair				2				
Bennett				1				
Taylor				1				
Purchase								5

M.C.C. Bowling

	O	M	R	W	O	M	R	W
Cumberland				2				2
Beauclerk				2				3

Umpires:

Close of Play: 1st day: ; 2nd day: ; 3rd day: .

Bennett appearing above is taken to be John Bennett. It is believed that his cousin James did not appear until 1798.

(Variant) The *Portsmouth Gazette* gives Hampshire (1) byes 0, total 76; Hampshire (2) Bennett 16, total 138; margin 125 runs but the version in Britcher is preferred.

M.C.C. v HAMPSHIRE

Played at Lord's Old Ground, Marylebone, August 14, 15, 16, 1797.

M.C.C. won by six wickets.

HAMPSHIRE

1	J.Small, jun	b Beauclerk	20	b Beauclerk	1
2	J.Harding	b J.Tufton	24	c Leycester	7
3	May	b Beauclerk	0	b Beauclerk	10
4	John Bennett	st H.J.Tufton	2	c Leycester	22
5	A.Freemantle	c J.Tufton	13	b J.Tufton	10
6	R.Purchase	b Beauclerk	25	c H.J.Tufton	4
7	White	c Lennox	3	b Beauclerk	0
8	T.Taylor	b J.Tufton	0	c Leycester	1
9	J.Small, sen	b J.Tufton	3	b Beauclerk	23
10	Witcher	b J.Tufton	2	b J.Tufton	1
11	D.Harris	not out	0	not out	0
	Byes				2
			92		81

FoW (1): 1- , 2- , 3- , 4- , 5- , 6- , 7- , 8- , 9- , 10-92
FoW (2): 1- , 2- , 3- , 4- , 5- , 6- , 7- , 8- , 9- , 10-81

M.C.C.

1	C.Lennox	b Purchase	4	b Purchase	6
2	G.Leycester	b Purchase	14	c White	14
3	Earl of Winchilsea	b Harris	2		
4	H.J.Tufton	c Freemantle	27	c J.Small, jun	0
5	J.Tufton	not out	39	not out	24
6	Lord F.Beauclerk	b Harris	14	b Purchase	5
7	E.Bligh	c Freemantle	2		
8	G.Louch	b Harris	9	not out	11
9	C.B.Codrington	lbw	1		
10	R.Stevens	c J.Small, jun	2		
11	R.B.Wyatt	b Purchase	0		
	Byes				
			114	(4 wickets)	60

FoW (1): 1- , 2- , 3- , 4- , 5- , 6- , 7- , 8- , 9- , 10-114
FoW (2): 1- , 2- , 3- , 4-

M.C.C. Bowling

	O	M	R	W	O	M	R	W
Beauclerk				3				4
J.Tufton				4				2

Hampshire Bowling

	O	M	R	W	O	M	R	W
Harris				3				
Purchase				3				2

Umpires:

Close of Play: 1st day: ; 2nd day: .

(Variant) The *Portsmouth Gazette* gives MCC (2) Beauclerk not out 24, Bligh b Purchase 5, J.Tufton dnb but the version in Britcher is preferred.

ENGLAND v M.C.C.

Played at Molesey Hurst, August 21, 22, 23, 1797.

M.C.C. won by six wickets.

ENGLAND

1	W.Fennex	b Beauclerk	24	b Wells		6
2	T.Walker	st Hammond	0	b Wells		0
3	H.Walker	st Hammond	0	b J.Tufton		39
4	R.Robinson	run out	11	b Beauclerk		12
5	J.Small, jun	c Wells	1	c Wells		0
6	J.Aylward	run out	5	c J.Tufton		35
7	A.Freemantle	c Wells	15	run out		4
8	T.Ray	b Beauclerk	3	run out		0
9	T.Boxall	b Beldham	1	b Wells		1
10	J.Crawte	c Beldham	0	not out		3
11	R.Purchase	not out	1	b Beauclerk		3
	Byes		1			
			62			103

FoW (1): 1- , 2- , 3- , 4- , 5- , 6- , 7- , 8- , 9- , 10-62
FoW (2): 1- , 2- , 3- , 4- , 5- , 6- , 7- , 8- , 9- , 10-103

M.C.C.

1	Lord F.Beauclerk	run out	24	b Fennex		3
2	E.Bligh	run out	4	not out		9
3	J.Tufton	lbw	0	b Boxall		3
4	J.Hammond	not out	83	not out		0
5	W.Beldham	c Ray	10			
6	John Wells	c Fennex	1			
7	N.Graham	run out	10			
8	C.Lennox	c Purchase	4	c Small		7
9	H.J.Tufton	st Freemantle	2	b Boxall		0
10	W.Barton	b Fennex	6			
11	C.B.Codrington	c H.Walker	0			
	Byes					
			144	(4 wickets)		22

FoW (1): 1- , 2- , 3- , 4- , 5- , 6- , 7- , 8- , 9- , 10-144
FoW (2): 1- , 2- , 3- , 4-

M.C.C. Bowling

	O	M	R	W	O	M	R	W
Beldham				1				
Beauclerk				2				2
Wells								3
J.Tufton								1

England Bowling

	O	M	R	W	O	M	R	W
Fennex				1				1
Boxall								2

Umpires:

Close of Play: 1st day: ; 2nd day: .

MCC had Beldham, Hammond and Wells as given men.

M.C.C. v ENGLAND

Played at Lord's Old Ground, Marylebone, August 28, 29, 30, 31, 1797.

England won by eight wickets.

M.C.C.

1	W.Barton	b Purchase	18	st Freemantle		15
2	W.Beldham	st Freemantle	19	c Ray		17
3	J.Tufton	c T.Walker	44	b Boxall		0
4	Lord F.Beauclerk	st T.Walker	32	c H.Walker		17
5	J.Hammond	run out	12	c Fennex		51
6	John Wells	c Fennex	8	not out		1
7	E.Bligh	run out	9	b Purchase		5
8	G.Louch	c Small	2	c Small		0
9	H.J.Tufton	st Freemantle	11	hit wkt		3
10	C.Lennox	not out	4	b T.Walker		4
11	C.B.Codrington	b Boxall	1	b Boxall		0
	Byes		1			3
			161			116

FoW (1): 1- , 2- , 3- , 4- , 5- , 6- , 7- , 8- , 9- , 10-161
FoW (2): 1- , 2- , 3- , 4- , 5- , 6- , 7- , 8- , 9- , 10-116

ENGLAND

1	J.Aylward	c H.J.Tufton	57			
2	H.Walker	b Wells	6			
3	T.Walker	b Hammond	64			
4	R.Robinson	b Bligh	37	not out		31
5	W.Fennex	not out	13			
6	J.Small, jun	b Beauclerk	5	run out		26
7	John Bennett	b Beauclerk	9	not out		4
8	A.Freemantle	run out	5	c H.J.Tufton		5
9	R.Purchase	b Beauclerk	1			
10	T.Ray	b Beauclerk	0			
11	T.Boxall	c Beauclerk	3			
	Byes		10			2
			210	(2 wickets)		68

FoW (1): 1- , 2- , 3- , 4- , 5- , 6- , 7- , 8- , 9- , 10-210
FoW (2): 1- , 2-

England Bowling

	O	M	R	W	O	M	R	W
Boxall				1				2
Purchase				1				1
T.Walker								1

M.C.C. Bowling

	O	M	R	W	O	M	R	W
Wells				1				
Beauclerk				4				
Hammond				1				
Bligh				1				

Umpires:

Close of Play: 1st day: ; 2nd day: ; 3rd day: .

MCC had Beldham, Hammond and Wells as given men.

M.C.C. v ENGLAND

Played at Lord's Old Ground, Marylebone, September 21, 22, 23, 25, 26, 1797.

M.C.C. won by four wickets.

ENGLAND
1	R.Robinson	b Wells	3	b Beauclerk		11
2	John Bennett	b Wells	7	c Beauclerk		0
3	H.Walker	b Beauclerk	9	b Hammond		3
4	T.Walker	c H.J.Tufton	0	b Beauclerk		49
5	J.Aylward	b Wells	7	c Lennox		23
6	J.Small, jun	c H.J.Tufton	5	b Hammond		26
7	W.Fennex	b Wells	12	c Hammond		3
8	A.Freemantle	c Wells	15	lbw		8
9	T.Ray	b Wells	0	c Hammond		22
10	R.Purchase	not out	7	not out		5
11	T.Boxall	c Barton	7	absent		-
	Byes		1			1
			73			151

FoW (1): 1- , 2- , 3- , 4- , 5- , 6- , 7- , 8- , 9- , 10-73
FoW (2): 1- , 2- , 3- , 4- , 5- , 6- , 7- , 8- , 9-151

M.C.C.
1	E.Bligh	b Boxall	2			
2	John Wells	b Boxall	22			
3	Lord F.Beauclerk	c Bennett	1	b Purchase		3
4	J.Tufton	c Ray	0	not out		35
5	J.Hammond	b T.Walker	21	b Fennex		24
6	H.J.Tufton	b Fennex	2	not out		24
7	W.Beldham	not out	55	c H.Walker		17
8	W.Barton	c Fennex	0	b Purchase		5
9	N.Graham	b Fennex	3			
10	T.Lord	c H.Walker	4	c Bennett		4
11	C.Lennox	b T.Walker	0	c Fennex		2
	Byes					1
			110	(6 wickets)		115

FoW (1): 1- , 2- , 3- , 4- , 5- , 6- , 7- , 8- , 9- , 10-110
FoW (2): 1- , 2- , 3- , 4- , 5- , 6-

M.C.C. Bowling

	O	M	R	W	O	M	R	W
Wells				5				
Beauclerk				1				2
Hammond								2

England Bowling

	O	M	R	W	O	M	R	W
Boxall				2				
Fennex				2				1
T.Walker				2				
Purchase								2

Umpires:

Close of Play: 1st day: ; 2nd day: ; 3rd day: ; 4th day: .

MCC had Beldham, Hammond and Wells as given men. Britcher says that Boxall, Bligh and Wells were all absent in the 2nd innings. They were probably unable to come when the match went into the Monday.

ENGLAND v SURREY

Played at Lord's Old Ground, Marylebone, June 6, 7, 8, 1798.

England won by 128 runs.

ENGLAND

1	W.Fennex	b T.Walker	17	c Kaye	8
2	T.Boxall	b T.Walker	17	c Beldham	0
3	J.Tufton	b T.Walker	25	c T.Walker	19
4	Lord F.Beauclerk	c Wells	0	b T.Walker	8
5	J.Hammond	b Wells	5	b Wells	2
6	J.Small, jun	b Wells	17	st Wells	1
7	B.Clifton	b Wells	8	c Wells	31
8	A.Freemantle	c Smith	23	c H.Walker	46
9	T.Ray	not out	17	b Wells	10
10	T.J.Burgoyne	st Wells	0	not out	7
11	J.Gibbons	b T.Walker	0	c H.Walker	7
	Byes		3		5
			132		144

FoW (1): 1- , 2- , 3- , 4- , 5- , 6- , 7- , 8- , 9- , 10-132
FoW (2): 1- , 2- , 3- , 4- , 5- , 6- , 7- , 8- , 9- , 10-144

SURREY

1	H.Walker	b Boxall	1	b Beauclerk	23
2	J.Walker	st Hammond	6	st Hammond	27
3	R.Robinson	b Beauclerk	14	c Freemantle	4
4	W.Beldham	b Boxall	7	c Ray	24
5	T.Walker	b Boxall	2	b Boxall	8
6	John Wells	b Boxall	0	not out	1
7	T.A.Smith	st Hammond	4	run out	2
8	J.L.Kaye	not out	3	b Boxall	1
9	Earl of Winchilsea	b Beauclerk	6	c Freemantle	0
10	P.Maitland	run out	5	run out	0
11	Z.Button	c Beauclerk	3	c Small	4
	Byes				3
			51		97

FoW (1): 1- , 2- , 3- , 4- , 5- , 6- , 7- , 8- , 9- , 10-51
FoW (2): 1- , 2- , 3- , 4- , 5- , 6- , 7- , 8- , 9- , 10-97

Surrey Bowling

	O	M	R	W	O	M	R	W
Wells				3				2
T.Walker				4				1

England Bowling

	O	M	R	W	O	M	R	W
Boxall				4				2
Beauclerk				2				1

Umpires:

Close of Play: 1st day: ; 2nd day: .

T.A.Smith, making his first appearance above, is the son of the T.A.Smith appearing in 'great' matches 1787-1794.

M.C.C. v MIDDLESEX

Played at Lord's Old Ground, Marylebone, June 20, 21, 1798.

Middlesex won by ten wickets.

M.C.C.
1	J.L.Kaye	b Boxall	0	not out	0
2	B.Clifton	c Booth	0	c Boxall	20
3	J.Tufton	c Ray	5	c Fennex	5
4	Lord F.Beauclerk	b Lord	7	b Fennex	12
5	H.J.Tufton	b Lord	3	c Fennex	3
6	C.Douglas	b Boxall	3	b Boxall	9
7	P.Maitland	run out	1	b Boxall	0
8	Earl of Winchilsea	c Boxall	4	run out	7
9	T.A.Smith	run out	2	b Fennex	25
10	J.Gibbons	not out	0	c Ray	0
11	Williams	b Lord	0	b Fennex	0
	Byes				4
			25		85

FoW (1): 1- , 2- , 3- , 4- , 5- , 6- , 7- , 8- , 9- , 10-25
FoW (2): 1- , 2- , 3- , 4- , 5- , 6- , 7- , 8- , 9- , 10-85

MIDDLESEX
1	N.Graham	st H.J.Tufton	5		
2	T.Boxall	c J.Tufton	7		
3	J.Hampton	c Kaye	17		
4	W.Fennex	b Clifton	14		
5	T.Ray	c Williams	28	not out	9
6	G.Booth	b Clifton	0		
7	T.Lord	c Beauclerk	4		
8	W.Beeston	c Beauclerk	8		
9	Sylvester	b Beauclerk	8		
10	T.J.Burgoyne	not out	1	not out	7
11	Stanhope	b Beauclerk	0		
	Byes		3		
			95	(no wicket)	16

FoW (1): 1- , 2- , 3- , 4- , 5- , 6- , 7- , 8- , 9- , 10-95

Middlesex Bowling
	O	M	R	W	O	M	R	W
Lord				3				
Boxall				2				2
Fennex								3

M.C.C. Bowling
	O	M	R	W	O	M	R	W
Clifton				2				
Beauclerk				2				

Umpires:

Close of Play: 1st day: .

Middlesex had Boxall as a given man.

M.C.C. v ENGLAND

Played at Lord's Old Ground, Marylebone, June 26, 27, 1798.

M.C.C. won by 17 runs.

M.C.C.

1	Earl of Winchilsea	run out	1	b Wells		3
2	J.Tufton	b Boxall	5	b Boxall		0
3	T.Walker	c Fennex	20	c Wells		13
4	J.Hammond	c Wells	0	b Boxall		8
5	Lord F.Beauclerk	b Boxall	21	b Lord		30
6	W.Beldham	b Wells	17	b Wells		8
7	B.Clifton	b Boxall	2	c Walker		0
8	T.A.Smith	b Wells	23	b Boxall		8
9	H.J.Tufton	hit wkt	4	b Boxall		6
10	J.Gibbons	b Fennex	7	c Crawte		5
11	Sylvester	not out	0	not out		1
	Byes					2
			100			84

FoW (1): 1- , 2- , 3- , 4- , 5- , 6- , 7- , 8- , 9- , 10-100
FoW (2): 1- , 2- , 3- , 4- , 5- , 6- , 7- , 8- , 9- , 10-84

ENGLAND

1	J.Crawte	c J.Tufton	2	c Beauclerk		3
2	J.Small, jun	c Hammond	4	b Beauclerk		6
3	R.Robinson	st Hammond	9	c Hammond		26
4	H.Walker	b Walker	0	c Walker		12
5	T.Ray	c H.J.Tufton	3	st H.J.Tufton		14
6	W.Fennex	run out	6	run out		0
7	John Wells	c Clifton	9	run out		5
8	A.Freemantle	c Beldham	29	c Beauclerk		10
9	J.Hampton	c Winchilsea	0	c H.J.Tufton		21
10	T.Boxall	st Hammond	5	b Walker		0
11	T.Lord	not out	0	not out		1
	Byes					2
			67			100

FoW (1): 1- , 2- , 3- , 4- , 5- , 6- , 7- , 8- , 9- , 10-67
FoW (2): 1- , 2- , 3- , 4- , 5- , 6- , 7- , 8- , 9- , 10-100

England Bowling

	O	M	R	W	O	M	R	W
Boxall				3				4
Wells				2				2
Fennex				1				
Lord								1

M.C.C. Bowling

	O	M	R	W	O	M	R	W
Walker				1				1
Beauclerk								1

Umpires:

Close of Play: 1st day: .

MCC had Beldham, Hammond and Walker as given men.

M.C.C. v ENGLAND

Played at Lord's Old Ground, Marylebone, July 11, 12, 13, 1798.

M.C.C. won by seven wickets.

ENGLAND

1	W.Fennex	b Walker	10	b Beldham		1
2	T.Ray	st Hammond	7	b Beauclerk		6
3	H.Walker	lbw	8	b Beldham		11
4	R.Robinson	c Hammond	33	c Tufton		10
5	A.Freemantle	b Walker	3	b Beauclerk		0
6	John Wells	c Maitland	12	c Tufton		9
7	J.Small, jun	c Whitehead	7	b Beldham		40
8	R.Purchase	b Walker	0	b Beauclerk		7
9	T.Lord	lbw	0	not out		9
10	Williams	c Hammond	1	b Walker		10
11	T.Boxall	not out	0	b Beldham		2
	Byes		1			2
			82			107

FoW (1): 1- , 2- , 3- , 4- , 5- , 6- , 7- , 8- , 9- , 10-82
FoW (2): 1- , 2- , 3- , 4- , 5- , 6- , 7- , 8- , 9- , 10-107

M.C.C.

1	Earl of Winchilsea	b Wells	0			
2	T.Walker	b Wells	5	b Wells		13
3	J.Tufton	b Wells	3	not out		31
4	Lord F.Beauclerk	c Walker	23	not out		34
5	W.Beldham	lbw	13			
6	J.Hammond	c Walker	10			
7	B.Clifton	b Boxall	9	lbw		12
8	R.Whitehead	b Wells	26			
9	J.Gibbons	b Wells	4			
10	P.Maitland	not out	0	c Walker		1
11	W.Turner	b Boxall	1			
	Byes		4			1
			98	(3 wickets)		92

FoW (1): 1- , 2- , 3- , 4- , 5- , 6- , 7- , 8- , 9- , 10-98
FoW (2): 1- , 2- , 3-

M.C.C. Bowling

	O	M	R	W	O	M	R	W
Walker				3				1
Beldham								4
Beauclerk								3

England Bowling

	O	M	R	W	O	M	R	W
Wells				5				1
Boxall				2				

Umpires:

Close of Play: 1st day: ; 2nd day: .

MCC had Beldham, Hammond and Walker as given men.

HAMPSHIRE v M.C.C.

Played at Stoke Down, Alresford, July 26, 27, 28, 1798.

M.C.C. won by 78 runs.

M.C.C.

1	John Wells	c J.Small, jun	3	c Freemantle	15
2	Sylvester	c Freemantle	6	b Grinham	5
3	J.Tufton	c Freemantle	30	b Purchase	12
4	Lord F.Beauclerk	c May	4	b Harris	11
5	B.Clifton	b Harris	5	b Harris	36
6	E.Bligh	c Freemantle	13	b Harris	7
7	Earl of Winchilsea	b Harris	6	c May	8
8	A.P.Upton	not out	15	not out	30
9	R.Whitehead	st Freemantle	2	b Harris	0
10	Williams	c Taylor	0	st Freemantle	3
11	N.Graham	b Harris	0	hit wkt	4
	Byes				4
			84		135

FoW (1): 1- , 2- , 3- , 4- , 5- , 6- , 7- , 8- , 9- , 10-84
FoW (2): 1- , 2- , 3- , 4- , 5- , 6- , 7- , 8- , 9- , 10-135

HAMPSHIRE

1	J.Small, jun	b Beauclerk	0	b Beauclerk	5
2	A.Freemantle	run out	18	c Whitehead	35
3	May	lbw	7	b Tufton	3
4	John Bennett	b Tufton	4	b Beauclerk	8
5	James Bennett	b Beauclerk	1	c Beauclerk	10
6	Wooldridge	c Winchilsea	7	b Clifton	4
7	J.Small, sen	b Beauclerk	2	run out	4
8	Grinham	not out	5	run out	2
9	R.Purchase	b Beauclerk	0	lbw	4
10	T.Taylor	b Clifton	2	c Graham	9
11	D.Harris	c Upton	1	not out	6
	Byes				4
			47		94

FoW (1): 1- , 2- , 3- , 4- , 5- , 6- , 7- , 8- , 9- , 10-47
FoW (2): 1- , 2- , 3- , 4- , 5- , 6- , 7- , 8- , 9- , 10-94

Hampshire Bowling

	O	M	R	W	O	M	R	W
Harris				3				4
Purchase								1
Grinham								1

M.C.C. Bowling

	O	M	R	W	O	M	R	W
Beauclerk				4				2
Tufton				1				1
Clifton				1				1

Umpires:

Close of Play: 1st day: ; 2nd day: .

MCC had Wells as a given man.

M.C.C. v HAMPSHIRE

Played at Lord's Old Ground, Marylebone, August 2, 3, 1798.

Hampshire won by 102 runs.

HAMPSHIRE

1	James Bennett	c Clifton	17	st Leycester	0
2	R.Purchase	c Upton	17	st Leycester	10
3	A.Freemantle	b Beauclerk	5	b Beauclerk	3
4	J.Small, jun	c Douglas	1	b Beauclerk	14
5	John Wells	b Beauclerk	31	c Leycester	4
6	T.Scott	b Douglas	9	b Tufton	15
7	John Bennett	not out	53	st Leycester	0
8	J.Small, sen	b Beauclerk	2	c Beauclerk	0
9	Grinham	b Tufton	1	c Upton	0
10	May	b Turner	22	b Beauclerk	0
11	D.Harris	c Winchilsea	3	not out	0
	Byes		14		
			175		46

FoW (1): 1- , 2- , 3- , 4- , 5- , 6- , 7- , 8- , 9- , 10-175
FoW (2): 1- , 2- , 3- , 4- , 5- , 6- , 7- , 8- , 9- , 10-46

M.C.C.

1	E.Bligh	b Harris	0	b Wells	0
2	R.Whitehead	c John Bennett	7	st Wells	3
3	Lord F.Beauclerk	b Wells	6	c J.Small, jun	16
4	G.Leycester	b Wells	3	st Wells	11
5	J.Tufton	c Freemantle	7	lbw	3
6	B.Clifton	c Harris	7	b Harris	0
7	A.P.Upton	run out	9	b Harris	5
8	C.Douglas	b Wells	11	b Wells	1
9	Earl of Winchilsea	c Grinham	0	c Freemantle	8
10	P.Maitland	st Wells	6	c Harris	2
11	W.Turner	not out	1	not out	2
	Byes		6		5
			63		56

FoW (1): 1- , 2- , 3- , 4- , 5- , 6- , 7- , 8- , 9- , 10-63
FoW (2): 1- , 2- , 3- , 4- , 5- , 6- , 7- , 8- , 9- , 10-56

M.C.C. Bowling

	O	M	R	W	O	M	R	W
Beauclerk				3				3
Tufton				1				1
Douglas				1				
Turner				1				

Hampshire Bowling

	O	M	R	W	O	M	R	W
Harris				1				2
Wells				3				2

Umpires:

Close of Play: 1st day: .

Hampshire had Wells as a given man. J Small, sen made his final appearance in 'great' matches at the age of 61.

ENGLAND v SURREY

Played at Lord's Old Ground, Marylebone, August 13, 14, 15, 1798.

England won by an innings and 1 run.

SURREY

1	John Wells	b Harris	0	b Hammond	5
2	R.Robinson	st Hammond	8	hit wkt	8
3	T.Walker	b Harris	0	hit wkt	24
4	W.Beldham	b Harris	7	c Beauclerk	28
5	H.Walker	c Clifton	8	run out	51
6	R.Whitehead	st Hammond	17	b Fennex	1
7	J.Walker	b Hammond	12	c Beauclerk	0
8	J.Hampton	b Beauclerk	1	b Beauclerk	8
9	Earl of Winchilsea	b Harris	1	c Hammond	0
10	W.Wells	b Harris	5	not out	10
11	W.Barton	not out	0	c Hammond	4
	Byes		2		4
			61		143

FoW (1): 1- , 2- , 3- , 4- , 5- , 6- , 7- , 8- , 9- , 10-61
FoW (2): 1- , 2- , 3- , 4- , 5- , 6- , 7- , 8- , 9- , 10-143

ENGLAND

1	W.Fennex	run out	5
2	J.Small, jun	c H.Walker	50
3	Lord F.Beauclerk	c Whitehead	3
4	J.Tufton	c Beldham	25
5	J.Hammond	c J.Wells	12
6	A.Freemantle	st Beldham	41
7	B.Clifton	run out	17
8	John Bennett	c J.Wells	3
9	J.Crawte	c H.Walker	30
10	T.Ray	c J.Wells	17
11	D.Harris	not out	0
	Byes		2
			205

FoW (1): 1- , 2- , 3- , 4- , 5- , 6- , 7- , 8- , 9- , 10-205

England Bowling

	O	M	R	W		O	M	R	W
Harris				5					
Beauclerk				1					1
Hammond				1					1
Fennex									1

Umpires:

Close of Play: 1st day: ; 2nd day: .

No one was bowled in the England innings so it is impossible to tell who took the wickets for Surrey.

ENGLAND v SURREY

Played at Lord's Old Ground, Marylebone, August 16, 17, 1798.

England won by 13 runs.

ENGLAND
1	J.Small, jun	c T.Walker	18	run out	9
2	T.Ray	b Wells	10	c Crawte	7
3	W.Barton	c Beldham	5	b Robinson	13
4	T.Lord	b Wells	2	b Wells	8
5	A.Freemantle	run out	2	st Wells	0
6	W.Fennex	b Wells	14	run out	0
7	Lord F.Beauclerk	not out	29	run out	10
8	J.Tufton	b T.Walker	1	c Beldham	4
9	J.Hammond	c Beldham	11	not out	53
10	John Bennett	b T.Walker	0	c T.Walker	1
11	P.Maitland	c Beldham	0	st Wells	0
	Byes		3		
			95		105

FoW (1): 1- , 2- , 3- , 4- , 5- , 6- , 7- , 8- , 9- , 10-95
FoW (2): 1- , 2- , 3- , 4- , 5- , 6- , 7- , 8- , 9- , 10-105

SURREY
1	Earl of Winchilsea	b Lord	0	c Tufton	4
2	T.Walker	not out	44	c Fennex	26
3	W.Beldham	b Hammond	12	b Beauclerk	5
4	R.Robinson	run out	2	b Fennex	15
5	John Wells	b Beauclerk	0	b Lord	41
6	H.Walker	b Hammond	5	c Hammond	1
7	J.Walker	b Hammond	3	not out	2
8	B.Clifton	c Hammond	10	b Hammond	1
9	J.Crawte	st Hammond	1	b Fennex	2
10	R.Whitehead	b Beauclerk	0	b Hammond	2
11	Briden	run out	1	b Hammond	4
	Byes		3		3
			81		106

FoW (1): 1- , 2- , 3- , 4- , 5- , 6- , 7- , 8- , 9- , 10-81
FoW (2): 1- , 2- , 3- , 4- , 5- , 6- , 7- , 8- , 9- , 10-106

Surrey Bowling

	O	M	R	W		O	M	R	W
Wells				3					1
T.Walker				2					
Robinson									1

England Bowling

	O	M	R	W		O	M	R	W
Lord				1					1
Hammond				3					3
Beauclerk				2					1
Fennex									2

Umpires:

Close of Play: 1st day: .

SURREY AND M.C.C. v ENGLAND

Played at Lord's Old Ground, Marylebone, July 30, 31, August 1, 1799.

Surrey and M.C.C. won by eight wickets.

ENGLAND

1	J.Small, jun	c H.Walker	25	b Wells	1
2	T.Boxall	hit wkt	19	c T.Walker	6
3	J.Hammond	c T.Walker	40	b Wells	28
4	W.Barton	c Wells	21	c Beldham	5
5	A.Freemantle	b Beldham	11	b T.Walker	0
6	W.Fennex	not out	37	c Wells	10
7	G.Booth	c Wells	1	c Robinson	5
8	T.Lord	c Leycester	7	b T.Walker	5
9	J.Beeston	c Whitehead	0	not out	0
10	Hockley	run out	3	st Leycester	2
11	W.Beeston	c Gibbons	0	c Wells	8
	Byes		1		1
			165		71

FoW (1): 1- , 2- , 3- , 4- , 5- , 6- , 7- , 8- , 9- , 10-165
FoW (2): 1- , 2- , 3- , 4- , 5- , 6- , 7- , 8- , 9- , 10-71

SURREY AND M.C.C.

1	G.Leycester	hit wkt	9	st Hammond	2
2	H.Walker	b Boxall	5		
3	T.Walker	b Boxall	10	not out	44
4	R.Robinson	b Lord	74	not out	44
5	W.Beldham	c Hammond	1		
6	John Wells	c Booth	9		
7	P.Maitland	b Lord	2		
8	R.Whitehead	b Lord	32	b Boxall	1
9	J.Gibbons	c Fennex	1		
10	S.Lushington	b Lord	3		
11	Sir H.W.Marten	not out	0		
	Byes				
			146	(2 wickets)	91

FoW (1): 1- , 2- , 3- , 4- , 5- , 6- , 7- , 8- , 9- , 10-146
FoW (2): 1- , 2-

Surrey and M.C.C. Bowling

	O	M	R	W	O	M	R	W
Beldham				1				
Wells								2
T.Walker								2

England Bowling

	O	M	R	W	O	M	R	W
Boxall				2				1
Lord				4				

Umpires:

Close of Play: 1st day: ; 2nd day: .

The winning team was 6 of MCC and 5 of Surrey.

R.WHITEHEAD'S XI v LORD YARMOUTH'S XI

Played at Lord's Old Ground, Marylebone, August 1, 2, 3, 1799.

Lord Yarmouth's XI won by four wickets.

R.WHITEHEAD'S XI

1	John Wells	b Fennex	7	b Lord		32
2	H.Walker	b Lord	22	st Hammond		32
3	S.Lushington	b Lord	4	run out		5
4	N.Graham	run out	7	not out		0
5	Hockley	run out	7	b Boxall		2
6	R.Whitehead	c Boxall	26	b Boxall		0
7	T.Walker	b Hammond	15	c Onslow		29
8	W.Beldham	c Small	53	b Robinson		27
9	A.Freemantle	b Hammond	30	c Hammond		14
10	W.Barton	c Hammond	0	b Boxall		19
11	W.Turner	not out	1	b Boxall		3
	Byes		5			7
			177			170

FoW (1): 1- , 2- , 3- , 4- , 5- , 6- , 7- , 8- , 9- , 10-177
FoW (2): 1- , 2- , 3- , 4- , 5- , 6- , 7- , 8- , 9- , 10-170

LORD YARMOUTH'S XI

1	T.Boxall	hit wkt	0			
2	J.Small, jun	b Wells	38	c H.Walker		88
3	R.Robinson	b Wells	26	c H.Walker		20
4	J.Hammond	c H.Walker	44	c T.Walker		51
5	P.Maitland	b Barton	20	not out		23
6	R.Stevens	b Barton	1	c T.Walker		2
7	T.Lord	c Freemantle	0			
8	D.Onslow	st Beldham	5	c Wells		3
9	J.Gibbons	b T.Walker	0	b Barton		0
10	W.Fennex	c Beldham	16	not out		6
11	J.Beeston	not out	0			
	Byes		1			4
			151	(6 wickets)		197

FoW (1): 1- , 2- , 3- , 4- , 5- , 6- , 7- , 8- , 9- , 10-151
FoW (2): 1- , 2- , 3- , 4- , 5- , 6-

Lord Yarmouth's XI Bowling

	O	M	R	W	O	M	R	W
Fennex				1				
Lord				2				1
Hammond				2				
Boxall								4
Robinson								1

R.Whitehead's XI Bowling

	O	M	R	W	O	M	R	W
Wells				2				
Barton				2				1
T.Walker				1				

Umpires:

Close of Play: 1st day: ; 2nd day: .

This match began the same day the previous one ended.

ENGLAND v SURREY

Played at Lord's Old Ground, Marylebone, August 13, 14, 15, 1799.

Surrey won by 143 runs.

SURREY

1	T.Walker	b Boxall	50	not out	82
2	W.Beldham	b Hammond	12	b Fennex	4
3	H.Walker	c Robinson	10	c Ray	6
4	A.Freemantle	c Ray	18	b Hammond	6
5	John Wells	b Hammond	16	b Hammond	30
6	W.Barton	b Boxall	0	c Small	14
7	T.J.Burgoyne	b Boxall	0	c Ray	6
8	R.Whitehead	st Hammond	0	c Robinson	5
9	S.Lushington	b Boxall	3	c Lord	2
10	Hockley	not out	0	c Ray	0
11	W.Turner	b Boxall	6	c Ray	3
	Byes		2		2
			117		160

FoW (1): 1- , 2- , 3- , 4- , 5- , 6- , 7- , 8- , 9- , 10-117
FoW (2): 1- , 2- , 3- , 4- , 5- , 6- , 7- , 8- , 9- , 10-160

ENGLAND

1	T.Boxall	run out	9	run out	3
2	J.Small, jun	b Wells	33	b T.Walker	36
3	R.Robinson	b T.Walker	4	b Wells	4
4	J.Hammond	c T.Walker	8	c Whitehead	2
5	W.Fennex	c Barton	7	b Wells	0
6	T.Ray	c Wells	2	b Wells	0
7	G.Booth	c Beldham	2	run out	1
8	T.Lord	c H.Walker	3	st Beldham	4
9	Woodroffe	b Wells	0	not out	0
10	Lord Yarmouth	c Barton	2	b Wells	0
11	N.Graham	not out	6	b Wells	3
	Byes				5
			76		58

FoW (1): 1- , 2- , 3- , 4- , 5- , 6- , 7- , 8- , 9- , 10-76
FoW (2): 1- , 2- , 3- , 4- , 5- , 6- , 7- , 8- , 9- , 10-58

England Bowling

	O	M	R	W	O	M	R	W
Boxall				5				
Hammond				2				2
Fennex								1

Surrey Bowling

	O	M	R	W	O	M	R	W
Wells				2				5
T.Walker				1				1

Umpires:

Close of Play: 1st day: ; 2nd day: .

ENGLAND v SURREY

Played at Lord's Old Ground, Marylebone, August 15, 16, 17, 1799.

Surrey won by an innings and 147 runs.

ENGLAND

1	G.Booth	c T.Walker	0	c H.Walker		2
2	T.Boxall	b Wells	3	not out		0
3	T.Lord	b Wells	4	b Turner		0
4	J.Hammond	c Wells	15	b Wells		4
5	J.Small, jun	c Beldham	14	run out		0
6	R.Robinson	b Beldham	34	c Ray		21
7	W.Fennex	c Wells	3	b T.Walker		15
8	A.Freemantle	b Beldham	10	c Burgoyne		1
9	R.Whitehead	not out	30	b Wells		0
10	J.Gibbons	b Beldham	0	b Turner		0
11	R.Stevens	b Beldham	7	b T.Walker		5
	Byes					2
			120			50

FoW (1): 1- , 2- , 3- , 4- , 5- , 6- , 7- , 8- , 9- , 10-120
FoW (2): 1- , 2- , 3- , 4- , 5- , 6- , 7- , 8- , 9- , 10-50

SURREY

1	John Wells	c Hammond	93
2	T.Walker	c Robinson	53
3	H.Walker	c Booth	5
4	W.Beldham	b Hammond	82
5	N.Graham	b Hammond	3
6	T.Ray	b Hammond	9
7	W.Barton	c Freemantle	13
8	T.J.Burgoyne	run out	30
9	Hockley	run out	5
10	W.Turner	b Robinson	12
11	Lord Yarmouth	not out	2
	Byes		10
			317

FoW (1): 1- , 2- , 3- , 4- , 5- , 6- , 7- , 8- , 9- , 10-317

Surrey Bowling

	O	M	R	W		O	M	R	W
Wells				2					2
Beldham				4					
Turner									2
T.Walker									2

England Bowling

	O	M	R	W
Hammond				3
Robinson				1

Umpires:

Close of Play: 1st day: ; 2nd day: .

This match began the same day as the previous one ended.

J.GIBBONS' XI v R.WHITEHEAD'S XI

Played at Lord's Old Ground, Marylebone, May 19, 20, 21, 1800.

R.Whitehead's XI won by 52 runs.

R.WHITEHEAD'S XI

#	Batsman	Dismissal	Runs	Dismissal (2)	Runs
1	T.Boxall	b Wells	1	c Fennex	0
2	H.Walker	b Wells	14	b Walker	10
3	J.Hammond	b Walker	8	st Wells	22
4	W.Beldham	c Booth	4	b Wells	3
5	J.Small, jun	b Wells	8	c Gibbons	13
6	G.Leycester	b Walker	3	b Wells	9
7	T.Ray	c Freemantle	5	b Wells	9
8	T.Mellish	c Robinson	7	b Walker	3
9	R.Whitehead	b Wells	0	st Walker	11
10	J.Tanner	not out	2	not out	4
11	Woodroffe	c Fennex	5	b Wells	0
	Byes		4		2
			61		86

FoW (1): 1- , 2- , 3- , 4- , 5- , 6- , 7- , 8- , 9- , 10-61
FoW (2): 1- , 2- , 3- , 4- , 5- , 6- , 7- , 8- , 9- , 10-86

J.GIBBONS' XI

#	Batsman	Dismissal	Runs	Dismissal (2)	Runs
1	T.Walker	b Beldham	0	b Beldham	16
2	W.Fennex	c Ray	6	c Small	0
3	R.Robinson	b Beldham	9	b Beldham	0
4	A.Freemantle	b Beldham	9	c Ray	1
5	J.Gibbons	b Beldham	4	b Boxall	1
6	John Wells	c Small	19	c Beldham	1
7	A.P.Upton	b Beldham	3	b Boxall	0
8	P.Maitland	b Beldham	4	run out	2
9	G.Booth	c Beldham	0	not out	4
10	T.J.Burgoyne	c Beldham	2	b Beldham	12
11	J.Eavers	not out	0	c Beldham	1
	Byes				1
			56		39

FoW (1): 1- , 2- , 3- , 4- , 5- , 6- , 7- , 8- , 9- , 10-56
FoW (2): 1- , 2- , 3- , 4- , 5- , 6- , 7- , 8- , 9- , 10-39

J.Gibbons' XI Bowling

	O	M	R	W	O	M	R	W
Wells				4				4
Walker				2				2

R.Whitehead's XI Bowling

	O	M	R	W	O	M	R	W
Beldham				6				3
Boxall								2

Umpires:

Close of Play: 1st day: ; 2nd day: .

Britcher gives 'Turner, Esq' (i.e. W.Turner) in three matches in 1800 where Bentley gives J.Tanner. Normally, Britcher would be preferred but the *Sporting Magazine* also gives Tanner in the two matches that it covers. Tanner is known to have been active and successful in good-quality metropolitan club cricket around this time so, on balance, the appearances in all three matches have been ascribed to him.

ENGLAND v SURREY

Played at Lord's Old Ground, Marylebone, June 11, 12, 13, 1800.

Surrey won by three wickets.

ENGLAND

1	G.Leycester	b T.Walker	4	b Wells		10
2	T.Boxall	b T.Walker	6	run out		9
3	J.Hammond	b Wells	29	not out		5
4	W.Fennex	run out	16	b Wells		4
5	W.Beldham	b T.Walker	3	b Wells		2
6	A.Freemantle	run out	8	run out		8
7	R.Purchase	c Wells	0	c H.Walker		0
8	J.Tanner	b T.Walker	0	b Wells		4
9	W.Barton	c Robinson	11	b T.Walker		2
10	J.Gibbons	not out	1	run out		0
11	C.Warren	b T.Walker	0	b Wells		0
	Byes		2			3
			80			47

FoW (1): 1- , 2- , 3- , 4- , 5- , 6- , 7- , 8- , 9- , 10-80
FoW (2): 1- , 2- , 3- , 4- , 5- , 6- , 7- , 8- , 9- , 10-47

SURREY

1	T.Walker	c Beldham	7			
2	H.Walker	b Beldham	1			
3	R.Robinson	b Boxall	5	b Boxall		17
4	John Wells	c Beldham	1	run out		33
5	J.Small, jun	b Beldham	3	c Freemantle		9
6	C.Lennox	b Boxall	2	b Boxall		11
7	R.Whitehead	b Beldham	0	b Boxall		18
8	Woodroffe	b Beldham	0	not out		0
9	J.Weller	b Boxall	10	not out		2
10	Sir H.W.Marten	b Boxall	0	run out		0
11	G.Cooper	not out	0	c Freemantle		7
	Byes		2			
			31	(7 wickets)		97

FoW (1): 1- , 2- , 3- , 4- , 5- , 6- , 7- , 8- , 9- , 10-31
FoW (2): 1- , 2- , 3- , 4- , 5- , 6- , 7-

Surrey Bowling

	O	M	R	W	O	M	R	W
Wells				1				5
T.Walker				5				1

England Bowling

	O	M	R	W	O	M	R	W
Beldham				4				
Boxall				4				3

Umpires:

Close of Play: 1st day: ; 2nd day: .

England had Beldham as a given man. See the note to the preceding game regarding J.Tanner. John Goulstone has established that J.Weller, making his first appearance in this match, changed his name to Ladbroke in 1819 following an inheritance and as J.W.Ladbroke became patron of the Godalming Club, which played 'important' matches in the 1820s. F.C.Ladbroke and J.W.Ladbroke were cousins, not brothers as is commonly stated. See the Supplementary Note on page 278.

ENGLAND v SURREY

Played at Lord's Old Ground, Marylebone, June 16, 17, 1800.

England won by thirteen wickets.

SURREY

1	John Wells	b Boxall	0	c Boxall		1
2	T.Walker	c Ray	15	run out		0
3	H.Walker	b Boxall	2	b Ward		2
4	J.Hampton	c Ray	11	c Boxall		0
5	W.Beldham	c Burgoyne	16	c Smith		1
6	R.Robinson	b Ward	4	c Boxall		8
7	J.Walker	c Fennex	0	c Hammond		13
8	James Wells	c Ray	0	c Ward		12
9	J.Tanner	hit wkt	0	c Ward		0
10	W.Wells	b Boxall	0	c Hammond		0
11	G.Beldham	not out	3	not out		31
	Byes		2			
			53			68

FoW (1): 1- , 2- , 3- , 4- , 5- , 6- , 7- , 8- , 9- , 10-53
FoW (2): 1- , 2- , 3- , 4- , 5- , 6- , 7- , 8- , 9- , 10-68

ENGLAND

1	T.Boxall	b T.Walker	7			
2	A.Freemantle	c H.Walker	24			
3	J.Small, jun	c W.Beldham	0			
4	W.Fennex	c H.Walker	4			
5	R.Whitehead	run out	11	not out		4
6	J.Ward	b T.Walker	6			
7	J.Hammond	c James Wells	0			
8	W.Barton	st James Wells	32	not out		0
9	T.Ray	c T.Walker	14			
10	J.Crawte	c W.Beldham	5			
11	T.J.Burgoyne	c H.Walker	0			
12	John Bennett	st James Wells	1			
13	J.Smith	b John Wells	10			
14	J.Harding	not out	3			
	Byes		1			
			118	(no wicket)		4

FoW (1): 1- , 2- , 3- , 4- , 5- , 6- , 7- , 8- , 9- , 10- , 11- , 12- , 13-118

England Bowling

	O	M	R	W		O	M	R	W
Boxall				3					
Ward				1					1

Surrey Bowling

	O	M	R	W		O	M	R	W
John Wells				1					
T.Walker				2					

Umpires:

Close of Play: 1st day: .

With James, John and W.Wells all appearing for Surrey, there is considerable uncertainty about some of the dismissals. All sources are clear that Smith was bowled by John Wells. SB also ascribes to John Wells the dismissals of Hammond, Barton and Bennett, but its source for this is unclear. Britcher gives them to 'Mr Wells' but lists both numbers 8 and 10 in the Surrey team as 'Mr Wells' without any differentiation, so it is not clear who is meant. The *Sporting Magazine* also gives these three dismissals to 'Mr Wells' but distinguishes in the Surrey team list between W.Wells and 'Mr Wells', i.e. presumably James Wells, and this has been accepted. In view of this, SM's version of England (2) has also been preferred to Britcher, who has Whitehead 2, Barton 2. Smith, in the England side, has sometimes been identified with T.A.Smith but the contemporary sources do not designate him as 'Esq' so a likelier candidate is J.Smith of Kent, still prominent in good quality club matches. Regarding J.Tanner, see the note under Gibbons v Whitehead, 19 May 1800.

ENGLAND v THE Ws AND Hs

Played at Lord's Old Ground, Marylebone, July 14, 15, 1800.

The Ws and Hs won by seven wickets.

ENGLAND

1	T.Mellish	b T.Walker	3	b T.Walker		1
2	J.Small, jun	c Hampton	10	b Hampton		52
3	W.Beldham	c H.Walker	49	c Whitehead		2
4	Lord F.Beauclerk	b John Wells	5	c Ward		0
5	R.Robinson	b Ward	9	b John Wells		37
6	A.Freemantle	b Ward	7	not out		16
7	W.Fennex	not out	18	b John Wells		4
8	T.Boxall	b Ward	0	b John Wells		4
9	J.Gibbons	b Ward	2	b John Wells		17
10	T.W.Coventry	c Ward	3	c H.Walker		1
11	Sir H.W.Marten	b John Wells	1	lbw		0
	Byes		10			6
			117			140

FoW (1): 1- , 2- , 3- , 4- , 5- , 6- , 7- , 8- , 9- , 10-117
FoW (2): 1- , 2- , 3- , 4- , 5- , 6- , 7- , 8- , 9- , 10-140

THE Ws AND Hs

1	J.Ward	b Beldham	5			
2	H.Walker	c Beldham	14			
3	T.Walker	c Beldham	88	run out		5
4	J.Weller	b Boxall	3			
5	John Wells	st Beldham	33	not out		21
6	J.Hammond	c Small	1	c Fennex		11
7	R.Whitehead	c Beldham	4	b Boxall		0
8	J.Hampton	not out	8	not out		34
9	W.Wells	run out	11			
10	Woodroffe	b Beauclerk	0			
11	J.Lawrell	c Mellish	8			
	Byes		12			
			187	(3 wickets)		71

FoW (1): 1- , 2- , 3- , 4- , 5- , 6- , 7- , 8- , 9- , 10-187
FoW (2): 1- , 2- , 3-

The Ws and Hs Bowling

	O	M	R	W	O	M	R	W
Ward				4				
T.Walker				1				1
John Wells				2				4
Hampton								1

England Bowling

	O	M	R	W	O	M	R	W
Beldham				1				
Boxall				1				1
Beauclerk				1				

Umpires:

Close of Play: 1st day: .

The *Morning Post* reports that C.Warren was due to appear for the Ws and Hs but dropped out and Lawrell replaced him.

ENGLAND v SURREY

Played at Lord's Old Ground, Marylebone, August 28, 29, 30, 1800.

England won by 51 runs.

ENGLAND

1	J.Crawte	run out	3			
2	J.Small, jun	c Waller	5			
3	A.Freemantle	c H.Walker	28	b Wells		0
4	J.Ward	b Wells	9			
5	Lord F.Beauclerk	c H.Walker	10	c Wells		20
6	W.Fennex	c Wells	1			
7	J.Hammond	c Robinson	52			
8	W.Barton	b Wells	22	b Wells		18
9	T.Ray	b T.Walker	12			
10	J.Weller	c Waller	0			
11	John Bennett	c Wells	1			
12	W.Ayling	run out	7	not out		0
13	C.Reed	c Chitty	6	run out		3
14	T.Boxall	not out	0			
	Byes		1			1
			157	(4 wickets, declared)		42

FoW (1): 1- , 2- , 3- , 4- , 5- , 6- , 7- , 8- , 9- , 10- , 11- , 12- , 13-157
FoW (2): 1- , 2- , 3- , 4-42

SURREY

1	G.Beldham	c Small	7	c Beauclerk		0
2	J.Walker	b Ward	0	c Reed		8
3	T.Walker	b Boxall	2	b Reed		26
4	R.Robinson	c Hammond	22	run out		28
5	W.Beldham	b Boxall	1	b Ward		5
6	John Wells	b Ward	0	b Boxall		4
7	H.Walker	run out	4	b Beauclerk		15
8	H.Hampton	st Hammond	5	run out		0
9	Earl of Winchilsea	c Ayling	7	st Hammond		0
10	H.J.Tufton	b Beauclerk	0	b Fennex		0
11	Waller	not out	6	c Weller		5
12	Chitty	b Beauclerk	0	not out		0
	Byes		1			2
			55			93

FoW (1): 1- , 2- , 3- , 4- , 5- , 6- , 7- , 8- , 9- , 10- , 11-55
FoW (2): 1- , 2- , 3- , 4- , 5- , 6- , 7- , 8- , 9- , 10- , 11-93

Surrey Bowling

	O	M	R	W	O	M	R	W
Wells				2				2
T.Walker				1				

England Bowling

	O	M	R	W	O	M	R	W
Boxall				2				1
Beauclerk				2				1
Ward				2				1
Fennex								1
Reed								1

Umpires:

Close of Play: 1st day: ; 2nd day: .

Surrey had Tufton as a given man. Buckley in *Fresh Light on Pre-Victorian Cricket*, citing the *Morning Post*, says, 'For Surrey, Winchilsea, Waller & Chitty vice Mr Wells [i.e. James Wells], Harding & J Hampton; H Hampton played.' England appear to have given up their second innings – declarations had not yet been invented.

The 'Lost' Great Matches

This list of eleven "lost" great matches (i.e., for which full scores have not been found) is restricted to those played between 1772 and 1800, the period covered by this book. Obviously, there were many such matches played before 1772 but these are not taken into account here. Also omitted are matches which were announced but for which no evidence has been found to prove they took place. All of the games included here have been authenticated from reliable sources and all of the them could be classified as "great" under the ACS criteria.

HAMPSHIRE v KENT
Played at Broad Halfpenny Down, Hambledon, August 10, 11, 1772.
Hampshire won by 50 runs.

HAMPSHIRE v KENT
Played at Merrow Down, Guildford, August 26, 27, 1772.
Kent won by an innings and 29 runs.
The Duke of Dorset scored 21 for Kent.

SURREY v HAMPSHIRE
Played at Merrow Down, Guildford, August 28, 29, 1772.
Hampshire won by 45 runs.

ENGLAND v HAMPSHIRE
Played at Laleham Burway Cricket Ground, July 12, 13, 1773.
England won by 114 runs.

SURREY v KENT
Played at Laleham Burway Cricket Ground, August 9, 10, 1773.
Surrey won by eight wickets.
Kent had two (unidentified) given men.

HAMPSHIRE v KENT
Played at Broad Halfpenny Down, Hambledon, July 13, 14, 1774.
Hampshire won by ten wickets.

KENT	HAMPSHIRE
Duke of Dorset	Mr T.Ridge
J.Minchin	J.Small
R.Miller	T.Sueter
May	G.Leer
J.Frame	J.Aylward
W.Bullen	J.Bayley
R.Simmons	R.Francis
J.Wood (Seal)	T.Brett
Pattenden	R.Nyren
Mr G.Louch	R.Purchase
J.Fish	W.Hogsflesh

The above were the advertised teams. It is unknown whether there were any changes. The Pattenden in the Kent side is almost certainly T.Pattenden as he played in their other matches this season. Looking at the Kent bowling strength, R.May is probably the May involved as he was a bowler.

HAMPSHIRE v KENT
Played at Merrow Down, Guildford, August 3, 4, 1775.
Kent won.
The margin of victory was not stated. Kent had two of Surrey, E.Stevens (Lumpy) and T.White, as given men.

KENT v SURREY
Played at Bourne Paddock, Bishopsbourne, July 21, 22, 23, 24, 1779.
Match abandoned as a draw.

SURREY	KENT
62	83 (8 wickets)

Rain interrupted the match and ended play on Friday morning for the rest of the day. There was no play at all on Saturday 24th. All bets were declared void. Kent had two (unidentified) given men from Hampshire but in the earlier match between the sides they were J.Aylward and R.A.Veck so it is probable that they were the two in this one as well.

WHITE CONDUIT CLUB v MIDDLESEX
Played at Lord's Old Ground, Marylebone, June 5, 6, 1787.
White Conduit Club won by ten wickets.

MIDDLESEX	WHITE CONDUIT CLUB
Mr G.T.Boult	Sir P.Burrell
C.Slater	Mr J.Peachey
J.Slater	Mr J.Dampier
Mr G.Louch	Capt.C.Cumberland
Stanhope	Mr G.East
N.Graham	Mr T.A.Smith
J.Weston	Mr G.Talbot
Livings	Mr R.N.Newman
Clark	Mr R.B.Wyatt
T.Lord	Mr E.Hussey
Hall	Mr G.Drummond
131 & ?	? & 39 (0 wickets)

Umpires: Earl of Winchilsea and Butcher.
Close 1st day: WCC 171/7 (Dampier 61*, Hussey 18 out).

Livings scored 56 and Graham 30 in Middlesex (1). On the second day Middlesex were dismissed in their second innings with an overall lead of 37. Burrell and Smith hit off the required runs for WCC without being parted. It is believed that Livings of Middlesex is T.Liffen of Brighton as that player's name sometimes appears as Living(s) in Brighton scores. Lord and Weston are shown as the Middlesex bowlers. Gilbert East hit an all-run six into the furthest corner of the ground, perhaps the first hit for six at Lord's. Middlesex had two (unidentified) given men, possibly Livings (Brighton?) and Clark (Hornchurch?).

HORNCHURCH v MIDDLESEX
Played at Langton Park, Hornchurch, July 5, 6, 1787.
Middlesex won by nine wickets.

HORNCHURCH
65 & 108

MIDDLESEX
124 & 50 (1 wicket)

HORNCHURCH v WHITE CONDUIT CLUB & MOULSEY HURST
Played at Langton Park, Hornchurch, August 2, 3, 1787.
White Conduit Club & Moulsey Hurst won by 100 runs.

WCC & MOULSEY HURST	HORNCHURCH
Earl of Winchilsea	Mr R.N.Newman
Sir P.Burrell	Mr R.B.Wyatt
Mr G.Talbot	Mr J.Russell
Mr G.East	Mr R.Denn
Mr G.Drummond	Rev G.Dupuis
Mr G.T.Boult	T.Clark
Slater	Davidson
Mr G.Louch	M.Rimmington
W.Bedster	N.Graham
E.Stevens (Lumpy)	Harvey
Davy	J.Martin
	Wickham
89 & more than 150	100 & 'not above 50'

The above were the advertised teams and it is not known whether there were any changes; however, twelve Hornchurch players were named so one must have dropped out. The team list gave Lumpy, Davy, Martin and Wickham as the bowlers. The match was scheduled to begin on July 31 but was put off until August 2.

SOURCES

Reading Mercury 17/8/1772; *General Evening Post* 29/8/1772; *Hampshire Chronicle* 31/8/1772; *Bath Chronicle* 31/8/1772; *Morning Post* 16/7/1773 and 9/8/1773; *Middlesex Journal* 19/7/1774; *Public Ledger* 26/7/1774; *Reading Mercury* 5/8/1775; *Kentish Post* 27/7/1779; *Morning Post* 3/8/1779; *The World* 6/6/1787; *The Times* 8/6/1787; *Maidstone Journal* 12/6/1787; *Chelmsford Chronicle* 13/7/1787 and 20/7/1787; *Kentish Post* 3/8/1787; *The World* 6/8/1787.

Supplementary Notes

Kent v Surrey (page 40): 19 July 1773
Kent v Surrey (page 42): 16 August 1773

The two matches between Kent and Surrey, at Bishopsbourne on 19 July and Sevenoaks Vine on 16 August, were the subject of two lengthy poems that provide a great deal of interesting information, besides casting light on a cricketing controversy of the time.

The first poem, *Surrey Triumphant or the Kentishmen's Defeat*, by Rev J.Duncombe, curate of Sundridge, was written (as its title suggests) to celebrate Surrey's success in the match at Bishopsbourne. This poem is printed in full in *Scores and Biographies* (page 9).

It provoked a riposte in the form of *The Kentish Cricketers*, by 'A Gentleman', which alleges that Surrey had won the match only by dubious means. The poem claims that Surrey, on winning the toss, had opted to pitch the wickets in a hollow rather than on a level part of the ground as convention required.

> Fortune, the Power to SURRY gave,
> The Ground to chuse they'd wish to have:
> Far from the usual Place of Play
> They pitch'd the wickets for the Day

Surrey, having won the toss, had choice of innings as well as ground, and batted first.

> The Whole of SURRY's skilful 'leven,
> Were out for Notches Seventy-seven.
> But when the KENTISH Men went in,
> Reason confess'd they could not win;
> For honest Lumpey did allow,
> He could not pitch but o'er a Brow:
> And KENTISH Sportsmen said, that they,
> Deep in a HOLE could never play.
> So SURRY did the Victory gain,
> By LUMPY, FORTUNE, ART, and RAIN.

After this defeat Kent's patron, the Duke of Dorset, challenged Surrey to a second match. The poem takes up the account.

> But, Oh, dire Omen! SURRY found,
> Fortune gave KENT the Choice of Ground;
> And Simmons sallied forth to pace
> The level Turf, the fairest Place:
> Candor, the KENTISH Sportsman taught,
> To pitch the Wickets as he ought.

Kent went on to win the second match by six wickets, thus proving, at least to the satisfaction of the poem's unidentified author, that in a fair contest on level ground

> KENT can conquer, if they please.

The poem has been quoted at some length because of what it reveals about the controversy arising from the Bishopsbourne match. It is reasonable to speculate that this was a factor in a significant change in the new version of the Laws issued the following year, which dispensed with the toss in most cases and provided instead that the visiting team 'shall have the choice of the innings and the pitching of the wickets, which shall be pitched within thirty yards of a centre fixed by the adversaries'.

It is also worth pointing out the context of the famous line about 'Lumpy' Stevens's supposed inability to pitch except 'o'er a Brow'. This is often quoted in isolation as if it were a general statement about his bowling technique, whereas it actually occurs in the course of a partisan poem by an aggrieved Kent supporter arguing that Surrey had won a match by unfairly pitching the wickets on uneven ground.

Despite the tendentious nature of both poems, it is notable that the details of play, so far as they can be checked, are exactly reflected in the surviving scores. This lends credibility to the many additional details the poems supply.

At Bishopsbourne:

Surrey won the toss. Palmer and Stone opened the batting in Surrey (1), and Stone was first out; play was interrupted by bad weather; Lewis played despite illness; and Wood of Kent suffered some unspecified, but apparently serious, foot injury. *Surrey Triumphant* confirms the identity of W.Bartholomew ('I a vicar's son': William was the son of the Rev Charles Bartholomew of Chertsey). *The Kentish Cricketers* refers to Stevens's bowling prowess and then specifically mentions Miller, Simmons, Louch and May. Why these four? The score tells us that Stevens bowled Simmons and T.May; Miller and Louch were caught, so maybe Stevens was the bowler. The same poem lists the Kent players in the following order: Miller, Dorset, Simmons, Mann, Davis, Hussey, R.May, T.May, Louch, Pattenden, Wood. It is notable that the gentlemen are not listed first so this may represent the intended, or the actual, batting order: but as this is not certain, the order has been left as in the sources. The poem also mentions Davis's skill as a wicket-keeper, but does not definitely state that he kept in this match.

At Sevenoaks:

Kent won the toss. Simmons then chose where to pitch the wickets, which may suggest he was captain. Note, however, that the Duke of Dorset was also playing. In Kent (1), Miller played Stevens so successfully that White was brought on to bowl instead.

Hornchurch v White Conduit Club and Moulsey Hurst (page 101): 15 May 1787

There is much doubt both about the venue of this match and about many of the players involved.

The match is not in Epps or Bentley and has not been traced in any newspaper or other contemporary source. Details are taken from SB, in which Haygarth says, 'It was not mentioned where this match was played, but it is presumed at Hornchurch, as the return [i.e. the match on 3 July] took place at Moulsey.' This was a reasonable suggestion on the basis of the information available to him, but it is called into question by the discovery that a third match took place at Hornchurch on 2 August (although the score has not survived). The *World* of 9 July, after reporting the second match, adds, 'There is to be another match at Cricket, between the White Conduit Club and the club at Hornchurch - the place again, Moulsey - the time, as it stands at present, the end of this month.' This sounds, although perhaps not unambiguously, like an announcement of something new; an impression strengthened by the fact that arrangements were still vague and explicitly open to change. Indeed, in the event the third match finally took place not in late July but in early August, and at Hornchurch, not Molesey. If the third match was an extra game arranged subsequently to the first two, it means that Haygarth's original speculation about the venue of the first match remains valid. A further point is that the first match appears to have escaped all the London papers. This is surely likelier if it was played at a relatively obscure venue like Hornchurch as opposed to the White Conduit ground, Molesey, or even Lord's: although all these remain possible.

The match also presents special difficulties in the matter of player identification. Three of the players, Butcher, Graham and Rimmington, share surnames with known Kent cricketers – too many to be a coincidence. It is assumed that they are the same.

- Butcher – Note his consistent record as a bowler in most matches in which he appears.

- Graham – It is probably significant that his only Kent match is against Essex at Hornchurch (27 September 1792), and Ashley-Cooper identifies him as N.Graham of either Crayford or Dartford (both just over the river from Essex).

- Rimmington – He must be one of the three players with this uncommon surname appearing in Kent matches 1780-83. The late H.S.Scales in his register of 18th-century players (Journal of the Cricket Society, Vols III-IV) suggests M.Rimmington: no reason is given but Scales is known to have had access to unpublished notes by Ashley-Cooper, now lost, so in the absence of other evidence M.Rimmington has been accepted, even though B.Rimmington appears to have been the most prominent in the earlier period.

Davidson is assumed to be the same man as appeared for England v Hants in 1784; also as a given man for Hornchurch in a match v Berks in 1785 (*Dawn of Cricket* p64).

Surrey v Hampshire (page 131): 30 July 1789

Altogether this is a strange game with big names on both sides but also some notable absentees and a large number of fringe players. A number of participants (Carpenter, Flint, Freemantle, Smith, Talbot, Vincent, J.Walker, Winchilsea) also appeared in the colts match between these counties in June (SB p90), in which several of them did well. Flint apparently bowled H.Walker in Surrey (2) and he has therefore been shown as a full substitute, although he does not appear to have batted in Hampshire (2). He had appeared for Surrey in the colts match so maybe he was a local man brought into the Hampshire side in emergency. All sources have James Wells rather than John and this is accepted, although the score of 80 might suggest otherwise.

England v Surrey and Sussex (page 186): 12 June 1793

Sporting Magazine lists the Surrey and Sussex team as follows: Winchilsea, Wells, Dehaney, T.Walker, Tufton, Nicoll, Crawte, J.Walker, H.Walker, Hammond, Beldham. With such prominent professionals listed last, this appears at first sight to make little sense either as a batting order or as the order of dismissal. The likely explanation is that the scoring at the top of the order was so heavy that the remaining professionals were held back to allow the amateurs more opportunity to bat. In 2010 an original Britcher was offered for sale which included a handwritten annotation to this game: 'An astonishing Match. I saw T.Walker and Ld. Winchilsea went in first & J.Wells went in when Ld. Winchilsea was bowled out.' This eyewitness account provides the first three to go in for Surrey and Sussex (and incidentally implies very large stands for the first two wickets). It also tends to confirm that the order in Bentley (Winchilsea, Tufton, Dehaney, Nicoll, T.Walker, Wells, J.Walker, J.Crawte, W.Beldham, H.Walker, Hammond) is that of going in but with amateurs listed first. Although it involves combining sources, this allows a reconstruction of this unusually high-scoring innings that is consistent with the apparent dismissal order in *Sporting Magazine*: 1. T.Walker (4th out); 2. Winchilsea (1st); 3. Wells (2nd); 4. Dehaney (3rd); 5. Tufton (5th); 6. Nicoll (6th); 7. J.Walker (8th); 8. Crawte (7th); 9. Beldham (10th); 10. H.Walker (9th); 11. Hammond (not out). If correct, this suggests that Beldham may have hit his wicket deliberately to give his side time to bowl England out again without extending the match into a fourth day. (Many thanks to Keith Warsop for his suggestions about the reconstruction of the innings and Beldham's dismissal.)

Earl of Winchilsea's XI v R Leigh's XI (page 224): 23 July 1795

Frederick Reynolds, who was a well-known dramatist, made his first appearance in 'great' matches, apparently as a last-minute replacement for a player taken ill. In his memoirs, published 1827, he recalled the game. 'I, for the first and last time, played against the celebrated formidable, Harris. In taking my place at the wicket, I almost felt as if I was taking my ground in a duel, and my terrors were so much increased by the mock sympathy of Hammond, Beldham and others round the wicket that when this mighty bowler, this *Jupiter tonans*, hurled his bolt at me, I shut my eyes in the intensity of my panic, and mechanically gave a random desperate blow, which, to my utter astonishment, was followed by a loud cry all over the ring of "*Run, run*". I did run; and with all my force; and getting *three* notches.' This vivid account, the details of which are supported by the score, tells us that Hammond was still batting when Reynolds arrived at the crease; also, that 'sledging' is no new phenomenon.

England v Surrey (page 267): 11 June 1800

Recent research by John Goulstone has clarified the appearances of J.Weller (later J.W.Ladbroke) and F.C.Ladbroke in major cricket. J.Weller played in 4 'great' and 'important' matches 1800-1802; following an inheritance in 1819 he changed his name to J.W.Ladbroke and appeared as such in a further 15 'important' matches 1821-1826, seven of which are incorrectly attributed to F.C.Ladbroke in the 1820-29 volume of the ACS scores series. His total career in 'great' and 'important' matches therefore comprised 19 appearances between 1800 and 1826, while the career of F.C.Ladbroke, whose involvement was mainly with the Homerton, Marylebone and Epsom clubs, amounted to 22 matches 1804-1822. Specifically, the appearances of F.C.Ladbroke in the following matches should be ascribed to J.W.Ladbroke.

3 Jul 1821	MCC v Godalming
9 Jul 1821	Godalming v MCC
1 Jul 1822	MCC v Godalming
16 Jun 1825	MCC v Godalming
23 Jun 1825	Godalming v MCC
17 Jul 1826	Sussex v Hampshire and Surrey
7 Aug 1826	Hampshire and Surrey v Sussex

Register of Matches

1772 (3)
Hampshire v England	Hambledon[1]	Jun 24-25
England v Hampshire	Guildford	Jul 23-24
England v Hampshire	Bishopsbourne	Aug 19-20

1773 (8)
Surrey v Kent	Laleham Burway	Jun 21-22
England v Hampshire	Sevenoaks	Jun 28-29
England v Hampshire	Finsbury	Jul 2-3
Kent v Surrey	Bishopsbourne	Jul 19-21
Hampshire v England	Hambledon[1]	Aug 4-5
Kent v Surrey	Sevenoaks	Aug 16-18
Surrey v Hampshire	Laleham Burway	Sep 16-18
Hampshire v Surrey	Hambledon[1]	Sep 27-28

1774 (5)
Hampshire v England	Hambledon[1]	Jun 22-24
England v Hampshire	Sevenoaks	Jul 7-8
Surrey v Hampshire	Guildford	Jul 20-21
Kent v Hampshire	Sevenoaks	Aug 8-10
Hampshire v Kent	Hambledon[1]	Aug 15-18

1775 (4)
Kent v Hampshire	Sevenoaks	Jun 14-15
Hampshire v Kent	Hambledon[1]	Jun 29-30
Surrey v Hampshire	Laleham Burway	Jul 6-8
Hampshire v Surrey	Hambledon[1]	Jul 13-17

1776 (7)
Hampshire v Kent	Molesey	Jun 5-7
Kent v Hampshire	Sevenoaks	Jun 25-26
Hampshire v Kent	Hambledon[1]	Jul 2-4
Kent v Hampshire	Sevenoaks	Jul 15-17
Hampshire v Kent	Hambledon[2]	Jul 22-24
Surrey v Hampshire	Laleham Burway	Aug 6-8
Hampshire v Surrey	Hambledon[1]	Aug 26-28

1777 (6)
England v Hampshire	Sevenoaks	Jun 18-20
Hampshire v England	Hambledon[1]	Jul 7-10
England v Hampshire	Laleham Burway	Jul 22-26
England v Hampshire	Guildford	Aug 18-20
Hampshire v England	Hambledon[1]	Sep 8-10
England v Hampshire	Finsbury	Sep 15-17

1778 (5)
England v Hampshire	Sevenoaks	Jun 29-30
Hampshire v England	Alresford	Jul 6-7
Chertsey v Hampshire	Laleham Burway	Sep 10-11
Hampshire v Surrey	Hambledon[1]	Sep 24-25
Surrey v Hampshire	Laleham Burway	Oct 6-8

1779 (5)
Hampshire v England	Alresford	Jun 14-15
England v Hampshire	Sevenoaks	Jun 23-26
Surrey v Kent	Laleham Burway	Aug 9-11
Hampshire v England	Hambledon[1]	Aug 23
England v Hampshire	Molesey	Sep 13-16

1780 (4)
Duke of Dorset's XI v
	Sir H.Mann's XI	Sevenoaks	Jun 27-28
Sir H.Mann's XI v
	Duke of Dorset's XI	Bishopsbourne	Aug 21-23
England v Hampshire	Bishopsbourne	Aug 30-Sep 1
Hampshire v England	Alresford	Sep 20-22

1781 (6)
Hampshire v Kent	Alresford	Jun 6-9
West Kent v East Kent	Sevenoaks	Jun 20-21
Kent v Hampshire	Bishopsbourne	Jul 18-20
Hampshire v Kent	Hambledon[1]	Jul 30-Aug 1
Sir H.Mann's XI v
	Duke of Dorset's XI	Bishopsbourne	Aug 8-11
Kent v Hampshire	Bishopsbourne	Aug 27-28

1782 (4)
Kent v Hampshire	Sevenoaks	Jul 3-5
Hampshire v Kent	Alresford	Jul 11-15
Kent v Hampshire	Bishopsbourne	Jul 25-26
Hampshire v England	Hambledon[3]	Aug 8-10

1783 (4)
West Kent v East Kent	Sevenoaks	Jun 25-26
Hampshire v Kent	Hambledon[3]	Jul 8-9
Kent v Hampshire	Bishopsbourne	Aug 6-9
Hampshire v England	Hambledon[3]	Aug 26-29

1784 (1)
England v Hampshire	Sevenoaks	Jun 1-2

1786 (5)
White Conduit Club v Kent	Islington	Jun 22-24
Kent v Hampshire	Sevenoaks	Jun 26-28
Hampshire v Kent	Hambledon[3]	Jul 13-15
A to C v Rest of the Alphabet	Molesey	Aug 2-5
Kent v White Conduit Club	Bishopsbourne	Aug 8-12

1787 (11)
Hornchurch v White Conduit Club
	and Moulsey Hurst	Hornchurch	May 15-16
Middlesex v Essex	Lord's	May 31
White Conduit Club v Middlesex
	Lord's	Jun 14-15
White Conduit Club v England	Lord's	Jun 20-22
White Conduit Club and
Moulsey Hurst v Hornchurch	Molesey	Jul 3-4
T.A.Smith's XI v
Earl of Winchilsea's XI	Ludgershall	Jul 16-17
Kent v Hampshire	Coxheath	Aug 7-10
Hampshire v Kent	Bishopsbourne	Aug 14-17
A to M v N to Z	Bishopsbourne	Aug 28-31
Hampshire v Kent	Hambledon[3]	Sep 3-5
A to M v N to Z	Lord's	Sep 10-12

1788 (11)
A to M v N to Z	Lord's	May 26-28
England v Hampshire and Kent	Lord's	Jun 5-7
Surrey v Hampshire	Molesey	Jun 9-10
Hampshire v England	Alresford	Jun 17-18
Hampshire v Surrey	Ludgershall	Jul 2-4
Surrey v Kent	Molesey	Jul 15-18
England v Hampshire	Sevenoaks	Jul 24-25
Kent v England	Coxheath	Jul 29-31
Kent v Surrey	Bishopsbourne	Aug 5-7
Hampshire v Surrey	Hambledon[3]	Aug 13-15
A to M v N to Z	Bishopsbourne	Aug 26-29

1789 (14)
Middlesex v
Gentlemen of England	Lord's	May 18-19
A to M v N to Z	Lord's	Jun 3-16
Surrey v Kent	Molesey	Jun 10-12
England v Kent	Lord's	Jun 25-Jul 2
East Kent v West Kent	Coxheath	Jun 29-30
MCC v Essex	Lord's	Jul 8-9
Hampshire v Kent	Hambledon[3]	Jul 13-14
England v Kent	Uxbridge	Jul 23-25
Surrey v Hampshire	Molesey	Jul 30-Aug 1
East Kent v West Kent	Coxheath	Aug 4-5
Hornchurch v MCC	Hornchurch	Aug 6-7
Kent v Surrey	Bishopsbourne	Aug 11-14
Kent v Hampshire	Bishopsbourne	Aug 18-21
England v Hampshire	Sevenoaks	Sep 2-5

1790 (12)
Left-Handed v Right-Handed	Lord's	May 10-12
MCC v Hornchurch	Lord's	May 20-21
Hampshire v Kent	Lord's	Jun 10-12
Hornchurch v MCC	Hornchurch	Jul 5-6
England v Hampshire	Sevenoaks	Jul 12-16

England v Hampshire	Burley	Jul 19-21
Hampshire and Surrey v Kent	Ludgershall	Jul 27-29
Earl of Darnley's XI v Earl of Winchilsea's XI	Hambledon³	Aug 4-7
MCC v Middlesex	Lord's	Aug 16
Middlesex x MCC	Uxbridge	Aug 19-20
England v Hampshire and MCC	Lord's	Aug 30-Sep 2
East Kent v West Kent	Bishopsbourne	Sep 7-11

1791 (14)

MCC v Middlesex	Lord's	May 16-18
MCC v Middlesex	Lord's	May 23-25
Gentlemen of England v Old Etonians	Lord's	May 30-Jun 2
MCC v Gentlemen of Kent	Lord's	Jun 2-3
MCC v Hornchurch	Lord's	Jun 13-14
England v Hampshire	Burley	Jun 20-22
Old Etonians v MCC	Burley	Jun 23-24
England v Hampshire	Sevenoaks	Jul 6-8
Hampshire v England	Hambledon³	Jul 13-15
Hampshire v England	Ludgershall	Jul 25-28
Hornchurch v MCC	Hornchurch	Aug 11-13
MCC v Kent	Lord's	Aug 15-18
Surrey v Hampshire	Wrecclesham	Aug 23-25
Brighton v Middlesex	Brighton	Sep 19-22

1792 (19)

MCC v Middlesex	Lord's	May 7-9
MCC v Middlesex	Lord's	May 15-17
E.Bligh's XI v Earl of Winchilsea's XI	Lord's	May 21-22
MCC v Brighton	Lord's	May 28-30
MCC v Berkshire	Lord's	May 31-Jun 1
MCC v England	Lord's	Jun 6-8
England v Kent	Lord's	Jun 21-23
Earl of Winchilsea's XI v T.A.Smith's XI	Burley	Jul 2-4
Hampshire v Surrey	Hambledon³	Jul 16-18
Hampshire v Surrey	Ludgershall	Jul 23-26
Berkshire v MCC	Bray	Aug 2-4
Kent v Hampshire	Cobham	Aug 15-17
Brighton v MCC	Brighton	Aug 20-23
Brighton v Hampshire and MCC	Brighton	Aug 23-25
Kent v Essex	Dartford¹	Aug 29-31
Brighton v Middlesex	Brighton	Sep 5-7
Kent v Hampshire	Dartford¹	Sep 17-19
Middlesex v Brighton	Lord's	Sep 20-24
Essex v Kent	Hornchurch	Sep 27-28

1793 (17)

Old Etonians v Old Westminsters	Lord's	May 13-14
MCC v Middlesex	Lord's	May 22-23
Hornchurch v MCC	Hornchurch	May 30-31
MCC v Hornchurch	Lord's	Jun 6-7
England v Surrey and Sussex	Lord's	Jun 12-14
MCC v Essex	Lord's	Jun 17-18
MCC v Kent	Lord's	Jun 20-21
MCC v Berkshire	Lord's	Jun 24-26
Kent v MCC	Dartford¹	Jun 27-28
Kent v MCC	Dartford¹	Jun 28-29
Earl of Winchilsea's XI v G.Louch's XI	Lord's	Jul 1-3
England v Surrey	Hambledon³	Jul 12-15
England v Surrey	Dartford¹	Jul 22-24
Oldfield v MCC	Bray	Jul 25-26
England v Surrey	Burley	Aug 5-7
Earl of Winchilsea's XI v R.Leigh's XI	Burley	Aug 7-10
R.N.Newman's XI v R.Leigh's XI	Navestock	Aug 19-20

1794 (16)

MCC v Middlesex	Lord's	May 26-29
England v Surrey	Lord's	Jun 9-11
R.Leigh's XI v E.G.Morant's XI	Bray	Jun 18-20
R.Leigh's XI v G.Louch's XI	Lord's	Jun 30-Jul 2
Oldfield v Middlesex and MCC	Bray	Jul 7-8
R.Leigh's XI v E.G.Morant's XI	Dartford¹	Jul 21-22
D.Harris' XI v T.Walker's XI	Dartford¹	Jul 23-24
MCC v Oldfield	Lord's	Jul 29-30
MCC v Hampshire and Kent	Lord's	Aug 7-11
MCC v Oldfield	Lord's	Aug 12-13
MCC v Oldfield	Lord's	Aug 13-14
Hampshire v Surrey and Kent	Alresford	Aug 19-20
Hampshire v Surrey and Kent	Alresford	Aug 21-23
Oldfield v Kent	Lord's	Aug 27-30
England v Surrey	Lord's	Sep 10-15
England v Surrey	Dartford¹	Sep 16-19

1795 (19)

MCC v Middlesex	Lord's	May 25-27
C.Lennox's XI v Earl of Winchilsea's XI	Lord's	Jun 1-3
Earl of Winchilsea's XI v C.Lennox's XI	Lord's	Jun 9-11
Surrey and MCC v England	Lord's	Jun 22-26
MCC v Middlesex	Lord's	Jun 26-29
Surrey v England	Molesey	Jul 6-8
C.Lennox's XI v Earl of Winchilsea's XI	Molesey	Jul 8-10
Middlesex v Oldfield	Lord's	Jul 16-18
Earl of Winchilsea's XI v R.Leigh's XI	Hambledon³	Jul 20-22
Earl of Winchilsea's XI v R.Leigh's XI	Alresford	Jul 23 1795-Jun 28 1796
MCC v Oldfield	Lord's	Aug 6-7
Surrey v England	Molesey	Aug 10-12
Surrey v England	Molesey	Aug 12-15
England v Hampshire	Dartford²	Aug 24-26
England v Hampshire	Dartford²	Aug 27-29
Kent v England	Maidstone	Aug 31-Sep 2
Sir H.Mann's XI v R.Leigh's XI	Margate	Sep 7-10
Sir H.Mann's XI v R.Leigh's XI	Margate	Sep 14-16
Earl of Darnley's XI	Margate	Sep 10-12

1796 (7)

Middlesex v Kent	Lord's	May 16-17
Earl of Darnley's XI v Earl of Winchilsea's XI	Lord's	Jun 13-15
Middlesex v Kent	Lord's	Jun 20-22
England v Surrey and Kent	Alresford	Jun 28-30
Middlesex v Surrey	Lord's	Aug 15-16
England v Surrey	Margate	Aug 22-23
England v Surrey	Margate	Aug 24-26

1797 (13)

C.Lennox's XI v Earl of Winchilsea's XI	Lord's	May 15-16
C.Lennox's XI v Earl of Winchilsea's XI	Lord's	May 19-20
England v Surrey	Lord's	Jun 6-9
England v Surrey	Lord's	Jun 19-Jul 3
C.Lennox's XI v Earl of Winchilsea's XI	Lord's	Jul 4-6
MCC v London	Lord's	Jul 10-12
Surrey and Middlesex v England	Walworth	Jul 12-13
Earl of Winchilsea's XI v C.Lennox's XI	Swaffham	Jul 20-21
Hampshire v MCC	Alresford	Aug 7-10
MCC v Hampshire	Lord's	Aug 14-16
England v MCC	Molesey	Aug 21-23
MCC v England	Lord's	Aug 28-31
MCC v England	Lord's	Sep 21-26

1798 (8)

England v Surrey	Lord's	Jun 6-8
MCC v Middlesex	Lord's	Jun 20-21
MCC v England	Lord's	Jun 26-27
MCC v England	Lord's	Jul 11-13
Hampshire v MCC	Alresford	Jul 26-28
MCC v Hampshire	Lord's	Aug 2-3
England v Surrey	Lord's	Aug 13-15
England v Surrey	Lord's	Aug 16-17

1799 (4)

Surrey and MCC v England	Lord's	Jul 30-Aug 1
R.Whitehead's XI v Lord Yarmouth's XI	Lord's	Aug 1-3
England v Surrey	Lord's	Aug 13-15
England v Surrey	Lord's	Aug 15-17

1800 (5)

J.Gibbons' XI v R.Whitehead's XI	Lord's	May 19-21
	Lord's	Jun 11-13
England v Surrey	Lord's	Jun 16-17
England v Surrey	Lord's	Jul 14-15
England v The Ws and Hs	Lord's	Aug 28-30

Register of Grounds

location	ground name	first match	last match	no
Alresford	Stoke Down, Alresford	1778	1798	12*
Bishopsbourne	Bourne Paddock, Bishopsbourne	1772	1790	17
Bray	Old Field, Bray	1792	1794	4
Brighton	Prince of Wales Ground, Brighton	1791	1792	4
Burley	The Park, Burley-on-the-Hill	1790	1793	6
Cobham	Cobham Park	1792	1792	1
Coxheath	Star Inn, Coxheath	1787	1789	4
Dartford (1)	Dartford Brent	1792	1794	8
Dartford (2)	Dartford Heath	1795	1795	2*
Finsbury	Honourable Artillery Company Ground, Finsbury	1773	1777	2
Guildford	Merrow Down, Guildford	1772	1777	3
Hambledon (1)	Broad Halfpenny Down, Hambledon	1772	1781	14*
Hambledon (2)	Chidden Holt, Hambledon	1776	1776	1
Hambledon (3)	Windmill Down, Hambledon	1782	1795	12
Hornchurch	Langton Park, Hornchurch	1787	1793	6
Islington	White Conduit Fields, Islington	1786	1786	1
Laleham Burway	Laleham Burway Cricket Ground	1773	1779	8
Lord's	Lord's Old Ground, Marylebone	1787	1800	82*
Ludgershall	Perham Down, Ludgershall	1787	1792	5
Maidstone	Penenden Heath	1795	1795	1
Margate	Dandelion Paddock, Margate	1795	1796	5
Molesey	Molesey Hurst	1776	1797	13*
Navestock	The Green Man, Navestock	1793	1793	1
Sevenoaks	Sevenoaks Vine Cricket Club Ground	1773	1791	20*
Swaffham	Racecourse Ground, Swaffham	1797	1797	1
Uxbridge	W.Fennex's New Ground, Uxbridge	1789	1790	2
Walworth	Aram's New Ground, Montpelier Gardens, Walworth	1797	1797	1*
Wrecclesham	Holt Pound Cricket Ground, Wrecclesham	1791	1791	1*

* denotes grounds used for important or first-class matches after 1800

Match in 1802

The score on the facing page came to light after the ACS had completed its initial classification of 'important' cricket matches in the period 1801-1863, but it clearly merits inclusion and this was formally ratified by the Association in March 2010. Consequently it should included in lists of 'important' matches and in the career figures for the players concerned. It appeared in the *Cricket Statistician* for Spring 2006 (where the date was incorrectly given as 1805), accompanied by an article by Keith Warsop. This is, however, believed to be its first publication in book form since its original appearance in Britcher.

At the same time as this match was added to the list of 'important' games, the ACS agreed to delete the match on 26 August 1803 at Rickmansworth between Mr H.C.Woolridge's XI and Hon W.R.Capel's XI. Further research has shown that a very high proportion of the players involved in the 1803 game were drawn from the Rickmansworth Club and in view of this the overall quality of the match does not justify 'important' status.

It should also be mentioned, for the avoidance of doubt, that the supposed match on 20-22 April 1842 at Cambridge between Cambridge Town and Cambridge University has been conclusively proved to be a hoax and should be deleted from the list of 'important' games.

C.LENNOX'S XI v G.LEYCESTER'S XI

Played at Lord's Old Ground, Marylebone, June 8, 1802.

Match drawn.

C.LENNOX'S XI

1	C.Lennox	b Walker	2	b Walker		5
2	Ashurst	b Walker	10	b Cumberland		2
3	John Wells	b Boxall	0	hit wkt		16
4	T.A.Smith	b Boxall	14	c Burrows		18
5	T.Lord	c Tanner	2	not out		1
6	J.Ward	not out	11	c Boxall		23
7	A.P.Upton	b Cumberland	7	c Barton		1
8	J.Weller	c Cooper	1	c Boxall		5
9	Morgan	b Walker	0	b Boxall		0
10	D.Onslow	hit wkt	0	b Boxall		0
11	J.Eavers	b Cumberland	0	c Burrows		1
	Extras	b 1	1			
			48			72

FoW (1): 1- , 2- , 3- , 4- , 5- , 6- , 7- , 8- , 9- , 10-48
FoW (2): 1- , 2- , 3- , 4- , 5- , 6- , 7- , 8- , 9- , 10-72

G.LEYCESTER'S XI

1	G.Leycester	b Ward	4	b Ward		13
2	T.J.Burgoyne	b Ward	0			
3	T.Boxall	b Ward	2			
4	W.Barton	run out	0			
5	T.Walker	c Lennox	9	(2) not out		13
6	J.Tanner	b Ward	7			
7	C.Cumberland	c Smith	11	(3) b Wells		0
8	G.Cooper	c Wells	1			
9	H.Burrows	run out	3			
10	H.Bentley	c Morgan	0			
11	W.Turner	not out	0			
	Extras	b 2	2			
			39	(2 wickets)		26

FoW (1): 1- , 2- , 3- , 4- , 5- , 6- , 7- , 8- , 9- , 10-39
FoW (2): 1- , 2-26

G.Leycester's XI Bowling

	O	M	R	W	O	M	R	W
Walker				3				1
Boxall				2				2
Cumberland				2				1

C.Lennox's XI Bowling

	O	M	R	W	O	M	R	W
Ward				4				1
Wells				(2)				1

Umpires: Toss:

Britcher says "this match is postponed" but it was apparently never resumed.

Index of Scorecards

A to C
  v Rest of the Alphabet   99
A to M
  v N to Z   109, 111, 112, 122, 124
Berkshire
  v M.C.C.   167, 173, 189
E.Bligh's XI
  v Earl of Winchilsea's XI   165
Brighton
  v Hampshire and M.C.C.   176
  v M.C.C.   166, 175
  v Middlesex   162, 178, 180
Chertsey
  v England   69
Earl of Darnley's XI
  v Sir H.Mann's XI   232
  v Earl of Winchilsea's XI   144, 235
Duke of Dorset's XI
  v Sir H.Mann's XI   77, 78, 85
East Kent
  v West Kent   82, 91, 127, 132, 148
England
  v Chertsey   69
  v Hampshire 34, 35, 36, 38, 39, 41, 45,
                 46, 61, 62, 63, 64, 65, 66,
                 67, 68, 72, 73, 75, 76, 79,
                 80, 90, 94, 95, 115, 118,
                 126, 136, 141, 142, 154,
                 156, 157, 158, 228, 229
  v Hampshire and Kent   113
  v Hampshire and M.C.C.   147
  v Kent   119, 130, 169, 230
  v M.C.C. 168, 251, 252, 253, 256, 257
  v Surrey 193, 194, 196, 200, 213, 214,
            220, 226, 227, 239, 240, 243,
            244, 254, 260, 261, 264, 265,
                        267, 268, 270
  v Surrey and Kent   237
  v Surrey and M.C.C.   218, 262
  v Surrey and Middlesex   247
  v Surrey and Sussex   186
  v White Conduit Club   104
  v The Ws and Hs   269
Essex
  v Kent   177, 181
  v M.C.C.   128, 187
  v Middlesex   102
Gentlemen of England
  v Middlesex   123
  v Old Etonians   151
Gentlemen of Kent
  v M.C.C.   152
J.Gibbons' XI
  v R.Whitehead's XI   266

Hampshire
  v England   34, 35, 36, 38, 39, 41, 45,
                46, 61, 62, 63, 64, 65, 66,
                67, 68, 72, 73, 75, 76, 79,
                80, 90, 94, 95, 115, 118,
                126, 136, 141, 142, 154,
                156, 157, 158, 228, 229
  v Kent   48, 49, 50, 51, 54, 55, 56, 57,
              58, 81, 83, 84, 86, 87, 88, 89,
            92, 93, 97, 98, 107, 108, 110,
                     129, 135, 139, 174, 179
  v M.C.C.   249, 250, 258, 259
  v Surrey   43, 44, 47, 52, 53, 59, 60,
              70, 71, 114, 116, 121, 131,
                          161, 171, 172
  v Surrey and Kent   210, 211
Hampshire and Kent
  v England   113
  v M.C.C.   207
Hampshire and M.C.C.
  v Brighton   176
  v England   147
Hampshire and Surrey
  v Kent   143
D.Harris' XI
  v T.Walker's XI   205
Hornchurch
  v M.C.C.   133, 138, 140, 153, 159, 184,
                                   185
  v White Conduit Club and
        Moulsey Hurst   101, 105
Kent
  v England   119, 130, 169, 230
  v Essex   177, 181
  v Hampshire 48, 49, 50, 51, 54, 55, 56,
                57, 58, 81, 83, 84, 86, 87,
                88, 89, 92, 93, 97, 98, 107,
                108, 110, 129, 135, 139,
                            174, 179
  v Hampshire and Surrey   143
  v M.C.C.   160, 188, 190, 191
  v Middlesex   234, 236
  v Oldfield   212
  v Surrey   37, 40, 42, 74, 117, 120,
                                 125, 134
  v White Conduit Club   96, 100
Left-Handed
  v Right-Handed   137
R.Leigh's XI
  v G.Louch's XI   202
  v Sir H.Mann's XI   231, 233
  v E.G.Morant's XI   201, 204
  v R.N.Newman's XI   198
  v Earl of Winchilsea's XI 197, 223, 224

C.Lennox's XI
  v Earl of Winchilsea's XI   216, 217,
                            221, 241, 242, 245, 248
London
  v M.C.C.   246
G.Louch's XI
  v R.Leigh's XI   202
  v Earl of Winchilsea's XI   192
Sir H.Mann's XI
  v Earl of Darnley's XI   232
  v Duke of Dorset's XI   77, 78, 85
  v R.Leigh's XI   231, 233
M.C.C.
  v Berkshire   167, 173, 189
  v Brighton   166, 175
  v England   168, 251, 252, 253,
                 256, 257
  v Essex   128, 187
  v Gentlemen of Kent   152
  v Hampshire   249, 250, 258, 259
  v Hampshire and Kent   207
  v Hornchurch   133, 138, 140, 153,
                 159, 184, 185
  v Kent   160, 188, 190, 191
  v London   246
  v Middlesex   145, 146, 149, 150,
               163, 164, 183, 199,
               215, 219, 255
  v Old Etonians   155
  v Oldfield   195, 206, 208, 209, 225
Middlesex
  v Brighton   162, 178, 180
  v Essex   102
  v Gentlemen of England   123
  v Kent   234, 236
  v M.C.C.   145, 146, 149, 150, 163,
          164, 183, 199, 215, 219, 255
  v Oldfield   222
  v Surrey   238
  v White Conduit Club   103
Middlesex and M.C.C.
  v Oldfield   203
E.G.Morant's XI
  v R.Leigh's XI   201, 204
N to Z
  v A to M   109, 111, 112, 122, 124
R.N.Newman's XI
  v R.Leigh's XI   198
Old Etonians
  v Gentlemen of England   151
  v M.C.C.   155
  v Old Westminsters   182
Old Westminsters
  v Old Etonians   182
Oldfield
  v Kent   212

  v M.C.C.   195, 206, 208, 209, 225
  v Middlesex   222
  v Middlesex and M.C.C.   203
Rest of the Alphabet
  v A to C   99
Right-Handed
  v Left-Handed   137
T.A.Smith's XI
  v Earl of Winchilsea's XI   106, 170
Surrey
  v England   193, 194, 196, 200, 213,
             214, 220, 226, 227, 239,
             240, 243, 244, 254, 260,
             261, 264, 265, 267, 268,
             270
  v Hampshire   43, 44, 47, 52, 53, 59,
             60, 70, 71, 114, 116, 121,
             131, 161,171, 172
  v Kent   37, 40, 42, 74, 117, 120,
             125, 134
  v Middlesex   238
Surrey and Kent
  v England   237
  v Hampshire   210, 211
Surrey and M.C.C.
  v England   218, 262
Surrey and Middlesex
  v England   247
Surrey and Sussex
  v England   186
T.Walker's XI
  v D.Harris' XI   205
West Kent
  v East Kent   82, 91, 127, 132, 148
White Conduit Club
  v England   104
  v Kent   96, 100
  v Middlesex   103
White Conduit Club and Moulsey Hurst
  v Hornchurch   101, 105
R.Whitehead's XI
  v J.Gibbons' XI   266
  v Lord Yarmouth's XI   263
Earl of Winchilsea's XI
  v E.Bligh's XI   165
  v Earl of Darnley's XI   144, 235
  v R.Leigh's XI   197, 223, 224
  v C.Lennox's XI   216, 217, 221, 241,
             242, 245, 248
  v G.Louch's XI   192
  v T.A.Smith's XI   106, 170
The Ws and Hs
  v England   269
Lord Yarmouth's XI
  v R.Whitehead's XI   263

Index of Players

ABURROW, Edward 34, 35, 36, 38, 39, 45, 46, 47, 48, 49, 50, 51, 52, 53, 55, 56, 57, 58, 59, 60, 61, 62, 63, 64, 65, 66, 67, 68, 70, 71, 72, 73, 75, 76, 79, 80, 81, 83, 84, 86, 87, 88, 89, 90
ALLEN, W. 103, 159, 187
AMHERST, Stephen 91, 96, 99, 100, 104, 107, 108, 112, 113, 117, 119, 120, 122, 123, 124, 125, 127, 129, 130, 132, 139, 143, 148, 152, 160, 163, 169, 174, 177, 181, 230
ANGUISH, Charles 128, 133, 138, 140, 142, 143, 145, 146, 147, 149, 150, 151, 152, 153, 154, 155, 158, 159, 161, 199, 200, 202, 203, 205, 206, 207, 208, 209, 210, 211, 215, 216
ANNETT, - 119, 121, 141, 156, 157, 171
ASTON, Henry Hervey 162, 165, 166, 167, 169, 172, 173, 174, 175, 176, 178, 180, 184
ATTFIELD, Henry 43, 44, 47, 52, 53, 59, 60, 63, 69, 70, 71, 74, 75, 76, 77, 79, 87, 114, 116, 121
AYLING, Robert 234, 236
AYLING, William 270
AYLWARD, James 38, 39, 41, 43, 44, 45, 46, 47, 48, 49, 50, 51, 52, 53, 54, 55, 56, 57, 58, 59, 60, 61, 62, 63, 64, 65, 66, 69, 72, 73, 74, 75, 76, 77, 78, 79, 81, 83, 84, 85, 86, 87, 88, 89, 90, 91, 92, 93, 94, 95, 96, 97, 98, 99, 100, 104, 107, 108, 109, 110, 111, 112, 113, 115, 117, 118, 119, 120, 122, 124, 125, 126, 127, 129, 130, 132, 134, 135, 136, 137, 139, 141, 142, 143, 144, 147, 148, 152, 154, 156, 157, 158, 160, 168, 169, 188, 190, 191, 192, 193, 194, 246, 247, 251, 252, 253
BAKER, - 66
BARBER, William 34, 35, 36, 38, 39, 41, 49, 51, 52, 53, 54, 55, 56, 58, 64
BARKER, - 102, 128, 133, 198
BARRYMORE, 7th Earl (Richard Barry) 162, 166
BARTHOLOMEW, William 40, 44, 69, 123
BARTON, William 215, 232, 233, 234, 238, 251, 252, 253, 260, 261, 262, 263, 264, 265, 267, 268, 270
BATES, - 127
BAYLEY, James 43, 44, 92, 93
BAYTON, John 58, 65
BEAUCLERK, Lord Frederick 152, 153, 215, 216, 234, 235, 236, 237, 239, 240, 241, 242, 243, 244, 246, 248, 249, 250, 251, 252, 253, 254, 255, 256, 257, 258, 259, 260, 261, 269, 270
BEDSTER, William 65, 66, 67, 68, 69, 70, 71, 72, 73, 74, 75, 76, 77, 78, 79, 80, 81, 82, 83, 84, 85, 86, 87, 88, 89, 90, 91, 92, 93, 94, 95, 99, 101, 102, 103, 105, 109, 123, 145, 146, 149, 150, 162, 163, 164, 165, 166, 168, 170, 172, 178, 181, 182, 183, 189, 195, 203, 208, 209
BEESTON, James 199, 215, 238, 246, 247, 262, 263
BEESTON, R. 146
BEESTON, William 146, 155, 255, 262
BELDHAM, George 268, 270
BELDHAM, John 213, 214, 220
BELDHAM, William 104, 106, 107, 108, 109, 110, 111, 112, 113, 114, 115, 116, 117, 118, 120, 121, 122, 124, 125, 126, 127, 130, 132, 134, 136, 137, 141, 142, 143, 144, 145, 146, 147, 149, 150, 152, 154, 156, 157, 158, 160, 161, 163, 164, 165, 168, 169, 170, 171, 172, 174, 176, 177, 179, 181, 186, 188, 190, 191, 193, 194, 196, 197, 198, 199, 200, 201, 202, 204, 205, 207, 210, 211, 213, 214, 215, 216, 217, 218, 220, 221, 223, 224, 226, 227, 228, 229, 230, 231, 232, 236, 237, 238, 239, 240, 243, 244, 245, 247, 248, 251, 252, 253, 254, 256, 257, 260, 261, 262, 263, 264, 265, 266, 267, 268, 269, 270
BENNETT, James 258, 259
BENNETT, John 249, 250, 252, 253, 258, 259, 260, 261, 268, 270
BERWICK, - 74, 75, 76, 77, 79, 80
BEXLEY, - 203
BLAKE, - 42
BLIGH, Hon Edward 133, 138, 139, 149, 150, 151, 152, 153, 154, 155, 158, 159, 160, 161, 162, 163, 164, 165, 166, 167, 168, 169, 170, 171, 172, 173, 174, 175, 176, 177, 178, 231, 232, 234, 235, 236, 237, 238, 241, 242, 243, 244, 245, 246, 249, 250, 251, 252, 253, 258, 259
BLISS, - 226

BLUNT, - 167
BOLTWOOD, - 69
BONHAM, Henry 71
BONICK, - 131
BOOKER, Francis 37, 42, 48, 49, 50, 51, 54, 55, 56, 57, 58, 61, 62, 67, 68, 72, 74, 77, 78, 87, 88, 89, 90, 91, 94, 95, 97, 98, 99, 100, 108, 109, 110, 111, 112, 113, 115, 117, 118, 119, 120, 122, 137, 141, 148
BOORMAN, John 35, 36, 39, 55, 56, 57, 58, 69, 74, 77, 78, 81, 84, 85, 86, 91, 96, 97, 98, 99, 100, 101, 102, 103, 108, 110, 111, 115, 117, 118, 119, 120, 125, 126, 127, 128, 129, 130, 132, 133, 134, 135, 139, 141, 142, 148, 153, 159, 165, 177, 181, 184, 185, 187, 198
BOOTH, George 255, 262, 264, 265, 266
BOULT, A. 102
BOULT, George T. 96, 98, 99, 101, 102, 105, 111, 123, 124, 128, 129, 130, 133, 145, 150, 163, 177, 181, 215, 222
BOULT, Zachariah 102
BOWRA, William 51, 54, 55, 56, 57, 58, 59, 60, 61, 62, 63, 64, 65, 66, 67, 68, 72, 73, 74, 75, 76, 77, 78, 79, 80, 81, 82, 83, 84, 85, 86, 87, 88, 89, 90, 91, 92, 93, 95, 97, 98, 99, 113, 118, 120, 162, 166, 175, 176, 178
BOXALL, Thomas 125, 143, 148, 157, 158, 160, 165, 168, 169, 170, 172, 174, 175, 176, 177, 179, 181, 183, 186, 188, 190, 191, 192, 193, 194, 196, 197, 198, 200, 201, 202, 204, 205, 207, 210, 211, 212, 213, 214, 216, 217, 218, 220, 221, 223, 224, 226, 227, 228, 229, 230, 231, 232, 233, 234, 235, 236, 237, 238, 239, 240, 241, 242, 243, 244, 245, 247, 251, 252, 253, 254, 255, 256, 257, 262, 263, 264, 265, 266, 267, 268, 269, 270
BRADES, - 225
BRAZIER, William 48, 49, 50, 51, 54, 55, 56, 57, 58, 59, 87, 88, 89, 90, 91, 92, 93, 94, 95, 97, 99, 107, 108, 109, 110, 111, 112, 113, 117, 118, 119, 120, 122, 124, 125, 126, 127, 129, 130, 132, 134, 135, 136, 137, 139, 141, 142, 144, 148, 212
BRETT, Thomas 34, 35, 36, 38, 39, 43, 44, 45, 46, 47, 48, 49, 50, 51, 52, 53, 54, 55, 56, 57, 58, 59, 60, 61, 62, 63, 64, 65, 67, 68, 70, 71
BRIDEN, - 261
BRIDGER, Henry 219
BROWN, - 248
BROWNING, Thomas 230
BROWNING, William 152, 230
BRUNDELL, Hon Robert 140, 163, 165, 187, 190, 191, 193, 196, 197
BULLEN, William 39, 46, 48, 49, 50, 51, 54, 55, 56, 57, 61, 62, 63, 64, 65, 66, 67, 68, 69, 72, 73, 74, 75, 76, 77, 78, 79, 80, 81, 82, 83, 84, 85, 86, 87, 88, 89, 90, 91, 92, 93, 94, 95, 96, 97, 98, 99, 100, 104, 107, 108, 109, 110, 111, 112, 113, 115, 117, 118, 119, 120, 122, 124, 125, 126, 127, 129, 130, 132, 134, 135, 136, 137, 139, 141, 142, 143, 144, 147, 148, 152, 154, 155, 156, 157, 158, 160, 179, 181, 182, 188, 190, 191, 192, 196, 198, 201, 204, 205, 207, 212, 224, 228, 229, 230, 231, 232, 233, 234, 235, 236, 237, 245
BULLER, Anthony 242
BURGESS, John 212, 233
BURGOYNE, Thomas John 246, 254, 255, 264, 265, 266, 268
BURRELL, Sir Peter 103, 104, 105, 117, 134, 141, 145
BUTCHER, - 101, 102, 103, 105, 106, 114, 116, 117, 120, 121, 125, 128, 131, 133, 134, 140, 142, 143, 144, 152, 190, 191, 192
BUTLER, - 123, 145, 162, 163, 164, 165, 166, 183, 225, 236, 246, 247
BUTTERLY, - 106
BUTTON, Zachariah 182, 254
CANTRELL, - 123, 149, 150, 162, 163, 164, 180
CAPEL, Hon Thomas Edward 140, 146, 147
CAPRON, - 175, 176, 180
CARPENTER, - 131
CARR, - 128, 138, 140, 159
CARTER, - 189, 195, 219, 222
CHILDS, - 34, 38, 39, 40, 42, 43, 44, 45
CHITTY, - 270
CHURCH, J. 127, 132, 219
CLAIR, - 249
CLARK, Thomas 101, 102, 105, 133, 138, 140, 153
CLARKE, - 145
CLEMENTS, - 101, 128, 133, 138, 140

CLIFFORD, Robert 62, 67, 72, 73, 74, 75, 76, 77, 78, 79, 80, 81, 82, 83, 84, 85, 86, 87, 88, 89, 90, 91, 92, 93, 94, 95, 96, 97, 98, 99, 100, 104, 107, 108, 109, 110, 111, 112, 113, 115, 117, 118, 119, 120, 122, 124, 125, 126, 127, 129, 130, 132, 134, 135, 136, 137, 139, 141, 142, 143, 144, 145, 146, 147, 148, 156, 160, 168, 177, 179, 181
CLIFTON, Benjamin 254, 255, 256, 257, 258, 259, 260, 261
CODRINGTON, Christopher Bethell 241, 242, 250, 251, 252
COLCHIN, Samuel 39, 46, 48, 49, 51, 54, 60, 65, 66, 69
COLE, J. 95, 115
COLLIER, - 100
COLLINS, - 156, 157, 161, 171, 175, 179
COOPER, G. 248, 267
COUCHMAN, - 91, 97
COURTENAY, William 248
COVENTRY, Hon Thomas William 269
CRAWTE, John 118, 120, 121, 122, 125, 127, 129, 130, 132, 134, 135, 136, 137, 139, 143, 144, 148, 156, 157, 160, 168, 169, 174, 177, 179, 181, 186, 193, 194, 196, 201, 204, 205, 210, 211, 213, 214, 218, 220, 221, 223, 224, 226, 227, 228, 229, 230, 238, 239, 240, 251, 256, 260, 261, 268, 270
CROSOER, Henry 98, 99, 107, 108, 132, 134, 135, 148
CUMBERLAND, Charles 151, 152, 153, 154, 155, 159, 160, 182, 183, 184, 185, 186, 188, 189, 195, 196, 197, 215, 218, 219, 222, 246, 249
DALE, - 123, 149, 150, 163, 164, 183, 199
DALKEITH, Earl of (Charles William Henry Montagu-Scott) 241, 242, 248
DAMPIER, John 96, 100, 104
DARNLEY, 4th Earl of (John Bligh) 133, 138, 139, 140, 142, 143, 144, 145, 146, 147, 151, 152, 153, 154, 155, 169, 174, 177, 184, 188, 190, 232, 235, 236
DAVIDSON, - 95, 101, 102
DAVIS, Sir John Brewer 37, 40
DAVIS, Thomas 41, 43, 44, 54, 56, 57
DAVY, - 105, 106, 114, 116
DEAN, - 103, 134, 135, 148
DE BURGH, Hon John Thomas 37
DEHANY, George 128, 133, 147, 151, 163, 164, 182, 183, 185, 186, 188, 189, 192, 195, 196, 197
DENN, Robert 101, 102, 105, 133, 138, 140, 153, 159, 177, 198
DORSET, 3rd Duke of (John Frederick Sackville) 37, 40, 41, 42, 45, 48, 49, 50, 51, 52, 53, 54, 55, 56, 57, 58, 61, 62, 63, 77, 92, 93, 94
DOUGLAS, Hon Charles 241, 246, 255, 259
DOWNHAM, - 233
DREW, John 232, 233
DRUMMOND, George 101, 103, 104, 106, 114, 116, 216
DUPUIS, George 105, 151, 152, 173
EAST, Gilbert 100, 103, 105, 113, 167, 173, 189, 195, 203, 206, 208, 209
EAVERS, J. 266
EDMEADS, John 34, 35, 36, 37, 47, 53, 59, 60, 63, 64, 65, 66, 69, 70, 71, 74, 76
EDMEADS, William 52
FENNEX, William 99, 108, 109, 110, 111, 112, 115, 118, 119, 122, 124, 126, 137, 145, 146, 149, 150, 152, 154, 156, 157, 158, 162, 163, 164, 165, 166, 168, 169, 170, 172, 177, 178, 179, 180, 181, 182, 183, 186, 187, 191, 192, 194, 197, 198, 199, 200, 201, 202, 204, 205, 212, 213, 214, 238, 240, 243, 244, 245, 247, 248, 251, 252, 253, 254, 255, 256, 257, 260, 261, 262, 263, 264, 265, 266, 267, 268, 269, 270
FIELDER, Richard 148, 169, 174, 177, 179, 181, 186, 188, 190, 191, 201, 212, 213, 214, 218, 226, 227, 230, 236
FINCH, John 167, 173, 189, 195, 199, 201, 203, 206, 208, 209, 212, 222, 225
FINCH, - 98
FISH, Jasper 42
FITZROY, Hon Henry William 114, 116, 128, 138, 139, 140, 145, 146, 148, 149, 150, 151, 152, 153, 154, 155, 159, 160, 161, 162, 165, 166, 167, 168, 169, 170, 172, 173, 174, 175, 176, 178, 184, 185, 187, 188, 189, 190, 191, 193, 194
FLINT, - 131
FOSTER, Francis 136
FRAME, John 34, 35, 39, 42, 43, 44, 46

FRANCIS, Richard 37, 40, 41, 42, 43, 44, 45, 46, 47, 48, 49, 50, 51, 52, 53, 54, 55, 56, 57, 58, 59, 60, 61, 62, 63, 64, 65, 66, 67, 68, 70, 71, 72, 73, 87, 88, 89, 90, 92, 93, 94, 95, 96, 117, 184, 185, 187
FRANCIS, - 51
FREEMANTLE, Andrew 121, 129, 131, 135, 136, 137, 141, 142, 143, 144, 147, 154, 156, 157, 158, 160, 161, 168, 169, 170, 171, 172, 174, 176, 179, 182, 186, 190, 191, 192, 193, 194, 196, 197, 198, 200, 201, 202, 204, 205, 207, 210, 211, 213, 214, 216, 217, 218, 220, 221, 223, 224, 226, 227, 228, 229, 230, 231, 232, 233, 235, 237, 239, 240, 243, 244, 245, 247, 249, 250, 251, 252, 253, 254, 256, 257, 258, 259, 260, 261, 262, 263, 264, 265, 266, 267, 268, 269, 270
FREEMANTLE, John 79, 80, 81, 83, 84, 86, 88
FRENCH, - 144
FUGGLES, James 34, 35, 36, 37
GATES, - 206, 208, 209, 212, 220, 222, 225
GIBBONS, John 242, 254, 255, 256, 257, 262, 263, 265, 266, 267, 269
GIBBS, - 103
GIBSON, - 77, 78
GILL, S. 167, 173, 189, 195, 203, 206, 208, 209, 212, 222, 225
GILL, - 34
GOLDHAM, John 155, 162, 163, 164, 168, 170, 175, 182, 183, 192, 199, 202, 203, 215, 225, 226, 227, 231, 233, 238, 246, 247
GOLDSMITH, John 171
GOODHEW, - 160, 212, 230
GOULSTONE, John 128, 133, 138, 140, 153, 159, 177, 181, 184, 185, 187, 198
GRAHAM, N. 101, 102, 103, 105, 123, 128, 133, 137, 147, 155, 163, 164, 165, 167, 170, 181, 182, 183, 192, 195, 199, 202, 203, 206, 215, 217, 219, 222, 225, 228, 229, 231, 232, 233, 234, 236, 238, 241, 242, 244, 245, 246, 247, 248, 251, 253, 255, 258, 263, 264, 265
GRANGE, - 145, 146, 149, 150, 151, 164, 178, 180
GREENSTREET, - 120
GREGORY, - 162, 166, 175, 178, 180
GRINHAM, - 258, 259
GROOMBRIDGE, - 185, 187
GROVER, John Septimus 138
GUNNELL, W. 247
HALE, Edward 131, 171, 249
HALL, W. 87
HALL, - 245
HAMMOND, John 148, 162, 166, 169, 175, 176, 178, 180, 186, 193, 194, 196, 198, 199, 200, 201, 202, 204, 205, 207, 210, 211, 212, 213, 214, 216, 217, 218, 219, 220, 221, 222, 223, 224, 225, 226, 227, 228, 229, 230, 231, 232, 233, 234, 235, 236, 237, 238, 239, 240, 243, 244, 245, 247, 248, 251, 252, 253, 254, 256, 257, 260, 261, 262, 263, 264, 265, 266, 267, 268, 269, 270
HAMPTON, Harry 270
HAMPTON, John 191, 192, 193, 194, 196, 197, 200, 202, 203, 206, 208, 209, 213, 214, 238, 255, 256, 260, 268, 269
HARBORD, Hon William Assheton 155, 159, 161
HARDING, James 171, 201, 210, 211, 212, 213, 214, 226, 227, 235, 237, 243, 250, 268
HARRIS, David 87, 88, 89, 90, 91, 92, 93, 94, 98, 99, 100, 104, 106, 108, 109, 110, 111, 112, 113, 114, 115, 116, 117, 118, 119, 120, 121, 122, 124, 126, 127, 129, 130, 132, 135, 136, 137, 139, 141, 147, 154, 156, 165, 168, 169, 172, 174, 176, 179, 193, 194, 196, 197, 198, 200, 201, 202, 204, 205, 207, 210, 211, 213, 214, 216, 217, 218, 220, 221, 223, 224, 225, 226, 227, 250, 258, 259, 260
HART, - 166
HARVEY, - 181, 184, 185, 187
HATCH, Isaac 96
HAWKINS, - 97, 98, 100, 106
HENEAGE, - 240
HIGGS, - 128, 133, 138
HOCKLEY, - 262, 263, 264, 265
HODGES, - 85
HOGBEN, - 83, 84, 85, 86, 88, 89
HOGSFLESH, William 34, 35, 36, 38, 39, 41, 43, 47, 48, 49, 50
HOLNESS, - 82
HOOKER, - 230, 231, 232
HORSEY, - 116, 131

HOSMER, Richard 77, 78, 82, 87, 91, 95, 96, 100, 104, 107, 112, 113, 117, 119, 123, 127, 132, 152
HUDSON, - 178
HUNT, - 116, 119, 128, 133
HUSSEY, Edward 37, 40, 96, 99, 100, 104, 107, 123, 138, 149, 150, 164, 165, 175, 176, 189, 234, 243
HYDE, - 162
INGRAM, Thomas 101, 113, 115, 117, 124, 126, 131, 134, 137, 153, 159, 163, 172, 177, 181, 184, 185, 187, 209, 246, 247
IRONS, - 69
JONES, Edward 197
JONES, - 102
JUTTEN, Thomas 162, 166, 175, 178, 180
KAYE, John Lister 105, 149, 151, 163, 167, 215, 254, 255
KENNETT, - 132
KNOWLES, - 242
LADBROKE, James Weller (see under WELLER, James)
LAMBERT, John 206, 207, 208, 209, 241, 242, 244
LAMBORN, - 63, 64, 65, 66, 67, 68, 69, 70, 71, 72, 73, 74, 75, 76, 79, 80, 81, 82, 83, 84, 85, 86
LAWRELL, James 269
LAWRENCE, Richard 103, 167, 173, 189, 195, 203, 206, 208, 209, 212, 222, 225
LEER, George 34, 35, 36, 38, 39, 41, 43, 44, 45, 46, 47, 48, 49, 50, 51, 52, 53, 55, 56, 57, 58, 59, 60, 61, 62, 63, 65, 66, 67, 68, 70, 71, 72, 73, 75, 76, 81, 83, 84, 86, 87, 88, 89, 90
LEGGATE, J. 123
LENNOX, Hon Charles 96, 123, 124, 125, 128, 138, 139, 140, 141, 145, 146, 147, 151, 153, 154, 155, 157, 158, 159, 160, 161, 215, 216, 217, 218, 219, 220, 221, 223, 226, 227, 241, 242, 243, 244, 245, 246, 248, 249, 250, 251, 252, 253, 267
LEWIS, M. 37, 40
LEYCESTER, George 138, 151, 152, 153, 158, 161, 173, 175, 176, 225, 226, 227, 228, 249, 250, 259, 262, 266, 267
LIFFEN, Thomas 162, 166, 175, 178, 180
LITTLER, John 159, 177, 181, 184, 185, 187, 189, 193
LLOYD, Thomas 173
LORD, Thomas 102, 109, 123, 145, 146, 149, 150, 151, 162, 163, 164, 165, 166, 167, 173, 178, 180, 182, 183, 187, 192, 195, 199, 203, 205, 206, 208, 209, 213, 215, 217, 219, 222, 225, 226, 227, 228, 229, 231, 232, 233, 234, 236, 238, 241, 242, 246, 248, 253, 255, 256, 257, 261, 262, 263, 264, 265
LOUCH, George 40, 42, 91, 100, 101, 102, 103, 105, 106, 108, 109, 110, 111, 112, 113, 115, 118, 119, 121, 122, 123, 124, 126, 128, 129, 130, 133, 135, 137, 138, 139, 140, 142, 143, 144, 145, 146, 147, 149, 150, 151, 152, 153, 154, 155, 157, 158, 159, 160, 161, 162, 163, 164, 165, 166, 167, 168, 169, 170, 171, 174, 175, 176, 178, 179, 180, 182, 183, 184, 185, 186, 187, 188, 189, 190, 192, 193, 194, 195, 196, 197, 199, 200, 202, 203, 204, 205, 206, 207, 208, 209, 210, 211, 215, 216, 217, 218, 219, 221, 222, 223, 224, 225, 227, 228, 230, 231, 232, 234, 235, 236, 237, 238, 241, 242, 243, 244, 245, 246, 249, 250, 252
LUCK, - 188, 190, 191
"LUMPY" (see under STEVENS, Edward)
LUSHINGTON, Stephen 262, 263, 264
MADDOX, J. 155
MAITLAND, Peregrine 254, 255, 257, 259, 261, 262, 263, 266
MANN, Sir Horatio 37, 40
MANN, Noah 64, 65, 66, 67, 68, 70, 71, 72, 73, 75, 76, 79, 80, 81, 82, 83, 84, 85, 86, 87, 88, 89, 90, 92, 93, 94, 95, 96, 97, 98, 99, 100, 104, 106, 107, 108, 109, 110, 111, 112, 113, 114, 115, 116, 118, 119, 121, 122, 124, 125, 126, 129, 130, 134, 135, 136
MANSFIELD, - 69
MARCHANT, J. 162, 166, 175, 176, 180
MARCLEW, - 233
MARTEN, Sir Henry William 241, 242, 262, 267, 269
MARTIN, J. 101, 102, 103, 105, 128, 133, 138, 140, 153, 183
MARTIN, T. 85, 91
MATTHEWS, - 123
MAY, Richard 34, 35, 36, 38, 40, 45, 50, 51, 54, 59, 74, 77, 78
MAY, Thomas 34, 35, 37, 38, 40
MAY, - 249, 250, 258, 259

MELLISH, Thomas 182, 184, 185, 187, 188, 199, 200, 216, 217, 234, 235, 236, 237, 241, 243, 244, 245, 246, 248, 249, 266, 269
MILES, - 187
MILLER, Joseph 47
MILLER, Richard 34, 35, 36, 37, 38, 40, 41, 42, 43, 44, 45, 46, 47, 48, 49, 50, 51, 52, 53, 54, 55, 56, 57, 61, 62, 63, 64, 65, 66, 67, 68, 69, 70, 71, 72, 73, 74, 75, 76, 77, 78, 79, 80, 81, 82, 83, 84, 85, 86, 88, 90, 91, 92, 93
MILLER, - 151
MILLS, - 69, 70, 71, 72, 73, 74, 77, 78, 82
MILSINGTON, Viscount (Thomas Charles Colyear) 170, 196, 197
MINCHIN, John 34, 35, 36, 38, 41, 42, 43, 44, 45, 46, 52, 53, 60, 61, 62, 63, 64, 67, 68, 69, 70, 71, 72, 73, 74, 75, 76, 77
MONK, - 167, 173, 189, 195, 203, 206, 208, 209, 222, 225
MONSON, Hon George Henry 96, 114, 170, 171, 172, 173, 174, 175, 176, 177
MORANT, Edward Gregory 197, 206, 222
MUGGERIDGE, - 47, 59, 60, 71
MUNDY, - 172, 249
MURRAY, - 101, 128, 133
NEALE, J. 121, 131, 171
NEWMAN, Richard Newman 37, 42, 78, 97, 101, 102, 103, 105, 184, 185, 188, 189, 190, 191, 192, 193, 194, 195, 198
NICHOLSON, - 119
NICOLL, Thomas Vere Richard 145, 151, 173, 182, 183, 184, 185, 186, 187, 188, 189, 199
NYREN, John 106, 110, 114, 131
NYREN, Richard 34, 35, 38, 39, 41, 44, 45, 46, 47, 48, 49, 50, 51, 52, 53, 54, 55, 56, 57, 58, 59, 60, 61, 62, 63, 64, 65, 66, 67, 68, 70, 71, 72, 73, 75, 76, 79, 80, 81, 83, 84, 86, 89, 90, 92, 93, 94, 95, 97
OLIVER, - 102
ONSLOW, Hon Denzil 235, 241, 242, 263
OXLEY, W. 140, 159, 177, 181, 184, 185, 187, 198
PACKER, - 146
PAGE, - 35, 42
PALMER, William 34, 36, 37, 39, 40, 41, 42, 43, 44, 45, 46, 47, 52, 53, 54, 59, 60
PALMER, - 125, 126, 127, 129, 130, 132, 135
PARK, - 219
PATTENDEN, Thomas 35, 36, 37, 38, 40, 41, 42, 48, 49, 50, 51, 54, 55, 56, 57, 58, 61, 74, 77, 78, 82, 83, 84, 85, 86, 87, 89, 91, 92, 93
PATTENDEN, William 78, 82, 85, 91, 98
PAYNE, T. 220
PEMMELL, - 66, 69, 82
PHILLIPS, Constantine 42, 64, 69
PILCHER, John 107, 110, 111, 112, 117, 120, 125, 126, 127, 129, 130, 132, 134, 135, 148, 156, 157, 160, 168, 179, 188, 190, 191, 207, 212, 233, 234, 235, 236, 239, 240
PITCAIRN, Alexander 150, 151, 152, 163, 166, 167, 170, 172, 173
POLDEN, - 69
PRIEST, - 180
PURCHASE, Richard 41, 43, 44, 45, 46, 47, 48, 84, 86, 88, 89, 90, 92, 93, 94, 95, 96, 97, 98, 99, 104, 106, 107, 108, 109, 110, 111, 112, 113, 114, 115, 116, 118, 119, 121, 122, 124, 126, 127, 129, 130, 132, 135, 136, 137, 139, 141, 142, 143, 144, 147, 148, 149, 150, 154, 155, 156, 157, 158, 160, 161, 168, 169, 170, 171, 172, 174, 175, 176, 178, 179, 180, 186, 190, 191, 192, 194, 196, 197, 198, 201, 202, 204, 205, 207, 210, 211, 214, 216, 217, 218, 219, 220, 221, 223, 224, 228, 229, 230, 231, 232, 233, 239, 240, 249, 250, 251, 252, 253, 257, 258, 259, 267
QUARME, Robert 167, 173, 189, 195
QUIDDINGTON, Thomas 47, 52, 53, 60
RAY, Thomas 167, 173, 178, 180, 182, 183, 189, 195, 199, 201, 202, 204, 212, 213, 214, 215, 217, 218, 219, 221, 222, 223, 224, 225, 226, 227, 228, 229, 231, 232, 233, 234, 235, 236, 237, 238, 239, 240, 241, 242, 244, 245, 246, 247, 248, 251, 252, 253, 254, 255, 256, 257, 260, 261, 264, 265, 266, 268, 270
READ, - 39
REDETT, C. 239
REED, Charles 270
REYNOLDS, Frederick 224, 239
RICE, James 215, 219, 231, 248

RIDGE, Thomas 36, 41, 48, 49, 50
RIMMINGTON, B. 72, 74, 77, 78, 79, 80, 81, 82, 83, 84, 85, 86, 91
RIMMINGTON, M. 81, 82, 101, 102, 103, 105, 153
RIMMINGTON, T. 78, 79, 80, 81
RING, George 239, 240
RING, John 87, 88, 89, 90, 91, 92, 93, 94, 95, 96, 97, 98, 100, 104, 107, 108, 109, 110, 111, 112, 113, 115, 119, 120, 124, 125, 126, 127, 129, 130, 132, 134, 135, 136, 137, 139, 141, 142, 143, 144, 148, 156, 157, 160, 169, 174, 177, 179, 181, 186, 188, 190, 191, 192, 193, 194, 196, 197, 200, 201, 202, 204, 205, 207, 210, 211, 212, 213, 214, 218, 220, 221, 223, 224, 225, 226, 227, 228, 229, 230, 231, 232, 233, 234, 235, 236, 237, 239, 240
ROBINSON, Robert 179, 183, 198, 200, 201, 202, 204, 205, 210, 211, 213, 214, 216, 217, 218, 220, 221, 223, 224, 226, 227, 228, 229, 230, 231, 232, 233, 237, 238, 239, 240, 243, 244, 245, 247, 251, 252, 253, 254, 256, 257, 260, 261, 262, 263, 264, 265, 266, 267, 268, 269, 270
RUBEGALL, - 199
RUSSELL, C. 230
RUSSELL, John 105, 138, 140, 153, 159, 198
SADLER, - 198
SALE, - 155, 167, 173, 182
SANDERSON, - 241
SCOTT, Thomas 135, 136, 141, 147, 156, 157, 158, 160, 161, 171, 174, 177, 179, 181, 186, 193, 194, 200, 201, 202, 204, 205, 207, 210, 211, 213, 214, 223, 259
SCOTT, - 183, 185, 249
SELBY, Thomas 148
SHACKLE, Thomas 123, 128, 133, 145, 146, 149, 150, 173, 178, 180, 189, 195, 203, 206, 208, 209, 212, 213, 214, 219, 222, 225, 229, 234, 236, 238
SHARPE, D. 180
SHELLEY, Sir John 175, 178, 206, 207, 208, 209, 215, 216
SHEPHEARD, George 238
SIMMONS, Richard 35, 36, 38, 40, 41, 42, 48, 49, 50, 51, 69, 70, 74
SIMMONS, - 138, 140, 153
SKINNER, T. 86
SLATER, C. 102, 103, 105
SMALL, Eli 235
SMALL, John sen. 34, 35, 36, 38, 39, 41, 43, 44, 45, 46, 47, 48, 49, 50, 51, 52, 53, 54, 55, 56, 57, 58, 59, 60, 61, 62, 63, 64, 65, 66, 67, 68, 70, 71, 72, 73, 75, 76, 79, 80, 81, 82, 83, 84, 85, 86, 87, 88, 89, 90, 92, 93, 94, 95, 96, 97, 98, 99, 100, 104, 106, 107, 108, 109, 110, 111, 112, 113, 114, 115, 116, 118, 119, 121, 122, 124, 126, 127, 129, 131, 132, 135, 136, 137, 139, 141, 142, 144, 147, 154, 156, 157, 158, 170, 171, 172, 179, 193, 194, 210, 211, 220, 221, 224, 228, 229, 235, 249, 250, 258, 259
SMALL, John jun. 95, 104, 106, 107, 108, 109, 110, 111, 112, 113, 114, 115, 116, 119, 121, 122, 124, 126, 129, 131, 132, 135, 136, 137, 139, 141, 142, 143, 144, 147, 154, 156, 157, 158, 160, 161, 168, 169, 170, 171, 172, 174, 176, 179, 193, 194, 196, 197, 198, 200, 201, 202, 204, 205, 207, 210, 211, 213, 214, 216, 217, 218, 220, 221, 223, 224, 226, 227, 228, 229, 230, 231, 232, 233, 235, 237, 239, 240, 243, 244, 245, 247, 248, 249, 250, 251, 252, 253, 254, 256, 257, 258, 259, 260, 261, 262, 263, 264, 265, 266, 267, 268, 269, 270
SMALL, - 119
SMITH, James 179, 181, 188, 191, 192, 204, 268
SMITH, Thomas Assheton sen. 101, 106, 114, 116, 129, 130, 131, 138, 139, 140, 142, 143, 144, 145, 146, 149, 150, 151, 152, 154, 155, 158, 159, 160, 161, 163, 164, 165, 166, 167, 168, 170, 171, 172, 173, 182, 183, 184, 185, 195, 199, 200, 201
SMITH, Thomas Assheton jun. 254, 255, 256
SOANE, - 220, 221
SPENCER, - 184
STANFORD, Richard 78, 82, 85, 91, 96, 100, 104, 107
STANHOPE, - 102, 103, 123, 128, 133, 255
STEVENS, Edward 34, 35, 36, 37, 38, 39, 40, 41, 42, 43, 44, 45, 46, 47, 48, 49, 50, 51, 52, 53, 55, 56, 57, 58, 59, 60, 61, 62, 63, 64, 65, 66, 67, 68, 69, 70, 71, 72, 73, 74, 75, 76, 77, 78, 79, 80, 81, 82, 83, 85, 87, 88, 89, 90, 91, 92, 93, 94, 95, 96, 97, 99, 100, 101, 105, 106, 109, 111, 112, 114, 115, 116, 117, 118, 120, 121, 122, 124, 125, 126, 131, 134, 136
STEVENS, John 128, 138, 140, 153, 159, 177, 181, 184, 185, 187, 198
STEVENS, Robert 250, 263, 265
STEWART, Henry 116, 135
STEWART, John 179, 249

293

STEWART, Peter 34, 35, 36, 38, 39, 43, 44, 45, 46, 47, 49, 54, 70, 71, 75, 76
STEWART, R. 151, 164
STONE, Robert 37, 40, 41, 45, 46, 68, 77, 78, 139, 140
STRATHAVON, Earl of (George Gordon) 101, 114, 164
STREETER, Edward 162, 166
SUETER, Thomas 34, 35, 36, 38, 39, 41, 43, 44, 45, 46, 47, 48, 49, 50, 51, 52, 53, 54, 55, 56, 57, 58, 59, 60, 61, 62, 63, 64, 65, 66, 67, 68, 70, 71, 72, 73, 75, 76, 79, 80, 81, 82, 83, 84, 85, 86, 87, 88, 89, 90, 92, 93, 94, 95, 97, 98, 117, 120, 121, 125, 131, 134, 136, 137, 141, 142, 144
SWAYNE, Thomas 69
SYLVESTER, - 165, 182, 183, 215, 217, 219, 238, 241, 242, 246, 248, 255, 256, 258
TALBOT, George 101, 103, 105, 106, 114, 116, 121, 123, 129, 130, 131, 150, 151, 152, 153, 154, 155, 158, 159, 161
TALMEGE, - 146
TANVERVILLE, 4th Earl of (Charles Bennett) 37, 40, 42, 43, 45, 46, 52, 53, 59, 60, 61, 62, 63, 64, 65, 66, 72, 73, 74, 75, 77, 78, 79, 80, 85
TANNER, John 247, 266, 267, 268
TAYLOR, Thomas 50, 51, 52, 53, 54, 55, 56, 57, 58, 59, 60, 61, 62, 63, 64, 65, 66, 67, 68, 70, 71, 72, 73, 75, 76, 79, 80, 81, 83, 84, 87, 88, 89, 90, 92, 94, 95, 96, 97, 98, 99, 100, 104, 106, 107, 108, 109, 110, 111, 112, 113, 114, 115, 116, 118, 119, 121, 122, 124, 126, 127, 129, 131, 135, 136, 137, 139, 141, 142, 143, 144, 147, 154, 155, 156, 157, 158, 161, 168, 170, 171, 172, 174, 176, 186, 204, 205, 207, 210, 211, 213, 214, 216, 220, 221, 223, 224, 247, 249, 250, 258
THANET, 9th Earl of (Sackville Tufton) 151, 152, 206, 208, 209
THOMPSON, - 167, 173, 189, 195, 203, 206, 208, 209, 212
TIMBER, - 167, 189, 195, 203, 206, 208, 209, 212, 222, 225
TOWELL, C. 155
TOWNSEND, - 91, 94, 95, 97, 98
TUFTON, Hon Henry James 186, 187, 189, 190, 191, 192, 195, 196, 197, 199, 200, 202, 203, 204, 205, 206, 207, 208, 209, 210, 211, 212, 215, 216, 217, 218, 219, 220, 221, 222, 223, 224, 225, 226, 227, 228, 229, 230, 231, 232, 233, 234, 236, 237, 239, 240, 241, 242, 243, 244, 245, 246, 249, 250, 251, 252, 253, 255, 256, 270
TUFTON, Hon John 190, 191, 192, 215, 216, 217, 218, 219, 220, 221, 222, 223, 224, 225, 226, 227, 228, 229, 230, 231, 232, 233, 234, 235, 236, 237, 239, 240, 241, 242, 243, 244, 245, 246, 248, 249, 250, 251, 252, 253, 254, 255, 256, 257, 258, 259, 260, 261
TURNBULL, - 239, 240
TURNER, Robert 123, 149, 150, 162, 163, 164, 165, 180, 182, 183, 195, 199, 203, 206, 207, 208, 209, 215, 219, 222, 246
TURNER, W. 123, 222, 229, 231, 257, 259, 263, 264, 265
TWISTLETON, Hon Thomas James 199, 200, 202, 237
TYSON, - 146, 182, 184, 185
UPTON, Hon Arthur Percy 217, 219, 234, 235, 241, 242, 243, 246, 248, 258, 259, 266
VALLANCE, J. 162, 166, 175, 178, 180
VALLANCE, P. 162, 166, 175, 176, 178, 180
VECK, Richard Aubrey 54, 55, 56, 57, 58, 59, 60, 61, 62, 63, 64, 65, 66, 67, 68, 70, 72, 73, 74, 75, 76, 79, 80, 81, 82, 83, 84, 86, 87, 88, 89, 90, 92, 93, 94, 95
VENNER, - 148
VINCENT, - 123, 130, 131
WALKER, Harry 97, 98, 99, 104, 106, 107, 108, 109, 110, 111, 112, 113, 114, 115, 116, 117, 118, 120, 121, 122, 124, 125, 126, 127, 131, 132, 134, 136, 137, 141, 142, 143, 144, 147, 156, 157, 158, 161, 168, 169, 170, 171, 172, 174, 179, 186, 192, 193, 194, 196, 197, 198, 200, 201, 202, 204, 205, 207, 210, 211, 213, 214, 216, 217, 218, 220, 221, 223, 224, 226, 227, 228, 229, 230, 237, 239, 240, 243, 244, 245, 247, 251, 252, 253, 254, 256, 257, 260, 261, 262, 263, 264, 265, 266, 267, 268, 269, 270
WALKER, John 125, 131, 156, 157, 161, 171, 186, 192, 193, 194, 196, 197, 200, 201, 204, 205, 210, 211, 213, 214, 218, 220, 223, 224, 226, 227, 228, 229, 231, 232, 233, 237, 238, 239, 240, 243, 244, 245, 247, 254, 260, 261, 268, 270
WALKER, Thomas 96, 97, 98, 99, 100, 104, 106, 107, 108, 109, 110, 111, 112, 113, 114, 115, 116, 117, 118, 119, 120, 121, 122, 124, 125, 126, 127, 130, 132, 134, 136, 137, 139, 141, 142, 143, 144, 147, 154, 155, 156, 157, 158, 159, 160, 161, 163, 164, 165, 168, 169, 170, 171, 172, 174, 176, 178, 179, 180, 183, 184, 185, 186, 188, 190, 191, 192, 193, 194, 196, 197, 198, 199,

200, 201, 202, 204, 205, 207, 210, 211, 213, 214, 216, 217, 218, 220, 221, 223, 224, 225, 226, 227, 228, 229, 230, 231, 232, 233, 234, 235, 236, 237, 238, 239, 240, 241, 242, 243, 244, 245, 247, 248, 251, 252, 253, 254, 256, 257, 260, 261, 262, 263, 264, 265, 266, 267, 268, 269, 270
WALKER, - 148
WALLER, - (Maidstone) 48, 49
WALLER, - (Surrey) 270
WALPOLE, Robert 182, 187
WARD, John 268, 269, 270
WARREN, Charles 215, 267
WEBB, T. 145, 146, 150, 180
WEBB, - 82, 83, 84, 85, 86
WELCH, Richard 155, 164, 165, 182, 183, 186, 187
WELLER, James 267, 269, 270
WELLS, James 94, 106, 107, 109, 110, 115, 117, 118, 120, 121, 122, 126, 131, 134, 156, 161, 171, 188, 213, 214, 268
WELLS, John 104, 106, 107, 108, 109, 110, 111, 113, 114, 115, 116, 117, 118, 120, 121, 122, 124, 125, 126, 127, 130, 132, 134, 136, 137, 141, 142, 143, 144, 147, 154, 156, 157, 158, 161, 165, 168, 169, 170, 171, 172, 174, 176, 186, 188, 190, 191, 193, 194, 196, 197, 198, 200, 201, 202, 204, 205, 207, 210, 211, 213, 214, 216, 217, 218, 220, 221, 223, 224, 226, 227, 228, 229, 234, 237, 238, 239, 240, 243, 244, 245, 247, 248, 251, 252, 253, 254, 256, 257, 258, 259, 260, 261, 262, 263, 264, 265, 266, 267, 268, 269, 270
WELLS, W. 149, 247, 260, 268, 269
WEST, - 203, 208
WESTON, J. 103
WHEELER, John 37
WHEELER, J. 199, 203, 219
WHITE, Jacob Thomas 149
WHITE, Thomas 34, 36, 37, 38, 39, 40, 41, 42, 43, 44, 45, 46, 47, 48, 49, 50, 52, 53, 54, 55, 56, 57, 58, 59, 60, 61, 62, 63, 67, 68, 70, 71, 73
WHITE, W. 102, 103, 105, 123, 126, 145, 146, 149, 150, 164
WHITE, - 131, 143, 250
WHITEHEAD, R. 219, 257, 258, 259, 260, 261, 262, 263, 264, 265, 266, 267, 268, 269
WILLIAMS, - 255, 257, 258
WILSON, - 248
WINCHILSEA, 9th Earl of (George Finch) 96, 97, 98, 99, 100, 101, 103, 104, 105, 106, 107, 108, 112, 114, 116, 117, 118, 120, 121, 124, 125, 128, 129, 130, 131, 133, 134, 135, 136, 138, 139, 140, 142, 143, 144, 145, 146, 147, 148, 149, 150, 151, 152, 153, 154, 155, 158, 159, 160, 161, 163, 164, 165, 166, 167, 168, 169, 170, 172, 173, 174, 175, 176, 177, 178, 182, 183, 184, 185, 186, 187, 188, 189, 190, 191, 192, 193, 194, 195, 196, 197, 199, 200, 203, 206, 207, 208, 209, 210, 211, 212, 215, 216, 217, 218, 219, 220, 221, 222, 223, 225, 226, 227, 234, 235, 236, 237, 238, 241, 242, 243, 244, 245, 246, 248, 249, 250, 254, 255, 256, 257, 258, 259, 260, 261, 270
WINDSOR, - 122
WINTER, Edward 203, 206, 208, 209, 212, 222, 235
WITCHER, - 250
WOMBWELL, Sir George 167
WOOD, John (Pirbright) 36, 37, 38, 39, 40, 41, 42, 43, 44, 45, 46, 47, 52, 53, 59, 60, 61, 62, 63, 64, 67, 68, 80
WOOD, John (Seal) 38, 39, 40, 42, 46, 50, 55, 56, 57, 58, 82, 94
WOOD, - 127, 148
WOODROFFE, - 264, 266, 267, 269
WOOLDRIDGE, - 258
WYATT, Richard B. 101, 102, 103, 105, 128, 133, 138, 140, 145, 149, 151, 153, 159, 177, 181, 184, 185, 188, 190, 250
YALDEN, William 34, 35, 36, 37, 38, 39, 40, 41, 42, 43, 44, 45, 47, 52, 53, 58, 59, 60, 60, 61, 62, 63, 64, 65, 66, 67, 68, 69, 70, 71, 73, 74, 75, 76, 77, 78, 79, 80, 81, 83, 85, 90, 92, 93, 94
YARMOUTH, Lord (Francis Charles Seymour-Conway) 264, 265

Abbreviations and Sources

Listed below are the main sources referred to for each match. Books (with page number) are shown first, followed by newspapers and other sources. Bentley has unnumbered pages. It is not the case that all sources listed agree entirely with the printed score – where sources differ, they have been considered in the light of the ground rules set out in the Preface in order to determine the 'best' version of the score.

Some newspapers were published every three or four days, and a particular issue may be dated, for example, 18th to 22nd July. In the list that follows, only the first date has been given. This will explain, in some cases, why the full score of a match appears in a newspaper dated earlier than the conclusion of that match.

Abbreviations

Bentley	*A Correct Account of all the Cricket Matches* (pub. 1823)
Britcher	*A Complete List of All the Grand Matches of Cricket* (pub. annually from 1790)
Epps	*A Collection of All the Grand Matches of Cricket* (pub. 1799)
FL18	G.B.Buckley, *Fresh Light on 18th Century Cricket* (pub. 1935)
FLPVC	G.B.Buckley, *Fresh Light on Pre-Victorian Cricket* (pub. 1937)
HCC	F.S.Ashley-Cooper, *The Hambledon Cricket Chronicle* (pub. 1924)
SB	*Scores & Biographies*, Volume 1 (pub. 1862)
WCS	H.T.Waghorn, *Cricket Scores 1730-1773* (pub. 1897)
WDC	H.T.Waghorn, *The Dawn of Cricket* (pub. 1906)

BathC	Bath Chronicle
CJ	Canterbury Journal
Courier	Courier & Evening Gazette
Craftsman	The Craftsman, or Say's Weekly Journal
Diary	The Diary, or Woodfall's Register
EM	Evening Mail
GA	General Advertiser
Gazetteer	The Gazetteer and New Daily Advertiser
GEP	General Evening Post
HC	Hampshire Chronicle
KC	Kentish Chronicle
KG	Kentish Gazette
KP	Kentish Post
LC	London Chronicle
LEP	London Evening Post
LlEP	Lloyd's Evening Post
LP	London Packet
MaJ	Maidstone Journal
MC	Morning Chronicle
MH	Morning Herald
MiddJ	Middlesex Journal
MS	Morning Star
Oracle	Oracle Bell's New World
PbG	Public Gazette
PG	Portsmouth Gazette

RM	Reading Mercury
SM	Sporting Magazine
Star	The Star
StJC	St James's Chronicle
StM	Stanford Mercury
Sun	The Sun
SWJ	Salisbury & Wiltshire Journal
TB	True Briton
Times	The Times
WEP	Westminster Evening Post
World	The World

Sources for Each Match

Page	
34	WDC p34, HCC p177, FL18 p57, RM 29/6, Gazetteer 6/7, Craftsman 11/7, GEP 25/6, MiddJ 27/6, WEP 4/7
35	WDC p35, HCC p178, MiddJ 25/7
36	SB p4, Epps p6, WCS p83, KG 18/8
37	SB p6, Epps p7, WCS p92, KG 23/6, GEP 24/6, LlEP 25/6
38	Epps p8, WCS p94, KG 30/6
39	SB p7, Epps p7, WCS p97, KG 7/7
40	SB p12, Epps p9, WCS p101, KG 17/7, KG 21/7
41	SB p12, Epps p10, WCS p108, KG 7/8
42	SB p14, Epps p11, WCS p110, KG 21/8
43	SB p15, Epps p12, WCS p114, RM 27/9, KG 18/9
44	HCC p178, RM 4/10
45	SB p21, Epps p17, RM 4/7, MiddJ 25/6, MC 28/6
46	SB p17, Epps p13, KG 9/7
47	SB p18, Epps p14, RM 25/7, StJC 28/7
48	SB p19, Epps p15, KG 10/8
49	SB p20, Epps p16, KG 31/8
50	SB p22, Epps p19, KG 14/6
51	SB p23
52	SB p24, Epps p20, KG 12/7, contemporary manuscript
53	SB p25, Epps p18, GEP 25/7, MiddJ 25/5, MC 27/7, MP 28/7, RM 24/7, KG 26/7
54	HCC p179, MiddJ 15/6, SWJ 17/6
55	SB p27, Epps p21, KG 26/6, RM 1/7
56	SB p28, Epps p22, KG 10/7, RM 15/7
57	SB p28, Epps p23, MiddJ 18/7, MC 19/7, KG 17/7
58	SB p29, Epps p24, KG 27/7, SWJ 29/7
59	HCC p180, FL18 p79, WDC p45, LEP 8/8, MC 9/8, MC 12/8
60	SB p30, SWJ 2/9
61	SB p31, Epps p25, RM 30/6, KP 21/6
62	SB p32, Epps p27
63	SB p33, Epps p26 & 29, KG 2/8
64	SB p34, Epps p28 & 29, LEP 21/8, StJC 21/8, MP 21/8, KG23/8, Dorset manuscript
65	SB p35, Dorset manuscript
66	SB p36, Dorset manuscript
67	SB p37, Epps p30, KP 4/7
68	SB p37, Epps p31, LP 13/7, KG 18/7
69	FL18 p86, GA 8/9, LEP 12/9, StJC 12/9, MP 14/9, MC 15/9, GA 15/9
70	GA 1/10, Cricket Statistician Spring 2010

Page
71 SB p38, Epps p32, StJC 8/10, MP 10/10, contemporary manuscript, contemporary printed scorecard
72 SB p39, Epps p33
73 SB p40, Epps p34
74 SB p41, Epps p35 & 37
75 SB p42, Epps p36
76 SB p42, Epps p38, MP 28/9, RM 27/9
77 SB p43, Epps p39, WEP 29/6, RM 3/7, KG 28/6
78 SB p44, Epps p40, KG 23/8
79 SB p45, Epps p41, KG30/8
80 SB p46, Epps p42, MP 30/9, KP 23/9
81 SB p47, Epps p44, KG 13/6
82 SB p47, Epps p45, KG 30/6
83 SB p48, Epps p46, KG 18/7
84 SB p49, Epps p47, KG 1/8
85 SB p49, Epps p48, KG 8/8
86 SB p50, Epps p49, KG 25/8
87 SB p51, Epps p50, KG 6/7
88 SB p53, Epps p51, KG 17/7
89 SB p53, Epps p52, KG 24/7
90 SB p54, Epps p53, KG 14/8
91 SB p56, Epps p55
92 SB p57, Epps p56, SWJ 14/7, KG 18/7
93 SB p58, Epps p57, KG 9/8
94 SB p59, Epps p58
95 SB p61, Epps p59, KG 6/6
96 SB p64, Bentley, Epps p61, LC 22/6, CJ 30/6
97 SB p65, Bentley, Epps p62, MP 21/8
98 SB p66, Bentley, Epps p63, WDC p76, KG 18/7, RM 24/7
99 SB p66, Bentley, Epps p64, MP 10/8, LC 8/8, GEP 8/8, KG 8/8, RM 14/8
100 SB p68, Bentley, Epps p65, MP 16/8, KG 11/8
101 SB p69
102 SB p70
103 FL18 p111, World 19/6
104 SB p71, Bentley, Epps p67, LC 21/6, World 21/6, World 23/6, KG 22/6, WEP 21/6, MC 25/6
105 SB p73
106 SB p74, BathC 26/7, WEP 21/7
107 SB p76, Bentley, Epps p69, WEP 4/8, CJ 7/8
108 SB p76, Bentley, Epps p70, CJ 14/8
109 SB p77, Bentley, Epps p71, KG 28/9
110 SB p78, Bentley, Epps p72, KG 4/9
111 SB p78, Bentley, Epps p73, MH 11/9, World 12/9
112 SB p81, Bentley, Epps p74, KG 27/5, GA 28/5, GA 29/5
113 SB p81, Bentley, Epps p75, KG 6/5
114 SB p82, Bentley, Epps p76
115 SB p83, Bentley, Epps p77
116 SB p84, Bentley, Epps p78
117 SB p85, Bentley, Epps p79
118 SB p85, Bentley, Epps p80, KC ?/?, GA 31/7
119 SB p86, Bentley, Epps p81, KC 29/7
120 SB p87, Bentley, Epps p82, WDC p92, KC 5/8, KG 5/8, GA 16/8
121 SB p87, Bentley, Epps p83
122 SB p88, Bentley, Epps p85, KC 26/8
123 WDC p99, World 15/5, KG 22/5

Page	
124	SB p91, Bentley, Epps p87, KG 16/6, Times 17/6
125	SB p92, Bentley, Epps p88, KG 16/6, Diary 18/6
126	SB p93, Bentley, Epps p89, Diary 29/6, MP 29/6, MS 29/6, World 29/6, Star 30/6, KG 3/7, Times 3/7
127	SB p93, Bentley, Epps p90, KG 3/7, Times 3/7
128	FL18 p138, MaJ 14/7
129	SB p94, Bentley, Epps p92, KG 17/7, MS 20/7
130	SB p95, Bentley, Epps p93, World 27/7
131	FLPVC p19, Oracle 6/8, MS 8/8, MP 8/8
132	SB p96, Bentley, Epps p94, WDC p100, MP 11/8, KG 7/8, Cricket Statistician Autumn 2009
133	FLPVC p20, MS 11/8, MP 11/8
134	SB p96, Bentley, Epps p95, KG 14/8, MP 17/8, MS 17/8
135	SB p97, Bentley, Epps p96, KG 18/8, MP 24/8, MS 24/8
136	SB p98, Bentley, Epps p97, KG 1/9
137	SB p101, Bentley, Epps p98, Britcher p3
138	Britcher p4
139	SB p103, Bentley, Epps p99, Britcher p6
140	Britcher p7
141	SB p104, Bentley, Epps p100, Britcher p8, KG 16/7
142	SB p104, Bentley, Epps p101, Britcher p9, StM 16/7, StM 23/7, StM 30/7
143	SB p105, Bentley, Epps p102, Britcher p10
144	SB p106, Bentley, Epps p103, Britcher p11
145	SB p106, Bentley, Britcher p12
146	SB p107, Bentley, Britcher p13
147	SB p108, Bentley, Epps p104, Britcher p14
148	SB p108, Bentley, Britcher p15, KG 7/9
149	SB p110, Bentley, Britcher p4, Star 19/5
150	SB p111, Bentley, Britcher p5
151	SB p111, Bentley, Britcher p6, Star 2/6
152	SB p112, Britcher p7, Bentley
153	SB p115, Bentley, Britcher p9, MH 16/7
154	SB p115, Bentley, Britcher p10, Star 28/6, StM 24/6
155	SB p116, Bentley, Britcher p11
156	SB p117, Bentley (both 1791 & 1792), Britcher (1791) p13, Britcher (1792) p14
157	SB p118, Bentley (both 1791 & 1792), , Britcher (1791) p14, Britcher (1792) p15, EM 18/7, MH 20/7, KG 18/7
158	SB p119, Bentley, Britcher p16, EM 29/7, KC 5/8
159	SB p121, Bentley, Britcher p17
160	SB p121, Bentley, Britcher p18, KG 23/8
161	SB p122, Bentley, Britcher p20, KG 2/9, KC 2/9
162	SB p125, Bentley, Britcher p26, KC 27/9
163	SB p128, Bentley, Britcher p4, Gazetteer 12/5
164	SB p129, Bentley, Britcher p5
165	SB p129, Bentley, Britcher p6, MH 25/5
166	SB p130, Bentley, Britcher p7
167	SB p131, Britcher p8
168	SB p132, Bentley, Britcher p9
169	SB p133, Bentley, Britcher p11
170	SB p134, Bentley, Britcher p12, StM 29/6, StM 6/7
171	SB p136, Bentley, Britcher p16
172	SB p137, Bentley, Britcher p18
173	SB p138, Britcher p19, Star 8/8
174	SB p140, Bentley, Britcher p21, MH 21/8, Gazette 22/8

Page	
175	SB p140, Bentley, Britcher p22, MH 23/8
176	SB p141, Bentley, Britcher p23
177	SB p142, Bentley, Britcher p24, KC 7/9, Gazette 4/9
178	SB p142, Bentley, Britcher p25
179	SB p143, Bentley, Britcher p26
180	Britcher p27
181	SB p144, Bentley
182	SB p146, Bentley, Britcher p3, SM May p122
183	SB p146, The Diary 31/5, Britcher p4, SM May p123
184	SB p147, Sun 3/6, Britcher p5, SM June p183
185	SB p148, Britcher p7, MP 8/6, SM June p184
186	SB p132 (date given as 1792), Bentley (date given as 1792), Britcher p8, World 10/6, June p186
187	SB p149, Britcher p9, MP 19/6, SM June p186
188	SB p149, Bentley, Britcher p10, SM June p187
189	SB p150, Britcher p11, MP 27/6, SM July p249
190	SB p151, Bentley, Britcher p12, MP 3/7, SM July p250
191	SB p151, Bentley, Britcher p13, SM July p251
192	SB p152, Bentley, Britcher p14, SM July p250
193	SB p154, Bentley, Britcher p17, SM July p253
194	SB p157, Bentley, Britcher p20, MH 26/7, MP 26/7
195	SB p157, Bentley, Britcher p21, MH 31/7, LEP 1/8, Sun 1/8
196	SB p158, Bentley, Britcher p22
197	SB p159, Bentley, Britcher p23, MP 14/8
198	SB p159, Bentley, Britcher p24, Sun 23/8
199	SB p164, Bentley, Britcher p5, SM June p173
200	SB p165, Bentley, Britcher p7
201	SB p165, Bentley, Britcher p8, SM July p226
202	SB p166, Bentley, Britcher p9, SM July p227
203	SB p167, Bentley, Britcher p10
204	SB p168, Bentley, Britcher p12
205	SB p169, Bentley, Britcher p13
206	SB p170, Britcher p15, SM August p285
207	SB p172, Britcher p19, Bentley, Star 13/8, KG 15/8, Oracle 4/8
208	SB p174, Britcher p21
209	SB p174, Britcher p22
210	SB p175, Bentley, Britcher p23
211	SB p175, Bentley, Britcher p24
212	SB p176, Bentley, Britcher p26
213	SB p176, Bentley, Britcher p28, KG 19/9
214	SB p177, Bentley, Britcher p29, KG 19/9
215	SB p180, Britcher p6
216	SB p180, Bentley, Britcher p7
217	SB p185, Bentley, Britcher p8
218	SB p184, Bentley, Britcher p12
219	SB p184, Britcher p13, SM July p209
220	SB p186, Bentley, Britcher p15, KC 17/7, SM July p210
221	SB p186, Bentley, Britcher p16, KC 21/7, Courier 18/7, SM July p211
222	SB p187, Britcher p17
223	SB p188, Bentley, Britcher p19, KC 25/7, MH 24/7, Courier 25/7, SM July p212
224	SB p188, Bentley, Britcher (1795) p21, Britcher (1796) p12, HC 3/8, PbG 21/8, HC 24/8
225	SB p189, Bentley, Britcher p23
226	SB p190, Bentley, Britcher p25

Page	
227	SB p190, Bentley, Britcher p26, KC 21/8, SM September p329
228	SB p191, Bentley, Britcher p27, SM September p330
229	SB p192, Bentley, Britcher p28, KC 4/9, SM September p330
230	SB p193, Bentley, Britcher p29, Courier 9/9, KG 8/9, KC 8/9, SM September p331
231	SB p193, Bentley, Britcher p30, WDC p144, Star 19/9, KG 11/9, SM September p332
232	SB p195, Bentley, Britcher p31, Courier 17/9, KG 15/9, KC 15/9, Star 23/9, SM October p52
233	SB p195, Bentley, Britcher p32, KG 18/9, SM September p332
234	SB p197, Bentley, Britcher p4
235	SB p199, Bentley, Britcher p9, Gazetteer 23/6, SM June p168
236	SB p200, Bentley, Britcher p10
237	SB p201, Bentley, Britcher p13
238	SB p208, Bentley, Britcher p25, WDC p138, SM August p279
239	SB p208, Bentley, Britcher p26, KG 26/8, Oracle 27/8, SM September p328
240	SB p209, Bentley, Britcher p27, Star 31/8
241	SB p214, Bentley, Britcher p4, WDC p146, KG 26/5
242	SB p215, Bentley, Britcher p5, SM May p105
243	SB p216, Bentley, Britcher p7, SM June p155
244	SB p218, Bentley, Britcher p9
245	SB p219, Bentley, Britcher p12
246	SB p220, Bentley, Britcher p13, MH 14/7
247	SB p220, Bentley, Britcher p14
248	SB p223, Bentley, Britcher p16
249	SB p224, Bentley, Britcher p20, LEP 12/8, PG 21/8
250	SB p225, Bentley, Britcher p23, PG 21/8
251	SB p226, Bentley, Britcher p24
252	SB p226, Bentley, Britcher p26
253	SB p228, Bentley, Britcher p28, MH 30/9, SM October p13
254	SB p233, Bentley, Britcher p6
255	SB p234, Bentley, Britcher p9
256	SB p235, Bentley, Britcher p11
257	SB p238, Bentley, Britcher p15
258	SB p240, Bentley, Britcher p19
259	SB p241, Bentley, Britcher p20
260	SB p243, Bentley, Britcher p22, WDC p149, Sun 17/8, TB 18/8, SM August p271
261	SB p244, Bentley, Britcher p24
262	SB p259, Bentley, Britcher p13, SM August p262
263	SB p259, Bentley, Britcher p14, SM August p243
264	SB p262, Bentley, Britcher p17, SM August p264
265	SB p263, Bentley, Britcher p18, SM August p265
266	SB p267, Britcher p(3), Bentley
267	SB p269, Bentley, Britcher p5, SM June p137
268	SB p269, Bentley, Britcher p6, SM June p137
269	SB p274, Bentley, Britcher p17, SM July p191
270	SB p279, Bentley, Britcher p32, SM October p28